DEATH IN LITERATURE

DEATH IN LITERATURE

ROBERT F. WEIR, EDITOR

COLUMBIA UNIVERSITY PRESS
NEW YORK   1980

For permission to reprint copyrighted material, acknowledgment is made to the publishers named on pp. 441–46, which constitute an extension of this copyright page.

Library of Congress Cataloging in Publication Data

Main entry under title:

Death in literature.

  Includes index.
  1. Death—Literary collections. 2. Literature—
Collections. I. Weir, Robert F.
PN6071.D4D43   1980   808.8′0354   80-16621
ISBN 0-231-04936-6
ISBN 0-231-04937-4 (pbk.)

Columbia University Press
New York

Copyright © 1980 Columbia University Press
Printed in the United States of America

To Jerry—
For her abiding love for me,
        our children,
        and the beneficial things in life—
            including good literature.

CONTENTS

5. CHILDREN, YOUTH, AND DEATH

6. DEATH BY KILLING

7. SUICIDE

PREFACE

THIS book will, I hope, do several things. First, it will show the richness and diversity of death as a subject in a variety of literary genres. Second, it will demonstrate the timelessness of the subject of death in literature, as evidenced by selections ranging from 2300 B.C. to A.D. 1979. Third, it will reflect a variety of cultural traditions through selections from India, China, Japan, Greece, Nigeria, Lebanon, Russia, Germany, England, France, Spain, Ireland, and the United States. Fourth, it will be a helpful book for teaching courses on death in the humanities and a beneficial book for all persons who want to enrich their lives by sensitizing themselves to the mortality shared by us all.

The introductions to the eleven sections provide an overview to some of the aspects of the subject of death. They are by no means exhaustive, but provide a map of the terrain for persons just beginning in the interdisciplinary field of thanatology. Many of these introductions contain brief descriptions of literary works which are used to illustrate a sectional theme and supplement the selections in a sectional unit. The shorter introductions to some of the individual literary works provide information on the authors and works which may aid in understanding what the authors said and why they said it.

As with any book, there are a number of persons whose names do not appear on the title page, but nevertheless are to be acknowledged for their advice, encouragement, and practical help. They are Carol Ahmad, Lionel Arnold, George Burris, Richard Bush, Hyla Converse, Ken Dollarhide, Phil Hamlin, Lloyd Huff, David Levine, Robert Radford, John Susky, and Ruth Ward. To each of these persons, my sincere thanks.

DEATH IN LITERATURE

1. THE INEVITABILITY OF DEATH

THERE is a Buddhist parable which nicely illustrates the inevitability of death and the perennial problem of accepting death as a fact of human existence. Called "The Parable of the Mustard Seed," the story is about a mother whose young son died unexpectedly. Bereaved by her son's death, she went throughout her neighborhood asking people for some medicine to give her son. Her neighbors scoffed at her stupidity: "Where did you ever get the idea there was a medicine to bring the dead back to life?"

Undeterred by their comments, the woman kept searching for a medicine for her son. Finally a wise man heard her story and suggested that she go tell her story to the Buddha. When the Buddha heard her request, he told her to go into the city and bring him some grains of mustard seed from the first house she found in which no one had ever died. Uplifted by the prospect of finding such a house, she carried her dead son into the city and began inquiring at houses to find one in which no person had died.

She soon discovered, of course, that she was engaged in an impossible task. At every house her request for the mustard-seed medicine was met with comments indicating the number of relatives who had died. No one was able to give her the medicine because no one could claim never to have experienced death in their family. At long last she realized what the Buddha was trying to teach her: death is a fact built into the very fabric of human existence, and her son, rather than having an unusual disease which might be cured, had succumbed to that lifeless condition which awaits all human beings. With that truth of human existence reluctantly discovered, she began to make plans for the disposal of her dead son's body.*

* *Buddhist Parables*, trans. by Eugene Watson Burlingame (New Haven: Yale University Press, 1922).

Like the mother in this parable, all persons are confronted with an undeniable fact of human existence: all who live, die. Yet, when confronted with this fact of mortality, the natural response appears to be to deny that it is true. Most of us go through life acting blissfully ignorant of the inevitable termination of that life process. We know that people die, of course, but we somehow cannot imagine that we personally will die. We may, if we are children, play games ("Bang, bang, you're dead!") in which no one really dies because all of the players are expected to resume the game after they have been "dead" for a short period of time. Or we may, if we are adults, play more serious games in which we try to deter death by blunting the aging process, using sophisticated life-prolonging machines, or joining the cryonics movement in the hopes of finding "cures" for death-dealing diseases.

In a variety of ways, we act as if we are exceptions to the fact of mortality. Rather than adjusting to the harsh reality that death is inevitable, we find it easier to believe that the ancient words of the Psalmist were written especially for us: "A thousand may fall at your side,/ten thousand at your right hand;/but it will not come near you" (Psalms 91:7).

This attitude of denial is nothing new. Anthropologists have often pointed out that attitudes toward death in folk societies were from the earliest stages of human development characterized by a denial of its inevitability. Apart from the deaths inflicted by enemies or induced by magic, persons in pre-scientific periods seem to have been persuaded that death was not a necessary feature of the human condition. The same general attitude, according to child psychologists, exists among children under the age of five. Because young children cannot imagine not being alive, they tend to think of death as an ongoing form of sleep. And, according to contemporary psychiatric studies, denial is the characteristic first response of patients when they are informed they have a terminal illness. They simply cannot believe that they, like all who have lived before them, are about to die.

Persons who write literature are, of course, caught up in this pervasive human tendency to deny that death is inevitable. Yet, in a strikingly perceptive way, there is a substantial body of literature which carries out the function Shakespeare ascribed to drama: namely, "to hold . . . the mirror up to nature" (*Hamlet*, III, 2). By using literature as a reflective device, poets, playwrights, and novelists often succeed in focusing our attention on that part of nature which we most want to ignore: the inevitability of death. By so doing, they call upon us to reflect on the meaning of human existence, the brevity of individual human lives, and the desirability of planning for that inevitable event which awaits us all.

It is from this perceptive body of literature that the following selections are taken. The writers of the first three selections are in agreement that death allows for no exceptions. The author of Psalm 90, an ancient Jewish prayer written after the Babylonian exile, emphasizes that "the years of our life . . . are soon gone." Two centuries later the writer of Ecclesiastes states simply that there is "a time to be born, and a time to die." With the passage of two more centuries, the Roman poet Lucretius writes that "all men must die, and no man can escape."

Several of the selections focus on the deaths of famous people to suggest that if even the rich and powerful succumb to death, so shall the rest of us. In the famous Yorick scene in *Hamlet*, Shakespeare has Hamlet point out that "Alexander died, Alexander was buried, Alexander returneth to dust. . . ." Thomas Gray's "Elegy Written in a Country Churchyard," the most famous example of the "graveyard school" of poetry, says that "the paths of glory lead but to the grave." Shelley's "Ozymandias" is a thought-provoking picture of a famous king who now is represented only by a deteriorating statue. The Aztec poem "Song of Nezahualcoyotl" and Bryant's "Thanatopsis" provide an interesting parallel to one another in that they point out that tribal chiefs and princesses, kings, poets, and sages have all met a common fate that has neutralized the privileges they once enjoyed.

Other selections highlight the changes wrought by time as young, talented, and beautiful people make their ways toward death. Edgar Allan Poe's "The Emperor Worm" depicts human existence as a long-playing drama whose ultimate hero is a worm. Emily Dickinson points out that young boys and girls inevitably end up as "quiet dust." Rabindranath Tagore, one of the great writers of modern India, reflects on the good and bad experiences that comprise the journey known as human life. Edwin Arlington Robinson and John Masefield both comment on the ravages of time and the destructiveness of death: in death, sparkling eyes, young bodies, laughter, and active brains are no more. And the Russian poet Yevgeny Yevtushenko laments the inevitable destruction of valuable, unrepeatable human lives.

The remaining selections provide unusual variations on the inevitability theme. Conrad Aiken, a contemporary American poet, describes death as a blind date who waits patiently in an amusement park to escort unsuspecting and unprepared young men and women to their final rendezvous with destiny. Mary Lavin, an Irish short-story writer, suggests that not only death, but many of the decisions made along life's way have a certain kind of inevitability about them. And Aleksandr Solzhenitsyn, the contemporary Russian novelist, tells a fascinating story in *The Cancer Ward* about a doctor who has specialized in oncology for years, yet is quite unprepared when she is diagnosed as having cancer.

PSALM 90 (RSV)
Anonymous (c.450 B.C.)

Lord, thou hast been our dwelling place
    in all generations.
Before the mountains were brought forth,
    or ever thou hadst formed the earth
      and the world,
    from everlasting to everlasting thou
      art God.
Thou turnest man back to the dust,
    and sayest, "Turn back, O children of
      men!"
For a thousand years in thy sight
    are but as yesterday when it is past,
    or as a watch in the night.
Thou dost sweep men away; they are like
      a dream,
    like grass which is renewed in the
      morning:
in the morning it flourishes and is
      renewed;
    in the evening it fades and withers.

For we are consumed by thy anger;
by thy wrath we are overwhelmed.
Thou hast set our iniquities before thee,
our secret sins in the light of thy
countenance.
For all our days pass away under thy
wrath,
our years come to an end like a sigh.
The years of our life are threescore and
ten,
or even by reason of strength fourscore;
yet their span is but toil and trouble;
they are soon gone, and we fly away.
Who considers the power of thy anger,
and thy wrath according to the fear of
thee?
So teach us to number our days
that we may get a heart of wisdom.
Return, O Lord! How long?
Have pity on thy servants!
Satisfy us in the morning with thy
steadfast love,
that we may rejoice and be glad all our
days.
Make us glad as many days as thou hast
afflicted us,
and as many years as we have seen evil.
Let thy work be manifest to thy servants,
and thy glorious power to their
children.
Let the favor of the Lord our God be
upon us,
and establish thou the work of our
hands upon us,
yea, the work of our hands establish
thou it.

ECCLESIASTES 3:1–9 (RSV)
Anonymous (c.250 B.C.)

For everything there is a season, and a
time for every matter under heaven:
>   a time to be born, and a time to die;
>   a time to plant, and a time to pluck up
>   what is planted;
>   a time to kill, and a time to heal;
>   a time to break down, and a time to
>   build up;
>   a time to weep, and a time to laugh;
>   a time to mourn, and a time to dance;
>   a time to cast away stones, and a time to
>   gather stones together;
>   a time to embrace, and a time to refrain
>   from embracing;
>   a time to seek, and a time to lose;
>   a time to keep, and a time to cast away;
>   a time to rend, and a time to sew;
>   a time to keep silence, and a time to
>   speak;
>   a time to love, and a time to hate;
>   a time for war, and a time for peace.
>   What gain has the worker from his toil?

from ON THE NATURE OF THINGS
Lucretius (c.94–55 B.C.)

DEATH
Is nothing to us, has no relevance
To our condition, seeing that the mind
Is mortal. Just as, long ago, we felt
Not the least touch of trouble when the wars
Were raging all around the shaken earth
And from all sides the Carthaginian hordes

Poured forth to battle, and no man ever knew
Whose subject he would be in life or death,
Which doom, by land or sea, would strike him down,
So, when we cease to be, and body and soul,
Which joined to make us one, have gone their ways,
Their separate ways, nothing at all can shake
Our feelings, not if earth were mixed with sea
Or sea with sky. Perhaps the mind or spirit,
After its separation from our body,
Has some sensation; what is that to us?
Nothing at all, for what we knew of being,
Essence, identity, oneness, was derived
From body's union with spirit, so, if time,
After our death, should some day reunite
All of our present particles, bring them back
To where they now reside, give us once more
The light of life, this still would have no meaning
For us, with our self-recollection gone.
As we are now, we lack all memory
Of what we were before, suffer no wound
From those old days. Look back on all that space
Of time's immensity, consider well
What infinite combinations there have been
In matter's ways and groupings. How easy, then,
For human beings to believe we are
Compounded of the very selfsame motes,
Arranged exactly in the selfsame ways
As once we were, our long-ago, our now
Being identical. And yet we keep
No memory of that once-upon-a-time,
Nor can we call it back; somewhere between
A break occurred, and all our atoms went
Wandering here and there and far away
From our sensations. If there lies ahead
Tough luck for any man, he must be there,
Himself, to feel its evil, but since death
Removes this chance, and by injunction stops

All rioting of woes against our state,
We may be reassured that in our death
We have no cause for fear, we cannot be
Wretched in nonexistence. Death alone
Has immortality, and takes away
Our mortal life. It does not matter a bit
If we once lived before.
                              So, seeing a man
Feel sorry for himself, that after death
He'll be a rotting corpse, laid in a tomb,
Succumb to fire, or predatory beasts,
You'll know he's insincere, just making noise,
With rancor in his heart, though he believes,
Or tries to make us think so, that death ends all.
And yet, I'd guess, he contradicts himself,
He does not really see himself as gone,
As utter nothingness, but does his best—
Not really understanding what he's doing—
To have himself survive, for, in his life,
He will project a future, a dark day
When beast or bird will lacerate his corpse.
So he feels sorry for himself; he fails
To make the real distinction that exists
Between his castoff body, and the man
Who stands beside it grieving, and imputes
Some of his sentimental feelings to it.
Resenting mortal fate, he cannot see
That in true death he'll not survive himself
To stand there as a mourner, stunned by grief
That he is burned or mangled. If in death
It's certainly no pleasure to be mauled
By beak of bird or fang of beast, I'd guess
It's no voluptuous revel to be laid
Over the flames, or packed in honey and ice,
Stiff on the surface of a marble slab,
Or buried under a great mound of earth.

                    . . . .

You well might think of saying to yourself:
"Even good Ancus closed his eyes on the light—
A better man than you will ever be,
You reprobate—and many lords and kings
Rulers of mighty nations, all have died.
Even that monarch, who once paved the way
Making the sea a highway for his legions
Where foot and horse alike could march dry-shod
While the deep foamed and thundered at the outrage,
Even he, great Xerxes, died and left the light,
And Scipio, the thunderbolt of war,
Terror of Carthage, gave his bones to earth
As does the meanest lackey. Add to these
Philosophers and artists, all the throng
Blessed by the Muses; Homer's majesty
Lies low in the same sleep as all the rest.
Democritus, warned by a ripe old age
That, with his memory, his powers of mind
Were also failing, gave himself to death;
And Epicurus perished, that great man
Whose genius towered over all the rest,
Making their starry talents fade and die
In his great sunlight. Who are you, forsooth,
To hesitate, resent, protest your death?
Your life is death already, though you live
And though you see, except that half your time
You waste in sleep, and the other half you snore
With eyes wide open, forever seeing dreams,
Forever in panic, forever lacking wit
To find out what the trouble is, depressed,
Or drunk, or drifting aimlessly around."

. . . .

Finally, what's this wanton lust for life
To make us tremble in dangers and in doubt?
All men must die, and no man can escape.
We turn and turn in the same atmosphere

In which no new delight is ever shaped
To grace our living; what we do not have
Seems better than everything else in all the world,
But should we get it, we want something else.
Our gaping thirst for life is never quenched.
We have to know what luck next year will bring,
What accident, what end. But life, prolonged,
Subtracts not even one second from the term
Of death's continuance. We lack the strength
To abbreviate that eternity. Suppose
You could contrive to live for centuries,
As many as you will. Death, even so,
Will still be waiting for you; he who died
Early this morning has as many years
Interminably before him, as the man,
His predecessor, has, who perished months
Or years, or even centuries ago.

from HAMLET (v, 1)
William Shakespeare (1564–1616)

This selection is from a scene in a church cemetery. Two gravediggers (called
clowns) are preparing a grave for Ophelia, who has committed suicide as a result
of her unsatisfied love for Hamlet. He has returned unexpectedly from his exile in
England. While standing at her gravesite with Horatio, Hamlet contemplates the
inevitability of death as he looks at the skull of Yorick, an adult companion during his childhood years.

HAMLET: What man dost thou dig it for?
FIRST CLOWN: For no man, sir.
HAMLET: What woman, then?
FIRST CLOWN: For none, neither.
HAMLET: Who is to be buried in 't?
FIRST CLOWN: One that was a woman, sir; but, rest her soul, she's dead.
HAMLET: How absolute the knave is! We must speak by the card, or
    equivocation will undo us. By the Lord, Horatio, this three years I
    have took note of it; the age is grown so picked that the toe of the

peasant comes so near the heel of the courtier, he galls his kibe. How long hast thou been a grave-maker?

FIRST CLOWN: Of all the days i' th' year, I came to 't that day that our last king Hamlet overcame Fortinbras.

HAMLET: How long is that since?

FIRST CLOWN: Cannot you tell that? Every fool can tell that. It was that very day that young Hamlet was born; he that is mad, and sent into England.

HAMLET: Ay, marry, why was he sent into England?

FIRST CLOWN: Why, because 'a was mad: 'a shall recover his wits there; or, if he do not, 't is no great matter there.

HAMLET: Why?

FIRST CLOWN: 'T will not be seen in him there; there the men are as mad as he.

HAMLET: How came he mad?

FIRST CLOWN: Very strangely, they say.

HAMLET: How "strangely"?

FIRST CLOWN: Faith, e'en with losing his wits.

HAMLET: Upon what ground?

FIRST CLOWN: Why, here in Denmark: I have been sexton here, man and boy, thirty years.

HAMLET: How long will a man lie i' th' earth ere he rot?

FIRST CLOWN: Faith, if 'a be not rotten before 'a die—as we have many pocky corses now-a-days, that will scarce hold the laying in—'a will last you some eight year or nine year. A tanner will last you nine year.

HAMLET: Why he more than another?

FIRST CLOWN: Why, sir, his hide is so tanned with his trade that 'a will keep out water a great while, and your water is a sore decayer of your whoreson dead body. Here's a skull now; this skull hath lain i' th' earth three and twenty years.

HAMLET: Whose was it?

FIRST CLOWN: A whoreson mad fellow's it was. Whose do you think it was?

HAMLET: Nay, I know not.

FIRST CLOWN: A pestilence on him for a mad rogue! 'A poured a flagon of Rhenish on my head once. This same skull, sir, was, sir, Yorick's skull, the King's jester.

HAMLET: This?

FIRST CLOWN: E'en that.

HAMLET: Let me see that. [*Takes the skull.*] Alas, poor Yorick! I knew him, Horatio; a fellow of infinite jest, of most excellent fancy. He hath borne me on his back a thousand times. And now how abhorred in my imagination it is! My gorge rises at it. Here hung those lips that I have kissed I know not how oft. Where be your gibes now, your gambols, your songs, your flashes of merriment, that were wont to set the table on a roar? Not one now, to mock your own grinning? Quite chop-fallen? Now get you to my lady's chamber, and tell her, let her paint an inch thick, to this favour she must come. Make her laugh at that. Prithee, Horatio, tell me one thing.

HORATIO: What's that, my lord?

HAMLET: Dost thou think Alexander looked o' this fashion i' th' earth?

HORATIO: E'en so.

HAMLET: And smelt so? Pah! [*Puts down the skull.*]

HORATIO: E'en so, my lord.

HAMLET: To what base uses we may return, Horatio! Why may not imagination trace the noble dust of Alexander, till 'a find it stopping a bung-hole?

HORATIO: 'T were to consider too curiously, to consider so.

HAMLET: No, faith, not a jot; but to follow him thither with modesty enough and likelihood to lead it; as thus: Alexander died, Alexander was buried, Alexander returneth to dust, the dust is earth, of earth we make loam, and why of that loam whereto he was converted might they not stop a beer-barrel?

> Imperious Caesar, dead and turn'd to clay,
> Might stop a hole to keep the wind away.
> O, that that earth, which kept the world in awe,
> Should patch a wall t' expel the winter's flaw!

ELEGY WRITTEN IN A COUNTRY CHURCHYARD
Thomas Gray (1716–1771)

The curfew tolls the knell of parting day,
    The lowing herd wind slowly o'er the lea,
The plowman homeward plods his weary way,
    And leaves the world to darkness and to me.

Now fades the glimmering landscape on the sight,
    And all the air a solemn stillness holds,
Save where the beetle wheels his droning flight,
    And drowsy tinklings lull the distant folds;

Save that from yonder ivy-mantled tower
    The moping owl does to the moon complain
Of such, as wandering near her secret bower,
    Molest her ancient solitary reign.

Beneath those rugged elms, that yew tree's shade,
    Where heaves the turf in many a moldering heap,
Each in his narrow cell forever laid,
    The rude forefathers of the hamlet sleep.

The breezy call of incense-breathing Morn,
    The swallow twittering from the straw-built shed,
The cock's shrill clarion, or the echoing horn,
    No more shall rouse them from their lowly bed.

For them no more the blazing hearth shall burn,
    Or busy housewife ply her evening care;
No children run to lisp their sire's return,
    Or climb his knees the envied kiss to share.

Oft did the harvest to their sickle yield,
    Their furrow oft the stubborn glebe has broke;
How jocund did they drive their team afield!
    How bowed the woods beneath their sturdy stroke!

Let not Ambition mock their useful toil,
    Their homely joys, and destiny obscure;
Nor Grandeur hear with a disdainful smile
    The short and simple annals of the poor.

The boast of heraldry, the pomp of power,
    And all that beauty, all that wealth e'er gave,
Awaits alike the inevitable hour.
    The paths of glory lead but to the grave.

Nor you, ye proud, impute to these the fault,
    If Memory o'er their tomb no trophies raise,
Where through the long-drawn aisle and fretted vault
    The pealing anthem swells the note of praise.

Can storied urn or animated bust
    Back to its mansion call the fleeting breath?
Can Honor's voice provoke the silent dust,
    Or Flattery soothe the dull cold ear of Death?

Perhaps in this neglected spot is laid
    Some heart once pregnant with celestial fire;
Hands that the rod of empire might have swayed,
    Or waked to ecstasy the living lyre.

But Knowledge to their eyes her ample page
    Rich with the spoils of time did ne'er unroll;
Chill Penury repressed their noble rage,
    And froze the genial current of the soul.

Full many a gem of purest ray serene,
    The dark unfathomed caves of ocean bear:
Full many a flower is born to blush unseen,
    And waste its sweetness on the desert air.

Some village Hampden, that with dauntless breast
    The little tyrant of his fields withstood;
Some mute inglorious Milton here may rest,
    Some Cromwell guiltless of his country's blood.

The applause of listening senates to command,
    The threats of pain and ruin to despise,
To scatter plenty o'er a smiling land,
    And read their history in a nation's eyes,

Their lot forbade: nor circumscribed alone
    Their growing virtues, but their crimes confined;

Forbade to wade through slaughter to a throne,
 And shut the gates of mercy on mankind,

The struggling pangs of conscious truth to hide,
 To quench the blushes of ingenuous shame,
Or heap the shrine of Luxury and Pride
 With incense kindled at the Muse's flame.

Far from the madding crowd's ignoble strife,
 Their sober wishes never learned to stray;
Along the cool sequestered vale of life
 They kept the noiseless tenor of their way.

Yet even these bones from insult to protect
 Some frail memorial still erected nigh,
With uncouth rhymes and shapeless sculpture decked,
 Implores the passing tribute of a sigh.

Their name, their years, spelt by the unlettered Muse,
 The place of fame and elegy supply:
And many a holy text around she strews,
 That teach the rustic moralist to die.

For who to dumb Forgetfulness a prey,
 This pleasing anxious being e'er resigned,
Left the warm precincts of the cheerful day,
 Nor cast one longing lingering look behind?

On some fond breast the parting soul relies,
 Some pious drops the closing eye requires;
Even from the tomb the voice of Nature cries,
 Even in our ashes live their wonted fires.

For thee, who mindful of the unhonored dead
 Dost in these lines their artless tale relate;
If chance, by lonely contemplation led,
 Some kindred spirit shall inquire thy fate,

Haply some hoary-headed swain may say,
 "Oft have we seen him at the peep of dawn
Brushing with hasty steps the dews away
 To meet the sun upon the upland lawn.

"There at the foot of yonder nodding beech
    That wreathes its old fantastic roots so high,
His listless length at noontide would he stretch,
    And pore upon the brook that babbles by.

"Hard by yon wood, now smiling as in scorn,
    Muttering his wayward fancies he would rove,
Now drooping, woeful wan, like one forlorn,
    Or crazed with care, or crossed in hopeless love.

"One morn I missed him on the customed hill,
    Along the heath and near his favorite tree;
Another came; nor yet beside the rill,
    Nor up the lawn, nor at the wood was he;

"The next with dirges due in sad array
    Slow through the churchway path we saw him borne.
Approach and read (for thou canst read) the lay,
    Graved on the stone beneath yon aged thorn."

THE EPITAPH

Here rests his head upon the lap of Earth
    A youth to Fortune and to Fame unknown
Fair Science frowned not on his humble birth,
    And Melancholy marked him for her own.

Large was his bounty, and his soul sincere,
    Heaven did a recompense as largely send:
He gave to Misery all he had, a tear,
    He gained from Heaven ('twas all he wished) a friend.

No farther seek his merits to disclose,
    Or draw his frailties from their dread abode
(There they alike in trembling hope repose),
    The bosom of his Father and his God.

OZYMANDIAS
Percy Bysshe Shelley (1792–1822)

I met a traveler from an antique land
Who said: Two vast and trunkless legs of stone
Stand in the desert. Near them, on the sand,
Half sunk, a shattered visage lies, whose frown,
And wrinkled lip, and sneer of cold command,
Tell that its sculptor well those passions read
Which yet survive, stamped on these lifeless things,
The hand that mocked them, and the heart that fed.
And on the pedestal these words appear:
"My name is Ozymandias, king of kings;
Look on my works, ye Mighty, and despair!"
Nothing beside remains. Round the decay
Of that colossal wreck, boundless and bare
The lone and level sands stretch far away.

SONG OF NEZAHUALCOYOTL
Aztec poem (c.1550)

This poem was written more than two centuries before William Cullen Bryant
was born. The similarities between this Native American poem and Bryant's
"Thanatopsis" are remarkable.

The fleeting pomps of the world are like the green willow trees, which,
aspiring to permanence, are consumed by a fire, fall before the ax, are
upturned by the wind, or are scarred and saddened by age.
The grandeurs of life are like the flowers in color and in fate; the beauty
of these remains so long as their chaste buds gather and store the rich
pearls of the dawn and saving it, drop it in liquid dew; but scarcely has
the Cause of All directed upon them the full rays of the sun, when their
beauty and glory fail, and the brilliant gay colors which decked forth
their pride wither and fade.
The delicious realms of flowers count their dynasties by short periods;
those which in the morning revel proudly in beauty and strength, by

evening weep for the sad destruction of their thrones, and for the mishaps which drive them to loss, to poverty, to death and to the grave.

All things of earth have an end, and in the midst of the most joyous lives, the breath falters, they fall, they sink into the ground.

All the earth is a grave, and naught escapes it; nothing is so perfect that it does not fall and disappear.

The rivers, brooks, fountains and waters flow on, and never return to their joyous beginnings; they hasten on to the vast realms of Tlaloc, and the wider they spread between their marges the more rapidly do they mold their own sepulchral urns.

That which was yesterday is not today; and let not that which is today trust to live tomorrow.

The caverns of the earth are filled with pestilential dust which once was the bones, the flesh, the bodies of great ones who sat upon thrones, deciding causes, ruling assemblies, governing armies, conquering provinces, possessing treasures, tearing down temples, flattering themselves with pride, majesty, fortune, praise, and dominion.

These glories have passed like the dark smoke thrown out by the fires of Popocatepetl, leaving no monuments but the rude skins on which they are written.

Ha! ha! Were I to introduce you into the obscure bowels of this temple, and were to ask you which of these bones were those of the powerful Achalchiuhtlanextin, first chief of the ancient Toltecs; of Necazecmitl, devout worshiper of the gods; if I inquire where is the peerless beauty of the glorious empress Xiuhtzal, where the peaceable Topiltzin, last monarch of the hapless land of Tulan; if I ask you where are the sacred ashes of our first father Xolotl; those of the bounteous Nopal; those of the generous Tlotzin; or even the still warm cinders of my glorious and immortal, though unhappy and luckless father Ixtlilxochitl; if I continued thus questioning about all our august ancestors, what would you reply?

The same that I reply—I know not, I know not; for first and last are confounded in the common clay.

What was their fate shall be ours, and of all who follow us.

Unconquered princes, warlike chieftains, let us seek, let us sigh for the heaven, for there all is eternal, and nothing is corruptible.

The darkness of the sepulchre is but the strengthening couch for the
glorious sun, and the obscurity of the night but serves to reveal the
brilliancy of the stars.
No one has power to alter these heavenly lights, for they serve to display
the greatness of their Creator, and as our eyes see them now, so saw
them our earliest ancestors, and so shall see them our latest posterity.

THANATOPSIS
William Cullen Bryant (1794–1878)

To him who in the love of Nature holds
Communion with her visible forms, she speaks
A various language; for his gayer hours
She has a voice of gladness, and a smile
And eloquence of beauty, and she glides
Into his darker musings, with a mild
And healing sympathy, that steals away
Their sharpness, ere he is aware. When thoughts
Of the last bitter hour come like a blight
Over thy spirit, and sad images
Of the stern agony, and shroud, and pall,
And breathless darkness, and the narrow house,
Make thee to shudder and grow sick at heart—
Go forth, under the open sky, and list
To Nature's teachings, while from all around—
Earth and her waters, and the depths of air—
Comes a still voice—Yet a few days, and thee
The all-beholding sun shall see no more
In all his course; nor yet in the cold ground,
Where thy pale form was laid, with many tears,
Nor in the embrace of ocean, shall exist
Thy image. Earth, that nourished thee, shall claim
Thy growth, to be resolved to earth again,
And, lost each human trace, surrendering up
Thine individual being, shalt thou go
To mix forever with the elements,

To be a brother to the insensible rock
And to the sluggish clod, which the rude swain
Turns with his share, and treads upon. The oak
Shall send his roots abroad, and pierce thy mold.

    Yet not to thine eternal resting place
Shalt thou retire alone, nor couldst thou wish
Couch more magnificent. Thou shalt lie down
With patriarchs of the infant world—with kings,
The powerful of the earth—the wise, the good,
Fair forms, and hoary seers of ages past,
All in one mighty sepulcher. The hills
Rock-ribbed and ancient as the sun—the vales
Stretching in pensive quietness between;
The venerable woods—rivers that move
In majesty, and the complaining brooks
That make the meadows green; and, poured round all,
Old Ocean's gray and melancholy waste—
Are but the solemn decorations all
Of the great tomb of man. The golden sun,
The planets, all the infinite host of heaven,
Are shining on the sad abodes of death,
Through the still lapse of ages. All that tread
The globe are but a handful to the tribes
That slumber in its bosom. Take the wings
Of morning, pierce the Barcan wilderness,
Or lose thyself in the continuous woods
Where rolls the Oregon, and hears no sound,
Save his own dashings—yet the dead are there;
And millions in those solitudes, since first
The flight of years began, have laid them down
In their last sleep—the dead reign there alone.
So shalt thou rest, and what if thou withdraw
In silence from the living, and no friend
Take note of thy departure? All that breathe
Will share thy destiny. The gay will laugh
When thou art gone, the solemn brood of care
Plod on, and each one as before will chase
His favorite phantom; yet all these shall leave

Their mirth and their employments, and shall come
And make their bed with thee. As the long train
Of ages glides away, the sons of men,
The youth in life's green spring, and he who goes
In the full strength of years, matron and maid,
The speechless babe, and the gray-headed man—
Shall one by one be gathered to thy side,
By those who in their turn shall follow them.

So live, that when thy summons comes to join
The innumerable caravan, which moves
To that mysterious realm where each shall take
His chamber in the silent halls of death,
Thou go not, like the quarry slave at night,
Scourged to his dungeon, but, sustained and soothed
By an unfaltering trust, approach thy grave,
Like one who wraps the drapery of his couch
About him, and lies down to pleasant dreams.

THE EMPEROR WORM
Edgar Allan Poe (1809–1849)

Lo! 'tis a gala night
    Within the lonesome latter years!
An angel throng, bewinged, bedight
    In veils, and drowned in tears,
Sit in a theatre, to see
    A play of hopes and fears,
While the orchestra breathes fitfully
    The music of the spheres.

Mimes, in the form of God on high,
    Mutter and mumble low,
And hither and thither fly—
    Mere puppets they, who come and go
At bidding of vast formless things
    That shift the scenery to and fro,
Flapping from out their Condor wings
    Invisible Woe!

That motley drama!—oh, be sure
    It shall not be forgot!
With its Phantom chased forever more,
    By a crowd that seize it not,
Through a circle that ever returneth in
    To the self-same spot,
And much of Madness and more of Sin
    And Horror the soul of the plot.

But see, amid the mimic rout,
    A crawling shape intrude!
A blood-red thing that writhes from out
    The scenic solitude!
It writhes!—it writhes!—with mortal pangs
    The mimes become its food,
And the seraphs sob at vermin fangs
    In human gore imbued.

Out—out are the lights—out all!
    And over each quivering form,
The curtain, a funeral pall,
    Comes down with the rush of a storm,
And the angels, all pallid and wan,
    Uprising, unveiling, affirm
That the play is the tragedy, "Man,"
    And its hero the Conqueror Worm.

THIS QUIET DUST
Emily Dickinson (1830–1886)

This quiet Dust was Gentlemen and Ladies
And Lads and Girls—
Was laughter and ability and Sighing
And Frocks and Curls.

This Passive Place a Summer's nimble mansion
Where Bloom and Bees
Exist an Oriental Circuit
Then cease, like these—

THE JOURNEY NEARS THE ROAD-END
Rabindranath Tagore (1861–1941)

Having written his first novel when he was nineteen, Tagore was awarded the Nobel Prize in Literature in 1913, especially for his *Gitanjali* (Song Offerings), the first Asian writer to receive this prize. A native of Bengal, he became an internationally known Indian poet, musician, dramatist, artist, and politician in this century. This poem, a Bengali original, was first published in 1924.

The journey nears the road-end
    where the shadows deepen with death.
The setting sun unties the last strings of its gifts,
    Squanders gold with both hands.
Death is lighted with festive colors;
    Life is before me.

With this word my breath will stop:
    I loved.
Love's overbrimming mystery
    joins death and life. It
Has filled my cup of pain
    with joy.

The *Vaisakh* storm lashed sorrow's road
    Where I walked, a lonely pilgrim,
Many nights bereft of light.
    Yet beckonings reached my heart.
Slander's thorn pricked me
    As a garland of triumph.

Gazing at the face of earth
    I never exhausted wonder.
Lakshmi, grace in the lotus of beauty,
    Touched me.
I caught in my flute
    The breath that rocks with laughs and cries.

I claimed for my soul
    Those human voices of the divine.
Many defeats, much fear and shame,
    Yet I saw greatness.

In the midst of agony and striving
    The door suddenly opened.

I gained the right of birth;
    That glory was mine.
I shared the stream that flows from ages,
    in wisdom, work, and thought.
If a vision were mine
    It belonged to all.

Sitting in the dust, I saw the supreme
    in light beyond the light,
Smaller than the smallest, great beyond the greatest,
    Transcending the senses.
I often beheld the unquenchable flame
    Rending the body.

Wherever a saint atoned,
    I gained.
Whoever triumphed over delusion,
    I knew myself in him;
Wherever a hero died with ease,
    My place is in his history.

Perfect beyond perfection, even if I forgot His name
    I offered Him worship.
The quiet sky reached me,
    At dawn I received the radiance.
My death will be fulfilled
    In this earth with the splendor of life.

Today in the farewell of the year,
    Death, remove your veil.
Much has fallen aside, love's tenderness often left me,
    Lightless memory faded on the road
But at this deathless moment of life, O Death
    Your hands are filled with treasure.

FOR A DEAD LADY
Edwin Arlington Robinson (1869–1935)

No more with overflowing light
Shall fill the eyes that now are faded,
Nor shall another's fringe with night
Their woman-hidden world as they did.
No more shall quiver down the days
The flowing wonder of her ways,
Whereof no language may requite
The shifting and the many-shaded.

The grace, divine, definitive,
Clings only as a faint forestalling;
The laugh that love could not forgive
Is hushed, and answers to no calling;
The forehead and the little ears
Have gone where Saturn keeps the years;
The breast where roses could not live
Has done with rising and with falling.

The beauty, shattered by the laws
That have creation in their keeping,
No longer trembles at applause,
Or over children that are sleeping;
And we who delve in beauty's lore
Know all that we have known before
Of what inexorable cause
Makes Time so vicious in his reaping.

THERE, ON THE DARKENED DEATHBED
John Masefield (1878–1967)

There, on the darkened deathbed, dies the brain
That flared three several times in seventy years;
It cannot lift the silly hand again,
Nor speak, nor sing, it neither sees nor hears.
And muffled mourners put it in the ground
And then go home, and in the earth it lies,
Too dark for vision and too deep for sound,
The million cells that made a good man wise.
Yet for a few short years an influence stirs,
A sense or wraith or essence of him dead,
Which makes insensate things its ministers
To those beloved, his spirit's daily bread;
Then that, too, fades; in book or deed a spark
Lingers, then that, too, fades; then all is dark.

BLIND DATE
Conrad Aiken (1889–1973)

No more the swanboat on the artificial lake
its paddled path through neon light shall take;
the stars are turned out on the immortal ferris wheel,
dark and still are the cars of the Virginia Reel.
Baby, it is the last of all blind dates,
and this we keep with the keeper of the golden gates.

For the last time, my darling, the chute-the-chutes,
the Tunnel of Love, the cry 'all men are brutes,'
the sweaty dance-hall with the juke-box playing,
pretzels and beer, and our young love a-Maying:
baby, it is the last of all blind dates,
and this we keep with the keeper of the golden gates.

The radios in a thousand taxis die;
at last man's music fades from the inhuman sky;

as, short or long, fades out the impermanent wave
to find in the ether or the earth its grave.
Baby, it is the last of all blind dates,
and this we keep with the keeper of the golden gates.

Hold hands and kiss, it will never come again,
look in your own eyes and remember the deep pain,
how hollow the world is, like a bubble burst,
yes, and all beauty by some wretchedness accursed!
Baby, it is the last of all blind dates,
and this we keep with the keeper of the golden gates.

Love now the footworn grass, the trampled flowers,
and the divided man of crowds, for he is ours—
love him, yes, love him now, this sundered being,
who most himself seeks when himself most fleeing—
baby, it is the last of all blind dates,
and this we keep with the keeper of the golden gates.

But look—the scenic railway is flashed from red to green—
and swiftly beneath our feet as this machine
our old star plunges down the precipitous sky,
down the hurrahs of space! So soon to die!—
But baby, it is the last of all blind dates;
and we shall keep it with the keeper of the golden gates.

STORY OF THE WIDOW'S SON
Mary Lavin (b. 1912)

Born in the United States, Mary Lavin has lived in Ireland since the age of ten. Although she has written several novels, she is best known as one of Ireland's leading short-story writers. The following story, with its alternative endings, explores the inevitability theme in an intriguing manner.

This is the story of a widow's son, but it is a story that has two endings.

There was once a widow, living in a small neglected village at the foot of a steep hill. She had only one son, but he was the meaning of her life. She lived for his sake. She wore herself out working for him. Every day she made a hundred sacrifices in order to keep him at a good school in the town, four miles away, because there was a better teacher there than the village dullard that had taught herself.

She made great plans for Packy, but she did not tell him about her plans. Instead she threatened him, day and night, that if he didn't turn out well, she would put him to work on the roads, or in the quarry under the hill.

But as the years went by, everyone in the village, and even Packy himself, could tell by the way she watched him out of sight in the morning, and watched to see him come into sight in the evening, that he was the beat of her heart, and that her gruff words were only a cover for her pride and her joy in him.

It was for Packy's sake that she walked for hours along the road, letting her cow graze the long acre of the wayside grass, in order to spare the few poor blades that pushed up through the stones in her own field. It was for his sake she walked back and forth to the town to sell a few cabbages as soon as ever they were fit. It was for his sake that she got up in the cold dawning hours to gather mushrooms that would take the place of foods that had to be bought with money. She bent her back daily to make every penny she could, and as often happens, she made more by industry, out of her few bald acres, than many of the farmers around her made out of their great bearded meadows. Out of the money she made by selling eggs alone, she paid for Packy's clothes and for the greater number of his books.

When Packy was fourteen, he was in the last class in the school, and the master had great hopes of his winning a scholarship to a big college in the city. He was getting to be a tall lad, and his features were beginning to take a strong cast. His character was strengthening too, under his mother's sharp tongue. The people of the village were beginning to give him the same respect they gave to the sons of the farmers who came from their fine colleges in the summer, with blue suits and bright ties. And whenever they spoke to the widow they praised him up to the skies.

One day in June, when the air was so heavy the scent that rose up from the grass was imprisoned under the low clouds and hung in the air, the widow was waiting at the gate for Packy. There had been no rain for some days and the hens and chickens were pecking irritably at the dry ground and wandering up and down the road in bewilderment.

A neighbor passed.

"Waiting for Packy?" said the neighbor, pleasantly, and he stood for a minute to take off his hat and wipe the sweat of the day from his face. He was an old man.

"It's a hot day!" he said. "It will be a hard push for Packy on that battered old bike of his. I wouldn't like to have to face into four miles on a day like this!"

"Packy would travel three times that distance if there was a book at the other end of the road!" said the widow, with the pride of those who cannot read more than a line or two without wearying.

The minutes went by slowly. The widow kept looking up at the sun. "I suppose the heat is better than the rain!" she said, at last.

"The heat can do a lot of harm, too, though," said the neighbor, absent-mindedly, as he pulled a long blade of grass from between the stones of the wall and began to chew the end of it. "You could get sunstroke on a day like this!" He looked up at the sun. "The sun is a terror," he said. "It could cause you to drop down dead like a stone!"

The widow strained out further over the gate. She looked up the hill in the direction of the town.

"He will have a good cool breeze on his face coming down the hill, at any rate," she said.

The man looked up the hill. "That's true. On the hottest day of the year you would get a cool breeze coming down that hill on a bicycle. You would feel the air streaming past your cheeks like silk. And in the winter it's like two knives flashing to either side of you, and peeling off your skin like you'd peel the bark off a sally-rod!" He chewed the grass meditatively. "That must be one of the steepest hills in Ireland," he said. "That hill is a hill worthy of the name of a hill." He took the grass out of his mouth. "It's my belief," he said, earnestly looking at the widow—"it's my belief that that hill is to be found marked with a name in the Ordnance Survey map!"

"If that's the case," said the widow, "Packy will be able to tell you all about it. When it isn't a book he has in his hand it's a map."

"Is that so?" said the man. "That's interesting. A map is a great thing. A map is not an ordinary thing. It isn't everyone can make out a map."

The widow wasn't listening.

"I think I see Packy!" she said, and she opened the wooden gate and stepped out into the roadway.

At the top of the hill there was glitter of spokes as a bicycle came into sight. Then there was a flash of blue jersey as Packy came flying downward, gripping the handlebars of the bike, with his bright hair blown back from his forehead. The hill was so steep, and he came down so fast, that it seemed to the man and woman at the bottom of the hill that he was not moving at all, but that it was the bright trees and bushes, the bright ditches and wayside grasses that were streaming away to either side of him.

The hens and chickens clucked and squawked and ran along the road looking for a safe place in the ditches. They ran to either side with feminine fuss and chatter. Packy waved to his mother. He came nearer and nearer. They could see the freckles on his face.

"Shoo!" cried Packy, at the squawking hens that had not yet left the roadway. They ran with their long necks straining forward.

"Shoo!" said Packy's mother, lifting her apron and flapping it in the air to frighten them out of his way.

It was only afterwards, when the harm was done, that the widow began to think that it might, perhaps, have been the flapping of her own apron that frightened the old clucking hen, and sent her flying out over the garden wall into the middle of the road.

The old hen appeared suddenly on top of the grassy ditch and looked with a distraught eye at the hens and chickens as they ran to right and left. Her own feathers began to stand out from her. She craned her neck forward and gave a distracted squawk, and fluttered down into the middle of the hot dusty road.

Packy jammed on the brakes. The widow screamed. There was a flurry of white feathers and a spurt of blood. The bicycle swerved and fell. Packy was thrown over the handlebars.

It was such a simple accident that, although the widow screamed, and although the old man looked around to see if there was help near, neither of them thought that Packy was very badly hurt, but when they ran over and lifted his head, and saw that he could not speak, they wiped the blood from his face and looked around, desperately, to measure the distance they would have to carry him.

It was only a few yards to the door of the cottage, but Packy was dead before they got him across the threshold.

"He's only in a weakness!" screamed the widow, and she urged the crowd that had gathered outside the door to do something for him. "Get a doctor!" she cried, pushing a young laborer towards the door. "Hurry! Hurry! The doctor will bring him around."

But the neighbors that kept coming in the door, quickly, from all sides, were crossing themselves, one after another, and falling on their knees, as soon as they laid eyes on the body, stretched out flat on the bed, with the dust and dirt and the sweat marks of life on his dead face.

When at last the widow was convinced that her son was dead, the other women had to hold her down. She waved her arms and cried out aloud, and wrestled to get free. She wanted to wring the neck of every hen in the yard.

"I'll kill every one of them. What good are they to me, now? All the hens in the world aren't worth one drop of human blood. That old clucking hen wasn't worth more than six shillings, at the very most. What is six shillings? Is it worth poor Packy's life?"

But after a time she stopped raving, and looked from one face to another.

"Why didn't he ride over the old hen?" she asked. "Why did he try to save an old hen that wasn't worth more than six shillings? Didn't he know he was worth more to his mother than an old hen that would be going into the pot one of these days? Why did he do it? Why did he put on the brakes going down one of the worst hills in the country? Why? Why?"

The neighbors patted her arm.

"There now!" they said. "There now!" and that was all they could think of saying, and they said it over and over again. "There now! There now!"

And years afterwards, whenever the widow spoke of her son Packy to the neighbors who dropped in to keep her company for an hour or two, she always had the same question to ask—the same tireless question.

"Why did he put the price of an old clucking hen above the price of his own life?"

And the people always gave the same answer.

"There now!" they said, "There now!" And they sat as silently as the widow herself, looking into the fire.

But surely some of those neighbors must have been stirred to wonder what would have happened had Packy not yielded to his impulse of fear, and had, instead, ridden boldly over the old clucking hen? And surely some of them must have stared into the flames and pictured the scene of the accident again, altering a detail here and there as they did so, and giving the story a different end. For these people knew the widow, and they knew Packy, and when you know people well it is as easy to guess what they would say and do in certain circumstances as it is to remember what they actually did say and do in other circumstances. In fact it is sometimes easier to invent than to remember accurately, and were this not so two great branches of creative art would wither in an hour: the art of the storyteller and the art of the gossip. So, perhaps, if I try to tell you what I myself think might have happened had Packy killed that cackling old hen, you will not accuse me of abusing my privileges as a writer. After all, what I am about to tell you is no more of a fiction than what I have already told, and I lean no heavier now upon your credulity than, with your full consent, I did in the first instance.

And moreover, in many respects the new story is the same as the old.

It begins in the same way too. There is the widow grazing her cow by the wayside, and walking the long roads to the town, weighted down with sacks of cabbages that will pay for Packy's schooling. There she is, fussing over Packy in the mornings in case he would be late for school. There she is in the evening watching the battered clock on the dresser for the hour when he will appear on the top of the hill at his return. And there too, on a hot day in June, is the old laboring man coming up the road, and pausing to talk to her, as she stood at the door. There he is dragging a blade of grass from between the stones of the wall, and putting it between his teeth to chew, before he opens his mouth.

And when he opens his mouth at last it is to utter the same remark.

"Waiting for Packy?" said the old man, and then he took off his hat and wiped the sweat from his forehead. It will be remembered that he was an old man. "It's a hot day," he said.

"It's very hot," said the widow, looking anxiously up the hill. "It's a hot day to push a bicycle four miles along a bad road with the dust rising to choke you, and sun striking spikes off the handlebars!"

"The heat is better than the rain, all the same," said the old man.

"I suppose it is," said the widow. "All the same, there were days when Packy came home with the rain dried into his clothes so bad they stood up stiff like boards when he took them off. They stood up stiff like boards against the wall, for all the world as if he was still standing in them!"

"Is that so?" said the old man. "You may be sure he got a good petting on those days. There is no son like a widow's son. A ewe lamb!"

"Is it Packy?" said the widow, in disgust. "Packy never got a day's petting since the day he was born. I made up my mind from the first that I'd never make a soft one out of him."

The widow looked up the hill again, and set herself to raking the gravel outside the gate as if she were in the road for no other purpose. Then she gave another look up the hill.

"Here he is now!" she said, and she raised such a cloud of dust with the rake that they could hardly see the glitter of the bicycle spokes, and the flash of blue jersey as Packy came down the hill at a breakneck speed.

Nearer and nearer he came, faster and faster, waving his hand to the widow, shouting at the hens to leave the way!

The hens ran for the ditches, stretching their necks in gawky terror. And then, as the last hen squawked into the ditch, the way was clear for a moment before the whirling silver spokes.

Then, unexpectedly, up from nowhere it seemed, came an old clucking hen and, clucking despairingly, it stood for a moment on the top of the wall and then rose into the air with the clumsy flight of a ground fowl.

Packy stopped whistling. The widow screamed. Packy yelled and the widow flapped her apron. Then Packy swerved the bicycle, and a cloud of dust rose from the braked wheel.

For a minute it could not be seen what exactly had happened, but Packy put his foot down and dragged it along the ground in the dust till he brought the bicycle to a sharp stop. He threw the bicycle down with a clatter on the hard road and ran back. The widow could not bear to look. She threw her apron over her head.

"He's killed the clucking hen!" she said. "He's killed her! He's killed her!" and then she let the apron fall back into place, and began to run up the hill herself. The old man spat out the blade of grass that he had been chewing and ran after the woman.

"Did you kill it?" screamed the widow, and as she got near enough to see the blood and feathers she raised her arm over her head, and her fist was clenched till the knuckles shone white. Packy cowered down over the carcass of the fowl and hunched up his shoulders as if to shield himself from a blow. His legs were spattered with blood, and the brown and white feathers of the dead hen were stuck to his hands, and stuck to his clothes, and they were strewn all over the road. Some of the short white inner feathers were still swirling with the dust in the air.

"I couldn't help it, Mother. I couldn't help it. I didn't see her till it was too late!"

The widow caught up the hen and examined it all over, holding it by the bone of the breast, and letting the long neck dangle. Then, catching it by the leg, she raised it suddenly above her head, and brought down the bleeding body on the boy's back, in blow after blow, spattering the blood all over his face and his hands, over his clothes and over the white dust of the road around him.

"How dare you lie to me!" she screamed, gaspingly, between the blows. "You saw the hen. I know you saw it. You stopped whistling! You called out! We were watching you. We saw." She turned upon the old man. "Isn't that right?" she demanded. "He saw the hen, didn't he? He saw it?"

"It looked that way," said the old man, uncertainly, his eye on the dangling fowl in the widow's hand.

"There you are!" said the widow. She threw the hen down on the road. "You saw the hen in front of you on the road, as plain as you see it now," she accused, "but you wouldn't stop to save it because you were in too big a hurry home to fill your belly! Isn't that so?"

"No, Mother. No! I saw her all right but it was too late to do anything."

"He admits now that he saw it," said the widow, turning and nodding triumphantly at the onlookers who had gathered at the sound of the shouting.

"I never denied seeing it!" said the boy, appealing to the onlookers as to his judges.

"He doesn't deny it!" screamed the widow. "He stands there as brazen as you like, and admits for all the world to hear that he saw the hen as plain as the nose on his face, and he rode over it without a thought!"

"But what else could I do?" said the boy, throwing out his hand; appealing to the crowd now, and now appealing to the widow. "If I'd put on the brakes going down the hill at such a speed I would have been put over the handlebars!"

"And what harm would that have done you?" screamed the widow. "I often saw you taking a toss when you were wrestling with Jimmy Mack and I heard no complaints afterwards, although your elbows and knees would be running blood, and your face scraped like a gridiron!" She turned to the crowd. "That's as true as God. I often saw him come in with his nose spouting blood like a pump, and one eye closed as tight as the eye of a corpse. My hand was often stiff for a week from sopping out wet clothes to put poultices on him and try to bring his face back to rights again." She swung back to Packy again. "You're not afraid of a fall when you go climbing trees, are you? You're not afraid to go up on the roof after a cat, are you? Oh, there's more in this than you want me to know. I can see that. You killed that hen on purpose—that's what I believe! You're tired of going to school. You want to get out of going away to college. That's it. You think if you kill the few poor hens we have there will be no money in the box when the time comes to pay for books and classes. That's it!" Packy began to redden.

"It's late in the day for me to be thinking of things like that," he said. "It's long ago I should have started those tricks if that was the way I felt. But it's not true. I want to go to college. The reason I was coming down the hill so fast was to tell you that I got the scholarship. The teacher told me as I was leaving the schoolhouse. That's why I was pedaling so hard. That's why I was whistling. That's why I was waving my hand. Didn't you see me waving my hand from once I came in sight of the top of the hill?"

The widow's hands fell to her side. The wind of words died down within her and left her flat and limp. She didn't know what to say. She could feel the neighbors staring at her. She wished that they were gone away about their business. She wanted to throw out her arms to the boy, to drag him against her heart and hug him like a small child. But she thought of how the crowd would look at each other and nod and snigger. A ewe lamb! She didn't want to satisfy them. If she gave in to her feelings now they would know how much she had been counting on his getting the scholarship. She wouldn't please them! She wouldn't satisfy them!

She looked at Packy, and when she saw him standing there before her, spattered with the furious feathers and crude blood of the dead hen, she felt a fierce disappointment for the boy's own disappointment, and a fierce resentment against him for killing the hen on this day of all days, and spoiling the great news of his success.

Her mind was in confusion. She started at the blood on his face, and all at once it seemed as if the blood was a bad omen of the future that was for him. Disappointment, fear, resentment, and above all defiance, raised themselves within her like screeching animals. She looked from Packy to the onlookers.

"Scholarship! Scholarship!" she sneered, putting as much derision as she could into her voice and expression.

"I suppose you think you are a great fellow now? I suppose you think you are independent now? I suppose you think you can go off with yourself now, and look down on your poor slave of a mother who scraped and sweated for you with her cabbages and her hens? I suppose you think to yourself that it doesn't matter now whether the hens are alive or dead? Is that the way? Well, let me tell you this! You're not as independent as you think. The scholarship may pay for your books and your teacher's fees but who will pay for your clothes? Ah ha, you forgot that, didn't you?" She put her hands on her hips. Packy hung his head. He no longer appealed to the gawking neighbors. They might have been able to save him from blows but he knew enough about life to know that no one could save him from shame.

The widow's heart burned at sight of his shamed face, as her heart burned with grief, but her temper too burned fiercer and fiercer, and she came to a point at which nothing could quell the blaze till it had burned itself out. "Who'll buy your suits?" she yelled. "Who'll buy your boots?" She paused to think of more humiliating accusations. "Who'll buy your breeches?" She paused again and her teeth bit against each other. What would wound deepest? What shame could she drag upon him? "Who'll buy your nightshirts or will you sleep in your skin?"

The neighbors laughed at that, and the tension was broken. The widow herself laughed. She held her sides and laughed, and as she laughed everything seemed to take on a newer and simpler significance. Things were not as bad as they seemed a moment before. She wanted Packy to laugh too. She looked at him. But as she looked at Packy her heart turned cold with a strange new fear.

"Get into the house!" she said, giving him a push ahead of her. She wanted him safe under her own roof. She wanted to get him away from the gaping neighbors. She hated them, man, woman, and child. She felt that if they had not been there things would have been different. And she wanted to get away from the sight of the blood on the road. She wanted to mash a few potatoes and make a bit of potato cake for Packy. That would comfort him. He loved that.

Packy hardly touched the food. And even after he had washed and scrubbed himself there were stains of blood turning up in the most unexpected places: behind his ears, under his fingernails, inside the cuff of his sleeve.

"Put on your good clothes," said the widow, making a great effort to be gentle, but her manners had become as twisted and as hard as the branches of the trees across the road from her, and even the kindly offers she made sounded harsh. The boy sat on the chair in a slumped position that kept her nerves on edge and set up a further conflict of irritation and love in her heart. She hated to see him slumping there in the chair, not asking to go outside the door, but still she was uneasy whenever he as much as looked in the direction of the door. She felt safe while he was under the roof; inside the lintel under her eyes.

Next day she went in to wake him for school, but his room was empty; his bed had not been slept in, and when she ran out into the yard and called him everywhere there was no answer. She ran up and down. She called at the houses of the neighbors but he was not in any house. And she thought she could hear sniggering behind her in each house that she left, as she ran to another one. He wasn't in the village. He wasn't in the town. The master of the school said that she should let the police have a description of him. He said he never met a boy as sensitive as Packy. A boy like that took strange notions into his head from time to time.

The police did their best but there was no news of Packy that night. A few days later there was a letter saying that he was well. He asked his mother to notify the master that he would not be coming back, so that some other boy could claim the scholarship. He said that he would send the price of the hen as soon as he made some money.

Another letter in a few weeks said that he had got a job on a trawler, and that he would not be able to write very often but that he would put aside some of his pay every week and send it to his mother whenever he got into port. He said that he wanted to pay her back for all she had done for him. He gave no address. He kept his promise about the money but he never gave any address when he wrote. . . . And so the people may have let their thoughts run on, as they sat by the fire with the widow, many a night, listening to her complaining voice saying the same thing over and over. "Why did he put the price of an old hen above the price of his own life?" And it is possible that their version of the story has a certain element of truth about it too. Perhaps all our actions have this double quality about them; this possibility of alternative, and that it is only by careful watching and absolute sincerity, that we follow the path that is destined for us, and, no matter how tragic that may be, it is better than the tragedy we bring upon ourselves.

from THE CANCER WARD
Aleksandr Solzhenitsyn (b. 1918)

The setting of this novel is a Russian hospital in the winter of 1955. Lyudmila Afanasyevna Dontsova has worked in the hospital for twenty years and is now the head of the radiology unit. She is also one of the hospital's oncologists. When she begins to suspect that she has cancer, she seeks out Tikhonovich Oreshchenkov, a retired radiologist and oncologist, for professional advice.

"Dormidont Tikhonovich, I've come to ask you whether you would come to the hospital to give me a gastro-intestinal examination. We'll arrange it for any day that's convenient for you."

She looked grey and her voice faltered. Oreshchenkov watched her steadily and unwaveringly, and his arched brows did not express a millimeter's surprise.

"Certainly, Lyudmila Afanasyevna. We'll pick a day. But tell me your symptoms now, anyway. And what you think yourself."

"I'll tell you my symptoms right away, but as for what I think—you know, I try not to think! That is, I think about it too much, I've begun to lose sleep, and it would be best if I didn't know. Seriously. You decide whether I ought to enter the hospital, and I'll enter, but I don't want to know more. If I'm to be operated on, I'd rather not know the diagnosis, so as not to be thinking during the operation: What can they do for me now? And what will they discover? Do you understand?"

Whether it was because of the deep armchair or her sagging shoulders, she did not look like a big, strong woman now. She had shrunk.

"Perhaps I understand, Lyudochka, but I don't agree. Why do you talk of an operation first thing?"

"Well, you have to be prepared . . ."

"Why didn't you come sooner, then? Of all people, *you* should know enough for that."

"It's hard to say, Dormidont Tikhonovich," sighed Dontsova. "That's the way life is, you get caught up in the whirl of things. Of course I should have come sooner. But don't think I've let it go far!" she protested vigorously to herself. Her rapid, businesslike manner of speech returned. "It seems unfair that I, an oncologist, should be stricken by an oncological ailment, when I know every one of them, when I imagine all the attendant effects, the consequences, and the complications."

"There's no injustice here," his deep and measured voice said persuasively. "This is the surest test of a doctor: to suffer an illness in his own specialty."

. . . .

Dontsova could not imagine how something she knew so well, knew through and through and inside out, could be so turned around to become entirely new and strange. She had been dealing with the ailments of others for thirty years. She had spent a good twenty years at the x-ray screen. She had read the screen, she had read the x-ray films, she had read the tortured, pleading eyes; she had compared analyses and consulted books, she had written articles, disputed with colleagues, argued with patients—and her entire experience, her tested point of view, had only become more unalterable, medical theory more ironclad. There was the etiology and pathogenesis, the symptoms, the diagnosis, the course of the disease, the treatment, prevention, and prognosis; but the resistance, doubts, and fears of the patients, although they were understandable human weaknesses and aroused the doctor's sympathy, were zeros when the methods were weighed. No place had been left for them in the logical quadrates.

Until now all human bodies had been arranged alike; the single anatomical atlas described them. The physiology of the vital processes and the physiology of sensations were uniform. The entirely authoritative texts logically explained everything that was normal and everything that was a deviation from the normal.

Then, suddenly, in a few days, her own body fell out of this harmonious and great system, struck the hard earth, and turned out to be a helpless sack filled with organs, each of which could ail and cry out at any moment.

In a few days everything had turned inside out, and what used to be comprised of elements she knew and had studied became *terra incognita* and frightening.

When her son had been a little boy, she had looked at drawings with him. The simplest household objects—a tea kettle, a spoon, a chair—when drawn from an unusual angle became unrecognizable.

Now she found the course of her own illness and its place in the treatment just as unrecognizable. Now she was not to be the wise, guiding force in the treatment, but the unreasoning, inert object of this force. Her first admission of the ailment's existence crushed her as if she were an ant. Her first adjustment to the illness was unbearable: the whole world was topsy-turvy, the whole order of things was capsized. Not yet dead, she had to take leave of her husband, her son, her daughter, her grandson and her work—although this work would now thunder over her and through her. In one day she had to put aside everything that constituted life, and then, as a pale-green shadow, still endure many torments, without knowing for a long time whether she would go on to a complete death or return to life.

Her life, it seemed, had been bare of luxuries, gaiety, or festivity—a round of work and cares, work and cares—but this life appeared so beautiful and desirable, so impossible to part with, that the thought of it drew a wail of anguish from her.

The whole of Sunday had been not Sunday to her, but a preparation of herself for the next day's x-ray examination.

At a quarter past eight on Monday, as they had agreed, Dormidont Tikhonovich, with Vera Gangart and another member of the staff, turned off the lights in the x-ray room and began to adjust the apparatus in the dark. Lyudmila Afanasyevna undressed and went behind the screen. As she took the first glass of barium solution from the orderly, she awkwardly spilled some; her hand, which, in rubber glove, had so many times pressed stomachs here, now shook.

They went through all the familiar procedures: feeling, pressing, turning, raising her arms, breathing in. They swung the apparatus horizontal, placed her on the table, and took x-ray pictures from various angles. Then they had to allow time for the contrasting mass to descend the digestive tract further. The x-ray apparatus could not be permitted to remain idle, and, while they waited, the doctor on duty took her regular patients. Lyudmila Afanasyevna even sat down to help her, but her mind was unable to focus on this and she was no help. Again the time came for her to stand behind the screen, drink the barium and lie down for filming.

. . . .

As she obeyed the instructions Lyudmila Afanasyevna could not think about them herself and did not try to find the explanations for them.

Nevertheless, once she let slip: "From what you're doing, I see what you're looking for!"

She thought they suspected a tumor, not of the stomach or the duodenum, but of the esophagus, which was the most difficult because it required partial opening of the chest cavity if there were to be an operation.

"Well, Lyu-udochka!" Oreshchenkov boomed in the darkness. "You want early diagnosis, but now you don't like our method. Would you rather wait three months? Then it would be easier to diagnose right off."

"No, thank you!"

She did not want to look at the big x-ray picture that they obtained toward the end of the day. She had lost her usual resolute, mannish gestures. She sat meekly under the bright ceiling light and waited for Oreshchenkov's concluding words—words, decision; but not diagnosis.

"Well, my esteemed colleague," Oreshchenkov benevolently spun it out, "the notables are divided in their opinions."

But from under his arched brows he kept watching her dismay. One might have expected greater strength from the resolute, austere Dontsova in this trial. Her sudden softening once again confirmed Oreshchenkov's opinion that modern man is helpless in the face of death, that he comes utterly unarmed to meet it.

PEOPLE
Yevgeny Yevtushenko (b. 1933)

No people are uninteresting.
Their fate is like the chronicle of planets.

Nothing in them is not particular,
and planet is dissimilar from planet.

And if a man lived in obscurity
making his friends in that obscurity
obscurity is not uninteresting.

To each his world is private,
and in that world one excellent minute.

And in that world one tragic minute.
These are private.

In any man who dies there dies with him
his first snow and kiss and fight.
It goes with him.

They are left books and bridges
and painted canvas and machinery.

Whose fate is to survive.
But what has gone is also not nothing:

by the rule of the game something has gone.
Not people die but worlds die in them.

Whom we knew as faulty, the earth's creatures.
Of whom, essentially, what did we know?

Brother of a brother? Friend of friends?
Lover of lover?

We who knew our fathers
in everything, in nothing.

They perish. They cannot be brought back.
The secret worlds are not regenerated.

And every time again and again
I make my lament against destruction.

2. DEATH PERSONIFIED

A WIDELY disparate literature exists in which death is depicted not as an impersonal event which occurs in all human lives, but as a personal agent residing in the universe and waiting to bring about loss of life for individual human beings at an appointed time. This personal agent, usually addressed as Death, is described in various poems, plays, and prose pieces as having humanlike characteristics, yet clearly not being limited in terms of time and space. Death is sometimes depicted in the literature of the East and West as having a humanlike body dressed in black or flaming red clothes, a face, eyes, hands (often holding a scythe, rope, spear, or other weapon), the capacity for human language, and an obsession for accurate timekeeping in appointments. In other pieces of world literature, death is described as a grotesque monster who, while having the capacity of human speech, possesses multiple heads and hands, a body which throws off flame, and an insatiable desire to kill and punish humans.

Numerous pieces of literature in Hinduism personify death. Characteristic of the Vedic period of Hinduism (1500–450 B.C.) is the personification of death as Yama, the first man ever to die and now the god of the dead. Yama is frequently depicted as sending forth noose-carrying messengers who, at the death of a human, seize the soul of the deceased and return with it to the realm of the dead. Sometimes, as in the Savitri story which follows, Yama is said to function himself as the messenger of death. As such, he appears differently to different people. To righteous persons, he appears kind and gentle; to unrighteous persons, he seems a terrifying figure bent on destruction and punishment.

While Yama continues to appear in later Hindu writings as death personified, there is an unusual personification of death as a woman in the *Mahabharata*. Vyasa, the legendary author of this epic poem, tells an ancient story whose purpose is to answer the question, "Whence is death?" According to the story, the god Brahma created humans to be immortal. With the passage of time, however, the earth was in danger of being overpopulated. The first solution considered by Brahma was simply to decimate the entire population with fire. The god Shiva approached Brahma and offered another solution: rather than destroying all humans and other living creatures, why not let them return to the earth through an endless process of repeated births and deaths? Suddenly from openings in the body of Brahma, the lord of creation, there came a beautiful woman with dark eyes. Brahma addressed her with the name "Death," and told her to go into the world and begin the process of slaying his creatures, the fools and the wise alike. When she hesitated and asked to be released from this dreadful duty, she was promised that the god Yama and diverse diseases would help her in establishing the process of life-death-rebirth. Moreover, Brahma assured her that the actual instruments of death would be covetousness, malice, jealousy, and "other stern passions" held by humans. With that assurance, the goddess Death began to take the lives of humans and other creatures when the appropriate time came.*

The literature of the West personifies death in a number of ways, ranging from the quite serious to the humorous. Several twentieth-century selections illustrate the variety of interpretations available. In *The Seventh Seal*, Ingmar Bergman's somber play set in the Middle Ages, death is personified as a pale-faced man dressed in a long black cloak. Having come to get a knight named Antonius Block, Death allows himself to be delayed in order to accept the knight's challenge to a game of chess. If Block can defeat him in chess, he will get a reprieve from having to die. The chess game continues throughout the play, with Death exhibiting a variety of moods and facial expressions, appearing in several geographical locations, demonstrating a remarkably cunning mind, and making himself visible or invisible as he chooses. He also, of course, demonstrates superior skill as a chess player.

In *Journey to Ixtlan*, one of Carlos Castaneda's books describing his adventures among the Yaqui Indians, death is personified as a hunter who continually stalks human beings just as some of them occasionally

---

* Frederick H. Holck, "Sutras and the Mahabharata Epic," in Frederick H. Holck, ed., *Death and Eastern Thought* (Nashville: Abingdon Press, 1974), pp. 53–78.

stalk other animals. As described by Don Juan, a Yaqui in his seventies, death is an eternal companion of all persons who watches tirelessly, waits patiently, always remains to a person's left, sometimes produces a shadow, occasionally has a chilling effect on human actions, gives advice when asked about life-threatening situations, and finally taps individuals on the shoulder when it is time for life to end. Generally unseen by humans, death is a constant companion whose presence can be felt by persons sensitive to it.

In a less serious vein, Woody Allen personifies death as a blundering fool in the one-act play *Death Knocks*. Dressed in a black-hooded cape and skintight black clothes, Death appears in a New York apartment as a middle-aged, white male who has come to pick up Nat Ackerman. Admitting that he can't play chess, he accepts Nat's challenge to play gin rummy to see if Nat can win an extra twenty-four hours of life. Drinking colas, eating candy, and exchanging insulting remarks with Nat, Death not only loses the game but ends up owing Ackerman money and accepting a challenge to play another game for double or nothing the following day.

Death is also sometimes personified in contemporary science fiction. A recent science fiction series depicts death as a humanlike alien being having superhuman powers. As the lord of evil and death, Thanos has a number of elaborate plans for destroying the earth, all of which are foiled (fortunately for us) through the efforts of Captain Marvel, Warlock, Moondragon, Iron Man, and other members of the Avengers.

The selections which follow demonstrate the various ways in which death is personified in literature. The Savitri story, taken from the *Mahabharata*, depicts the god Yama as a majestic figure dressed in red garments and carrying a noose with which he intends to end the life of Savitri's husband. In the passage from *Richard II*, Shakespeare describes death as a powerful clownlike figure who amuses himself with the pretensions of kings before causing their deaths. John Donne's "Death, Be Not Proud" suggests that death can be addressed personally and ultimately is unable to control the destiny of human beings. And in one of the more unusual passages in literature, John Milton in *Paradise Lost* describes death as a black, gruesome, terrifying figure who guards the gates of hell and threatens to beat Satan with a whip of scorpions.

The other selections are taken from the past two centuries. Walt

Whitman describes death as a veiled female figure with maternalistic instincts, capable of loving, soothing, and ultimately comforting human beings. Emily Dickinson suggests that Death is accompanied by Immortality, and the two companions travel around in a carriage picking up human passengers bound for eternity. James Weldon Johnson depicts death as a compassionate messenger sent by God on a white horse to relieve humans of their pain and take them to heaven where they can be comforted. Somerset Maugham personifies death as a woman who engages in human conversation, sometimes associates with humans in crowds, and keeps appointments with humans at predetermined locations. Alan Seeger, who was killed in the first World War, writes of death in the context of war, suggesting prophetically that soldiers sometimes have a rendezvous with a figure who closes their eyes, takes them by the hand, and leads them away from the battlefield into his dark land. And Amos Tutuola, a Nigerian author writing in eccentric English, provides an intriguing account of death as a personal agent who converses in human language, carries a club, lives in a house, tends a garden, uses human bones as tools and utensils, and travels throughout the world killing people.

from THE MAHABHARATA
Anonymous (c.200 B.C.–A.D. 200)

Along with the *Ramayana*, the *Mahabharata* is one of the two great epic poems of India. Some of the material in the poem may have been in existence as early as 500 B.C., but the poem in its present written form is dated from the classical period of Hinduism. Consisting of over 100,000 couplets, it is the longest poem produced in human history. It actually contains numerous poems (the most famous being the *Bhagavad Gita*), prayers, and stories. The story of Savitri, her husband Satyavan (whose death after one year of marriage had been predicted by Narad), and the god Yama is one of the more famous stories in the epic poem. The following selection takes place when Savitri and Satyavan have been married one year.

So, pure and dutiful, she sought that place
Where sat the King and Queen, and, bending low,
Murmured request: "My husband goeth straight
To the great forest, gathering fruits and flowers;
I pray your leave that I may be with him.
To make the Agnihotra sacrifice
Fetcheth he those, and will not be gainsaid,

But surely goeth. Let me go. A year
Hath rolled since I did fare from th' hermitage
To see our groves in bloom. I have much will
To see them now."
                          The old King gently said:
"In sooth it is a year since she was given
To be our son's wife, and I mind me not
Of any boon the loving heart hath asked,
Nor any one untimely word she spake;
Let it be as she prayeth. Go, my child;
Have care of Satyavan, and take thy way."

So, being permitted of them both, she went—
That beauteous lady—at her husband's side,
With aching heart, albeit her face was bright.
Flower-laden trees her large eyes lighted on,
Green glades where pea-fowl sported, crystal streams,
And soaring hills whose green sides burned with bloom,
Which oft the Prince would bid her gaze upon;
But she as oft turned those great eyes from them
To look on him, her husband, who must die
(For always in her mind were Narad's words).
And so she walked behind him, guarding him,
Bethinking at what hour her lord must die,
Her true heart torn in twain, one half to him
Close-cleaving, one half watching if Death come.

Then, having reached where woodland fruits did grow,
They gathered those, and filled a basket full;
And afterwards the Prince plied hard his axe,
Cutting the sacred fuel. Presently
There crept a pang upon him; a fierce throe
Burned through his brows, and, all asweat, he came
Feebly to Savitri, and moaned: "O wife,
I am thus suddenly too weak for work;
My veins throb, Savitri; my blood runs fire;
It is as if a threefold fork were plunged
Into my brain. Let me lie down, fair Love!
Indeed, I cannot stand upon my feet."

Thereon that noble lady, hastening near,
Stayed him, that would have fallen, with quick arms;
And, sitting on the earth, laid her lord's head
Tenderly in her lap. So bent she, mute,
Fanning his face, and thinking 'twas the day—
The hour—which Narad named—the sure fixed date
Of dreadful end—when, lo! before her rose
A shade majestic. Red his garments were,
His body vast and dark; like fiery suns
The eyes which burned beneath his forehead-cloth;
Armed was he with a noose, awful of mien.
This Form tremendous stood by Satyavan,
Fixing its gaze upon him. At the sight
The fearful Princess started to her feet.
Heedfully laying on the grass his head,
Up started she, with beating heart, and joined
Her palms for supplication, and spake thus
In accents tremulous: "Thou seem'st some god;
Thy mien is more than mortal; make me know
What god thou art, and what thy purpose here."
And Yama said (the dreadful God of death):
"Thou art a faithful wife, O Savitri,
True to thy vows, pious, and dutiful;
Therefore I answer thee. Yama I am!
This Prince, thy lord, lieth at point to die;
Him will I straightway bind and bear from life;
This is my office, and for this I come."

Then Savitri spake sadly: "It is taught,
Thy messengers are sent to fetch the dying;
Why is it, Mightiest, thou art come thyself?"

In pity of her love, the Pitiless
Answered—the King of all the Dead replied:
"This was a Prince unparalleled, thy lord;
Virtuous as fair, a sea of goodly gifts,
Not to be summoned by a meaner voice
Than Yama's own: therefore is Yama come."

With that the gloomy God fitted his noose,
And forced forth from the Prince the soul of him—
Subtile, a thumb in length—which being reft,
Breath stayed, blood stopped, his body's grace was gone,
And all life's warmth to stony coldness turned.
Then, binding it, the Silent Presence bore
Satyavan's soul away toward the South.

But Savitri the Princess followed him;
Being so bold in wifely purity,
So holy by her love: and so upheld,
She followed him.
                              Presently Yama turned.
"Go back," quoth he; "pay him the funeral dues.
Enough, O Savitri! is wrought for love;
Go back! too far already hast thou come."

Then Savitri made answer: "I must go
Where my lord goes, or where my lord is borne;
Nought other is my duty. Nay, I think,
By reason of my vows, my services
Done to the Gurus, and my faultless love,
Grant but thy grace, I shall unhindered go.
The sages teach that to walk seven steps,
One with another, maketh good men friends;
Beseech thee, let me say a verse to thee:—

  'Be master of thyself, if thou wilt be
  Servant of Duty. Such as thou shalt see
  Not self-subduing, do no deeds of good
  In youth or age, in household or in wood.
  But wise men know that virtue is best bliss,
  And all by some one way may reach to this.
  It needs not men should pass through orders four
  To come to knowledge: doing right is more
  Than any learning; therefore sages say
  Best and most excellent is Virtue's way.'"

Spake Yama then: "Return! yet I am moved
By those soft words; justly their accents fell,

And sweet and reasonable was their sense.
See, now, thou faultless one. Except this life
I bear away, ask any boon from me;
It shall not be denied."

Savitri said:
"Let, then, the King, my husband's father, have
His eyesight back, and be his strength restored,
And let him live anew, strong as the sun."

"I give this gift," Yama replied: "thy wish,
Blameless, shall be fulfilled. But now go back;
Already art thou wearied, and our road
Is hard and long. Turn back, lest thou, too, die."

The Princess answered: "Weary am I not,
So I walk nigh my lord. Where he is borne,
Thither wend I. Most mighty of the gods,
I follow whereso'er thou takest him.
A verse is writ on this, if thou wouldst hear:—
    'There is nought better than to be
    With noble souls in company:
    There is nought dearer than to wend
    With good friends faithful to the end.
    This is the love whose fruit is sweet;
    Therefore to bide therein is meet.'"

Spake Yama, smiling: "Beautiful! Thy words
Delight me; they are excellent, and teach
Wisdom unto the wise, singing soft truth.
Look, now! except the life of Satyavan,
Ask yet another—any—boon from me."

Savitri said: "Let, then, the pious King,
My husband's father, who hath lost his throne,
Have back the Raj; and let him rule his realm
In happy righteousness. This boon I ask."

"He shall have back the throne," Yama replied,
"And he shall reign in righteousness: these things
Will surely fall. But thou, gaining thy wish,
Return anon; so shalt thou 'scape sore ill."

"Ah, awful god! who hold'st the world in leash,"
The Princess said, "restraining evil men,
And leading good men—even unconscious—there
Where they attain, hear yet these famous words:—

'The constant virtues of the good are tenderness and love
To all that lives—in earth, air, sea—great, small—below, above,
Compassionate of heart, they keep a gentle thought for each,
Kind in their actions, mild in will, and pitiful of speech;
Who pitieth not he hath not faith; full many an one so lives,
But when an enemy seeks help the good man gladly gives.'"

"As water to the thirsting," Yama said,
"Princess, thy words melodious are to me.
Except the life of Satyavan thy lord,
Ask one boon yet again, for I will grant."

Answer made Savitri: "The King, my sire,
Hath no male child. Let him see many sons
Begotten of his body, who may keep
The royal line long regnant. This I ask."

"So it shall be!" the Lord of death replied;
"A hundred fair preservers of his race
Thy sire shall boast. But this wish being won,
Return, dear Princess; thou hast come too far."

"It is not far for me," quoth Savitri,
"Since I am near my husband; nay, my heart
Is set to go as far as to the end;
But hear these other verses, if thou wilt:—

'By that sunlit name thou bearest,
Thou, Vaivaswata! art dearest;
Those that as their Lord proclaim thee,
King of Righteousness do name thee:
Better than themselves the wise
Trust the righteous. Each relies
Most upon the good, and makes
Friendship with them. Friendship takes
Fear from hearts; yet friends betray,
In good men we may trust alway.'"

"Sweet lady," Yama said, "never were words
Spoke better; never truer heard by ear;
Lo! I am pleased with thee. Except this soul,
Ask one gift yet again, and get thee home."

"I ask thee, then," quickly the Princess cried,
"Sons, many sons, born of my body: boys;
Satyavan's children; lovely, valiant, strong;
Continuers of their line. Grant this, kind God."

"I grant it," Yama answered; "thou shalt bear
Those sons thy heart desireth, valiant, strong.
Therefore go back, that years be given thee.
Too long a path thou treadest, dark and rough."

But, sweeter than before, the Princess sang:—
   "In paths of peace and virtue
   Always the good remain;
   And sorrow shall not stay with them,
   Nor long access of pain;
   At meeting or at parting
   Joys to their bosom strike;
   For good to good is friendly,
   And virtue loves her like.
   The great sun goes his journey
   By their strong truth impelled;
   By their pure lives and penances
   Is earth itself upheld;
   Of all which live or shall live
   Upon its hills and fields,
   Pure hearts are the 'protectors,'
   For virtue saves and shields.

   "Never are noble spirits
   Poor while their like survive;
   True love has gems to render,
   And virtue wealth to give.
   Never is lost or wasted
   The goodness of the good;
   Never against a mercy,

Against a right, it stood;
And seeing this, that virtue
Is always friend to all,
The virtuous and true-hearted,
Men their 'protectors' call."

"Line for line, Princess! as thou sangest so,"
Quoth Yama, "all that lovely praise of good,
Grateful to hallowed minds, lofty in sound,
And couched in dulcet numbers—word by word—
Dearer thou grew'st to me. O thou great heart,
Perfect and firm! ask any boon from me,—
Ask an incomparable boon!"

                She cried
Swiftly, no longer stayed: "Not heaven I crave,
Nor heavenly joys, nor bliss incomparable,
Hard to be granted even by thee; but *him*,
My sweet lord's life, without which I am dead;
Give me that gift of gifts! I will not take
Aught less without him—not one boon—no praise,
No splendors, no rewards—not even those sons
Whom thou didst promise. Ah, thou wilt not, now,
Bear hence the father of them, and my hope!
Make thy free word good; give me Satyavan
Alive once more."

             And thereupon the God—
The Lord of Justice, high Vaivaswata—
Loosened the noose and freed the Prince's soul,
And gave it to the lady, saying this,
With eyes grown tender: "See, thou sweetest queen
Of women, brightest jewel of thy kind!
Here is thy husband. He shall live and reign
Side by side with thee—saved by thee—in peace,
And fame, and wealth, and health, many long years;
For pious sacrifices world-renowned.
Boys shalt thou bear to him, as I did grant—
Kshatriya kings, fathers of kings to be,

Sustainers of thy line. Also, thy sire
Shall see his name upheld by sons of sons,
Like the immortals, valiant, Malavas."

These gifts the awful Yama gave, and went
Unto his place; but Savitri—made glad,
Having her husband's soul—sped to the glade
Where his corse lay. She saw it there, and ran,
And, sitting on the earth, lifted its head,
And lulled it on her lap full tenderly.
Thereat warm life returned: the white lips moved;
The fixed eyes brightened, gazed, and gazed again;
As when one starts from sleep and sees a face—
The well-beloved's—grow clear, and, smiling, wakes,
So Satyavan. "Long have I slumbered, Dear,"
He sighed, "why didst thou not arouse me? Where
Is gone that gloomy man that haled at me?"

Answered the Princess: "Long, indeed, thy sleep,
Dear Lord, and deep; for he that haled at thee
Was Yama, God of Death; but he is gone;
And thou, being rested and awake, rise now,
If thou canst rise; for, look, the night is near!"

from RICHARD II (III, 2)
William Shakespeare (1564–1616)

And nothing can we call our own but death
And that small model of the barren earth
Which serves as paste and cover to our bones.
For God's sake, let us sit upon the ground
And tell sad stories of the death of kings:
How some have been deposed; some slain in war;
Some haunted by the ghosts they have deposed;
Some poison'd by their wives; some sleeping kill'd;
All murder'd: for within the hollow crown

That rounds the mortal temples of a king
Keeps Death his court, and there the antic sits,
Scoffing his state and grinning at his pomp,
Allowing him a breath, a little scene,
To monarchize, be fear'd and kill with looks,
Infusing him with self and vain conceit,
As if this flesh which walls about our life
Were brass impregnable, and humour'd thus
Comes at the last and with a little pin
Bores through his castle wall, and farewell king!

DEATH, BE NOT PROUD
John Donne (1572–1631)

Death, be not proud, though some have called thee
Mighty and dreadful, for thou art not so;
For those whom thou think'st thou dost overthrow
Die not, poor Death, nor yet canst thou kill me.
From rest and sleep, which but thy pictures be,
Much pleasure; then from thee much more must flow,
And soonest our best men with thee do go,
Rest of their bones, and soul's delivery.
Thou art slave to fate, chance, kings, and desperate men,
And dost with poison, war, and sickness dwell,
And poppy or charms can make us sleep as well
And better than thy stroke; why swell'st thou then?
One short sleep past, we wake eternally
And death shall be no more; Death, thou shalt die.

from PARADISE LOST (Book II)
John Milton (1608–1674)

This epic poem was written, according to Milton, to "assert Eternal Providence, and justify the ways of God to men." Beginning with the biblical story of the Fall, Milton presents a cosmic drama played out on three levels of existence (heaven, earth, hell) by God, Christ, Satan, and a huge supporting cast. The scene which follows occurs when Satan, having rebelled against God and landed in hell, decides to pass through the gates of hell to explore the newly created earth and the original pair of humans who live there. He discovers at the gate two guards, one of whom is Death.

Meanwhile the Adversary of God and Man,
Satan, with thoughts inflamed of highest design,
Puts on swift wings, and toward the gates of Hell
Explores his solitary flight: sometimes
He scours the right hand coast, sometimes the left;
Now shaves with level wing the deep, then soars
Up to the fiery concave towering high.
As when far off at sea a fleet descried
Hangs in the clouds, by equinoctial winds
Close sailing from Bengala, or the isles
Of Ternate and Tidore, whence merchants bring
Their spicy drugs; they on the trading flood,
Through the wide Ethiopian to the Cape,
Ply stemming nightly toward the pole: so seemed
Far off the flying Fiend. At last appear
Hell-bounds, high reaching to the horrid roof,
And thrice threefold the gates; three folds were brass,
Three iron, three of adamantine rock,
Impenetrable, impaled with circling fire,
Yet unconsumed. Before the gates there sat
On either side a formidable Shape.
The one seemed woman to the waist, and fair,
But ended foul in many a scaly fold,
Voluminous and vast—a serpent armed
With mortal sting. About her middle round
A cry of Hell-hounds never-ceasing barked

With wide Cerberean mouths full loud, and rung
A hideous peal; yet, when they list, would creep,
If aught disturbed their noise, into her womb,
And kennel there; yet there still barked and howled
Within unseen. Far less abhorred than these
Vexed Scylla, bathing in the sea that parts
Calabria from the hoarse Trinacrian shore;
Nor uglier follow the night-hag, when, called
In secret, riding through the air she comes,
Lured with the smell of infant blood, to dance
With Lapland witches, while the laboring moon
Eclipses at their charms. The other Shape—
If shape it might be called that shape had none
Distinguishable in member, joint, or limb;
Or substance might be called that shadow seemed,
For each seemed either—black it stood as Night,
Fierce as ten Furies, terrible as Hell,
And shook a dreadful dart: what seemed his head
The likeness of a kingly crown had on.
Satan was now at hand, and from his seat
The monster moving onward came as fast
With horrid strides; Hell trembled as he strode.
Th' undaunted Fiend what this might be admired—
Admired, not feared (God and his Son except,
Created thing naught valued he nor shunned),
And with disdainful look thus first began:—

   "Whence and what art thou, execrable Shape,
That dar'st, though grim and terrible, advance
Thy miscreated front athwart my way
To yonder gates? Through them I mean to pass,
That be assured, without leave asked of thee.
Retire; or taste thy folly, and learn by proof,
Hell-born, not to contend with Spirits of Heaven."

   To whom the Goblin, full of wrath, replied:—
"Art thou that traitor Angel? art thou he,
Who first broke peace in Heaven and faith, till then
Unbroken, and in proud rebellious arms

Drew after him the third part of Heaven's sons,
Conjured against the Highest—for which both thou
And they, outcast from God, are here condemned
To waste eternal days in woe and pain?
And reckon'st thou thyself with Spirits of Heaven,
Hell-doomed, and breath'st defiance here and scorn,
Where I reign king, and, to enrage thee more,
Thy king and lord? Back to thy punishment,
False fugitive; and to thy speed add wings,
Lest with a whip of scorpions I pursue
Thy lingering, or with one stroke of this dart
Strange horror seize thee, and pangs unfelt before."
   So spake the grisly Terror, and in shape,
So speaking and so threatening, grew tenfold,
More dreadful and deform. On th' other side,
Incensed with indignation, Satan stood
Unterrified, and like a comet burned,
That fires the length of Ophiuchus huge
In th' arctic sky, and from his horrid hair
Shakes pestilence and war. Each at the head
Leveled his deadly aim; their fatal hands
No second stroke intend; and such a frown
Each cast at th' other as when two black clouds,
With heaven's artillery fraught, come rattling on
Over the Caspian—then stand front to front
Hovering a space, till winds the signal blow
To join their dark encounter in mid-air.
So frowned the mighty combatants that Hell
Grew darker at their frown; so matched they stood;
For never but once more was either like
To meet so great a foe. And now great deeds
Had been achieved, whereof all Hell had rung,
Had not the snaky Sorceress, that sat
Fast by Hell-gate and kept the fatal key,
Risen, and with hideous outcry rushed between.
   "O father, what intends thy hand," she cried,
"Against thy only son? What fury, O son,

Possesses thee to bend that mortal dart
Against thy father's head? And know'st for whom?
For him who sits above, and laughs the while
At thee, ordained his drudge to execute
Whate'er his wrath, which he calls justice, bids—
His wrath, which one day will destroy ye both!"
　　She spake, and at her words the hellish Pest
Forbore: then these to her Satan returned:—
　　"So strange thy outcry, and thy words so strange
Thou interposest, that my sudden hand,
Prevented, spares to tell thee yet by deeds
What it intends, till first I know of thee
What thing thou art, thus double-formed, and why,
In this infernal vale first met, thou call'st
Me father, and that phantasm call'st my son.
I know thee not, nor ever saw till now
Sight more detestable than him and thee."
　　T' whom thus the Portress of Hell-gate replied:—
"Hast thou forgot me, then; and do I seem
Now in thine eye so foul?—once deemed so fair
In Heaven, when at th' assembly, and in sight
Of all the Seraphim with thee combined
In bold conspiracy against Heaven's King,
All on a sudden miserable pain
Surprised thee, dim thine eyes and dizzy swum
In darkness, while thy head flames thick and fast
Threw forth, till on the left side opening wide,
Likest to thee in shape and countenance bright,
Then shining heavenly fair, a goddess armed,
Out of thy head I sprung. Amazement seized
All th' host of Heaven; back they recoiled afraid
At first, and called me *Sin*, and for a sign
Portentous held me; but, familiar grown,
I pleased, and with attractive graces won
The most averse—thee chiefly, who, full oft
Thyself in me thy perfect image viewing,
Becam'st enamoured; and such joy thou took'st

With me in secret that my womb conceived
A growing burden. Meanwhile war arose,
And fields were fought in Heaven: wherein remained
(For what could else?) to our Almighty Foe
Clear victory; to our part loss and rout
Through all the Empyrean. Down they fell,
Driven headlong from the pitch of Heaven, down
Into this Deep; and in the general fall
I also: at which time this powerful key
Into my hands was given, with charge to keep
These gates for ever shut, which none can pass
Without my opening. Pensive here I sat
Alone; but long I sat not, till my womb,
Pregnant by thee, and now excessive grown,
Prodigious motion felt and rueful throes.
At last this odious offspring whom thou seest,
Thine own begotten, breaking violent way,
Tore through my entrails, that, with fear and pain
Distorted, all my nether shape thus grew
Transformed: but he my inbred enemy
Forth issued, brandishing his fatal dart,
Made to destroy. I fled, and cried out *Death!*
Hell trembled at the hideous name, and sighed
From all her caves, and back resounded *Death!*
I fled; but he pursued (though more, it seems,
Inflamed with lust than rage), and, swifter far,
Me overtook, his mother, all dismayed,
And, in embraces forcible and foul
Engendering with me, of that rape begot
These yelling monsters, that with ceaseless cry
Surround me, as thou saw'st—hourly conceived
And hourly born, with sorrow infinite
To me; for, when they list, into the womb
That bred them they return, and howl, and gnaw
My bowels, their repast; then, bursting forth
Afresh, with conscious terrors vex me round,
That rest or intermission none I find.

Before mine eyes in opposition sits
Grim Death, my son and foe, who sets them on,
And me, his parent, would full soon devour
For want of other prey, but that he knows
His end with mine involved, and knows that I
Should prove a bitter morsel, and his bane,
Whenever that shall be: so Fate pronounced.
But thou, O father, I forewarn thee, shun
His deadly arrow; neither vainly hope
To be invulnerable in those bright arms,
Though tempered heavenly; for that mortal dint,
Save he who reigns above, none can resist."

THE CAROL OF DEATH
Walt Whitman (1819–1892)

A close personal friend of Lincoln, Whitman was terribly upset when he heard of the assassination. One of the ways of expressing his grief was through an elegy entitled "When Lilacs Last in the Dooryard Bloomed." The following carol occurs near the end of that poem.

Come lovely and soothing death,
Undulate round the world, serenely arriving, arriving,
In the day, in the night, to all, to each,
Sooner or later delicate death.

Praised be the fathomless universe,
For life and joy, and for object and knowledge curious,
And for love, sweet love—but praise! praise! praise!
For the sure-enwinding arms of cool-enfolding death.

Dark mother always gliding near with soft feet,
Have none chanted for thee a chant of fullest welcome?
Then I chant it for thee, I glorify thee above all,
I bring thee a song that when thou must indeed come, come
    unfalteringly.

Approach strong deliveress,
When it is so, when thou hast taken them I joyously sing the dead,

Lost in the loving floating ocean of thee,
Laved in the flood of thy bliss O death.

From me to thee glad serenades,
Dances for thee I propose saluting thee, adornments and feastings for
    thee,
And the sights of the open landscape and the high-spread sky are fitting,
And life and the fields, and the huge and thoughtful night.

The night in silence under many a star,
The ocean shore and the husky whispering wave whose voice I know,
And the soul turning to thee O vast and well-veiled death,
And the body gratefully nestling close to thee.

Over the treetops I float thee a song,
Over the rising and sinking waves, over the myriad fields and the prairies
    wide,
Over the dense-packed cities all and the teeming wharves and ways,
I float this carol with joy, with joy to thee O death.

BECAUSE I COULD NOT STOP FOR DEATH
Emily Dickinson (1830–1886)

Because I could not stop for Death,
He kindly stopped for me;
The carriage held but just ourselves
And Immortality.

We slowly drove, he knew no haste,
And I had put away
My labor, and my leisure too,
For his civility.

We passed the school where children played,
Their lessons scarcely done;
We passed the fields of gazing grain,
We passed the setting sun.

We paused before a house that seemed
A swelling on the ground;

The roof was scarcely visible,
The cornice but a mound.

Since then 'tis centuries; but each
Feels shorter than the day
I first surmised the horses' heads
Were toward eternity.

GO DOWN DEATH
James Weldon Johnson (1871–1938)

Weep not, weep not,
She is not dead;
She's resting in the bosom of Jesus.
Heart-broken husband—weep no more;
Grief-stricken son—weep no more;
Left-lonesome daughter—weep no more;
She's only just gone home.

Day before yesterday morning,
God was looking down from his great, high heaven,
Looking down on all his children,
And his eye fell on Sister Caroline,
Tossing on her bed of pain.
And God's big heart was touched with pity,
With the everlasting pity.

And God sat back on his throne,
And he commanded that tall, bright angel standing at his right hand:
Call me Death!
And that tall, bright angel cried in a voice
That broke like a clap of thunder:
Call Death!—Call Death!
And the echo sounded down the streets of heaven
Till it reached away back to that shadowy place,
Where Death waits with his pale, white horses.

And Death heard the summons,
And he leaped on his fastest horse,

Pale as a sheet in the moonlight.
Up the golden street Death galloped,
And the hoofs of his horse struck fire from the gold,
But they didn't make no sound.
Up Death rode to the Great White Throne,
And waited for God's command.

And God said: Go down, Death, go down,
Go down to Savannah, Georgia,
Down in Yamacraw,
And find Sister Caroline.
She's borne the burden and heat of the day,
She's labored long in my vineyard,
And she's tired—
She's weary—
Go down, Death, and bring her to me.

And Death didn't say a word,
But he loosed the reins on his pale, white horse,
And he clamped the spurs to his bloodless sides,
And out and down he rode,
Through heaven's pearly gates,
Past suns and moons and stars;
On Death rode,
And the foam from his horse was like a comet in the sky;
On Death rode,
Leaving the lightning's flash behind;
Straight on down he came.

While we were watching round her bed,
She turned her eyes and looked away,
She saw what we couldn't see;
She saw Old Death. She saw Old Death.
Coming like a falling star.
But Death didn't frighten Sister Caroline;
He looked to her like a welcome friend.
And she whispered to us: I'm going home,
And she smiled and closed her eyes.

And Death took her up like a baby,
And she lay in his icy arms,

But she didn't feel no chill.
And Death began to ride again—
Up beyond the evening star,
Out beyond the morning star,
Into the glittering light of glory,
On to the Great White Throne.
And there he laid Sister Caroline
On the loving breast of Jesus.

And Jesus took his own hand and wiped away her tears,
And he smoothed the furrows from her face,
And the angels sang a little song,
And Jesus rocked her in his arms,
And kept a-saying: Take your rest,
Take your rest, take your rest.

Weep not—weep not,
She is not dead;
She's resting in the bosom of Jesus.

APPOINTMENT IN SAMARRA
W. Somerset Maugham (1874–1965)

Death speaks: There was a merchant in Bagdad who sent his servant to market to buy provisions and in a little while the servant came back, white and trembling, and said, Master, just now when I was in the market-place I was jostled by a woman in the crowd and when I turned I saw it was Death that jostled me. She looked at me and made a threatening gesture; now, lend me your horse, and I will ride away from this city and avoid my fate. I will go to Samarra and there Death will not find me. The merchant lent him his horse, and the servant mounted it, and he dug his spurs in its flanks and as fast as the horse could gallop he went. Then the merchant went down to the market-place and he saw me standing in the crowd and he came to me and said, Why did you make a threatening gesture to my servant when you saw him this morning? That was not a threatening gesture, I said, it was only a start of surprise. I was astonished to see him in Bagdad, for I had an appointment with him tonight in Samarra.

I HAVE A RENDEZVOUS WITH DEATH
Alan Seeger (1888–1916)

I have a rendezvous with Death
At some disputed barricade,
When Spring comes back with rustling shade
And apple blossoms fill the air—
I have a rendezvous with Death
When Spring brings back blue days and fair.

It may be he shall take my hand
And lead me into his dark land
And close my eyes and quench my breath—
It may be I shall pass him still.
I have a rendezvous with Death
On some scarred slope of battered hill,
When Spring comes round again this year
And the first meadow flowers appear.

God knows 'twere better to be deep
Pillowed in silk and scented down,
Where Love throbs out in blissful sleep,
Pulse nigh to pulse and breath to breath,
Where hushed awakenings are dear. . . .
But I've a rendezvous with Death
At midnight in some flaming town,
When Spring trips north again this year,
And I to my pledged word am true,
I shall not fail that rendezvous.

from THE PALM-WINE DRINKARD
Amos Tutuola (b. 1920)

Growing up as a Yoruba in Nigeria, Tutuola inherited many childhood folk tales which made no separation between the world of the living and the world of the dead. In this novel he retells several of these folk tales by updating them with contemporary elements and weaving them together into a fascinating story. In the episode which follows, the narrator has learned the pleasure of drinking palm wine only to have his palm-wine tapster fall out of a tree and die. The narrator sets out to search for his palm-wine tapster among the living dead.

When it was early in the morning of the next day, I had no palm-wine to drink at all, and throughout that day I felt not so happy as before; I was seriously sat down in my parlor, but when it was the third day that I had no palm-wine at all, all my friends did not come to my house again, they left me there alone, because there was no palm-wine for them to drink.

But when I completed a week in my house without palm-wine, then I went out and, I saw one of them in the town, so I saluted him, he answered but he did not approach me at all, he hastily went away.

Then I started to find out another expert palm-wine tapster, but I could not get me one who could tap the palm-wine to my requirement. When there was no palm-wine for me to drink I started to drink ordinary water which I was unable to taste before, but I did not satisfy with it as palm-wine.

When I saw that there was no palm-wine for me again, and nobody could tap it for me, then I thought within myself that old people were saying that the whole people who had died in this world, did not go to heaven directly, but they were living in one place somewhere in this world. So that I said that I would find out where my palm-wine tapster who had died was.

One fine morning, I took all my native juju and also my father's juju with me and I left my father's hometown to find out whereabouts was my tapster who had died.

But in those days, there were many wild animals and every place was covered by thick bushes and forests; again, towns and villages were not near each other as nowadays, and as I was traveling from bushes to bushes and from forests to forests and sleeping inside it for many days and months, I was sleeping on the branches of trees, because spirits, etc., were just like partners, and to save my life from them; and again I could spend two or three months before reaching a town or village. Whenever I reached a town or a village, I would spend almost four months there, to find out my palm-wine tapster from the inhabitants of that town or village and if he did not reach there, then I would leave there and continue my journey to another town or village. After the seventh month that I had left my home town, I reached a town and went to an old man, this old man was not really a man, he was a god and he was eating with his wife when I reached there. When I entered the house I saluted both of them, they answered me well, although nobody should enter his house like that as he was a god, but I myself was a god and juju-man. Then I told the old man (god) that I am looking for my palm-wine tapster who had died in my town some time ago, he did not answer to my question but asked me first what was my name? I replied that my name was "Father of gods" who could do everything in this world, then he said: "was that true" and I said yes; after that he told me to go to his native black-smith in an unknown place, or who was living in another town, and bring the right thing that he had told the black-smith to make for him. He said that if I could bring the right thing that he told the black-smith to make for him, then he would believe that I was the "Father of gods who could do everything in this world" and he would tell me where my tapster was.

Immediately this old man told or promised me so, I went away, but after I had traveled about one mile away then I used one of my juju and at once I changed into a very big bird and flew back to the roof of the old man's house; but as I stood on the roof of his house, many people saw me there. They came nearer and looked at me on the roof, so when the old man noticed that many had surrounded his house and were looking at the roof, he and his wife came out from the house and when he saw me (bird) on the roof, he told his wife that if he had not sent me to his native black-smith to bring the bell that he told the black-smith to make for him, he would tell me to mention the name of the bird. But at the same time that he said so, I knew what he wanted from the black-smith and I flew away to his black-smith, then when I reached there I told the black-smith that the old man (god) told me to bring his bell which he had told him to make for him. So the black-smith gave me the bell; after that I returned to the old man with the bell and when he saw me with the bell, he and his wife were surprised and also shocked at that moment.

After that he told his wife to give me food, but after I had eaten the food, he told me again, that there remained another wonderful work to do for him, before he would tell me whereabouts my tapster was. When it was 6:30 A.M. of the following morning, he (god) woke me up, and gave me a wide and strong net which was the same in color as the ground of that town. He told me to go and bring "Death" from his house with the net. When I left his house or the town about a mile, there I saw a junction of roads and I was doubtful when I reached the junction, I did not know which was Death's road among these roads, and when I thought within myself that as it was the market day, and all the market goers would soon be returning from the market—I lied down on the middle of the roads, I put my head to one of the roads, my left hand to one, right hand to another one, and my both feet to the rest, after that I pretended as I had slept there. But when all the market goers were returning from the market, they saw me lied down there and shouted thus:—"Who was the mother of this fine boy, he slept on the roads and put his head towards Death's road."

Then I began to travel on Death's road, and I spent about eight hours to reach there, but to my surprise I did not meet anybody on this road until I reached there and I was afraid because of that. When I reached his (Death's) house, he was not at home by that time, he was in his yam garden which was very close to his house, and I met a small rolling drum in his verandah, then I beat it to Death as a sign of salutation. But when he (Death) heard the sound of the drum, he said thus:—"Is that man still alive or dead?" Then I replied "I am still alive and I am not a dead man."

But at the same time that he heard so from me, he was greatly annoyed and he commanded the drum with a kind of voice that the strings of the drum should tight me there; as a matter of fact, the strings of the drum tighted me so that I was hardly breathing.

When I felt that these strings did not allow me to breathe and again every part of my body was bleeding too much, then I myself commanded the ropes of the yams in his garden to tight him there, and the yam stakes should begin to beat him also. After I had said so and at the same time, all the ropes of the yams in his garden tighted him hardly, and all the yam stakes were beating him repeatedly, so when he (Death) saw that these stakes were beating him repeatedly, then he commanded the strings of the drum which tighted me to release me, and I was released at the same time. But when I saw that I was released, then I myself commanded the ropes of the yams to release him and the yam stakes to stop beating him, and he was released at once. After he was released by the ropes of yams and yam stakes, he came to his house and met me at his verandah, then we shook hands together, and he told me to enter the house, he put me to one of his rooms, and after a while, he brought food to me and we ate it together, after that we started conversations which went thus:—He (Death) asked me from where did I come? I replied that

I came from a certain town which was not so far from his place. Then he asked what did I come to do? I told him that I had been hearing about him in my town and all over the world and I thought within myself that one day I should come and visit or to know him personally. After that he replied that his work was only to kill the people of the world, after that he got up and told me to follow him and I did so.

He took me around his house and his yam garden too, he showed me the skeleton bones of human-beings which he had killed since a century ago and showed me many other things also, but there I saw that he was using skeleton bones of human-beings as fuel woods and skull heads of human-beings as his basins, plates and tumblers, etc.

Nobody was living near or with him there, he was living lonely, even bush animals and birds were very far away from his house. So when I wanted to sleep at night, he gave me a wide black cover cloth and then gave me a separate room to sleep inside, but when I entered the room, I met a bed which was made with bones of human-beings; but as this bed was terrible to look at or to sleep on it, I slept under it instead, because I knew his trick already. Even as this bed was very terrible, I was unable to sleep under as I lied down there because of fear of the bones of human-beings, but I lied down there awoke. To my surprise was that when it was about two o'clock in the mid-night, there I saw somebody enter into the room cautiously with a heavy club in his hands, he came nearer to the bed on which he had told me to sleep, then he clubbed the bed with all his power, he clubbed the center of the bed thrice and he returned cautiously, he thought that I slept on that bed and he thought also that he had killed me.

But when it was 6 o'clock early in the morning, I first woke up and went to the room in which he slept, I woke him up, so when he heard my voice, he was frightened, even he could not salute me at all when he got up from his bed, because he thought that he had killed me last night.

But the second day that I slept there, he did not attempt to do anything again, but I woke up by two o'clock of that night, and went to the road which I should follow to the town and I traveled about a quarter of a mile to his house, then I stopped and dug a pit of his (Death's) size on the center of that road, after I spread the net which the old man gave me to bring him (Death) with on that pit, then I returned to his house, but he did not wake up as I was playing this trick.

When it was 6 o'clock in the morning, I went to his door and woke him up as usual, then I told him that I wanted to return to my town this morning, so that I wanted him to lead me a short distance; then he got up from his bed and he began to lead me as I told him, but when he led me to the place that I had dug, I told him to sit down, so I myself sat down on the road side, but as he sat down on the net, he fell into the pit, and without any ado I rolled up the net with him and put him on my head and I kept going to the old man's house who told me to go and bring him Death.

As I was carrying him along the road, he was trying all his efforts to escape or to kill me, but I did not give him a chance to do that. When I had traveled about eight hours, then I reached the town and went straight to the old man's house who told me to go and bring Death from his house. When I reached the old man's house, he was inside his room, then I called him and told him that I had brought Death that he told me to go and bring. But immediately he heard from me that I had brought Death and when he saw him on my head, he was greatly terrified and raised alarm that he thought nobody could go and bring Death from his house, then he told me to carry him (Death) back to his house at once, and he (old man) hastily went back to his room and started to close all his doors and windows, but before he could close two or three of his windows, I threw Death before his door and at the same time that I threw him down, the net cut into pieces and Death found his way out.

Then the old man and his wife escaped through the windows and also the whole people in that town ran away for their lives and left their properties there. (The old man had thought that Death would kill me if I went to his house, because nobody could reach Death's house and return, but I had known the old man's trick already).

So that since the day that I had brought Death out from his house, he has no permanent place to dwell or stay, and we are hearing his name about in the world. . . .

3. PERSONAL VIEWS OF THE DYING

MICHAEL CRISTOFER'S award-winning play *The Shadow Box* is indicative of considerable recent literary interest in the personal views of individuals about to die. The setting of the play consists of three cottages on the grounds of a large hospital. Each cottage houses a person who is terminally ill, along with relatives and friends who relate in various ways to the person who is dying.

Joe is dying in the first cottage. Married and the father of a teenage son, Joe is acutely aware that he is dying. He discusses his impending death with his wife, admits uncertainty as to the cause of his abbreviated life, and tells of a recurring dream in which first all of his friends disappear and then he himself disappears in the midst of a blinding white light. His dying is made difficult by his wife's inability to accept his terminal condition, and her refusal to tell their son Steve that his father will not be going home from the hospital.

Brian is dying in the second cottage. Since finding out that he has an untreatable condition, he has written two novels, scores of poems and short stories, and four autobiographies which he hopes will capture part of the literary market devoted to the views of dying persons. He has, in addition, painted several pictures, written letters to his friends and enemies, done some traveling, put his business affairs in order, and established a relationship with a homosexual named Mark. When Beverly, his former wife, visits him, he explains his recent activities by saying that he wants to leave nothing unsaid or undone when he dies.

Felicity is dying in the third cottage. She is in her sixties, blind, in pain, dependent upon a wheelchair and her middle-aged daughter Agnes, and frequently out of touch with reality. Having survived numerous operations, she has lived longer than her doctors and her daughter expected. She refers to herself as a living corpse, but generally appears to deny that she is actually dying. She lives in the midst of confusion, false hopes, and deception, thinking that her younger daughter Claire, who died several years ago, is soon going to visit her.

As suggested by this play, individuals respond in a variety of ways to the terminal phase of life. Elisabeth Kübler-Ross has described a series of emotional reactions or stages which some persons experience as they are dying.* The initial response to learning about a terminal condition is *denial*. Rather than facing the painful reality of having to die, individuals usually convince themselves that some kind of mistake has been made in their diagnosis or that some miraculous therapy will defer their dying indefinitely. Denial thus serves as a psychological defense mechanism to cushion the impact that death is going to occur much sooner than anticipated. For Felicity and the dying patients she represents, denial is a recurring response to a terminal condition; for Ted Rosenthal, Stewart Alsop, Cornelius Ryan, and numerous other persons, denial is a necessary but temporary reaction during the process of dying.

A second emotional reaction to dying is *anger*. Having come to grips with the fact that they are dying, many persons become angry at the unfairness of the situation in which they—often young, talented, productive—are dying while other persons remain alive with apparently many years yet to live. Johnny Gunther and Cornelius Ryan demonstrate this understandable response to their dying, and Ted Rosenthal shows that the anger of dying patients can be intensified through the insensitivity or negligence of hospital personnel.

Another response to dying is *bargaining*—with God, the hospital staff, or someone in the hopes of postponing death for a definite period of time. By making promises of good behavior or setting up self-imposed deadlines, dying persons often attempt to secure an extension on life. Felicity at times seems to have bargained that she would not have to die until she saw her daughter Claire; possible bargains made by persons in this section include Johnny Gunther's admission to Harvard, Ted Rosenthal's cabin in the California wilderness, and Cornelius Ryan's completion of his third major book.

Most persons who are dying experience *depression* along the way. At times the depression is brought about by intensified pain, loss of independence, financial difficulties, smashed dreams and plans, and the inability to carry out other valuable activities. At other times the

* Elisabeth Kübler-Ross, *On Death and Dying* (New York: Macmillan, 1969).

depression is brought about through the impending loss of everything valued and everyone loved. Ted Rosenthal, Stewart Alsop, and Cornelius Ryan repeatedly demonstrate the pervasiveness of depression among dying persons who deeply value life.

Finally, some dying persons get to the point of *acceptance* of their impending deaths. They are not happy or resigned to the inevitable, but have a sense of having finished their business, put their affairs in order, and said farewell to their loved ones. Of the characters in *The Shadow Box*, Brian demonstrates some of the features of this phase; of the persons in this section, Stewart Alsop describes it best when he writes of having neared the end of "the process of adjustment whereby one comes to terms with death."

Not all dying persons experience all of these emotional responses and, of those who do, the emotional phases do not always follow the same sequence, nor do they last for predictable periods of time. Moreover, as illustrated by Ted Rosenthal's anger at being placed in stereotypical categories, harm can be done by making these emotional responses to dying normative for all patients.

It is therefore helpful, in addition to looking at emotional responses to dying, to discuss the needs of the dying. One of the needs, and probably the most important one, is pain control. Burn patients, cancer patients, emphysema patients, and others who are dying often experience a great deal of pain which can sometimes, but not always, be relieved with drugs such as morphine and diamorphine. At the present time considerable experimentation is being done using alcohol, marijuana, LSD, heroin, methadone, and a pain-relief "cocktail" called Brompton's mixture for the control of pain connected with terminal conditions. A second need of dying persons is a feeling of dignity or self-worth. Individuals who have long been accustomed to making decisions about their own lives need to feel that, even though they are dying, they can still exercise a measure of control over the terminal phase of their lives. Rather than being regarded as bodies containing diseases, they need to regard themselves and be regarded by others as *persons*. In addition, dying persons need love and affection. Rather than being left isolated and alone, they need companionship: someone to talk with, to touch, to hold—to care.*

* Richard Schulz, *The Psychology of Death, Dying, and Bereavement* (Reading, Mass.: Addison-Wesley, 1978), pp. 57–84.

The selections rather easily divide into two groups. The first group contains several poems, a short story, and passages from one of the world's great novels. Cervantes' *Don Quixote* depicts a man who, having sought adventure in his own world of fantasy, changes his perspective drastically when he is dying and puts forth views which are rational and realistic. The Tichborne and Nashe poems contain thought-provoking reflections on the meaning of life even as their authors' lives are threatened by execution and plague. The pre-Columbian Ojibwa poem reveals equanimity even at the prospect of dying in a strange land. Emily Dickinson's poem, while written in a humorous vein, points out that dying persons often have to make critically important decisions about business and legal matters. In "The Jilting of Granny Weatherall," Katherine Anne Porter, a contemporary American writer, describes a dying woman whose mind keeps moving from the present to the past. And in the final poem, Abū al-Qāsim al-Shābbī, a twentieth-century Arab poet, provides another reflective view on the meaning of life in the face of death.

The second group contains the views of persons actually in the process of dying. In *Death Be Not Proud*, John Gunther describes the ordeal of his son Johnny, who died at the age of seventeen after having suffered the effects of a brain tumor for over a year. In *How Could I Not Be Among You?* Ted Rosenthal records a number of views held in the final months of his life, which was abbreviated by leukemia at the age of thirty-four. Stewart Alsop, an internationally known journalist and reporter, contracted an unusual form of cancer whose multiple effects are candidly described in *Stay of Execution*. The dying experiences of Cornelius Ryan, another internationally known writer, are described with equal candor in *A Private Battle*.

from DON QUIXOTE
Miguel de Cervantes Saavedra (1547–1616)

This novel is one of the most widely read pieces of literature in the world. Cervantes tells of the adventures of Don Quixote, a self-proclaimed knight whose reading of books of chivalry has made distinctions between reality and fantasy unimportant, and his faithful squire named Sancho Panza. Motivated by visions of justice and grandeur, the two men have numerous experiences together. At last, Don Quixote is tired, disappointed, ill, and dying.

As all human things, especially the lives of men, are not eternal, and even their beginnings are but steps to their end, and as Don Quixote was under no special dispensation of Heaven, he was snatched away by death when he least expected it. Whether his sickness was caused by his melancholic reflections on his defeat, or whether it was so preordained by Providence, he was stricken down by a violent fever that confined him to his bed for six days. All that time his good friends, the priest, the bachelor, and the barber, often visited him, and his trusty squire, Sancho Panza, never left his bedside. They were convinced that his sickness was due to his sorrow at having been defeated and his disappointment in the matter of Dulcinea's disenchantment; and so, they tried in every way to cheer him up. The bachelor begged him to pluck up his spirits and get up from his bed so that they might begin their pastoral life, adding that he had already written an eclogue that would put Sannazaro's nose out of joint, and that he had bought with his own money from a shepherd of Quintanar two pedigreed dogs to watch the flock, one called Barcino and the other Butron. But this had no effect, for Don Quixote continued to mope as before. A physician was sent for, who, after feeling his pulse, took a rather gloomy view of the case and told him that he should provide for his soul's health, for that of his body was in dangerous condition. Don Quixote received the news calmly and serenely, but his niece, his housekeeper, and his squire began to weep as bitterly as if he had been laid out already. The physician was of the opinion that melancholy and mortification had brought him to death's door. Don Quixote then asked them to leave him for a little while, as he wished to sleep. They retired, and he slept at a stretch, as they say, for more than six hours, and the housekeeper and the niece were afraid that he might not waken from it. At length he did awaken and cried out in a loud voice: "Blessed be the Almighty for this great benefit He has granted me! Infinite are His mercies, and undiminished even by the sins of men."

The niece, who was listening very attentively to these words of her uncle, found more sense in them than there was in his usual talk, at least since he had fallen ill, and she questioned him: "What do you mean, uncle? Has anything strange taken place? What mercies and what sins of men are you talking about?"

"Mercies," answered Don Quixote, "that God has just this moment granted to me in spite of all my sins. My judgment is now clear and unfettered, and that dark cloud of ignorance has disappeared, which the continual reading of those detestable books of knight-errantry had cast over my understanding. Now I see their folly and fraud, and my sole regret is that the discovery comes too late to allow me to amend my ways by reading others that would enlighten my soul. I find, dear niece, that my end approaches, but I would have it remembered that though in my life I was reputed a madman, yet in my death this opinion was not confirmed. Therefore, my dear child, call my good friends, the priest, the bachelor Sanson Carrasco, and Master Nicholas, the barber, for I wish to make my confession and my will."

There was no need for the niece to go to the trouble, for presently all three arrived at the house, and Don Quixote no sooner saw them than he said: "My dear friends, welcome the happy news! I am no longer Don Quixote of La Mancha, but Alonso Quixano, the man whom the world formerly called the Good, owing to his virtuous life. I am now the sworn enemy of Amadis of Gaul and his innumerable brood; I now abhor all profane stories of knight-errantry, for I know only too well, through Heaven's mercy and through my own personal experience, the great danger of reading them."

When his three friends heard him talk thus, they concluded that he was stricken with some new madness. Sanson then said to him: "What does all this mean, Don Quixote? Now that we have just received news that Lady Dulcinea is disenchanted, and now that we are just about to become shepherds and spend our days singing and living like princes, you talk about turning yourself into a hermit. No more foolish tales, I beg you, and come back to your senses."

"Those foolish tales," replied Don Quixote, "that up to now have been my bane may with Heaven's help turn to my advantage at my death. Dear friends, I feel that I am rapidly sinking; therefore, let us put aside all jesting. I want a priest to hear my confession, and a notary to draw up my will. At such a moment a man must not deceive his soul; therefore, I beg you to send for the notary while the priest hears my confession."

Don Quixote's words amazed his hearers, but though they were at first skeptical about the return of his sanity, they were forced to take him at his word. One of the symptoms that made them fear he was near the point of death was the suddenness with which he had recovered his intellect, for after what he had already said, he conversed with such good sense and displayed such true Christian resignation that they believed his wits had been restored at last. The curate, therefore, told the company to leave the room, and he confessed Don Quixote. In the meantime the bachelor hastened to fetch the notary, and presently he returned with him and with Sancho Panza. The latter (who had already heard from the bachelor the news of his master's plight), finding the niece and the housekeeper in tears, began to make wry faces and finally burst out crying. After the priest had heard the sick man's confession, he came out saying: "There is no doubt that Alonso Quixano is at the point of death, and there is also no doubt that he is in his entire right mind; so, we should go in and enable him to make his will."

These sad tidings burst open the floodgates of the housekeeper's, the niece's, and the good squire's swollen eyes; their tears flowed fast and furious, and a thousand sighs rose from their breasts, for, indeed, as it has been noted, the sick gentleman, whether as Alonso Quixano the Good or as Don Quixote of La Mancha, had always been so good-natured and so agreeable that he was beloved not only by his family, but by all who knew him.

The notary, with the rest of the company, then went into the sick man's chamber, and Don Quixote stated the preamble to the will, commending his soul to Heaven and including the customary Christian declarations. When he came to the legacies he said:

"Item, I give and bequeath to Sancho Panza, whom in my madness I made my squire, whatever money he has of mine in his possession; and whereas there are accounts and reckonings to be settled between us for what he has received and disbursed, my will and pleasure is that he should not be required to furnish any account of such sums, and whatever may remain due to me, which must be but little, be enjoyed by him as my free gift, and may he prosper with it. And as when I was mad, he was through my means made governor of an island, I would now, in my right senses, give him the government of a kingdom, were it in my power, for his honesty and his faithfulness deserve it.

"And now, my friend," said he, turning to Sancho, "forgive me for making you appear as mad as I was myself, and for drawing you into my errors and persuading you that there have been and still are knights-errant in the world."

"Woe is me!" cried Sancho all in tears. "Don't die on me; but take my advice and live on for many a year; the maddest trick a man can play in his life is to yield up the ghost without more ado, and without being knocked on the head or stabbed through the belly to mope away and die of the doldrums. Shame on you, master; don't let the grass grow under your feet. Up with you this instant, out of your bed, and let us put on our shepherd's clothing and off with us to the fields as we had resolved a while back. Who knows but we may find Lady Dulcinea behind a hedge, disenchanted and as fresh as a daisy. If it's your defeat that is tearing your heart, lay the blame on me and say that it was my fault in not tightening Rozinante's girths enough, and that was why you were unhorsed. You must remember, too, sir, from your books on knight-errantry how common it was for knights to jostle one another out of the saddle, and he who's lying low today may be crowning his victory tomorrow."

"Just so," said Sanson; "there is good sense in what honest Sancho says."

"Go softly, I pray you, gentlemen," replied Don Quixote; "one should never look for birds of this year in the nests of yesteryear. I was mad, but I am now in my senses; I was once Don Quixote of La Mancha, but I am now, as I said before, Alonso Quixano the Good, and I hope that my repentance and my sincere words may restore me to the same esteem as you had for me before. So now proceed, Mr. Notary.

"Item, I declare and appoint Antonia Quixano, my niece, here present, sole heiress of all my estate, both real and personal, after all my just debts and legacies have been paid and deducted out of my goods and chattels; and the first charges on the estate shall be salaries due to my housekeeper, together with twenty ducats over and above her salary wages, which I leave and bequeath her to buy a gown.

"Item, I appoint the curate and the bachelor Sanson Carrasco, here present, to be the executors of this my last will and testament.

"Item, it is my will that if my niece Antonia Quixano should wish to marry, it will be with none but a person who, upon strict investigation, shall be found never to have read a book of knight-errantry in his life; but if it should be ascertained that he is acquainted with such books and she still insists on marrying him, she is then to lose all rights to my bequest, which my executors may then distribute in charity as they think fit.

"Item, I entreat the said executors that if at any time they happen to meet with the author of a certain book entitled *The Second Part of the Exploits of Don Quixote of La Mancha*, they will in my name most heartily beg his pardon for my having been unwittingly the cause of his writing such an amount of folly and triviality as he has done. Indeed, as I depart from this life my conscience troubles me that ever I was the cause of his publishing such a book."

After finishing the will, he swooned away and stretched his body to its full length in the bed. The company were alarmed and ran to his assistance; but these fainting attacks were repeated with great frequency during the three days that he lived after he had made his will. The household was in grief and confusion; and yet, after all, the niece continued to eat her meals, the housekeeper drowned her sorrows in wine, and Sancho Panza puffed himself up with satisfaction, for the thought of a legacy possesses a magic power to remove, or at least to soothe, the pangs that the heir should otherwise feel for the death of his friend.

At length Don Quixote's last day came, after he had received all the sacraments and expressed his abhorrence of books of knight-errantry. The notary, who was present, said that he had never read of any knight who ever died in his bed so peacefully and like a good Christian as Don Quixote. And so, amid the tears and lamentations of his friends, who knelt by his beside, he gave up the ghost, that is to say, he died. . . .

ELEGY, WRITTEN WITH HIS OWN HAND IN THE TOWER BEFORE HIS EXECUTION
Chidiock Tichborne (c.1558–1586)

My prime of youth is but a frost of cares,
 My feast of joy is but a dish of pain,
My crop of corn is but a field of tares,
 And all my good is but vain hope of gain:
The day is past, and yet I saw no sun,
And now I live, and now my life is done.

My tale was heard, and yet it was not told,
 My fruit is fall'n, and yet my leaves are green,
My youth is spent, and yet I am not old,
 I saw the world, and yet I was not seen:
My thread is cut, and yet it is not spun,
And now I live, and now my life is done.

I sought my death, and found it in my womb,
 I looked for life, and saw it was a shade,
I trod the earth, and knew it was my tomb,
 And now I die, and now I was but made:
My glass is full, and now my glass is run,
And now I live, and now my life is done.

A LITANY IN TIME OF PLAGUE
Thomas Nashe (1567–1601)

Adieu, farewell, earth's bliss;
This world uncertain is;
Fond are life's lustful joys;
Death proves them all but toys;
None from his darts can fly;
I am sick, I must die.
 Lord, have mercy on us!

Rich men, trust not in wealth,
Gold cannot buy you health;

Physic himself must fade.
All things to end are made,
The plague full swift goes by;
I am sick, I must die.
    Lord, have mercy on us!

Beauty is but a flower
Which wrinkles will devour;
Brightness falls from the air;
Queens have died young and fair;
Dust hath closed Helen's eye.
I am sick, I must die.
    Lord, have mercy on us!

Strength stoops unto the grave,
Worms feed on Hector brave;
Swords may not fight with fate,
Earth still holds ope her gate.
"Come, come!" the bells do cry.
I am sick, I must die.
    Lord, have mercy on us!

Wit with his wantonness
Tasteth death's bitterness;
Hell's executioner
Hath no ears for to hear
What vain art can reply.
I am sick, I must die.
    Lord, have mercy on us!

Haste, therefore, each degree,
To welcome destiny;
Heaven is our heritage,
Earth but a player's stage;
Mount we unto the sky.
I am sick, I must die.
    Lord, have mercy on us.

SONG OF A MAN ABOUT TO DIE IN A STRANGE LAND
Ojibwa poem (c.1400)

If I die here in a strange land,
If I die in a land not my own,
Nevertheless, the thunder,
The rolling thunder,
Will take me home.

If I die here, the wind,
The wind rushing over the prairie,
The wind will take me home.

The wind and the thunder,
They are the same everywhere,
What does it matter, then,
If I die here in a strange land?

I HEARD A FLY BUZZ—WHEN I DIED
Emily Dickinson (1830–1886)

I heard a Fly buzz—when I died—
The Stillness in the Room
Was like the Stillness in the Air—
Between the Heaves of Storm—

The Eyes around—had wrung them dry—
And Breaths were gathering firm
For that last Onset—when the King
Be witnessed—in the Room—

I willed my Keepsakes—Signed away
What portion of me be
Assignable—and then it was
There interposed a Fly—

With Blue—uncertain stumbling Buzz—
Between the light—and me—
And then the Windows failed—and then
I could not see to see—

THE JILTING OF GRANNY WEATHERALL
Katherine Anne Porter (b. 1890)

She flicked her wrist neatly out of Doctor Harry's pudgy careful fingers and pulled the sheet up to her chin. The brat ought to be in knee breeches. Doctoring around the country with spectacles on his nose! "Get along now, take your schoolbooks and go. There's nothing wrong with me."

Doctor Harry spread a warm paw like a cushion on her forehead where the forked green vein danced and made her eyelids twitch. "Now, now, be a good girl, and we'll have you up in no time."

"That's no way to speak to a woman nearly eighty years old just because she's down. I'd have you respect your elders, young man."

"Well, Missy, excuse me." Doctor Harry patted her cheek. "But I've got to warn you, haven't I? You're a marvel, but you must be careful or you're going to be good and sorry."

"Don't tell me what I'm going to be. I'm on my feet now, morally speaking. It's Cornelia. I had to go to bed to get rid of her."

Her bones felt loose, and floated around in her skin, and Doctor Harry floated like a balloon around the foot of the bed. He floated and pulled down his waistcoat and swung his glasses on a cord. "Well, stay where you are, it certainly can't hurt you."

"Get along and doctor your sick," said Granny Weatherall. "Leave a well woman alone. I'll call for you when I want you. . . . Where were you forty years ago when I pulled through milk-leg and double pneumonia? You weren't even born. Don't let Cornelia lead you on," she shouted, because Doctor Harry appeared to float up to the ceiling and out. "I pay my own bills, and I don't throw my money away on nonsense!"

She meant to wave good-by, but it was too much trouble. Her eyes closed of themselves, it was like a dark curtain drawn around the bed. The pillow rose and floated under her, pleasant as a hammock in a light wind. She listened to the leaves rustling outside the window. No, somebody was swishing newspapers: no, Cornelia and Doctor Harry were whispering together. She leaped broad awake, thinking they whispered in her ear.

"She was never like this, *never* like this!" "Well, what can we expect?" "Yes, eighty years old. . . ."

Well, and what if she was? She still had ears. It was like Cornelia to whisper around doors. She always kept things secret in such a public way. She was always being tactful and kind. Cornelia was dutiful; that was the trouble with her. Dutiful and good: "So good and dutiful," said Granny, "that I'd like to spank her." She saw herself spanking Cornelia and making a fine job of it.

"What'd you say, Mother?"

Granny felt her face tying up in hard knots.

"Can't a body think, I'd like to know?"

"I thought you might want something."

"I do. I want a lot of things. First off, go away and don't whisper."

She lay and drowsed, hoping in her sleep that the children would keep out and let her rest a minute. It had been a long day. Not that she was tired. It was always pleasant to snatch a minute now and then. There was always so much to be done, let me see: tomorrow.

Tomorrow was far away and there was nothing to trouble about. Things were finished somehow when the time came; thank God there was always a little margin over for peace: then a person could spread out the plan of life and tuck in the edges orderly. It was good to have everything clean and folded away, with the hair brushes and tonic bottles sitting straight on the white embroidered linen: the day started without fuss and the pantry shelves laid out with rows of jelly glasses and brown jugs and white stone-china jars with blue whirligigs and words painted on them: coffee, tea, sugar, ginger, cinnamon, allspice: and the bronze clock with the lion on top nicely dusted off. The dust that lion could collect in twenty-four hours! The box in the attic with all those letters tied up, well she'd have to go through that tomorrow. All those letters—George's letters and John's letters and her letters to them both—lying around for the children to find afterwards made her uneasy. Yes, that would be tomorrow's business. No use to let them know how silly she had been once.

While she was rummaging around she found death in her mind and it felt clammy and unfamiliar. She had spent so much time preparing for death there was no need for bringing it up again. Let it take care of itself now. When she was sixty she had felt very old, finished, and went around making farewell trips to see her children and grandchildren, with a secret in her mind: This is the very last of your mother, children! Then she made her will and came down with a long fever. That was all just a notion like a lot of other things, but it was lucky too, for she had once for all got over the idea of dying for a long time. Now she couldn't be worried. She hoped she had better sense now. Her father had lived to be one hundred and two years old and had drunk a noggin of strong hot toddy on his last birthday. He told the reporters it was his daily habit, and he owed his long life to that. He had made quite a scandal and was very pleased about it. She believed she'd just plague Cornelia a little.

"Cornelia! Cornelia!" No footsteps, but a sudden hand on her cheek. "Bless you, where have you been?"

"Here, mother."

"Well, Cornelia, I want a noggin of hot toddy."

"Are you cold, darling?"

"I'm chilly, Cornelia. Lying in bed stops the circulation. I must have told you that a thousand times."

Well, she could just hear Cornelia telling her husband that Mother was getting childish and they'd have to humor her. The thing that most annoyed her was that Cornelia thought she was deaf, dumb, and blind. Little hasty glances and tiny gestures tossed around her and over her head saying, "Don't cross her, let her have her way, she's eighty years old," and she sitting there as if she lived in a thin glass cage. Sometimes Granny almost made up her mind to pack up and move back to her own house where nobody could remind her every minute that she was old. Wait, wait, Cornelia, till your own children whisper behind your back!

In her day she had kept a better house and had got more work done. She wasn't too old yet for Lydia to be driving eighty miles for advice when one of the children jumped the track, and Jimmy still dropped in and talked things over: "Now, Mammy, you've got a good business head, I want to know what you think of this? . . ." Old Cornelia couldn't change the furniture around without asking. Little things, little things! They had been so sweet when they were little. Granny wished the old days were back again with the children young and everything to be done over. It had been a hard pull, but not too much for her. When she thought of all the food she had cooked, and all the clothes she had cut and sewed, and all the gardens she had made—well, the children showed it. There they were, made out of her, and they couldn't get away from that. Sometimes she wanted to see John again and point to them and say, Well, I didn't do so badly, did I? But that would have to wait. That was for tomorrow. She used to think of him as a man, but now all the children were older than their father, and he would be a child beside her if she saw him now. It seemed strange and there was something wrong in the idea. Why, he couldn't possibly recognize her. She had fenced in a hundred acres once, digging the post holes herself and clamping the wires with just a negro boy to help. That changed a woman. John would be looking for a young woman with the peaked Spanish comb in her hair and the painted fan. Digging post holes changes a woman. Riding country roads in the winter when women had their babies was another thing: sitting up nights with sick horses and sick negroes and sick children and hardly ever losing one. John, I hardly ever lost one of them! John would see that in a minute, that would be something he could understand, she wouldn't have to explain anything!

It made her feel like rolling up her sleeves and putting the whole place to rights again. No matter if Cornelia was determined to be everywhere at once, there were a great many things left undone on this place. She would start tomorrow and do them. It was good to be strong enough for everything, even if all you made melted and changed and slipped under your hands, so that by the time you finished you almost forgot what you were working for. What was it I set out to do? she asked herself intently, but she could not remember. A fog rose over the valley, she saw it marching across the creek swallowing the trees and moving up the hill like an army of ghosts. Soon it would be at the near edge of the orchard, and then it was time to go in and light the lamps. Come in, children, don't stay out in the night air.

Lighting the lamps had been beautiful. The children huddled up to her and breathed like little calves waiting at the bars in the twilight. Their eyes followed the match and watched the flame rise and settle in a blue curve, then they moved away from her. The lamp was lit, they didn't have to be scared and hang on to mother any more. Never, never, never more. God, for all my life I thank thee. Without Thee, my God, I could never have done it. Hail, Mary, full of grace.

I want you to pick all the fruit this year and see that nothing is wasted. There's always someone who can use it. Don't let good things rot for want of using. You waste life when you waste good food. Don't let things get lost. It's bitter to lose things. Now, don't let me get to thinking, not when I am tired and taking a little nap before supper. . . .

The pillow rose about her shoulders and pressed against her heart and the memory was being squeezed out of it: oh, push down the pillow, somebody: it would smother her if she tried to hold it. Such a fresh breeze blowing and such a green day with no threats in it. But he had not come, just the same. What does a woman do when she has put on the white veil and set out the white cake for a man and he doesn't come? She tried to remember. No, I swear he never harmed me but in that. He never harmed me but in that . . . and what if he did? There was the day, the day, but a whirl of dark smoke rose and covered it, crept up and over into the bright field where everything was planted so carefully in orderly rows. That was hell, she knew hell when she saw it. For sixty years she had prayed against remembering him and against losing her soul in the deep pit of hell, and now the two things were mingled in one and the thought of him was a smoky cloud from hell that moved and crept in her head when she had just got rid of Doctor Harry and was trying to rest a minute. Wounded vanity, Ellen, said a sharp voice in the top of her mind. Don't let your wounded vanity get the upper hand of you. Plenty of girls get jilted. You were jilted, weren't you? Then stand up to it. Her eyelids wavered and let in streamers of blue-gray light like tissue paper over her eyes. She must get up and pull the shades down or she'd never sleep. She was in bed again and the shades were not down. How could that happen? Better turn over, hide from the light, sleeping in the light gave you nightmares. "Mother, how do you feel now?" and a stinging wetness on her forehead. But I don't like having my face washed in cold water!

Hapsy? George? Lydia? Jimmy? No, Cornelia, and her features were swollen and full of little puddles. "They're coming, darling, they'll all be here soon." Go wash your face, child, you look funny.

Instead of obeying, Cornelia knelt down and put her head on the pillow. She seemed to be talking but there was no sound. "Well, are you tongue-tied? Whose birthday is it? Are you going to give a party?"

Cornelia's mouth moved urgently in strange shapes. "Don't do that, you bother me, daughter."

"Oh, no, Mother, Oh, no. . . ."

Nonsense. It was strange about children. They disputed your every word. "No what, Cornelia?"

"Here's Doctor Harry."

"I won't see that boy again. He just left five minutes ago."

"That was this morning, Mother. It's night now. Here's the nurse."

"This is Doctor Harry, Mrs. Weatherall. I never saw you look so young and happy!"

"Ah, I'll never be young again—but I'd be happy if they'd let me lie in peace and get rested."

She thought she spoke up loudly, but no one answered. A warm weight on her forehead, a warm bracelet on her wrist, and a breeze went on whispering, trying to tell her something. A shuffle of leaves in the everlasting hand of God. He blew on them and they danced and rattled. "Mother, don't mind, we're going to give you a little hypodermic." "Look here, daughter, how do ants get in this bed? I saw sugar ants yesterday." Did you send for Hapsy too?

It was Hapsy she really wanted. She had to go a long way back through a great many rooms to find Hapsy standing with a baby on her arm. She seemed to herself to be Hapsy also, and the baby on Hapsy's arm was Hapsy and himself and herself, all at once, and there was no surprise in the meeting. Then Hapsy melted from within and turned flimsy as gray gauze and the baby was a gauzy shadow, and Hapsy came up close and said, "I thought you'd never come," and looked at her very searchingly and said, "You haven't changed a bit!" They leaned forward to kiss, when Cornelia began whispering from a long way off, "Oh, is there anything you want to tell me? Is there anything I can do for you?"

Yes, she had changed her mind after sixty years and she would like to see George. I want you to find George. Find him and be sure to tell him I forgot him. I want him to know I had my husband just the same and my children and my house like any other woman. A good house too and a good husband that I loved and fine children out of him. Better than I hoped for even. Tell him I was given back everything he took away and more. Oh, no, oh, God, no, there was something else besides the house and the man and the children. Oh, surely they were not all? What was it? Something not given back. . . . Her breath crowded down under her ribs and grew into a monstrous frightening shape with cutting edges; it bored up into her head, and the agony was unbelievable: Yes, John, get the doctor now, no more talk, my time has come.

When this one was born it should be the last. The last. It should have been born first, for it was the one she had truly wanted. Everything came in good time. Nothing left out, left over. She was strong, in three days she would be as well as ever. Better. A woman needed milk in her to have her full health.

"Mother, do you hear me?"

"I've been telling you—"

"Mother, Father Connolly's here."

"I went to Holy Communion only last week. Tell him I'm not so sinful as all that."

"Father just wants to speak to you."

He could speak as much as he pleased. It was like him to drop in and inquire about her soul as if it were a teething baby, and then stay on for a cup of tea and a round of cards and gossip. He always had a funny story of some sort, usually about an Irishman who made his little mistakes and confessed them, and the point lay in some absurd thing he would blurt out in the confessional showing his struggles between native piety and original sin. Granny felt easy about her soul. Cornelia, where are your manners? Give Father Connolly a chair. She had her secret comfortable understanding with a few favorite saints who cleared a straight road to God for her. All as surely signed and sealed as the papers for the new Forty Acres. Forever . . . heirs and assigns forever. Since the day the wedding cake was not cut, but thrown out and wasted. The whole bottom dropped out of the world, and there she was blind and sweating with nothing under her feet and the walls falling away. His hand had caught her under the breast, she had not fallen, there was the freshly polished floor with the green rug on it, just as before. He had cursed like a sailor's parrot and said, "I'll kill him for you." Don't lay a hand on him, for my sake leave something to God. "Now, Ellen, you must believe what I tell you. . . ."

So there was nothing, nothing to worry about any more, except sometimes in the night one of the children screamed in a nightmare, and they both hustled out shaking and hunting for the matches and calling, "There, wait a minute, here we are!" John, get the doctor now, Hapsy's time has come. But there was Hapsy standing by the bed in a white cap. "Cornelia, tell Hapsy to take off her cap. I can't see her plain."

Her eyes opened very wide and the room stood out like a picture she had seen somewhere. Dark colors with the shadows rising towards the ceiling in long angles. The tall black dresser gleamed with nothing on it but John's picture, enlarged from a little one, with John's eyes very black when they should have been blue. You never saw him, so how do you know how he looked? But the man insisted the copy was perfect, it was very rich and handsome. For a picture, yes, but it's not my husband. The table by the bed had a linen cover and a candle and a crucifix. The light was blue from Cornelia's silk lampshades. No sort of light at all, just frippery. You had to live forty years with kerosene lamps to appreciate honest electricity. She felt very strong and she saw Doctor Harry with a rosy nimbus around him.

"You look like a saint, Doctor Harry, and I vow that's as near as you'll ever come to it."

"She's saying something."

"I heard you, Cornelia. What's all this carrying-on?"

"Father Connolly's saying——"

Cornelia's voice staggered and bumped like a cart in a bad road. It rounded corners and turned back again and arrived nowhere. Granny stepped up in the cart very lightly and reached for the reins, but a man sat beside her and she knew him by his hands, driving the cart. She did not look in his face, for she knew without seeing, but looked instead down the road where the trees leaned over and bowed to each other and a thousand birds were singing a Mass. She felt like singing too, but she put her hand in the bosom of her dress and pulled out a rosary, and Father Connolly murmured Latin in a very solemn voice and tickled her feet. My God will you stop that nonsense? I'm a married woman. What if he did run away and leave me to face the priest by myself? I found another a whole world better. I wouldn't have exchanged my husband for anybody except St. Michael himself, and you may tell him that for me with a thank you in the bargain.

Light flashed on her closed eyelids, and a deep roaring shook her. Cornelia, is that lightning? I hear thunder. There's going to be a storm. Close all the windows. Call the children in. . . . "Mother, here we are, all of us." "Is that you, Hapsy?" "Oh, no, I'm Lydia. We drove as fast as we could." Their faces drifted above her, drifted away. The rosary fell out of her hands and Lydia put it back. Jimmy tried to help, their hands fumbled together, and Granny closed two fingers around Jimmy's thumb. Beads wouldn't do, it must be something alive. She was so amazed her thoughts ran round and round. So, my dear Lord, this is my death and I wasn't even thinking about it. My children have come to see me die. But I can't, it's not time. Oh, I always hated surprises. I wanted to give Cornelia the amethyst set—Cornelia, you're to have the amethyst set, but

Hapsy's to wear it when she wants, and, Doctor Harry, do shut up. Nobody sent for you. Oh, my dear Lord, do wait a minute. I meant to do something about the Forty Acres, Jimmy doesn't need it and Lydia will later on, with that worthless husband of hers. I meant to finish the altar cloth and send six bottles of wine to Sister Borgia for her dyspepsia. I want to send six bottles of wine to Sister Borgia, Father Connolly, now don't let me forget.

Cornelia's voice made short turns and tilted over and crashed. "Oh, Mother, oh, Mother, oh, Mother. . . ."

"I'm not going, Cornelia. I'm taken by surprise. I can't go."

You'll see Hapsy again. What about her? "I thought you'd never come." Granny made a long journey outward, looking for Hapsy. What if I don't find her? What then? Her heart sank down and down, there was no bottom to death, she couldn't come to the end of it. The blue light from Cornelia's lampshade drew into a tiny point in the center of her brain, it flickered and winked like an eye, quietly it fluttered and dwindled. Granny lay curled down within herself, amazed and watchful, staring at the point of light that was herself; her body was now only a deeper mass of shadow in an endless darkness and this darkness would curl around the light and swallow it up. God, give a sign!

For the second time there was no sign. Again no bridegroom and the priest in the house. She could not remember any other sorrow because this grief wiped them all away. Oh, no, there's nothing more cruel than this—I'll never forgive it. She stretched herself with a deep breath and blew out the light.

IN THE SHADOW OF THE VALLEY OF DEATH
Abū al-Qāsim al-Shābbī (1909–1934)

Born in southern Tunisia, al-Shābbī is considered one of the outstanding modern Arab poets of North Africa. His poems are collected under the title *Aghānī al-Hayāh* (Songs of Life).

We walk, as all around walks on creation . . . yet, to what goal?
With the birds we sing to the sun, as the spring plays on its flute;
We read out to Death the tale of Life . . . yet, how ends that tale?
Thus I spoke to the winds, and thus they answered: ask of Being itself
    how it began.

Covered over in mist, in bitter weariness cried out my soul:
Whither shall I go?
I said: walk on with Life; it replied: what reaped I as I walked before?
Collapsed like parched and withered plant I cried: Where, o heart, is my
   rake?
Bring it, that I may trace my grave in the dark silence, bury myself,
Bring it, for darkness is dense around me, and the mists of sorrow are
   settled on high.
Dawn fills the goblets of passion, yet they shatter in my hands;
Proud youth has fled into the past, and left on my lips a lament.
Come, o heart! We are two strangers who made of life an art of sorrow;
We have fed long on life, sung long with youth,
And now with night go barefooted over the rocky paths—and bleed.
We are satiated with dust, our thirst quenched with tears,
Left and right we have scattered dreams, love, pain, and sorrow,
And then? I, remote from the joy of the world and its song,
In the darkness of death bury the days of my life, cannot even mourn their
   passing,
And the flowers of life, in grievous, troubling silence, fall at my feet.
The magic of life is dry: come, o my weeping heart, let us now try death.
   Come!

from DEATH BE NOT PROUD
John Gunther (1901–1970)

This book is a reflective recording of a courageous teenager's dying. Johnny
Gunther was sixteen when he and his parents discovered, in 1946, that he had a
brain tumor. A student at the Deerfield Academy at the time, Johnny struggled
valiantly for fifteen months against hopeless odds—to finish Deerfield, to be
admitted to Harvard, to continue living. His is a story of a brilliant, talented, and
sensitive young man whose life was cut short before he entered college. The story
is told by his father.

   The first time I saw Johnny really frightened came at about this time,
when he got ready for the first x-ray. He kept saying that "surely" this
must be "just for taking pictures." He said to me again and again,
anxiously, "It's just for *pictures*, isn't it?" Then he knew from the time
he spent under the machine that something much more serious than tak-

ing pictures was going on, and that this must be a form of treatment. He turned to me firmly and asked, "Does this mean that I have cancer?" Then he murmured to Frances later, "I have so much to do! And there's so little time!"

. . . .

A major problem continued to be what to tell him. If the tumor was indeed mostly gone, how then explain the continued bulging? But beyond this there were larger questions. *Why* was Johnny being subjected to this merciless experience? I tried to explain that suffering is an inevitable part of most lives, that none of this ordeal was without some purpose, that pain is a constituent of all the processes of growth, that perhaps the entire harrowing episode would make his brain even finer, subtler, and more sensitive than it was. He did not appear to be convinced. Then there was a question I asked myself incessantly. Why—of all things— should Johnny be afflicted in that part of him which was his best, the brain? What philosophical explanation could one find for that? Was all this a dismal accident, purely barren and fortuitous? Beethoven was struck deaf and Milton blind and I met a singer once who got a cancer of the vocal cords. But if the connection of circumstances was not fortui- tous, not accidental, where was justice?

. . . .

Now occurred the most remarkable of all remarkable things in the story of this struggle. Johnny accepted with disappointment but good spirit that he could not return to Deerfield—I broke the news to him—and he set out diligently to make up his lost school hours by tutor- ing. He could hardly walk without swaying; he could scarcely move his left fingers; he had lost half the sight of each eye; he was dazed with the poison from the bump; a portion of his brain had been eaten away; and yet he worked.

Frances found him two tutors and set them into their routine smoothly, while Johnny himself planned his daily endeavor like a general directing a battle. He helped map out the lessons himself, and knew with complete assurance and precision just what he wanted each tutor to cover in every session.

. . . .

My sister was with Johnny and me when he got the news that the eyes were normal. I never knew till this moment just how anguishing was the strain that he strove so hard to conceal. He jumped bolt upright; then slowly, proudly, very slowly and proudly, he relaxed downward to the pillow, while across his face spread the most beatifically happy expression I have ever seen on a human being, and his eyes—normal eyes now—filled just to the brim with tears, but did not spill over, as he smiled with relief, pride, and the exhaustion that comes with release from intolerable strain.

. . . .

Straight through March and April, despite everything, Johnny worked on and on. He was utterly obsessed about getting into Harvard in the fall. But to achieve this he had to complete making up his work at Deerfield and graduate as well as pass the college entrance exams, a double task that seemed impossible. Then on March 18 we learned that he had caught up with his history course at Deerfield—though he hadn't been there for eleven months—and on April 7 he had a letter from Mr. Boyden that gave him radiant happiness: he had passed his English examination satisfactorily and so was abreast of this course too. I took him to the science room in the Public Library, where he did some advanced work, and he proceeded to write up no fewer than fifty-four chemistry experiments! Then Frances found out about the New York Tutoring School, where Mr. Matthew is a wise and considerate headmaster, and we enrolled him there. Johnny's marks after six weeks were 90 in English, 95 in history, 95 in trig. This in a boy with half a brain!

. . . .

The effort to pretend that the tumor was nothing cost him dearly; the price of his invincible fight was great fatigue. It took a miserable lot out of him to pretend to ignore what he must have now known to be the truth, that he wasn't getting any better. The faraway look was in his eyes more often now. But it was impossible for us not to support his optimism, because any discouragement would have been a crushing blow. All he had now was his will to live. We had to keep that up at any cost. The cord of life was wearing very thin, and if we took away hope, it would be bound to snap.

from HOW COULD I NOT BE AMONG YOU?
Ted Rosenthal (1938–1972)

In September 1969, Ted Rosenthal found out that he had acute leukemia and was going to die. Married and with two young children, he entered Memorial Hospital in New York for treatment. During a recuperative period he recorded many of his views regarding cancer treatment, hospitals, dying, and living. After these words were spoken and written, he had a remission which allowed him to return to California to begin building a house in the wilderness. A filmed version of this book won first prize at the 1972 American Film Festival.

I was confused if anything, but I did have certain positive feelings and one was that the total sympathy I would get from all people by making a kind of a grandstand play and announcing it. And it was almost a sadistic feeling. I called up countless people, person after person and said, "Guess what's happened to me?" And that felt good. And everybody came over and kissed me and loved me and hugged me. But there was this undercurrent of sinking despair feeling underneath it all. I was scared.

. . . .

They train you at the hospital not to think in terms of the future at all. They never speak in terms of dates or lengths of time and they don't promise you anything. Therefore when they give you good news, all they are essentially telling you is that you're not dead. All those people who say that you are predictable and that you will die in the same way that everyone else dies, they are right. I resented that at first. I resented them saying "Oh you are at the two week stage. You're feeling, doing this. You're free. You're at the angry stage. I understand that. You're depressed. You're lost. Three and one half weeks after you find this out you always feel lost."

Well, they're right. It works that way with me. I am following patterns. I am following the guidelines for dying-of-terminal-cancer-patients down to the letter. They all told me how this would be, how I would be reacting. It's fiendish. No matter what I say, they say, "Hm. That's what we thought you'd say." Especially the nurses—and the doctors, too. All of them.

. . . .

My only request was—the thing I was most concerned about was that should I die, I wanted a warning in advance of dying so that I could get out of the hospital, get back to California, get into the country and die there. And I was shocked when the doctor said, "We'll do the best we can." I thought he would say more than that. I thought he could say, "Sure we'll do that for you," but he said "We'll do the best we can."

. . . .

Dying is a matter of feeling. I think dying is no different than being born. When I was told that I was going to die in five months I felt that was the same as telling me that I was going to die that afternoon. And the whole idea of going through an awful lot of pain or frustration or embarrassment from one day to the next to prolong my life a few days or a few weeks or a few months or even a year or so was frightening in itself.

. . . .

To live in the moment you literally have to have the sense of having nothing to live for. Not in the sense of future economic opportunities and that sort of thing, but just realizing that there is no real purpose to life and being able to live life fully from moment to moment. And that's something I can't even tell myself how to do and I can't tell anybody else how to do it.

I'm changed; I'll always be changed. I'll always be happier for what I have gone through, only because it has enabled me to have the courage to open myself up to anything that happens and I am no longer afraid of death. At least I am not afraid of death the way I might have been had I not become sick. But I do forget that it is me. The days are ticking off and I hate that.

Asparaginase, the drug that I have been on for the last couple of weeks, causes acute nausea that no drug, no pill will do anything to help. So my doctor came rushing in one day when I was lying on my back underneath this bottle of asparaginase and said, "Do you have any weed? Do you have any access to weed?" And I said, "What kind of weed do you mean?" and he said, "Grass, pot, marijuana." So I got some that night and I sat there and I decided to wait until I thought I was at my worst. I sat there with a bowl in my lap, ready to vomit and a pipe of pot in my other hand. And just as I was about to let loose, I took a puff and, whee, it was gone. I felt fine. I went right in after two or three puffs and I ate a dozen crabs and a huge lobster and a piece of chocolate cake on top of that, then I went rushing back to the doctor the next day and told him and he said, "Fantastic." So he has me on pot now.

. . . .

My medical condition was such that it changed dramatically from moment to moment, from day to day, with bone marrows that I had taken, with blood tests constant all day long. I was never able to synchronize my feelings with information that came, and every bit of information had to alter my feelings about myself in terms of survival and where I stood in relation to the future and even that moment. I became frightened.

How long do I have to live?

That's not the sort of thing that happens to me.

People die from that, isn't that so?

from STAY OF EXECUTION
Stewart Alsop (1913–1974)

Alsop was a famous journalist and political analyst when, at the age of fifty-seven, he was diagnosed as having acute myeloblastic leukemia. Over the next three years he tried to "better the odds" against death by undergoing chemotherapy and other cancer treatments at the National Institutes of Health. John Glick and other physicians at NIH finally decided that he had an unusual form of cancer known as smoldering leukemia. While under treatment, Alsop wrote a remarkable account of his dying—and his changing perspective toward "Uncle Thanatos."

Before I got sick I hardly ever thought about death, because the subject is an unpleasant one. Since John Glick quoted those odds to me, I have had to think a lot about death, and I have learned something from the thinking. I learned something especially from those twenty days of unexplained viremia, or whatever it was (John Glick still does not know for sure). What I learned is something that most healthy people do not fully understand when they think about their own death.

If you are young and in good spirits and full of health, the thought of dying is not only utterly abhorrent but inherently incredible. The inherent incredibility of death to a healthy young man acts as a protective mechanism and helps to keep a combat soldier sane.

But the fear of death in battle is quite different from the fear of death on a hospital bed. It is, for one thing, much rarer. Most people do not die a violent death, whether on the battle field or in the streets. Most people die in bed, because they are very sick or because they are very old or both. But their sickness or their oldness also acts as a protective mechanism. Sickness and age do not make death at all incredible. They do make death less than utterly abhorrent.

In short, for people who are sick, to be a bit sicker—sick unto death itself—holds far fewer terrors than for people who feel well. Both Cy Sulzberger and Bill Attwood wrote me letters in which they referred to death as the Greek god, Thanatos. It was at this point that I began to think of death as Uncle Thanatos. When I felt sick enough, I even felt a certain affection for Thanatos, and much less fear of him than I had before.

. . . .

On Thursday, all the top specialists at NIH—Dr. Henderson, Dr. Carbone, Dr. Gralnick, and others, as well as John—had a morning meeting to decide on an Alsop diagnosis and an Alsop treatment. John called up about it in the afternoon, and we also talked about it at 5 P.M., when I went to NIH for a platelet transfusion.

The diagnosis is smoldering leukemia—smoldering, subacute, aleukemic leukemia. John said there had been only about a dozen cases under the same heading in the history of NIH. Therefore, treatment and prognosis were both difficult, the more so because my case was not exactly like any of the others.

Because I had had a near remission in the fall, John is hopeful that I will be especially responsive to drugs—in other words, that the bad cells will retreat more easily than usual. Moreover, the prognosis is certainly more hopeful than it would have been if I had had AML. Almost anything is more hopeful.

I am to have a marrow test on Wednesday, May 17 (my fifty-eighth birthday—nice birthday present), and if the bad cells are still increasing (which John obviously expects) I am to have a one-week course of steroids, tapering off thereafter. Most people react to steroids at first with euphoria, followed by depression when they are withdrawn. John Glick will try to control the depression by tapering off the treatments. I think I'll be euphoric if the treatment works and depressed if it doesn't. But maybe that's too rational.

. . . .

This is being written in late May 1973, in one of NIH's drearily familiar hospital rooms (except for the reproductions from the National Gallery of Art opposite each bed, they are all exactly alike). I came here, on John Glick's orders, a week ago, on May 19.

I felt queer on the way out. In fact, I had been feeling queer for some two months. Since mid-March, I had been having those familiar atypical symptoms, night sweats and low-grade fevers, the same unexplained symptoms I had had in September 1971 and intermittently since. But I felt especially queer on Saturday, so when we got to Needwood I went to bed. About five in the afternoon I woke up, feeling not queer but sick, really sick. I took my temperature, and it was over 104. We called John Glick, and he ordered me into NIH. By eight that night, after thumping my back and peering at a chest x-ray, he had made his diagnosis—pneumonia again.

In the two months of night sweats and fevers, my blood counts had sunk inexorably. I needed hemoglobin transfusions more frequently than before, and my poor brother Joe had had to join forces with Bob Park as a platelet donor, spending three to six hours of every busy week with a needle in his arm in the plasma pharesis laboratory. But the worst of my counts was the granulocyte count. For weeks it had been 100 or less. Statistically and medically, I was an easy mark for a galloping infection, the kind that kills a leukemic in a matter of hours.

I felt very sick on Saturday night, and I had a feeling, quite a strong feeling, that this time I would not leave NIH on my two feet; that this was what the Bible calls "the end of the days." Given my counts, this was not at all an irrational feeling. But I seem to have been wrong. As this is written, a week after being admitted, I have had no temperature for forty-eight hours, for the first time in more than eight weeks, and John Glick reports that the pneumonia is contained. He is very complimentary about my granulocytes, which, though few in number, seem to be brave and resourceful; John compares them to Napoleon's Old Guard. The granulocytic Old Guard could not have saved me, of course, without the cidal antibiotics that are dripping into my left arm as I type. In any case, I seem to have had yet another stay of execution.

John Glick can make no prognosis about what may happen next.

Perhaps I shall drift back into the fever-and-night-sweats routine. Perhaps, as after the October penumonia, I shall make a halfway comeback, with no fever and feeling reasonably well as long as I get my hemoglobin and platelet transfusions. And just perhaps, although miracles, like lightning, rarely strike twice in the same place, I shall have another remission, as I had after my bout of flu in the autumn of 1971.

In any case, one contrast strikes me. At the beginning of this book, I described the trapped and desperate feeling that came over me after I had been told that I would die quite soon. Last Saturday night, when I felt so sick, I felt rather sure that I would die quite soon, and perhaps very soon, within the next day or so. I did not at all welcome the prospect, but it filled me with no sense of panic. I kissed Tish a fond good night at ten, took some Benadryl, and went easily off to sleep. Why the difference?

Perhaps the state of the nation has something—a very little something—to do with the difference. For weeks now I have been haunted and depressed by a sense that the American system, in which I have always believed in an unquestioning sort of way, the way a boy believes in his family, really is falling apart; by a sense that we are a failed nation, a failed people. And Watergate is surely a peculiarly depressing way to say farewell to all our greatness. It is a whimper—a sleazy little whimper, a grubby little whimper—rather than a bang.

The thought has occurred to me quite often in recent weeks that perhaps this is a good time to bow out. No doubt it was the state of Alsop, far more than the state of the nation, that caused this thought to occur to me so often. The fact is that I have been depressed, the more so because John Glick, on whom I have become excessively dependent, leaves in a few weeks to take up a new post in California. Moreover, I have been feeling lousy.

Since mid-March, when the fevers and the night sweats began, I have written my column for *Newsweek* and worked on this book and driven downtown to dictate letters to Amanda, make telephone calls, and make dates for business lunches. Tish and I, as usual better guests than hosts, have gone out to dinner several times a week and talked and laughed with friends. I have lived, in short, what John Glick calls "a normal life."

But it has not been altogether normal. It is not normal to wake up every night just before dawn, with a fever of 101 or so, take a couple of pills, and settle down to sweat like a hog for four or five hours. It is not normal to feel so weak you can't play tennis or go trout fishing. And it is not normal either to feel a sort of creeping weariness and a sense of being terribly dependent, like a vampire, on the blood of others. After eight weeks of this kind of "normal" life, the thought of death loses some of its terror.

But the most important reason why I felt no panic fear last Saturday was, I think, the strange, unconscious, indescribable process which I have tried to describe in this book—the process of adjustment whereby one comes to terms with death. A dying man needs to die, as a sleepy man needs to sleep, and there comes a time when it is wrong, as well as useless, to resist.

There was a time, after I first got sick, when I liked to recall another of my small collection of Churchillisms, the familiar story of how Churchill visited his old school, Harrow, in his extreme old age, and the headmaster asked him to say a few words to the boys.

"Never give up," Churchill said. "Never. Never. Never. Never." There is no doubt that the old man lived beyond his allotted span by a tremendous effort of a tremendous will. He lived so long because he never gave up. But to what good end?

I saw Churchill once again, after that lucheon at Chartwell. A year or so before he died, I was in the visitors' gallery of the House of Commons on a reporting trip to London when Sir Winston unexpectedly appeared on the floor. There was a hush as the old man waddled feebly toward his accustomed seat, hunched over and uncertain of every step. He sat down heavily and looked around the House, owlishly, unseeing, as if for some long-vanished familiar face, and then, as the debate resumed, his big head slumped forward grotesquely on his chest. He was an empty husk of a man, all the wit and elegance and greatness drained out of him by age. Like my mother, he should have died herebefore.

There is a time to live, but there is also a time to die. That time has not yet come for me. But it will. It will come for all of us.

from A PRIVATE BATTLE
Cornelius Ryan (1920–1974) and Kathryn Morgan Ryan

This unusual account of dying is the work of two authors. When Cornelius Ryan, author of military histories of the second World War, found out in 1970 that he had prostate cancer, he began secretly recording his reactions and experiences.

After his death, his wife discovered his tapes and, a writer herself, decided to supplement his views with her own recollections and the technical records supplied by the doctors in the case. The following selections are some of his views while dying.

On this Saturday, July 25, 1970, only the big synchronous clock on the wall across the room from my desk makes its customary noise. It has just flapped over another minute. The time is 6:13 A.M. Just under twelve hours ago—at precisely 6:35 P.M. yesterday—my wife and I were told by a prominent New York urologist that I have a primary carcinoma of the prostate. He meant that I've got cancer. In these tormented hours this is the first time I've said that word out loud.

. . . .

Now cancer will be my closest possession, going with me from office to house, to conferences and dinner parties, as I go myself. I have got to get used to having it always here. I have got to think about what influence it may assume in time, not only over me but on my family, friends, and work. This seems as good a time as any to start to talk it out on tape. I want to spare Kathryn and the children as much as possible. I will only be able to deal candidly with this subject through the tape recorder or in notebooks I will have to hide somewhere among the research material only I delve into. For now, the space behind the Russian atlas seems as safe a place as any. The book is within arm's reach on the shelf where I keep translations and no one ever looks at them but me.

What comes to mind immediately is how fast cancer alienates one from the usual routines and behavior. I suppose I'm less alive than I was yesterday and by tomorrow I'll be dying more than I am today. Not in the manner of the old cliché that you began to die the minute you are born. That is not much consolation. There's not a time limit inherent in that old bromide. My time as of now is most definitely limited, predetermined by cancer survival statistics and the absence of real progress against the disease.

I feel such a terrible sense of injustice. What did I do to deserve this? Yet, that's just the kind of question I've got to eliminate from my mind. I do not exactly trust my ability to maintain objectivity publicly unless I can release the body quakes and shocks in private. And how can you make people who haven't got cancer understand what's happened to you without having to endure their pity as well? I'm damned if I want pity. Self-pity is bad enough.

. . . .

Just now I thought of something that is probably the closest comparison to my present predicament I have ever experienced. During World War II I found myself caught up with a patrol in a minefield. My reaction, and I remember it so very well, had two distinct plateaus: how did I get myself into this situation? and, now, let's get out of it!

Curiously, back then, I cannot remember experiencing fear. Neither do I recall any great surge of courage. I think my reaction was almost mechanical. There was no point in dwelling on the fact that we were in the minefield. The sole objective was to get through it safely—and somehow we all did. Luck would appear to play a rather large factor in life. At the moment mine seems to be running out. Now, as in those wartime days, I don't know what steps will bring me through this grave ordeal, but I can't stay rooted to one spot forever.

Unless, unwittingly, I have already stayed too long. It may be too late to extricate myself, for, if one uses the approximate time of the pathological expert's diagnosis, I began dying forty-two hours ago.

No, let me correct that. The first indication I had that something was wrong occurred about four months back. So presumably I have been dying for the better part of this, my fiftieth, year.

There's a mosquito in here buzzing around the desk. If it stings me I hope the damn thing gets cancer.

. . . .

Memorial's bill, excluding surgeons and specialists, is $3,453.65. I am amazed at all it includes, and looking at the list, I am somewhat astounded that the bill isn't higher. There is, of course, room and board. The little room, 904, was $119 per day. Can most patients afford that? Still, included in the bill are costs for the use of the operating room, for the blood bank, transfusion services, plasma, anesthesia, pathology. And there are other tests and services also in the overall charge: hematology, cytology, diagnostic radiology, bacteriology, urinology, EKG, biochemistry. Even the physical therapists and special-duty nurses are included in the bill. Little enough to save a life, if one gets to the right place and into the hands of the right people.

But I am out of pocket in many other ways: the telephone calls to Europe and throughout Europe, plane fares, hotels, specialists' fees. Since July I have spent close to $7,000 for cancer research and treatment. Major medical insurances are essentials for partial payments of hospitalization but they cannot cover the trips and research I undertook. How few people could have afforded to do what I have done! That makes the collation of facts and methods of treatment all the more essential. Every man, woman, and child in the world should have the right to the best and most complete medical information available in order to reduce costs but, more important, in order to save their lives. The horror is that far too often, as I might have done, they will fall into the hands of a doctor using therapy which is already obsolete.

. . . .

There is nothing more appalling than the state I am in at present. I thought I had experienced the full spectrum of humiliations. I was wrong. I am sitting in a wheelchair in the office because I cannot walk back and forth to my desk. Each day Kathryn helps me propel a walker down the few steps from our rooms to the foyer and then gets me into this chair and backs out the front door to start the walk that has become a journey. There are seventeen steps from the front door to the driveway, with one landing where Katie can rest. I don't know where she gets the reserves of strength to haul me around. She straps me into the chair so I won't fall out and raises the front wheels high in the air while she takes me down with the large back wheels, sliding them gently off each riser and down to the next. I try not to moan because she does do it gently and should not be doing it at all. At the bottom we rest for a moment on the driveway before Katie starts for the office. Our drive has a slight downward elevation and a couple of times she has not been able to hold the chair except by dragging her feet behind it. I have tried to help by attempting to slow the back wheels with my hands and although I've rubbed some skin off, it does impede the forward speed.

Nearing the office the driveway rises again and this is the hardest part for Katie. I can propel the wheels with my hands quite successfully now, which saves her from having to push all my weight up the incline. Then she turns me around again and we back into the office. I want to cry every trip we make because I would rather be gone for good than for her to have to do this kind of thing. I am hoping to get some young lad to come and do the pushing and pulling because I simply cannot have Katie exerting herself like this.

Other aspects of my present condition are far worse. I am incontinent. It is the most embarrassing, god-awful thing in the world. I have a car robe over my knees and a urinal bottle on the far side of my desk. I cannot get up and get to the bathroom, so I have to use the bottle and very often I have had to ask Annie to leave the room quickly in the middle of dictation or work on copy. I cannot tell when I have to use the urinal and the need is often upon me before I can prepare myself or Katie or Annie.

. . . .

It is my impression that a great many people think I won't be around much longer. In fact, I had the same thought myself shortly after arriving home. People called in and I didn't remember seeing them. Then one night—it could not have been more than a day or two after I came home—I felt very strange. I had no sensation of pain, no urgency to get to the bathroom, no recollection of past or present. It was quite peaceful to lie there like that, and yet I rather felt I should do something about it, because I felt a bit unnatural.

I must have dozed off because it was morning and Katie was bending over me, yelling something about waking up. I was too tired to open my eyes. I could feel her hands on my face, chest, and arms. She tried to move me but I didn't feel like moving. I had come to like my condition and I was more comfortable than I can remember being in days. The next I knew, Neligan was there, and he poked around my body and, like Katie, talked to me. I could hear him perfectly well but I thought if I didn't answer he would just go away. Quite frankly I didn't care what he did as long as he left me alone. That was the precise time I thought I might be dying—and I didn't care.

. . . .

Each morning for the past two or three years when I have wakened the first words I've said are, "Thank you, God, for this fine day." It has not mattered if the weather was bad or good. What has been important is that God had seen me through the night and given me another day to work and to be with my family. I continue to thank Him. He has allowed me to do what was important.

I have received more than my share of blessings. I have been able to cram so much into my life that it has been brimful of happiness. The most rewarding moments, the best writing I think I've ever done, the love I'd had from my wife and children and the joy I've taken in their accomplishments—all have been realized in the years I've had cancer. But I will still continue to fight it. I don't have time to die.

4. DEATH SCENES

MUCH of the world's literature depicts death scenes of individuals. Sometimes the individuals are real persons in history; sometimes they are creations of an author's imaginative mind. Sometimes the dying person is historically important; other times the person is historically unimportant or merely fictional. In any case, as illustrated by the following literary examples, the depiction of an individual's death is often the focal point or culminating event of a real-life story or of a poem, play, short story, or novel.

Generally regarded as the greatest novel of China, the *Dream of the Red Chamber* builds up to a climactic death scene. Its author, Tsao Hsueh-Chin (1724–1764), describes the complex events—both comical and tragic—which take place in the house of Chia, an extensive family of five generations living in two households in Peking. The central theme of the novel is the ill-fated love between Pao-yu, a boy who represents anticipated greatness for the house of Chia, and his cousin Black Jade.

Like the love of Romeo and Juliet, the love of Pao-yu and Black Jade is not meant to be. Pao-yu declares his love for Black Jade early in the story, but cannot marry her because Phoenix, the matriarchal leader of the house of Chia, decides that he must marry Precious Virtue instead. Black Jade, already in poor health, simply cannot adjust to this crushing disappointment. Her physical condition deteriorates rapidly as the marriage date approaches, and she voices a wish to die as quickly as possible. In an emotionally gripping scene toward the end of the novel, Black Jade in her weakened condition asks a servant to burn the gifts Pao-yu has given her, then lapses into a semiconscious state. At approximately the hour of the wedding between Pao-yu and Precious Virtue, Black Jade regains consciousness long enough to cry out as she dies, "Pao-yu, Pao-yu, how——?"

A death scene is also the culminating point in Franz Kafka's story "A Hunger Artist." Kafka, a Czech existentialist writer, tells a story about a man who for years had professionally engaged in periods of fasting. Accompanied by his manager, he had toured the cities of Europe and captivated observers with his ability to fast for periods of forty days. Crowds gathered, people expressed amazement, and some of the onlookers remained throughout the night to assure themselves that the hunger artist did not sneak a meal. Then, after years of fascination with the hunger artist, people lost interest in his professional abilities. Instead of being the center of attention, the hunger artist found himself relegated to the menagerie of circuses, his cage vying with the animal cages for the attention of passersby. Now nobody seemed interested in his endurance. Now nobody even knew when he passed the fortieth day of fasting. Now nobody, until it was time to clean out his cage, even remembered that he was there. Finally, when they did clean his cage, they discovered his emaciated body in a heap of straw. When asked why he had fasted without end, he explained simply that he had never found any food he particularly liked to eat. With that unusual statement, he died in his cage.

Love Story, Erich Segal's contemporary American novel, is centered entirely on the impending death of a young woman in love with her husband and with life. As a student at Radcliffe, Jenny falls in love with a Harvard student named Oliver Barrett IV. She comes from a not particularly rich, Catholic family; he stands to inherit great wealth if he abides by his father's views regarding a proper daughter-in-law. Against his father's wishes, and at the cost of his inheritance, Oliver and Jenny marry.

The first three years of marriage are financially difficult, with Jenny teaching school and Oliver trying to complete law school. Then, after his graduation and with the potential of a financially successful legal career in front of them, they unexpectedly find out that she is terminally ill at the age of twenty-four with a form of leukemia which is too advanced to be treated. Any plans they have had for the future, for a new home, or for children are dashed against the reality of an untreatable disease. Her death scene climaxes the novel, with Oliver sitting on her hospital bed and at her request holding her tightly in his arms. With that last embrace and parting words of thanks to him, she dies.

The selections in this section further demonstrate how death scenes often figure prominently in literature. The first selection comes from *The Epic of Gilgamesh*, the oldest piece of literature extant. Comprised of mythological stories depicting the extraordinary adventures of the god-man Gilgamesh, the epic has as its focal point the death of Gilgamesh's friend Enkidu, a death which ends an unusually strong friendship and causes Gilgamesh to search for the possibility of immortality in this life. The account of the Buddha's death in the *Digha-nikaya* describes conversations which took place during his final hours in the city of Kusinara, as well as parting words of advice to his disciples prior to his passing into nirvana. Plato's account of the death of Socrates also contains parting words of advice for Socrates' students, as well as the famous portrayal of a man who chose to die rather than break the laws of his country or attempt an escape to save his life. And the account of Jesus' death in the gospel of Mark depicts a man who was convicted on questionable legal charges, humiliated by an angry crowd and unsympathetic soldiers, and sentenced to die as a criminal.

The other selections show varied ways of incorporating death scenes into literature. Tennyson's "Morte d'Arthur" is an imaginative portrayal in poetic verse of what King Arthur's death might have been like. John Gunther, after having depicted the ordeal of dying endured by his son (see the previous section), provides a poignant description of Johnny's death in a hospital and the physicians who stood by, unable to prevent it from happening. *Eric*, written by Doris Lund, is another account of a teenager's valiant but losing struggle against death. Like Johnny Gunther, Eric had a promising future cut short by his death in a hospital. The death scene described by Margaret Craven, an American journalist and short-story writer, is fictional and portrays the lonely death of a logger in the Canadian Northwest. And Ghassan Kanafani, a Palestinian Arab now living in Lebanon, provides a critical look at hospital deaths in his short story "The Death of Bed Number 12."

from THE EPIC OF GILGAMESH
Anonymous (c.2300 B.C.)

Written 1500 years before the Homeric epics, this story describes the adventures of Gilgamesh, a king who reigned in Uruk of Mesopotamia at some time during the first half of the third millennium. The epic tells of an unusual friendship between Gilgamesh, said to be two parts god and one part man, and Enkidu, a "natural man" who had grown up with wild animals. The friendship is short-lived, however, because they offend a Sumarian goddess who in turn places a death-causing curse on Enkidu.

This day on which Enkidu dreamed came to an end and he lay stricken with sickness. One whole day he lay on his bed and his suffering increased. He said to Gilgamesh, the friend on whose account he had left the wilderness, "Once I ran for you, for the water of life, and I now have nothing." A second day he lay on his bed and Gilgamesh watched over him but the sickness increased. A third day he lay on his bed, he called out to Gilgamesh, rousing him up. Now he was weak and his eyes were blind with weeping. Ten days he lay and his suffering increased, eleven and twelve days he lay on his bed of pain. Then he called to Gilgamesh, "My friend, the great goddess cursed me and I must die in shame. I shall not die like a man fallen in battle; I feared to fall, but happy is the man who falls in the battle, for I must die in shame." And Gilgamesh wept over Enkidu. With the first light of dawn he raised his voice and said to the counsellors of Uruk:

"Hear me, great ones of Uruk,
I weep for Enkidu, my friend,
Bitterly moaning like a woman mourning
I weep for my brother.
O Enkidu, my brother,
You were the ax at my side,
My hand's strength, the sword in my belt,
The shield before me,
A glorious robe, my fairest ornament;
An evil Fate has robbed me.
The wild ass and the gazelle
That were father and mother,
All long-tailed creatures that nourished you
Weep for you,
All the wild things of the plain and pastures;
The paths that you loved in the forest of cedars
Night and day murmur.
Let the great ones of strong-walled Uruk
Weep for you;
Let the finger of blessing

Be stretched out in mourning;
Enkidu, young brother. Hark,
There is an echo through all the country
Like a mother mourning.
Weep all the paths where we walked together;
And the beasts we hunted, the bear and hyena,
Tiger and panther, leopard and lion,
The stag and the ibex, the bull and the doe.
The river along whose banks we used to walk,
Weeps for you,
Ula of Elam and dear Euphrates
Where once we drew water for the water-skins.
The mountain we climbed where we slew the Watchman,
Weeps for you.
The warriors of strong-walled Uruk
Where the Bull of Heaven was killed,
Weep for you.
All the people of Eridu
Weep for you Enkidu.
Those who brought grain for your eating
Mourn for you now;
Who rubbed oil on your back
Mourn for you now;
Who poured beer for your drinking
Mourn for you now.
The harlot who anointed you with fragrant ointment
Laments for you now;
The women of the palace, who brought you a wife,
A chosen ring of good advice,
Lament for you now.
And the young men your brothers
As though they were women
Go long-haired in mourning.
What is this sleep which holds you now?
You are lost in the dark and cannot hear me."
He touched his heart but it did not beat, nor did he lift his eyes again.
When Gilgamesh touched his heart it did not beat. So Gilgamesh laid a

veil, as one veils the bride, over his friend. He began to rage like a lion, like a lioness robbed of her whelps. This way and that he paced round the bed, he tore out his hair and strewed it around. He dragged off his splendid robes and flung them down as though they were abominations.

In the first light of dawn Gilgamesh cried out, "I made you rest on a royal bed, you reclined on a couch at my left hand, the princes of the earth kissed your feet. I will cause all the people of Uruk to weep over you and raise the dirge of the dead. The joyful people will stoop with sorrow; and when you have gone to the earth I will let my hair grow long for your sake, I will wander through the wilderness in the skin of a lion." The next day also, in the first light, Gilgamesh lamented; seven days and seven nights he wept for Enkidu, until the worm fastened on him. Only then he gave him up to the earth, for the Anunnaki, the judges, had seized him.

Then Gilgamesh issued a proclamation through the land, he summoned them all, the coppersmiths, the goldsmiths, the stoneworkers, and commanded them, "Make a statue of my friend." The statue was fashioned with a great weight of lapis lazuli for the breast and of gold for the body. A table of hard-wood was set out, and on it a bowl of carnelian filled with honey, and a bowl of lapis lazuli filled with butter. These he exposed and offered to the Sun; and weeping he went away.

from the DIGHA-NIKAYA
Anonymous (c.480 B.C.)

As the founder of Buddhism, the Buddha (563–483 B.C.) put forth an extensive body of teachings and established a community of monks that continues to be active in Buddhist countries in the modern world. The Buddha's death is described at great length in the *Digha-nikaya*, a collection of the Buddha's discourses whose written form is dated from the first Buddhist council in 480 B.C. The death scene contains several exchanges between the Buddha (referred to as the Tathagata, or "Truthfinder"), Ananda (a cousin and personal attendant of the Buddha), and other close disciples in Kusinara.

Then The Blessed One addressed the venerable Ananda:

"Let us go hence, Ananda. To the further bank of the Hirannavati river, and to the city of Kusinara and the sal-tree grove Upavattana of the Mallas will we draw near."

"Yes, Reverend Sir," said the venerable Ananda to The Blessed One in assent.

. . . .

When The Blessed One had thus spoken, the venerable Ananda spoke to him as follows:

"Reverend Sir, let not The Blessed One pass into Nirvana in this wattel-and-daub town, this town of the jungle, this branch village. For there are other great cities, Reverend Sir, to wit, Campa, Rajagaha, Savatthi, Saketa, Kosambi, and Benares. Let The Blessed One pass into Nirvana in one of them. In them are many wealthy men of the warrior caste, many wealthy men of the Brahman caste, and many wealthy householders who are firm believers in The Tathagata, and they will perform the funeral rites for The Tathagata."

"O Ananda, say not so! O Ananda, say not so, that this is a wattel-and-daub town, a town of the jungle, a branch village. There was once, Ananda, a king called Sudassana the Great, who was a Universal Monarch, a virtuous king of justice, a victorious ruler of the four quarters of the earth, possessing a secure dominion over his territory and owning the seven precious gems. This city Kusinara, Ananda, was the capital of king Sudassana the Great, and had then the name of Kusavati."

. . . .

"Go thou, Ananda, and enter the city Kusinara, and announce to the Kusinara-Mallas:

"'To-night, O ye Vasetthas, in the last watch, The Tathagata will pass into Nirvana. Be favorable, be favorable, O ye Vasetthas, and suffer not that afterwards ye feel remorse, saying, "The Tathagata passed into Nirvana while in our borders, but we did not avail ourselves of the opportunity of being present at the last moment of The Tathagata."'"

. . . .

Then The Blessed One addressed the venerable Ananda:

"It may be, Ananda, that some of you will think, 'The word of The Teacher is a thing of the past; we have now no Teacher.' But that, Ananda, is not the correct view. The Doctrine and Discipline, Ananda, which I have taught and enjoined upon you is to be your teacher when I am gone. But whereas now, Ananda, all the priests address each other with the title of 'brother,' not so must they address each other after I am gone. A senior priest, Ananda, is to address a junior priest either by his given name, or by his family name, or by the title of 'brother'; a junior priest is to address a senior priest with the title 'reverend sir,' or 'venerable.' If the Order, Ananda, wish to do so, after I am gone they may abrogate all the lesser and minor precepts."

. . . .

Then the venerable Ananda spoke to The Blessed One as follows:

"It is wonderful, Reverend Sir! It is marvelous, Reverend Sir! Reverend Sir, I have faith to believe that in this congregation of priests not a single priest has a doubt or perplexity respecting either The Buddha or the Doctrine or the Order or the Path or the course of conduct."

"With you, Ananda, it is a matter of faith, when you say that; but with The Tathagata, Ananda, it is a matter of knowledge that in this congregation of priests not a single priest has a doubt or perplexity respecting either The Buddha or the Doctrine or the Order of the Path or the course of conduct. For of all these five hundred priests, Ananda, the most backward one has become converted, and is not liable to pass into a lower state of existence, but is destined necessarily to attain supreme wisdom."

Then The Blessed One addressed the priests:

"And now, O priests, I take my leave of you; all the constituents of being are transitory; work out your salvation with diligence."

And this was the last word of the Tathagata.

from PHAEDO
Plato (427–347 B.C.)

Plato, the most brilliant student of Socrates (469–399 B.C.), provides us through his dialogues with a record of the events leading up to the death of his teacher. Those events include a widespread misunderstanding of Socrates' views, a trial by a jury of Athenian citizens (one of the charges was atheism), a conviction and death sentence, and an opportunity to escape his execution. In the following passage Plato has Phaedo telling Echecrates about Socrates' last conversation with Criton (Crito), another of his students, after Socrates has decided not to escape his death sentence.

When he had spoken, Criton said, "Ah well, Socrates, what injunctions have you for these friends or for me, about your children or anything else? What could we do for you to gratify you most?"

"What I always say, Criton," he said, "nothing very new: Take good care of yourselves, and you will gratify me and mine and yourselves whatever you do, even if you promise nothing now. But if you neglect yourselves, and won't take care to live your lives following the footsteps, so to speak, of both this last conversation and those we have had in former times, you will do no good even if you promise ever so much at present and ever so faithfully."

"Then we will do our best about that," he said; "but how are we to bury you?"

"How you like," said he, "if you catch me and I don't escape you." At the same time, laughing gently and looking towards us, he said, "Criton doesn't believe me, my friends, that this is I, Socrates now talking with you and laying down each of my injunctions, but he thinks me to be what he will see shortly, a corpse, and asks, if you please, how to bury me! I have been saying all this long time, that when I have drunk the potion, I shall not be here then with you; I shall have gone clear away to some bliss of the blest, as they call it. But he thinks I am talking nonsense, just to console myself, yes and you too. Then go bail for me to Criton," he said, "the opposite of the bail he gave to those judges. He gave bail that I would remain; you please, give bail that I will not remain after I die, but I shall get off clear and clean, that Criton may take it more easily, and may not be vexed by seeing my body either being burnt or buried; don't let him worry for me and think I'm in a dreadful state, or say at the funeral that he is laying out or carrying out or digging in Socrates. Be sure, Criton, best of friends," he said, "to use ugly words not only is out of tune with the event, but it even infects the soul with something evil. Now, be confident and say you are burying my body, and then bury it as you please and as you think would be most according to custom."

With these words, he got up and retired into another room for the bath, and Criton went after him, telling us to wait. So we waited discussing and talking together about what had been said, or sometimes speaking of the great misforture which had befallen us, for we felt really as if we had lost a father and had to spend the rest of our lives as orphans. When he had bathed, and his children had been brought to see him—for he had two little sons, and one big—and when the women of his family had come, he talked to them before Criton and gave what instructions he wished. Then he asked the women and children to go, and came back to us. It was now near sunset, for he had spent a long time within. He came and sat down after his bath, and he had not talked long after this when the servant of the Eleven came in, and standing by him said, "O Socrates! I have not to complain of you as I do of others, that they are angry with me, and curse me, because I bring them word to drink their potion, which my officers make me do! But I have always found you in this time most generous and gentle, and the best man who ever came here. And now too, I know well you are not angry with me, for you know who are responsible, and you keep it for them. Now you know what I came to tell you, so farewell, and try to bear as well as you can what can't be helped."

Then he turned and was going out, with tears running down his cheeks. And Socrates looked up at him and said, "Farewell to you also, I will do so." Then, at the same time turning to us, "What a nice fellow!" he said. "All the time he has been coming and talking to me, a real good sort, and now how generously he sheds tears for me! Come along, Criton, let's obey him. Someone bring the potion, if the stuff has been ground; if not, let the fellow grind it."

Then Criton said, "But, Socrates, I think the sun is still over the hills, it has not set yet. Yes, and I know of others who, having been told to drink the poison, have done it very late; they had dinner first and a good one, and some enjoyed the company of any they wanted. Please don't be in a hurry, there is time to spare."

But Socrates said, "Those you speak of have very good reason for doing that, for they think they will gain by doing it; and I have good reasons why I won't do it. For I think I shall gain nothing by drinking a little later, only that I shall think myself a fool for clinging to life and sparing when the cask's empty. Come along," he said, "do what I tell you, if you please."

And Criton, hearing this, nodded to the boy who stood near. The boy went out, and after spending a long time, came in with the man who was to give the poison carrying it ground ready in a cup. Socrates caught sight of the man and said, "Here, my good man, you know about these things; what must I do?"

"Just drink it," he said, "and walk about till your legs get heavy, then lie down. In that way the drug will act of itself."

At the same time, he held out the cup to Socrates, and he took it quite cheerfully, Echecrates, not a tremble, not a change in color or looks; but looking full at the man under his brows, as he used to do, he asked him, "What do you say about this drink? What of a libation to someone? Is that allowed, or not?"

He said, "We only grind so much as we think enough for a moderate potion."

"I understand," he said, "but at least, I suppose, it is allowed to offer a prayer to the gods and that must be done, for good luck in the migration from here to there. Then that is my prayer, and so may it be!"

With these words he put the cup to his lips and, quite easy and contented, drank it up. So far most of us had been able to hold back our tears pretty well; but when we saw him begin drinking and end drinking, we could no longer. I burst into a flood of tears for all I could do, so I wrapped up my face and cried myself out; not for him indeed, but for my own misfortune in losing such a man and such a comrade. Criton had got up and gone out even before I did, for he could not hold the tears in. Apollodoros had never ceased weeping all this time, and now he burst out into loud sobs, and by his weeping and lamentations completely broke down every man there except Socrates himself. He only said, "What a scene! You amaze me. That's just why I sent the women away, to keep them from making a scene like this. I've heard that one ought to make an end in decent silence. Quiet yourselves and endure."

When we heard him we felt ashamed and restrained our tears. He walked about, and when he said that his legs were feeling heavy, he lay down on his back, as the man told him to do; at the same time the one who gave him the potion felt him, and after a while examined his feet and legs; then pinching a foot hard, he asked if he felt anything; he said no. After this, again, he pressed the shins; and, moving up like this, he showed us that he was growing cold and stiff. Again he felt him, and told us that when it came to his heart, he would be gone. Already the cold had come nearly as far as the abdomen, when Socrates threw off the covering from his face—for he had covered it over—and said, the last words he uttered, "Criton," he said, "we owe a cock to Asclepios; pay it without fail."

"That indeed shall be done," said Criton. "Have you anything more to say?"

When Criton had asked this, Socrates gave no further answer, but after a little time, he stirred, and the man uncovered him, and his eyes were still. Criton, seeing this, closed the mouth and eyelids.

This was the end of our comrade, Echecrates, a man, as we would say, of all then living we had ever met, the noblest and the wisest and most just.

MARK 15:1–39 (RSV)
Anonymous (A.D. c.70)

Each of the four gospels in the New Testament provides an account of Jesus' death. The Markan version is the oldest and most concise. Death by crucifixion was a Roman penalty reserved for slaves and selected criminals, with the condemned person usually dying from a combination of exhaustion and exposure.

And as soon as it was morning the chief priests, with the elders and scribes, and the whole council held a consultation; and they bound Jesus and led him away and delivered him to Pilate. And Pilate asked him, "Are you the King of the Jews?" And he answered him, "You have said so." And the chief priests accused him of many things. And Pilate again asked him, "Have you no answer to make? See how many charges they bring against you." But Jesus made no further answer, so that Pilate wondered.

Now at the feast he used to release for them one prisoner whom they asked. And among the rebels in prison, who had committed murder in the insurrection, there was a man called Barabbas. And the crowd came up and began to ask Pilate to do as he was wont to do for them. And he answered them, "Do you want me to release for you the King of the Jews?" For he perceived that it was out of envy that the chief priests had delivered him up. But the chief priests stirred up the crowd to have him release for them Barabbas instead. And Pilate again said to them, "Then what shall I do with the man whom you call the King of the Jews?" And they cried out again, "Crucify him." And Pilate said to them, "Why, what evil has he done?" But they shouted all the more, "Crucify him."

So Pilate, wishing to satisfy the crowd, released for them Barabbas; and having scourged Jesus, he delivered him to be crucified.

And the soldiers led him away inside the palace (that is, the praetorium); and they called together the whole battalion. And they clothed him in a purple cloak, and plaiting a crown of thorns they put it on him. And they began to salute him, "Hail, King of the Jews!" And they struck his head with a reed, and spat upon him, and they knelt down in homage to him. And when they had mocked him, they stripped him of the purple cloak, and put his own clothes on him. And they led him out to crucify him.

And they compelled a passer-by, Simon of Cyrene, who was coming in from the country, the father of Alexander and Rufus, to carry his cross. And they brought him to the place called Golgotha (which means the place of a skull). And they offered him wine mingled with myrrh; but he did not take it. And they crucified him, and divided his garments among them, casting lots for them, to decide what each should take. And it was the third hour, when they crucified him. And the inscription of the charge against him read, "The King of the Jews." And with him they crucified two robbers, one on his right and one on his left. And those who passed by derided him, wagging their heads, and saying, "Aha! You who would destroy the temple and build it in three days, save yourself, and come down from the cross!" So also the chief priests mocked him to one another with the scribes, saying, "He saved others; he cannot save himself. Let the Christ, the King of Israel, come down now from the cross, that we may see and believe." Those who were crucified with him also reviled him.

And when the sixth hour had come, there was darkness over the whole land until the ninth hour. And at the ninth hour Jesus cried with a loud voice, "Eloi, Eloi, lama sabach-thani?" which means, "My God, my God, why hast thou forsaken me?" And some of the bystanders hearing it said, "Behold, he is calling Elijah." And one ran and, filling a sponge full of vinegar, put it on a reed and gave it to him to drink, saying, "Wait, let us see whether Elijah will come to take him down." And Jesus uttered a loud cry, and breathed his last. And the curtain of the temple was torn in two, from top to bottom. And when the centurion, who stood facing him, saw that he thus breathed his last, he said, "Truly this man was the Son of God!"

MORTE d'ARTHUR
Alfred, Lord Tennyson (1809–1892)

So all day long the noise of battle rolled
Among the mountains by the winter sea,
Until King Arthur's table, man by man,
Had fallen in Lyonness about their lord,
King Arthur; then, because his wound was deep,
The bold Sir Bedivere uplifted him,
Sir Bedivere, the last of all his knights,
And bore him to a chapel nigh the field,
A broken chancel with a broken cross,
That stood on a dark strait of barren land.
On one side lay the Ocean and on one
Lay a great water, and the moon was full.
Then spake King Arthur to Sir Bedivere:
"The sequel of today unsolders all
The goodliest fellowship of famous knights
Whereof this world holds record. Such a sleep
They sleep—the men I loved. I think that we
Shall never more, at any future time,
Delight our souls with talk of knightly deeds,
Walking about the gardens and the halls
Of Camelot, as in the days that were.
I perish by this people which I made—
Tho' Merlin sware that I should come again
To rule once more—but let what will be, be,
I am so deeply smitten thro' the helm
That without help I cannot last till morn.
Thou therefore take my brand Excalibur,
Which was my pride; for thou rememberest how
In those old days, one summer noon, an arm
Rose up from out the bosom of the lake,
Clothed in white samite, mystic, wonderful,
Holding the sword—and how I rowed across
And took it, and have worn it, like a king;
And, wheresoever I am sung or told

In aftertime, this also shall be known.
But now delay not; take Excalibur,
And fling him far into the middle mere;
Watch what thou seest, and lightly bring me word."
To him replied the bold Sir Bedivere:
"It is not meet, Sir King, to leave thee thus,
Aidless, alone, and smitten thro' the helm.
A little thing may harm a wounded man.
Yet I thy hest will all perform at full,
Watch what I see, and lightly bring thee word."
So saying, from the ruined shrine he stept
And in the moon athwart the place of tombs,
Where lay the mighty bones of ancient men,
Old knights, and over them the sea-wind sang
Shrill, chill, with flakes of foam. He, stepping down
By zigzig paths, and juts of pointed rock,
Came on the shining levels of the lake.
There drew he forth the brand Excalibur,
And o'er him, drawing it, the winter moon,
Brightening the skirts of a long cloud, ran forth
And sparkled keen with frost against the hilt;
For all the haft twinkled with diamond sparks,
Myriads of topaz-lights, and jacinth-work
Of subtlest jewellery. He gazed so long
That both his eyes were dazzled, as he stood,
This way and that dividing the swift mind,
In act to throw; but at the last it seemed
Better to leave Excalibur concealed
There in the many-knotted waterflags,
That whistled stiff and dry about the marge.
So strode he back slow to the wounded king.
Then spake King Arthur to Sir Bedivere:
"Hast thou performed my mission which I gave?
What is it thou hast seen? or what hast heard?"
And answer made the bold Sir Bedivere:
"I heard the ripple washing in the reeds,
And the wild water lapping on the crag."

To whom replied King Arthur, faint and pale:
"Thou hast betrayed thy nature and thy name,
Not rendering true answer, as beseemed
Thy fealty, nor like a noble knight;
For surer sign had followed, either hand,
Or voice, or else a motion of the mere.
This is a shameful thing for men to lie.
Yet now, I charge thee, quickly go again
As thou art lief and dear, and do the thing
I bade thee, watch, and lightly bring me word."
Then went Sir Bedivere the second time
Across the ridge, and paced beside the mere,
Counting the dewy pebbles, fixed in thought;
But when he saw the wonder of the hilt,
How curiously and strangely chased, he smote
His palms together, and he cried aloud:
"And if indeed I cast the brand away,
Surely a precious thing, one worthy note.
Should thus be lost forever from the earth,
Which might have pleased the eyes of many men.
What good should follow this, if this were done?
What harm, undone? deep harm to disobey,
Seeing obedience is the bond of rule.
Were it well to obey then, if a king demand
An act unprofitable, against himself?
The King is sick, and knows not what he does.
What record, or what relic of my lord
Should be to aftertime, but empty breath
And rumors of a doubt? but were this kept,
Stored in some treasure-house of mighty kings,
Some one might show it at a joust of arms,
Saying 'King Arthur's sword, Excalibur,
Wrought by the lonely maiden of the lake;
Nine years she wrought it, sitting in the deeps
Upon the hidden bases of the hills.'
So might some old man speak in the aftertime
To all the people, winning reverence;

But now much honor and much fame were lost."
So spake he, clouded with his own conceit,
And hid Excalibur the second time,
And so strode back slow to the wounded King.
Then spoke King Arthur, breathing heavily:
"What is it thou hast seen? or what hast heard?"
And answer made the bold Sir Bedivere:
"I heard the water lapping on the crag,
And the long ripple washing in the reeds."
To whom replied King Arthur, much in wrath:
"Ah, miserable and unkind, untrue,
Unknightly, traitor-hearted! Woe is me!
Authority forgets a dying king,
Laid widowed of the power in his eye
That bowed the will. I see thee what thou art,
For thou, the latest-left of all my knights,
In whom should meet the offices of all,
Thou wouldst betray me for the precious hilt;
Either from lust of gold, or like a girl
Valuing the giddy pleasure of the eyes.
Yet, for a man may fail in duty twice,
And the third time may prosper, get thee hence;
But, if thou spare to fling Excalibur,
I will arise and slay thee with my hands."
Then quickly rose Sir Bedivere, and ran,
And, leaping down the ridges lightly, plunged
Among the bulrush-beds, and clutched the sword,
And strongly wheeled and threw it. The great brand
Made lightnings in the splendor of the moon,
And flashing round and round, and whirled in an arch,
Shot like a streamer of the northern morn,
Seen where the moving isles of winter shock
By night, with noises of the northern sea.
So flashed and fell the brand Excalibur;
But ere he dipt the surface, rose an arm
Clothed in white samite, mystic, wonderful
And caught him by the hilt, and brandished him

Three times, and drew him under in the mere.
And lightly went the other to the King.
Then spoke King Arthur, drawing thicker breath:
"Now see I by thine eyes that this is done. .
Speak out; what is it thou hast heard, or seen?"
And answer made the bold Sir Bedivere:
"Sir King, I closed mine eyelids, lest the gems
Should blind my purpose, for I never saw,
Nor shall see, here or elsewhere, till I die,
Not tho' I live three lives of mortal men,
So great a miracle as yonder hilt.
Then with both hands I flung him, wheeling him;
But when I looked again, behold an arm,
Clothed in white samite, mystic, wonderful,
That caught him by the hilt, and brandished him
Three times, and drew him under in the mere."
And answer made King Arthur, breathing hard:
"My end draws nigh; 'tis time that I were gone.
Make broad thy shoulders to receive my weight,
And bear me to the margin; yet I fear
My wound hath taken cold, and I shall die."
So saying, from the pavement he half rose,
Slowly, with pain, reclining on his arm,
And looking wistfully with wide blue eyes
As in a picture. Him Sir Bedivere
Remorsefully regarded thro' his tears,
And would have spoken, but he found not words,
Then took with care, and kneeling on one knee,
O'er both his shoulders drew the languid hands,
And rising bore him thro' the place of tombs.
But, as he walked, King Arthur panted hard,
Like one that feels a nightmare on his bed
When all the house is mute. So sighed the King,
Muttering and murmuring at his ear, "Quick, quick!"
I fear it is too late, and I shall die."
But the other swiftly strode from ridge to ridge,
Clothed with his breath, and looking, as he walked,

Larger than human on the frozen hills.
He heard the deep behind him, and a cry
Before. His own thought drove him like a goad.
Dry clashed his harness in the icy caves
And barren chasms, and all to left and right
The bare black cliff clanged round him, as he based
His feet on juts of slippery crag that rang
Sharp-smitten with the dint of armed heels—
And on a sudden, lo! the level lake,
And the long glories of the winter moon.
Then saw they how there hove a dusky barge,
Dark as a funeral scarf from stem to stern,
Beneath them; and descending they were ware
That all the decks were dense with stately forms
Black-stoled, black-hooded, like a dream—by these
Three Queens with crowns of gold—and from them rose
A cry that shivered to the tingling stars,
And, as it were one voice, an agony
Of lamentation, like a wind, that shrills
All night in a waste land, where no one comes,
Or hath come, since the making of the world.
Then murmured Arthur, "Place me in the barge,"
And to the barge they came. There those three queens
Put forth their hands, and took the king, and wept.
But she, that rose the tallest of them all
And fairest, laid his head upon her lap,
And loosed the shattered casque, and chafed his hands,
And called him by his name, complaining loud
And dropping bitter tears against his brow
Striped with dark blood; for all his face was white
And colorless, and like the withered moon
Smote by the fresh beam of the springing east;
And all his greaves and cuisses dashed with drops
Of onset; and the light and lustrous curls—
That made his forehead like a rising sun
High from the dais-throne—were parched with dust;
Or, clotted into points and hanging loose,

Mixed with the knightly growth that fringed his lips.
So like a shattered column lay the king;
Not like that Arthur who, with lance in rest,
From spur to plume a star of tournament,
Shot thro' the lists at Camelot, and charged
Before the eyes of ladies and of kings.
Then loudly cried the bold Sir Bedivere:
"Ah! my Lord Arthur, whither shall I go?
Where shall I hide my forehead and my eyes?
For now I see the true old times are dead,
When every morning brought a noble chance,
And every chance brought out a noble knight.
Such times have been not since the light that led
The holy Elders with the gift of myrrh.
But now the whole Round Table is dissolved
Which was an image of the mighty world;
And I, the last, go forth companionless,
And the days darken round me, and the years,
Among new men, strange faces, other minds."
And slowly answered Arthur from the barge:
"The old order changeth, yielding place to new,
And God fulfils himself in many ways,
Lest one good custom should corrupt the world.
Comfort thyself: what comfort is in me?
I have lived my life, and that which I have done
May He within himself make pure! but thou,
If thou shouldst never see my face again,
Pray for my soul. More things are wrought by prayer
Than this world dreams of. Wherefore, let thy voice
Rise like a fountain for me night and day.
For what are men better than sheep or goats
That nourish a blind life within the brain,
If, knowing God, they lift not hands of prayer
Both for themselves and those who call them friend?
For so the whole round earth is every way
Bound by gold chains about the feet of God.
But now farewell. I am going a long way

With these thou seest—if indeed I go—
(For all my mind is clouded with a doubt)
To the island-valley of Avilion;
Where falls not hail, or rain, or any snow,
Nor ever wind blows loudly; but it lies
Deep-meadowed, happy, fair with orchard lawns
And bowery hollows crowned with summer sea,
Where I will heal me of my grievous wound."
So said he, and the barge with oar and sail
Moved from the brink, like some fullbreasted swan
That, fluting a wild carol ere her death,
Ruffles her pure cold plume, and takes the flood
With swarthy webs. Long stood Sir Bedivere
Revolving many memories, till the hull
Looked one black dot against the verge of dawn,
And on the mere the wailing died away.

from DEATH BE NOT PROUD
John Gunther (1901–1970)

Johnny Gunther had struggled against death for over a year. His divorced parents had spent as much time as they could with him. Then, because of a cerebral hemorrhage, he made a sudden and irreversible turn for the worse—on the same day he received his admission papers from Harvard.

The ambulance men came and we moved Johnny to a nearby hospital rather than Neurological, since Mount did not think that he could survive more than a very brief trip, and the hospital was just around the corner. Everything went wrong. First there were laborious and cruel negotiations on the phone. It was as if the whole fabric of our surroundings and even the most commonplace things had broken at last under this unendurably brutal strain, as if nothing at all would work, as if everything had been torn apart. It was a kind of revolt both of nature and the animate. The emergency door was locked at the hospital; its phone switchboard went to pieces crazily; a helpless nurse did not know what to do about anything; one of the attendants downstairs was hysterical; at the end, the taxi driver who took us back reeled and drove like someone very drunk, which indeed he was.

Johnny went under oxygen, of course; he was given every known medicament that could possibly help, and a youthful doctor explored, as always with difficulty, the veins in his leg for the glucose infusion and transfusion. We got to the hospital at a little after six. Frances and I sat with Johnny or paced the hall or talked on an open terrace at the end of the corridor for a series of long, vacant hours. It was a very hot, clear, dark night. Johnny slept on his side, restfully. He never regained consciousness. He died absolutely without fear, and without pain, and without knowing that he was going to die.

At a few minutes to eleven we thought we ought to go into his room; we had stepped out on the balcony for a brief second, and presently, with infinite depth, very slowly and at spaced intervals, three great quivering gasps came out of him. He had regained color just before; he had some final essential spark of animation; he was still fighting. But now these shatteringly deep breaths, arising from something so deep down that his whole body shook and trembled, told us their irrevocable message. Someone started ringing an emergency bell. After all those months of doctors and doctors and doctors, it happened that no doctor was there at that precise moment. Not that they could have done anything. Traeger had just gone home, and he came back of course. Another doctor was in the interns' room, and he slipped up briskly. All the doctors!—helpless flies now, climbing across the granite face of death.

Johnny died at 11:02 P.M. Frances reached for him through the ugly, transparent, raincoat-like curtain of the oxygen machine. I felt his arms, cupping my hands around them, and the warmth gradually left them, receding very slowly upward from his hands. For a long time some warmth remained. Then little by little the life-color left his face, his lips became blue, and his hands were cold. What is life? It departs covertly. Like a thief Death took him.

from ERIC
Doris Lund (b. 1919)

Eric was seventeen when, in 1967, he was diagnosed as having acute leukemia and given six months to two years to live. Over the next four years he attended the University of Connecticut, starred on its soccer team, traveled across the country, held a part-time job, received a variety of in-patient and out-patient treatments for leukemia, had six remissions, and fell in love with a nurse named MaryLou. The story of his struggle to live and love is told by his mother.

I went in to see him alone. There was a hush in the room. A nurse and an intern were quietly checking dials, needles, charts. But I saw only the figure on the bed. I had been frightened at the thought of watching Eric die. The actual moment when he would cease to exist. Wouldn't it be more than I could bear? Wouldn't my heart stop, too? Yet here, close to the end, there was no fear.

In the hour of his death, I searched Eric's face with wonder and awe, much as I'd searched it the day he was born. A son! From darkness he had come, the mystery of who he was still hidden behind the small brow, the closed eyes. Into darkness he was going (not fighting off the oxygen mask any longer . . . going . . . accepting), eyes closed once again, taking with him still too much of the mystery of who he was, yet leaving me unbelievably rich.

Pain waited for me when this hour was over. I had no time for it now. All the life force in my body was focused on knowing what little there was left to know. No tears, for I wanted to see. No faintness, for I wanted to be *there* in case he came back once more from the blackness. Only sixteen or so hours ago—was it afternoon, was it morning?—he'd opened his eyes for a moment, after hours of unconsciousness, and struggled to speak through broken lips.

"Come closer. Mom? Come closer——

"Have to get to Westport," he gasped. "Can't find the way. Please, Mom—help me? Westport?"

"You'll get there," I whispered back, not knowing what he meant, thinking he was delirious but wanting to comfort him. "You'll find the way, Eric. I know you will."

He hadn't roused again. And it was half an hour since Dr. Dowling had said he was dying. I took his hand. The cool, translucent fingers lay very still in mine, not responding, not curling in the fierce life grip of the baby. Strange, strange, I never thought you'd grow old before I did, Eric, that you'd die while I held your hand——

MaryLou darted in at that moment and came up to me. Urgently she whispered, "Talk to him! I just remembered, hearing is the last sense to go. Say something to him quickly." She left us.

Now! Now it must happen. I put my hand on his shoulder and bent close to the pale curved ear, the delicate microphone waiting for its last message. What could I tell him for the journey?

"I love you," I said. "I'm here with you, Eric, and you're almost there."

Suddenly I thought I understood. Westport! Scene of hard-won victories on the playing field, where he and his soccer companions became county champions long ago. There was one more game to be played, and he wanted to play it well. Death is an act to be well performed. It seemed to me he was out on the field again, lone player running through the darkness, trying to head off the enemy, trying to score just one more time before he went down forever.

"You're beautiful, Eric. You were beautiful all the way. You did it just right. You're almost there. I love you!"

He died in MaryLou's arms a few minutes later. Her head was on the pillow next to his. It was a good and gentle death, the death she'd promised him with peace and dignity. Her last great gift.

Most of us had spoken to him by then, given him our messages for the journey. The words were not remarkable in any way.

"I told him, 'You're a good brother,'" said Mark.

"I told him, 'Eric, it's good to be with you. I love you,'" said his father.

Love is the only message, after all.

We stood together in the doorway just outside his room to stop them if they tried to have a Code Alert.

A nurse came out and started to run.

"No Code," we said.

She stopped, surprised. No paddles for the heart, no holes or tubes for the throat, no machinery for the lungs?

"But—" she said.

Sidney looked at her hard. "No Code," he said again.

Afterward. I'd forgotten there would be an "afterward." We stood in the hallway, crying, hugging, once in a while laughing. We had suddenly lost our balance. The center of our world, on which we'd all been focused for so long, had suddenly been taken away. We were swaying dizzily around the edges, holding on to each other, feeling tears on each other's cheeks, not knowing yet how to let go.

I held MaryLou and said, "You've lost your lover and your best friend. But you haven't lost us as a family. We'll be yours as long as you need us and want us."

The I remembered Mrs. Hardy. Let her not hear it from anyone but me. I walked quickly down the hall to her ward. She was sitting by her bed, little frail bird of a woman with sandpiper legs, a foolish ruffled shower cap covering her bald head, reading *McCall's* magazine. I saw the headline: Fashions for Spring.

She looked up as I came nearer, and her eyes were frightened.

"I'm sorry I have to tell you this. Eric lost his fight."

She cried, then, and I was afraid she might drown because she didn't have a whole face left to cry with. I put my arms around her and kissed her cheek; it was burning. She pulled away, signaling me to wait while she found her pad and began to write feverishly. Her handwriting was getting harder and harder to read. But I made out, "God bless you and give you peace. You were a wonderful mother."

We hugged once more. "I'll try to come and see you," I said. "I really will."

There were others to tell, others to comfort. I remembered what Eric had told me about the night Abby died. "Her husband tried to comfort *us*—he didn't want us to give up or be afraid because Abby died."

I remembered, and now I understood. I tried to think of what to say to the ones I knew.

There was the autopsy form. "Sign here, please." There was the Eye Bank form. "Sign here—below." Eric had already signed it himself. And there were two brown shopping bags with the possessions of Eric Lund. The nurse who handed them to us said, "We're sorry it turned out this way." Then she turned to me. "Do you want a tranquilizer?"

"No, thank you." I know all the stops from Librium to Miltown, from the hills of Dexamil to the Valium of tranquillity, and there isn't a pill in the world that can put things right now. I'll take my pain straight, undulled, and with the glory of knowing how much he was, the sense of his strength shoring up my life. Even though all seems to be lost, much will be found again. I want it all—as Eric wanted it all. I can wait. And trust. Life will begin again.

"Let's go home," I said.

from I HEARD THE OWL CALL MY NAME
Margaret Craven (b. 1902)

This novel tells the story of a young minister who comes to the Indian village of Kingcome in British Columbia. Unaware that he has a terminal condition, Mark Brian sets out to help the Indians in the village as well as other persons scattered in remote locations throughout his isolated parish. Often accompanied by an Indian friend named Jim, Mark learns valuable lessons about life and death from the Indians he came to teach. On one occasion Mark and Jim stop to visit an old logger named Calamity.

Mark and Jim spent five days in the other villages and on the way home, when they went through Whale Pass and could see the white Kingcome Mountains, they passed the A-frame on Calamity's float, and, as he always did, Mark looked to see if smoke was coming from Calamity's little shack. None was.

"He's probably away," Jim said. "All the big camps are still closed because of snow. Nothing but a skeleton crew left anywhere. I expect some logging boat stopped and took him out."

"Pull up alongside, Jim. I'd better check."

How many times he had stopped to hide out a gale or to chat, and always Calamity had taken out the carved walrus tusk which was the cribbage board, and always he had said, "Just one game, Mark, while I put on a mite of supper."

But this time when he knocked at the door, no rough voice answered him, and he opened the door and stepped in. There was the table with its ancient oil cloth cover, and the coffee pot, doubtless half full of grounds, waiting for Calamity to toss in a handful of coffee and boil it up again. There was the broken easy chair, and on the cot in the corner lay Calamity.

Mark pulled the chair close to the cot and sat down, and he reached over and touched the shoulder.

"What's the matter, old-timer? Did you get hit by a widow-maker?"

"I knew you'd come, lad. I been waiting. I went upside to check the snow and damned if I didn't slip off the cliff and wake up with the tide lickin' at my boots. Had to drag myself to the shack."

"How long have you been here?"

"Four days, maybe. All I need is some food within reach and the stove going, and I'd take it kindly if you'd move the cot so I can put in a stick now and then."

Mark went over him carefully.

"I think you've broken a hip, Calamity. What you need is a trip to Alert Bay. If the hospital ship's close enough, she'll take you, and if she's too far to get here, I'll take you."

"Damn waste of money. First thing they'd do is take off my red long-johns and I'd die of pneumonia." And Mark asked of himself, "And what do you think you're doing now?"

While Mark built the fire, Jim sent out an emergency on the radio-telephone, but the hospital ship was too far away to come and the gale warnings were out and the straits too rough to cross. But it didn't matter. It was too late for help and Mark knew it, and Calamity knew it also.

Mark sat beside the cot.

"I ain't much of a church man, Mark. Guess you might say I'm an agnostic. I don't know."

"There's a good bit of agnostic in all of us, Calamity. None of us knows much—only enough to trust to reach out a hand in the dark."

"Under my pillow there's a map of Knight's Inlet. I put a cross on the place where I cut trees once. I always thought that when it was my time to conk out, I'd kind of like my ashes—"

"I'll do it, Calamity. It's a promise."

"Don't say no fine words about me; we'll both know they're lies. Do it in the spring, on some fine day."

Mark sat by Calamity through the deep night, until the hand he held slipped from his, and the period between breaths grew longer and longer. At dawn the old hand-logger sighed deeply and was done. Then Mark covered the body with a blanket and returned to the boat to catch the first weather report, which promised that by noon the straits might be navigable. By radio-telephone he managed at last to reach his friend, the sergeant, and tell him what had happened, and ask permission to bring the body of Calamity for cremation, and this he was given. Then he lay down for a few hours' sleep.

. . . .

When the little seaplane lifted and was gone, Mark turned back to his boat, checked the oil and water, and started to Knight's Inlet to keep his promise to Calamity Bill. Already nothing looked the same because it was going to end, because he was going to leave it, and the thought filled him with a twinge of sudden anguish and the little, unexpected fear that precedes any big change, sad or joyous.

. . . .

Now, beside the compass, he placed the map he had taken from under Calamity's pillow, watching for the narrow finger of the sea on the left side of the inlet, found and entered it, slowing the boat until it barely moved, seeking the cove Calamity had marked with a cross. When he saw it, he stopped the engine and let the boat drift slowly in.

At flood tide no eddy moved, no ripple marred the surface. On the water Mark saw reflected the cliffs that rose above the narrow fingerling, the green spruce and cedar, and one huge hemlock that must have been growing when Christ was a little lad. Here he gave the ashes of Calamity to the sea, and when he came to the last words of the committal, "Rest eternal grant unto him, O Lord," he heard the echo of the words come back to him from across the narrow channel, softly and eerily, as if from another world. Then there was no sound but the soft mewing of the gulls nesting in the cliffs.

THE DEATH OF BED NUMBER 12
Ghassan Kanafani (b. 1936)

Dear Ahmed,

I have chosen you in particular to be the recipient of this letter for a reason which may appear to you commonplace, yet since yesterday my every thought has been centered on it. I chose you in particular because when I saw him yesterday dying on the high white bed I remembered how you used to use the work "die" to express anything extreme. Many is the time I've heard you use such expresssions as "I almost died laughing," "I was dead tired," "Death itself couldn't quench my love," and so on. While it is true that we all use such words, you use them more than anybody. Thus it was that I remembered you as I saw him sinking down in the bed and clutching at the coverlet with his long, emaciated fingers, giving a convulsive shiver and then staring out at me with dead eyes.

But why have I not begun at the beginning? You know, no doubt, that I am now in my second month at the hospital. I have been suffering from a stomach ulcer, but no sooner had the surgeon plugged up the hole in

my stomach than a new one appeared in my head, about which the surgeon could do nothing. Believe me, Ahmed, that an "ulcer" on the brain
is a lot more stubborn than one in the stomach. My room leads on to the
main corridor of the Internal Diseases Wing, while the window overlooks
the small hospital garden. Thus, propped up by a pillow, I can observe
both the continuous flow of patients passing the door as well as the birds
which fly past the window incessantly. Amidst this hubbub of people who
come here to die in the serene shadow of the scalpel and whom I see,
having arrived on their own two feet, leaving after days or hours on the
death trolley, wrapped round in a covering of white; in this hubbub I find
myself quite unable to make good those holes that have begun to open up
in my head, quite incapable of stopping the flow of questions that mercilessly demand an answer of me.

I shall be leaving the hospital in a few days, for they have patched up
my insides as best they can. I am now able to walk leaning on the arm of
an old and ugly nurse and on my own powers of resistance. The hospital,
however, has done little more than transfer the ulcer from my stomach to
my head, for in this place, as the ugly old woman remarked, medicine
may be able to plug up a hole in the stomach but it can never find the
answers required to plug up holes in one's thinking. The day she said this
the old woman gave a toothless laugh as she quietly led me off to the
scales.

What, though, is such talk to do with us? What I want to talk to you
about is death. Death that takes place in front of you, not about that death
of which one merely hears. The difference between the two types of death
is immeasurable and cannot be appreciated by someone who has not been
a witness to a human being clutching at the coverlet of his bed with all the
strength of his trembling fingers in order to resist that terrible slipping into
extinction, as though the coverlet can pull him back from that colossus
who, little by little, wrests from his eyes this life about which we know
scarcely anything.

As the doctors waited around him, I examined the card that hung at
the foot of his bed. I had slipped out of my room and was standing there,
unseen by the doctors, who were engaged in a hopeless attempt to save
the dying man. I read: "Name: Mohamed Ali Akbar. Age: 25. Na-
tionality: Omani." I turned the card over and this time read:
"Leukemia." Again I stared into the thin brown face, the wide frightened

eyes and the lips that trembled like a ripple of purple water. As his eyes turned and came to rest on my face it seemed that he was appealing to me for help. Why? Because I used to give to him a casual greeting every morning? Or was it that he saw in my face some understanding of the terror that he was undergoing? He went on staring at me and then—quite simply—he died.

It was only then that the doctor discovered me and dragged me off angrily to my room. But he would never be able to banish from my mind the scene that is ever-present there. As I got on to my bed I heard the voice of the male nurse in the corridor alongside my door saying in a mater-of-fact voice:

"Bed number 12 has died!"

I said to myself: "Mohamed Ali Akbar has lost his name, he is Bed number 12." What do I mean now when I talk of a human being whose name was Mohamed Ali Akbar? What does it matter to him whether he still retains his name or whether it has been replaced by a number? Then I remembered how he wouldn't allow anyone to omit any part of his name. Every morning the nurse would ask him, "And how are you, Mohamed Ali?" and he would not reply, for he regarded his name as being Mohamed Ali Akbar—just like that, all in one—and that this Mohamed Ali to whom the nurse was speaking was some other person.

Though the nurses found a subject for mirth in this insistence on his whole name being used, Mohamed Ali Akbar continued to demand it; perhaps he regarded his right to possessing his name in full as being an insistence that he at least owned something, for he was poor, extremely poor, a great deal more so than you with your fertile imagination could conceive as you lounge around in the cafe; poverty was something engraved in his face, his forearms, his chest, the way he ate, into everything that surrounded him.

When I was able to walk for the first time after they had patched me up, I paid him a visit. The back of his bed was raised and he was sitting up, lost in thought. I sat on the side of the bed for a short while, and we exchanged a few brief, banal words. I noticed that alongside his pillow was an old wooden box with his name carved on it in semi-Persian style writing; it was securely tied with twine. Apart from this he owned nothing except his clothes, which were kept in the hospital cupboard. I remembered that on that day I had asked the nurse:

"What's in the old box?"

"No one knows," she answered, laughing. "He refuses to be parted from the box for a single instant."

The she bent over me and whispered:

"These people who look so poor are generally hiding some treasure or other—perhaps this is his!"

During my stay here no one visted him at the hospital. As he knew no one I used to send him some of the sweets with which my visitors inundated me. He accepted everything without enthusiasm. He was not good at expressing gratitude and his behavior over this caused a certain fleeting resentment in me.

I did not concern myself with the mysterious box. Though Mohamed Ali Akbar's condition steadily worsened, his attitude toward the box did not change, which caused the nurse to remark to me that if there had been some treasure in it he would surely have given it away or willed it to someone, seeing that he was heading for death at such speed. Like some petty philosopher I had laughed that day saying to myself that the stupidity of this nurse scarcely knew any bounds, for how did she expect Mohamed Ali Akbar to persuade himself that he was inevitably dying, that there was not a hope of his pulling through? His insistence on keeping the box was tantamount to hanging on to his hope of pulling through and being reunited with his box.

When Mohamed Ali Akbar died I saw the box at his side, where it had always been, and it occurred to me that the box ought to be buried unopened with him. On going to my room that night I was quite unable to sleep. While Mohamed Ali Akbar had been deposited in the autopsy room, wrapped up in a white covering, he was, at the same time, sitting in my room and staring at me, passing through the hospital wards and searching about in his bed; I could almost hear the way he would gasp for breath before going to sleep. When day dawned across the trees of the hospital garden, I had created a complete story about him for myself.

Mohamed Ali Akbar was a poor man from the western quarter of the village of Abkha in Oman; a thin, dark-skinned young man, with aspirations burning in his eyes that could find no release. True he was poor, but what does poverty matter to a man if he has never known anything else? The whole of Abkha suffered from being poor, a poverty identical to Mohamed Ali Akbar's; it was, however, a contented poverty, a poverty that was deep-seated and devoid of anything that prompted one to feel that it was wrong and that there was something called "riches." And so it was that the two water-skins Mohamed Ali Akbar carried across his shoulders as he knocked on people's doors to sell them water, were the two scales which set the balance of his daily round. Mohamed Ali Akbar was aware of a certain dizziness when he laid down the water-skins, but when taking them up again the next morning he would feel that his existence was progressing tranquilly and that he had ensured for himself a balanced, undeviating journey through life.

Mohamed Ali Akbar's life could have continued in this quiet and ordered fashion, had fate emulated civilization—in not reaching faraway Oman. But fate was present even in far-off Oman and it was inevitable that Mohamed Ali Akbar should suffer a little from its capricious ways.

It happened on a scorchingly hot morning. Though the sun was not yet at the meridian, the surface of the road was hot and the desert blew gusts of dust-laden wind into his face. He knocked at a door which was answered by a young, brown-skinned girl with wide black eyes, and everything happened with the utmost speed. Like some clumsy oaf who has lost his way, he stood in front of the door, the water-skins swinging to and fro on his lean shoulders. Abstractedly he stared at her, hoping like someone overcome with a mild attack of sunstroke that his eyes would miraculously be capable of clasping her to him. She stared back at him in sheer astonishment, and, unable to utter a word, he turned his back on her and went off home with his water-skins.

Though Mohamed Ali Akbar was exceptionally shy even with his own family, he found himself forced to pour out his heart to his elder sister. As his mother had died of smallpox a long time ago and his father was helplessly bedridden, it was to his sister that he turned for help, for he had unswerving confidence that Sabika possessed the necessary intelligence and judgment for solving a problem of this sort. Seated before him on the rush mat, shrouded in her coarse black dress, she did not break her silence till Mohamed Ali Akbar had 'gasped out the last of his story.

"I shall seek her hand in marriage," she then said. "Isn't that what you want?"

"Yes, yes, is it possible?"

Removing a straw from the old rush mat, his sister replied:

"Why not? You are now a young man and we are all equal in Abkha."

Mohamed Ali Akbar spent a most disturbed night. When morning came he found that his sister was even more eager than himself to set off on her mission. They agreed to meet up at noon when she would tell him of the results of her efforts, and from there they would both make the necessary arrangements for bringing the matter to completion.

Mohamed Ali Akbar did not know how to pass the time wandering through the lanes with the water-skins on his shoulders. He kept looking at his shadow and beseeching God to make it into a circle round his feet so that he might hurry back home. After what seemed an eternity, he made his way back and was met at the door by his sister.

"It seems that her mother is agreeable. But it must all be put to her father, who will give his answer in five days."

Deep down within him Mohamed Ali Akbar felt that he was going to be successful in making the girl his wife. As far as he was able to imagine he began from henceforth to build up images of his future with this young and beautiful brown-skinned girl. His sister Sabika looked at the matter with a wise and experienced eye, but she too was sure they would be successful, for she was convinced that her brother's name was without blemish among the people of Abkha; she had, in addition, given a lot of attention to gaining the approval of the girl's mother, knowing as she did how a woman was able to put over an idea to her husband and make him believe that it was his own. Sabika, therefore, awaited the outcome of the matter with complete composure.

On the fifth day Sabika went to the girl's house in order to receive the answer. When she returned, however, her disconsolate face showed that she had failed. She stood in a corner of the room, unable to look Mohamed Ali Akbar in the eye, not knowing how to begin recounting what had happened.

"You must forget her, Mohamed Ali," she said when she had managed to pluck up her courage.

Not knowing what to say, he waited for his sister to finish.

"Her father died two days ago," continued Sabika, finding an opportunity in his silence to continue. "His dying wish to his family was that they should not give her to you in marriage."

Mohamed Ali Akbar heard these words as though they were addressed to someone else.

"But why, Sabika—why?" was all he could ask.

"He was told that you were a scoundrel, that you lived by stealing sheep on the mountain road, trading what you steal with the foreigners."

"I?"

"They think you are Mohamed Ali," said Sabika in a trembling voice she was unable to control. "You know—the scoundrel Mohamed Ali? Her father thought that you were he . . ."

"But I am not Mohamed Ali," he replied, palms outstretched like a child excusing himself for some misdeed he has not committed. "I'm Mohamed Ali Akbar."

"There's been a mistake—I told them at the beginning that your name was Mohamed Ali. I didn't say Mohamed Ali Akbar because I saw no necessity for doing so."

Mohamed Ali Akbar felt his chest being crushed under the weight of the blow. However, he remained standing where he was, staring at his sister Sabika without fully seeing her. Blinded by anger, he let fly a final arrow:

"Did you tell her mother that I'm not Mohamed Ali but Mohamed Ali Akbar?"

"Yes, but the father's last wish was that they shouldn't marry her to you."

"But I'm Mohamed Ali Akbar the water-seller, aren't I?"

What was the use, though, of being so stricken? Everything had, quite simply, come to an end, a single word had lodged itself in the gullet of his romance and it had died. Mohamed Ali Akbar, however, was unable to forget the girl so easily and spent his time roaming about near her house in the hope of seeing her once again. Why? He did not know. His failure brought in its wake a savage anger which turned to hate; soon he was no longer able to pass along that road for fear that his fury would overcome him and he would pelt the window of her house with stones.

From that day onwards he refused to be called by anything but his name in full: Mohamed Ali Akbar, all in one. He refused to answer to anyone who called him Mohamed or Mohamed Ali and this soon became a habit with him. Even his sister Sabika did not dare to use a contracted form of his name. No longer did he experience his former contentment, and Abkha gradually changed to a forbidding graveyard in his eyes. Refusing to give in to his sister's insistence that he should marry, a worm called "wealth" began to eat its way into his brain. He wanted to take revenge on everything, to marry a woman with whom he could challenge the whole of Abkha, all those who did not believe that he was Mohamed Ali Akbar but Mohamed Ali the scoundrel. Where, though, to find wealth? Thus he decided to sail away to Kuwait.

The distance between Abkha and Ras al-Khaima is two hours by foot, and from Ras al-Khaima to Kuwait by sea is a journey of three days, the fare for which, on an antiquated boat, was seventy rupees. After a year or two he would be able to return to Oman and strut about proudly in the alleyways of Abkha wearing a snow-white *aba* trimmed with gold, like the one he had seen round the shoulder of a notable from Ras al-Khaima who had come to his village to take the hand of a girl the fame of whose beauty had reached all the way there.

The journey was a hard one. The boat which took that eager throng across the south and then made its way northwards to the corner of the Gulf was continually exposed to a variety of dangers. But ebullient souls accustomed to life's hardships paid no heed to such matters; all hands cooperated in the task of delivering safely that small wooden boat floating on the waves of the great sea. And when the sails of the ships lying in Kuwait's quiet harbor came into view, Mohamed Ali Akbar experienced a strange feeling: the dream had now fallen from the colored world of fantasy into the realm of reality and he had to search around for a starting point, for a beginning to his dream. It seemed to him that the fantasies nourished by his hate for Abkha and for which he now sought vengeance were not of sufficient moment. As the frail craft approached, threading its way among the anchored boats, he was slowly drained of his feeling and it appeared to him that his long dreams of wealth were merely a solace for his sudden failure and that they were quite irrational. The packed streets, the buildings with their massive walls, the grey sky, the scorching heat, the warm air of the north wind, the roads crammed with cars, the serious faces, all these things appeared to him as barriers standing between him and his dream. He hurried aimlessly through this ocean of people, conscious of a deep feeling of loss which resembled vertigo, almost convinced that these many faces which did not glance at him were his first enemy, that all these people were the walls obstructing the very beginning of the road to his dream. The story was not as simple as in Abkha. Here it was without beginning, without end, without landmarks. It seemed to him that all the roads along which he walked were endless, that they circuited a rampart that held everything—every single thing—within its embrace. When, at sunset, a road led him to the seashore and he once again saw the sea, he stood staring across at the far horizon that joined up with the water: out there was Abkha, enveloped in tranquillity. It existed, every quarter had its beginning and its end, every wall carried its own particular lineaments; despite everything it was close to his heart. He felt lost in a rush of scalding water and for the first time he had no sense of shame as he lifted his hand to wipe salty tears from his cheeks.

Mohamed Ali Akbar wept without embarrassment, perhaps for the first time since he grew up, involuntarily, he had been overcome by a ferocious yearning for the two water-skins he used to carry across his shoulders. He was still staring out at the horizon while night gradually settled down around him. It made him feel in a way that he was present in a certain place at a certain time and that this night was like night in Abkha: people were sleeping behind their walls, the streets bore the lineaments of fatigue and silence, the sea rumbled heavily under the light of the moon. He felt relief. Wanting to laugh and yet unable to, he wept once again.

Dawn brought him an upsurge of fresh hope. He rose and went running through the streets. He realized that he must find someone from

Oman with whom he could talk and that he would, sooner or later, find such a person, and from there he would learn where he was destined to proceed, from where to make a start.

And so Mohamed Ali Akbar attained his position as errand boy at a shop and was provided with a bicycle on which to carry out his duties. It was from this bicycle that the features of the streets, the qualities of the walls, registered themselves in his head. He felt a certain intimacy with them, but it was an intimacy imposed upon a background of a forbidding impression that he was being dogged by the eyes of his sister Sabika, the chinks in the girl's window, and Mohamed Ali the scoundrel who, unwittingly, had caused such dire disaster.

Months passed with the speed of a bicycle's wheels passing over the surface of a road. The wealth he had dreamed of began to come in and Mohamed Ali Akbar clung to this tiny fortune with all his strength, lest some passing whim should sweep it away or some scoundrel lay his hands on it. Thus it was that it occurred to him to make a sturdy wooden box in which to keep his fortune.

But what did Mohamed Ali Akbar's fortune consist of? Something that could not be reckoned in terms of money. When he had collected a certain amount of money he had bought himself a diaphanous white *aba* with gold edging. Every evening, alone with his box, he would take out the carefully folded *aba*, pass his thin brown fingers tenderly over it and spread it before his eyes; on it he would spill out his modest dreams, tracing along its borders all the streets of his village, the low, latticed windows from behind which peeped the eyes of young girls. There, in a corner of the *aba*, reposed the past which he could not bring himself to return to but whose existence was necessary in order to give the *aba* its true value. The thin fingers would fold it gently once again, put it safely back in its wooden box, and tie strong cord round the box. Then, and only then, did sleep taste sweet.

The box also contained a pair of china earrings for his sister Sabika, which he would give her on his return to Abkha, a bottle of pungent perfume, and a white purse holding such money as God in His bounty had given him and which he hoped would increase day by day.

As for the end, it began one evening. He was returning his bicycle to the shop when he felt a burning sensation in his limbs. He was alarmed at the thought that he had grown so weak, and with such speed, but did not take a great deal of notice, having had spells of trembling whenever he felt exceptionally homesick for Sabika and Abkha; he had already experienced just such a sensation of weakness when savagely yearning for all those things he hated and loved and had left behind, those things that made up the whole of his past. And so Mohamed Ali Akbar hastened along the road to his home with these thoughts in mind. But his feeling of weakness and nostalgia stayed with him till the following midday. When he made the effort to get up from bed, he was amazed to find that he had slept right through to noon instead of waking up at his usual early hour. What alarmed him even more was that he was still conscious of the feeling of weakness boring into his bones. Slightly afraid, he thought for a while and imagined himself all at once standing on the seashore with the glaring sun reflected off the water almost blinding him, the two water-skins on his shoulders, conscious of a sensation of intense exhaustion. The reflection of the sun increased in violence, yet he was unable to shut his eyes—they were aflame. Abruptly he slid back into sleep.

Here time as usually understood came to an end for Mohamed Ali Akbar. From now on everything happened as though he were raised above the ground, as though his legs were dangling in mid-air: like a man on a gallows, he was moving in front of Time's screen, a screen as inert as a rock of basalt. His part as a practicing human had been played out; his part as a mere spectator had come. He felt that there was no bond tying him to anything, that he was somewhere far away and that the things that moved before his eyes were no more than fish inside a large glass tumbler; his own eyes, too, were open and staring as though made of glass.

When he woke up again he realized that he was being carried by his arms and legs. Though he felt exhausted, he found the energy to recall that there was something which continued to be necessary to him and called out in a faint voice:

"The box . . . the box!"

No one, however, paid him any attention. With a frenzied movement he rose so as to get back to his box. His chest panting with the effort of getting to his feet, he called out:

"The box!"

But once again no one heard him. As he reached the door he clung to it and again gasped out in a lifeless voice:

"The box . . ."

Overcome by his exertions, he fell into a trance that was of the seashore itself. This time he felt that the tide was rising little by little over his feet and that the water was intensely cold. His hands were grasping a square-shaped rock with which he plunged downwards. When he awoke again he found himself clasping his old box tied round with cord. While spectres passed to and fro in front of him, a needle was plunged into his arm, and a face bent over him.

Long days passed. But for Mohamed Ali Akbar nothing really happened at all. The mercilessness of the pain continued on its way, and he was not conscious of its passing. He was conscious only of its constant presence. The sea became dissolved into windows behind wooden shutters low against the side of the street, a pair of china earrings, an *aba* wet with salt water, a ship suspended motionless above the waves, and an old wooden box.

Only once was he aware of any contact with the world. This was when he heard a voice beside him say:

"What's in the old box?"

He looked at the source of the voice and saw, as in a dream, the face of a young, clean-shaven man with fair hair who was pointing at the box and looking at something.

The moment of recollection was short. He returned to gazing silently at the sea, though the face of the clean-shaven, blond young man also remained in front of him. After this he felt a sudden upsurge of energy; for no particular reason things had become clear to him. He distinctly saw, for the first time since he had collapsed, the rising of the sun. It seemed to him that he was capable of getting up from his bed and returning to his bicycle. Everything had grown clear to him: the box was alongside him, bound round as it had always been. Feeling at peace, he moved so as to get up, when a crowd of men in white clothes suddenly descended upon him, standing round him and regarding him with curiosity. Mohamed Ali Akbar tried to say something but was unable to. Suddenly he felt that the tide had risen right up to his waist and that the water was unbearably cold. He could feel nothing. He stretched out his arms to seize hold of something lest he should drown, but everything slid away from under his fingers. Suddenly he saw the clean-shaven face of the blond young man again; he stared at him, somewhat frightened of him on account of his box, while the water continued to rise higher and higher until it had screened off that fair, clean-shaven face from his gaze.

"Bed number 12 has died."

As the male nurse called out I was unable to free myself from Mohamed Ali Akbar's eyes staring out at me before he died. I imagined that Mohamed Ali Akbar, who refused to have his name mutilated, would now be satisfied at being merely "Bed number 12" if only he could be assured about the fate of his box.

This, my dear Ahmed, is the story of Mohamed Ali Akbar, Bed number 12, who died yesterday evening and is now lying wrapped round in a white cloth in the autopsy room—the thin brown face that shifted an ulcer from my intestines to my brain and who caused me to write to you, so you don't again repeat your famous phrase "I almost died laughing" in my prescence.

Ever yours,

I haven't yet left the hospital. My health is gradually getting back to normal and the method by which I gauge this amuses me. Do you know how I measure my strength? I stand smoking on the balcony and throw the cigarette end with all my strength so that it falls along the strips of green grass in the garden. In past weeks the cigarette would fall just within the fourth strip, but today it was much nearer the sixth.

From your letter I understood you to say that you were in no need of being a witness to Mohamed Ali Akbar's death to know what death is. You wrote saying that the experience of death does not require the tragic prologues with which I described Mohamed Ali Akbar's life and that people die with far greater matter-of-factness: the man who fell down on the pavement and so let off the loaded pistol he had with him, whose bullet ripped open his neck (he was in the company of a strikingly beautiful girl), or the one who had a heart attack in the street one April evening, having become engaged to be married only a week before. Yes, that's all very true, my dear Ahmed, all very true, but the problem doesn't lie here at all, the problem of death is in no way that of the dead man, it is the problem of those who remain, those who bitterly await their turn so that they too may serve as a humble lesson to the eyes of the living. Of all the things I wrote in my last letter what I want to say now is that we must transfer our thinking from the starting point to the end. All thinking must set forth from the point of death, whether it be, as you say, that of a man who dies contemplating the charms of the body of a wonderfully beautiful girl, or whether he dies staring into a newly shaven face which frightens him because of an old wooden box tied round with string. The unsolved question remains that of the end; the question of non-existence, of eternal life—or what? Or what, my dear Ahmed?

Anyway, let's stop pouring water into a sack with a hole in it. Do you know what happened after I sent you my last letter? I went to the doctor's room and found them writing a report about Mohamed Ali Akbar. And they were on the point of opening the box. Oh, Ahmed, how imprisoned we are in our bodies and minds! We are always endowing others with our own attributes, always looking at them through a narrow fissure of our own views and way of thinking, wanting them, as far as we can, to become "us." We want to squeeze them into our skins, to give them our eyes to see with, to clothe them in our past and our own way of facing up to life. We place them within a framework outlined by our present understanding of time and place.

Mohamed Ali Akbar was none of the things I imagined. He was the father of three boys and two girls. We have forgotten that over there men marry early. Also, Mohamed Ali Akbar was not a water-seller, water being plentiful in Oman, but had been a sailor on one of the sailing ships that ply between the ports of the south and the Gulf, before settling down here quite a time ago.

It was in fact four years ago that Mohamed Ali Akbar arrived in Kuwait. After unimaginably hard effort he managed—only two months ago—to open what passed for a shop on one of the pavements of New Street. As to how he provided for his children in Oman, we simply don't know.

I read in the doctor's report that the patient had lost his sight six hours before death and so it would seem that Mohamed Ali Akbar had not in fact been staring into my face at the moment of his death as he was then blind. The doctor also wrote that as the address of the patient's family was not known, his burial would be attended solely by the hospital grave-diggers.

The doctor read out the report to his colleague. It was concise and extremely condensed, merely dealing in technical terms with the man's illness. The doctor's voice was lugubrious and colorless. When he had finished reading he proceeded to untie the string round the box. At this point I thought of leaving the room, for it was none of my business: the Mohamed Ali Akbar I knew had died and this person they had written about was someone else; this box, too, was some other box. I knew for certain what Mohamed Ali Akbar's box contained. Why should I bother myself about some new problem?

And yet I was unable to go to the door, but stood in the corner, trembling slightly.

The box was soon opened and the doctor quickly ran his fingers through the contents. Then he pushed it to one side.

Fearfully I looked into the box: it was filled with recent invoices for sums owed by the shop to the stores which supplied it; in one corner was an old photo of a bearded face, an old watch strap, some string, a small candle, and several rupees among the papers.

I must be truthful and say that I was sadly disappointed. Before leaving the room, though, I saw something that stunned me: the nurse had pushed aside Mohamed Ali Akbar's invoices and revealed a long china earring that glittered. In a daze I went to the box and picked up the earring. I don't know why it was that I looked at the nurse and said:

"He bought this earring for his sister Sabika—I happen to know that."

For a brief instant she stared at me in some surprise—then she laughed uproariously. The doctor, too, laughed at the joke.

You are no doubt aware that nurses are required to humor patients with stomach ulcers in case they should suffer a relapse.

Yours ever—

5. CHILDREN, YOUTH, AND DEATH

CHILDREN in the modern world are often shielded from the reality of death. In part, they are shielded because in their urbanized, technological world death is something that seems to happen only on the television screen or in the hidden confines of a hospital room from which they are often barred because of their young ages. In part, they are shielded because their parents and other adults persist in giving them false images about death: "Grandmother went to sleep," or "Uncle George is taking a long trip," or "Mother has gone away and can't come back home," or "God took Daddy to heaven because He loves him," or "I lost Granddaddy in 1978," and so forth. Added to this failure to be truthful with children about death is the tendency by many parents to protect their children from witnessing death by disposing of dead animals before the children discover them, having pets "put to sleep" in a veterinarian's office, and encouraging children not to attend relatives' funerals.

Although many children do not now have the personal and natural experiences with death that once were common in an agrarian society, they nevertheless have vivid imaginations about what death means and how it relates to them. Preschool children, as illustrated by the excerpt from James Agee's novel, generally regard death as a form of temporary separation. The separation may be imagined to be like sleep (Mother and Daddy are always at home in the early morning), or it may be thought of in terms of some other kind of separation the child has experienced (Daddy, and often Mother, leaves for work, but always returns in the evening). Children in the younger elementary grades, like the boy in Joan Fassler's story, come to realize that death does happen and that it is not a temporary condition, but they generally regard it as happening to older persons than themselves and their friends. Children at this stage of development have active imaginations about death and the possibility of some kind of life after death, with vivid images and serious questions (as well as games and jokes) about cemeteries, ghosts, angels, heaven, skeletons, and related matters. Preadolescents, like the daughter in Peter De Vries' novel, begin to understand that death will be a part of their own futures. While psychologically regarding themselves as exceptions (just as teenagers and adults do) to the rule that all who live will die, they nevertheless begin the task of grasping intellectually that death is both inevitable and universal.*

Fortunately there are a number of children's books which can help children (and their parents) understand more about death. Some of the books are intended for preschool or younger elementary children. Complete with colorful illustrations, these books can easily be read to younger children and generally depict death as a part of a natural cycle involving plants, animals, and humans. *The Dead Tree*, by Alvin Tresselt, tells about an oak tree which had grown for over one hundred years. The tree benefited birds, squirrels, and people, but problems developed with carpenter ants, termites, woodpeckers, and fungus all attacking the tree over the years. Finally a strong wind blew the weakened tree down and it gradually returned to the earth as rich loam. Margaret Wise Brown's *The Dead Bird* tells about some children finding a dead bird. They knew it was dead because its body was cold and stiff, and its heart didn't beat. With loving care, they buried the bird in the woods and used a rock as its marker. Judith Liberman's *The Bird's Last Song* uses the death of a bird to point out the continuity of life. Death is presented as a natural part of an unending cycle which involves all living things. *The Tenth Good Thing About Barney*, by Judith Viorst, is a delightful first-person narration by a child who has been saddened by the death of his cat, Barney. At the suggestion of his mother, he tries to think of ten good things to say about Barney when they have a funeral. At last, following the funeral and burial in their yard, he thinks of the tenth good thing: Barney is in the ground and helping the flowers grow. Sandel Stoddard Warburg's *Growing Time* also depicts the adjustment of a small child to the death of a pet. Additionally it points out the inadequacy of many adult explanations about death when the death in question, as in this story, is the death of a dearly loved and seemingly irreplaceable dog.

* Maria H. Nagy, "The Child's View of Death," in Herman Feifel, ed., *The Meaning of Death* (New York: McGraw-Hill, 1959), pp. 79–98.

Other books about death are intended for elementary children who can read for themselves, understand that death is a feature of human life as well as the natural world, and begin to grapple with the emotional problems which arise when a loved one dies. A classic example is *Charlotte's Web*, E. B. White's story about a spider who devoted her life to ensuring the survival of a pig named Wilbur and her own unborn offspring. Blessed with human speech and mental powers, Charlotte lived to see her plans brought to fruition and then announced that she would soon be dead. Wilbur's response to her death depicts some of the emotional reactions brought about when a loved one—even a spider—dies. *Annie and the Old One*, by Miska Miles, is the story of a Navajo girl's adjustment to the impending death of her grandmother. While in the process of learning to weave, Annie is told by her grandmother that when the new rug is completed, it will be time for the grandmother to go to Mother Earth. After trying to delay this inevitable event, Annie is taught to understand that people, like the cactus plant, cannot bloom forever. *Why Did He Die?*, by Audrey Harris, depicts a young boy's adjustment to the death of a close friend's grandfather. In responding to his question, his mother explains that all machines, plants, animals, and people wear out or die, and that the death of people is necessary to prevent the world from being overpopulated. Eda LeShan's *Learning to Say Good-By* explores the emotional problems children have when a parent dies. Guilt, fear, resentment, and withdrawal are presented as normal responses for children undergoing bereavement, and suggestions are made regarding adjusting to the death of a parent and reestablishing a normal life in the absence of the parent.

Several excellent books on death are available for preadolescents and teenagers. *The Magic Moth*, by Virginia Lee, depicts the suffering that ten-year-old Maryanne Foss undergoes because of a congenital heart defect. Her brother, Mark-O, is six and has difficulty accepting the fact that Maryanne's death is imminent. He gets to tell Maryanne good-bye before she dies, then attends her funeral and burial. Later, in attempting to understand her death, he thinks of her in terms of a "magic moth" who continues to live in a changed form, just like a white moth which emerged from a cocoon on the evening of Maryanne's death. Doris Buchanan Smith's *A Taste of Blackberries* is a first-person narration of a close, adventure-filled friendship between the narrator and Jamie, a boy who lived nearby. One day, unexpectedly, Jamie was stung by a bee and, before anyone thought much about it, suddenly died from an allergic reaction to the bee. His friend's reaction involved denial, guilt, confusion, loneliness, and many unanswerable questions. After going to the funeral and cemetery, he found it very difficult to think about God—or to accept explanations involving God—when he realized that something as small as a bee had killed his best friend. Constance C. Greene's *Beat the Turtle Drum* is another first-person narration of an extremely close friendship, this time between two sisters aged eleven and thirteen. Kate, the older sister, tells about her sister's birthday celebration. Having received some birthday money, Joss spent it to rent a horse for a week and had a glorious time sharing riding with Kate and other friends. While on a picnic that week with Kate, however, Joss fell out of a tree and instantly died from a broken neck. Kate was shattered emotionally and for the next month alternated between denial and anger. Adult explanations regarding "God's will" only intensified her emotional pain. And in a different vein *The Summer of the Great-Grandmother*, by Madelein L'Engle, provides a realistic account of the benefits and problems brought to a family unit by an older adult who has difficulties with senility in her last months of living. Suffering, frustration, moments of compassion, and labors of love combine to make the story beneficial reading for both young people and adults.

The selections which follow focus on two aspects of the general subject of children, youth, and death. Some of the selections concentrate on the deaths of children and teenagers, and reveal in profound ways the depth and duration of grief brought about by these premature deaths. Other selections provide insights into the ways children and young people respond to the deaths of friends, parents, and other significant adults in their lives.

Seven of the selections are poems. Yamonoue Okura, a poet during the Taika and early Nara periods of Japanese history, writes about the grief experienced by parents when their young son became ill and they watched helplessly as he died. Kao Ch'i, a poet during the Ming dynasty in China, writes about his own grief over the death of his six-year-old daughter. Emily Dickinson's short poem describes the drowning death of a young boy. A. E. Housman's "To an Athlete Dying Young" is a moving description of a young man's funeral procession which retraces the course he once traveled victoriously as an athlete. Robert Frost's "Out, Out—" is a remarkable portrayal of the suddenness and unexpectedness with which death can occur in a young person's life. Edna St. Vincent Millay's "Lament" depicts the difficulty—bordering on the impossible—of explaining a parent's tragic death to young children. And Jeff Irish's poem reveals the profound experience of loss he has had with the death of his older brother.

The remaining selections are prose pieces. The excerpt from James Agee's *A Death in the Family* describes the difficulty young children have in understanding the finality of death and the frustrating limitations placed on any adult who has the task of explaining to children the tragic and unexpected death of a parent. In a virtual mirror image, Peter De Vries' *Blood of the Lamb* describes the difficulty parents have in understanding the premature death of a young person and the frustrating limitations of all available theories which try to explain such deaths. *My Grandpa Died Today*, by Joan Fassler, presents one child's process of adjustment to the death of a grandfather. And "To Hell with Dying," a short story by Alice Walker, a contemporary black writer, suggests that children of all ages sometimes have emotional problems adjusting to and accepting the deaths of persons important to them.

AN ELEGY ON THE DEATH OF FURUHI
Yamanoue Okura (660–733)

What worth to me the seven treasures,
So prized and desired by all the world?
Furuhi, born of us two,
Our love, our dear white pearl,
With dawn, with the morning star,
Frolicked about the bed with us, standing or sitting;
When dusk came with the evening star,
He pulled our hands, urged us to bed,

"Leave me not, father and mother,
Let me sleep between you,
Like *saki-kusa*, the three-stalked plant."
So spoke that lovely mouth.
Then we trusted, as one trusts in a great ship,
That he would grow up as time passed by,
And we should watch him, both in weal and woe.
But, as of a sudden sweeps the storm,
Illness caught our son.
Helpless and in grief,
I braced my sleeves with white cord,
Grasped my shining mirror,
And gazing up into the sky
I appealed to the gods of heaven;
Dropping my forehead to the ground
Madly I prayed to the gods of earth:
"It is yours to decide his fate,
To cure him or to let him die."
Nothing availed my prayers,
He languished day by day,
His voice failed each morning,
His mortal life ebbed out.
Wildly I leapt and kicked the floor,
Cried, stared up, stared down,
And beat my breast in grief.
But the child from my arms has flown;
So goes the world. . . .

ENVOYS
So young he will not know the way;
Here is a fee for you,
O courier from the Nether World,
Bear him on your back.
With offerings I beseech you,
Be true and lead him up
Straight along the road to heaven!

WRITTEN ON SEEING THE FLOWERS, AND REMEMBERING MY DAUGHTER
Kao Ch'i (1336–1374)

I grieve for my second daughter,
Six years I carried her about,
Held her against my breast and helped her eat,
Taught her rhymes as she sat on my knee.
She would arise early and copy her elder sister's dress,
Struggling to see herself in the dressing table mirror.
She had begun to delight in pretty silks and lace
But in a poor family she could have none of these.
I would sigh over my own recurring frustrations,
Treading the byways through the rain and snow.
But evenings when I returned to receive her greeting
My sad cares could be transformed into contentment.
What were we to do, that day when illness struck?
The worse because it was during the crisis of war;
Frightened by the alarming sounds, she sank quickly into death.
There was no time even to fix medicines for her.
Distraught, I prepared her poor little coffin;
Weeping, accompanied it to that distant hillside.
It is already lost in the vast void.
Disconsolate, I still grieve deeply for her.
I think how last year, in the spring,
When the flowers bloomed by the pond in our old garden
She led me by the hand along under the trees
And asked me to break off a pretty branch for her.
This year again the flowers bloom;
Now I live far from home, here by this river's edge.
All the household are here, only she is gone.
I look at the flowers, and my tears fall in vain.
A cup of wine brings me no comfort.
The wind makes desolate sounds in the night curtains.

HOW THE WATERS CLOSED ABOVE HIM
Emily Dickinson (1830–1886)

How the Waters closed above Him
We shall never know—
How He stretched His Anguish to us
That—is covered too—

Spreads the Pond Her Base of Lilies
Bold above the Boy
Whose unclaimed Hat and Jacket
Sum the History—

TO AN ATHLETE DYING YOUNG
A. E. Housman (1859–1936)

The time you won your town the race
We chaired you through the market-place;
Man and boy stood cheering by,
And home we brought you shoulder-high.

Today, the road all runners come,
Shoulder-high we bring you home,
And set you at your threshold down,
Townsman of a stiller town.

Smart lad, to slip betimes away
From fields where glory does not stay,
And early though the laurel grows
It withers quicker than the rose.

Eyes the shady night has shut
Cannot see the record cut,
And silence sounds no worse than cheers
after earth has stopped the ears:

Now you will not swell the rout
Of lads that wore their honors out,
Runners whom renown outran
And the name died before the man.

So set, before its echoes fade,
The fleet foot on the sill of shade,
And hold to the low lintel up
The still-defended challenge-cup.

And round that early-laureled head
Will flock to gaze the strengthless dead,
And find unwithered on its curls
The garland briefer than a girl's.

"OUT, OUT——"
Robert Frost (1874–1963)

The title of this poem is taken from Macbeth's speech when he hears that his wife
has died (*Macbeth*, v, 6). By using this title, Frost follows Shakespeare in suggesting that life is like a candle whose flame is snuffed out suddenly—and too
soon.

The buzz-saw snarled and rattled in the yard
And made dust and dropped stove-length sticks of wood,
Sweet-scented stuff when the breeze drew across it.
And from there those that lifted eyes could count
Five mountain ranges one behind the other
Under the sunset far into Vermont.
And the saw snarled and rattled, snarled and rattled,
As it ran light, or had to bear a load.
And nothing happened: day was all but done.
Call it a day, I wish they might have said
To please the boy by giving him the half hour
That a boy counts so much when saved from work.
His sister stood beside them in her apron
To tell them "Supper." At the word, the saw,
As if to prove saws knew what supper meant,
Leaped out at the boy's hand, or seemed to leap—
He must have given the hand. However it was,
Neither refused the meeting. But the hand!
The boy's first outcry was a rueful laugh,
As he swung toward them holding up the hand
Half in appeal, but half as if to keep
The life from spilling. Then the boy saw all—

Since he was old enough to know, big boy
Doing a man's work, though a child at heart—
He saw all spoiled. "Don't let him cut my hand off—
The doctor, when he comes. Don't let him, sister!"
So. But the hand was gone already.
The doctor put him in the dark of ether.
He lay and puffed his lips out with his breath.
And then—the watcher at his pulse took fright.
No one believed. They listened at his heart.
Little—less—nothing!—and that ended it.
No more to build on there. And they, since they
Were not the one dead, turned to their affairs.

LAMENT
Edna St. Vincent Millay (1892–1950)

Listen, children:
Your father is dead.
From his old coats
I'll make you little jackets;
I'll make you little trousers
From his old pants.
There'll be in his pockets
Things he used to put there,
Keys and pennies
Covered with tobacco;
Dan shall have the pennies
To save in his bank;
Anne shall have the keys
To make a pretty noise with.
Life must go on,
And the dead be forgotten;
Life must go on,
Though good men die;
Anne, eat your breakfast;
Dan, take your medicine;
Life must go on;
I forget just why.

from A DEATH IN THE FAMILY
James Agee (1910–1955)

This Pulitzer Prize-winning novel tells the story of a family's varied reactions to an unexpected death. Jay, the husband and father of the family, was killed in a car accident one evening on his way home. After the other grieving relatives had returned to their own homes, Aunt Hannah stayed with Mary and the children to help them cope with the tragic loss. Early the next morning Mary told the young children that God let their father "go to sleep and took him straight away with Him to heaven." Unable to comprehend the full significance of their mother's statements, Catherine and Rufus reluctantly joined Aunt Hannah for breakfast.

Catherine did not like being buttoned up by Rufus or bossed around by him, and breakfast wasn't like breakfast either. Aunt Hannah didn't say anything and neither did Rufus and neither did she, and she felt that even if she wanted to say anything she oughtn't. Everything was queer, it was so still and it seemed dark. Aunt Hannah sliced the banana so thin on the Post Toasties it looked cold and wet and slimy. She gave each of them a little bit of coffee in their milk and she made Rufus' a little bit darker than hers. She didn't say, "Eat"; "Eat your breakfast, Catherine"; "Don't dawdle," like Catherine's mother; she didn't say anything. Catherine did not feel hungry, but she felt mildly curious because things tasted so different, and she ate slowly ahead, tasting each mouthful. Everything was so still that it made Catherine feel uneasy and sad. There were little noises when a fork or spoon touched a dish; the only other noise was the very thin dry toast Aunt Hannah kept slowly crunching and the fluttering sipping of the steamy coffee with which she wet each mouthful of dry crumbs enough to swallow it. When Catherine tried to make a similar noise sipping her milk, her Aunt Hannah glanced at her sharply as if she wondered if Catherine was trying to be a smart aleck but she did not say anything. Catherine was not trying to be a smart aleck but she felt she had better not make that noise again. The fried eggs had hardly any pepper and they were so soft the yellow ran out over the white and the white plate and looked so nasty she didn't want to eat it but she ate it because she didn't want to be told to and because she felt there was some special reason, still, why she ought to be a good girl. She felt very uneasy, but there was nothing to do but eat, so she always took care to get a good hold on her tumbler and did not take too much on her spoon, and hardly spilled at all, and when she became aware of how little she was spilling it made her feel like a big girl and yet she did not feel any less uneasy, because she knew there was something wrong. She was not as much interested in eating as she was in the way things were, and listening carefully, looking mostly at her plate, every sound she heard and the whole quietness which was so much stronger than the sounds, meant that things were not good. What it was was that he wasn't here. Her mother wasn't either, but she was upstairs. He wasn't even upstairs. He was coming home last night but he didn't come home and he wasn't coming home now either, and her mother felt so awful she cried, and Aunt Hannah wasn't saying anything, just making all that noise with the toast and big loud sips with the coffee and swallowing, *grrmmp*, and then the same thing over again and over again, and every time she made the noise with the toast it was almost scary, as if she was talking about some awful thing, and every time she sipped it was like crying or like when Granma sucked in air between her teeth when she hurt herself, and every time she swallowed, *crrmmp*, it meant it was all over and there was nothing to do about it or say or even ask, and then she would take another bite of toast as hard and shivery as gritting your teeth, and start the whole thing all over again. Her mother said he wasn't coming home ever any more. That was what she said, but why wasn't he home eating breakfast right this minute? Because he was not with them eating breakfast it wasn't fun and everything was so queer. Now maybe in just a minute he would walk right in and grin at her and say, "Good morning, merry sunshine," because her lip was sticking out, and even bend down and rub her cheek with his whiskers and then sit down and eat a big breakfast and then it would be all fun again and she would watch from the window when he went to work and just before he went out of sight he would turn around and she would wave but why wasn't he right here now where she wanted him to be and why didn't he come home? Ever any more. He won't come home again ever any more. Won't come home again ever. But he will, though, because it's home. But why's he not here? He's up seeing Grampa Follet. Grampa Follet is very, very sick. But Mama didn't feel awful then, she feels awful now. But why didn't he come back when she said he would? He went to heaven and now Catherine could remember about heaven, that's where God lives, way up in the sky. Why'd he do that? God took him there. But why'd he go there and not come home like Mama said? Last night Mama said he was coming home last night. We could even wait up a while and when he didn't and we had to go to bed she *promised* he would come if we went to sleep and she promised he'd be here at breakfast time and now its breakfast time and she says he won't come home ever any more. Now her Aunt Hannah folder her napkin, and folded it again more narrowly, and again still more narrowly, and pressed the butt end of it against her mouth, and laid it beside her plate, where it slowly and slightly unfolded, and, looking first at Rufus and then at Catherine and then back at Rufus, said quietly, "I think you ought to know about your father. Whatever I can tell you. Because your mother's not feeling well."

Now I'll know when he *is* coming home, Catherine thought.

All through breakfast, Rufus had wanted to ask questions, but now he felt so shy and uneasy that he could hardly speak. "Who hurt him?" he finally asked.

"Why nobody hurt him, Rufus," she said, and she looked shocked. "What on earth made you think so?"

Mamma said so, Catherine thought.

"Mama said he got hurt so bad God put him to sleep," Rufus said.

Like the kitties, Catherine thought; she saw a dim, gigantic old man in white take her tiny father by the skin of the neck and put him in a huge slop jar full of water and sit on the lid, and she heard the tiny scratching and the stifled mewing.

"That's true he was hurt, but nobody hurt him," her Aunt Hannah was saying. How could that be, Catherine wondered. "He was driving home by himself. That's all, all by himself, in the auto last night, and he had an accident."

Rufus felt his face get warm and he looked warningly at his sister. He knew it could not be that, not with his father, a grown man, besides, God wouldn't put you to sleep for *that*, and it didn't hurt, anyhow. But Catherine might think so. Sure enough, she was looking at her aunt with astonishment and disbelief that she could say such a thing about her father. Not in his *pants*, you dern fool, Rufus wanted to tell her, but his Aunt Hannah continued: "A *fatal* accident"; and by her voice, as she spoke the strange word, "fatal," they knew she meant something very bad. "That means that, just as your mother told you, that he was hurt so badly that God put him to sleep right away."

Like the rabbits, Rufus remembered, all torn white bloody fur and red insides. He could not imagine his father like that. Poor little things, he remembered his mother's voice comforting his crying, hurt so terribly that God just let them go to sleep.

If it was in the auto, Catherine thought, then he wouldn't be in the slop jar.

They couldn't be happy any more if He hadn't, his mother had said. They could never get well.

Hannah wondered whether they could comprehend it at all and whether she should try to tell them. She doubted it. Deeply uncertain, she tried again.

"He was driving home last night," she said, "about nine, and apparently something was already wrong with the steering mech—with the wheel you guide the machine with. But your father didn't know it. Because there wasn't any way he could know until something went wrong and then it was too late. But one of the wheels struck a loose stone in the road and the wheel turned aside very suddenly, and when . . ." She paused and went on more quietly and slowly: "You see, when your father tried to make the auto go where it should, stay on the road, he found he couldn't, he didn't have any control. Because something was wrong with the steering gear. So, instead of doing as he tried to make it, the auto twisted aside because of the loose stone and ran off the road into a deep ditch." She paused again. "Do you understand?"

They kept looking at her.

"Your father was thrown from the auto," she said. "Then the auto went on without him up the other side of the ditch. It went up an eight-foot embankment and then it fell down backward, turned over and landed just beside him.

"They're pretty sure he was dead even before he was thrown out. Because the only mark on his whole body," and now they began to hear in her voice a troubling intensity and resentment, "was right—here!" She pressed the front of her forefinger to the point of her chin, and looked at them almost as if she were accusing them.

They said nothing.

I suppose I've got to finish, Hannah thought; I've gone this far.

"They're pretty sure how it happened," she said. "The auto gave such a sudden terrible *jerk*"—she jerked so violently that both children jumped, and startled her; she demonstrated what she saw next more gently: "that your father was thrown forward and struck his chin, very hard, against the wheel, the steering wheel, and from that instant he never knew anything more."

She looked at Rufus, at Catherine, and again at Rufus. "Do you understand?" They looked at her.

After a while Catherine said, "He hurt his chin."

"Yes, Catherine. He did," she replied. "They believe he was *instantly killed*, with that one single blow, because it happened to strike just exactly where it did. Because if you're struck very hard in just that place, it jars your whole head, your brain so hard that—sometimes people die in that very instant." She drew a deep breath and let it out long and shaky. "Concussion of the brain, that is called," she said with most careful distinctness, and bowed her head for a moment; they saw her thumb make a small cross on her chest.

She looked up. "Now do you understand, children?" she asked earnestly. "I know it's very hard to understand. You please tell me if there's anything you want to know and I'll do my best to expl—tell you better."

Rufus and Catherine looked at each other and looked away. After a while Rufus said, "Did it hurt him bad?"

"He could never have felt it. That's the one great mercy" (or *is* it, she wondered); "the doctor is sure of that."

Catherine wondered whether she could ask one question. She thought she'd better not.

"What's an eightfoot embackmut?" asked Rufus.

"Em-bank-ment," she replied. "Just a bank. A steep little hill, eight feet high. Bout's high's the ceiling."

He and Catherine saw the auto climb it and fall backward rolling and come to rest beside their father. Unbackmut, Catherine thought; em-*bank*-ment, Rufus said to himself.

"What's instintly?"

"Instantly is—quick's that"; she snapped her fingers, more loudly than she had expected to; Catherine flinched and kept her eyes on the fingers. "Like snapping off an electric light," Rufus nodded. "So you can be very sure, both of you, he never felt a moment's pain. Not one moment."

"When's . . ." Catherine began.

"What's . . ." Rufus began at the same moment; they glared at each other.

"What is it, Catherine?"

"When's Daddy coming home?"

"Why *good golly*, Catherine," Rufus began. "Hold your tongue!" his Aunt Hannah said fiercely, and he listened, scared, and ashamed of himself.

"Catherine, he *can't* come home," she said very kindly. "That's just what all this means, child." She put her hand over Catherine's hand and Rufus could see that her chin was trembling. "He died, Catherine," she said. "That's what your mother means. God put him to sleep and took him, took his soul away with Him. So he can't come home . . ." She stopped, and began again. "We'll see him once more," she said, "tomorrow or day after; that I promise you," she said, wishing she was sure of Mary's views about this. "But he'll be asleep then. And after that we won't see him any more in this world. Not until God takes us away too.

"Do you see, child?" Catherine was looking at her very seriously. "Of course you don't, God bless you"; she squeezed her hand. "Don't ever try too hard to understand, child. Just try to understand it's so. He'd come if he could but he simply can't because God wants him with Him. That's all." She kept her hand over Catherine's a little while more, while Rufus realized much more clearly than before that he really could not and would not come home again: because of God.

"He would if he could but he can't," Catherine finally said, remembering a joking phrase of her mother's.

Hannah, who knew the joking phrase too, was startled, but quickly realized that the child meant it in earnest, "That's it," she said gratefully.

But he'll come once more, anyway, Rufus realized, looking forward to it. Even if he *is* asleep.

"What was it you wanted to ask, Rufus?" he heard his aunt say.

He tried to remember and remembered. "What's kuh, kunkush, kuh . . .?"

"Con-*cus*-sion, Rufus. Concus-sion of the brain. That's the doctor's name for what happened. It means, it's as if the brain were hit very hard and suddenly, and joggled loose. The instant that happens, your father was—he . . ."

"Instantly killed."

She nodded.
"Then it was that, that put him to sleep."
"Hyess."
"*Not* God."
Catherine looked at him, bewildered.

from BLOOD OF THE LAMB
Peter De Vries (b. 1910)

In this powerful novel, De Vries depicts the love and sorrow of a father whose eleven-year-old daughter becomes terminally ill. Having survived the suicide of his wife, the father is now confronted with the suffering and impending death of his daughter Carol—a death which seems to demonstrate the absurdity of human existence. He prays desperately for a remission, then has to cope with her death.

I walked out past St. Catherine's to the bar and grill and back again so often through so many hospitalizations that I cannot remember which time it was that I stopped in the church on the way back to sit down and rest. I was dead-drunk and stone-sober and bone-tired, my head split and numbed by the plague of voices in eternal disputation. I knew why I was delaying my return to the hospital. The report on the morning's aspiration would be phoned up to the ward from the laboratory any minute, and what I died to learn I dreaded to hear.

I got up and walked to the center aisle, where I stood looking out to the high altar and the soaring windows. I turned around and went to the rear corner, where stood the little shrine to St. Jude, Patron of Lost Causes and Hopeless Cases. Half the candles were burning. I took a taper and lit another. I was alone in the church. The gentle flames wavered and shattered in a mist of tears spilling from my eyes as I sank to the floor.

"I do not ask that she be spared to me, but that her life be spared to her. Or give us a year. We will spend it as we have the last, missing nothing. We will mark the dance of every hour between the snowdrop and the snow: crocus to tulip to violet to iris to rose. We will note not only the azalea's crimson flowers but the red halo that encircles a while the azalea's root when her petals are shed, also the white halo that rings for a week the foot of the old catalpa tree. Later we will prize the chrysan-

themums which last so long, almost as long as paper flowers, perhaps because they know in blooming not to bloom. We will seek out the leaves
turning in the little-praised bushes and the unadvertised trees. Everyone
loves the sweet, neat blossom of the hawthorn in spring, but who lingers
over the olive drab of her leaf in autumn? We will. We will note the lost
yellows in the tangles of that bush that spills over the Howards' stone
wall, the meek hues among which it seems to hesitate before committing
itself to red, and next year learn its name. We will seek out these modest
subtleties so lost in the blare of oaks and maples, like flutes and wood-
winds drowned in brasses and drums. When winter comes, we will let no
snow fall ignored. We will again watch the first blizzard from her
window like figures locked snug in a glass paperweight. 'Pick one out and
follow it to the ground,' she will say again. We will feed the plain birds
that stay to cheer us through the winter, and when spring returns we shall
be the first out, to catch the snowdrop's first white whisper in the wood.
All this we ask, with the remission of our sins, in Christ's name. Amen."

. . . .

Summer passed into autumn, and when in November a few white
flakes sifted down out of the sky, Mrs. Brodhag decided to make the
journey to her sister in Seattle of which she had for so long restively
spoken. Perhaps she would make "other connections" there, in view of
my having the house on the market. If I sold it—a result little
foreshadowed by the processions marching through it behind an ever-
changing leadership of brokers—and did move into a city apartment, I
would hardly be needing her help. The trip to the airport was the first
down the Parkway since the days when we had made so many. "—In
both our prayers—" she raged in my ear against the roar of jets. I
pressed into her hand a St. Christopher medal, extricated with difficulty
from the chain of the crucifix with which it had become entangled in my
pocket. We smiled as she nodded thanks. Then she was a bird in the sky,
then a bee, then nothing.

It was as many months again before I could bring myself to explore at
any length the bright front bedroom, than only because the sudden sale
of the house required its cleaning out. Dresses and toys and bureau articles were put into boxes and carried into the garage for the charity truck
to haul away. Among the books and papers in a large desk drawer was a

class letter from the sixth grade, a monumental scroll on which each individual note was pasted, wound upon two sticks like an ancient document. I read a few before stowing it into a carton of things to be kept for a still further future. One was a note from a boy reputed to have lost his heart to her, commanding her early return and with a P.S. reading, "You and I up in a tree, k-i-s-s-i-n-g." Into the carton were also tucked the home movies still sealed in their original tins. At last I found the courage to turn on the tape recorder.

I carried it down into the living room, of which the windows were open, the year being now once again well advanced into spring. It was twilight, and I turned on all the lamps.

After a whir of scratches and laughing whispers began some absurd dialogue Carol had picked up between Mrs. Brodhad and me, without our knowing it, about leaking eaves and how they should be got at. "You might as well be married the way she nags you," Carol said into the machine she had herself initiated with this prank. Then followed some of her piano pieces, including the Chopin Nocturne I had managed to get on the tape the night of the unfortunate television program. I stood at the window with a heavy drink as each molten note dropped out of nowhere onto my heart. There was a long silence after the music, and I was about to end the entertainment as a poor idea when my hand was arrested at the switch by the sound of her voice. This time she read a selection to which she had a few words of preface:

"I want you to know that everything is all right, Daddy. I mean you mustn't worry, really. You've helped me a lot—more than you can imagine. I was digging around in the cabinet part at the bottom of the bookshelves for something to read that you would like. I mean, not something from your favorite books of poetry and all, but something of your own. What did I come across but that issue of the magazine put out by your alma mater, with the piece in it about your philosophy of life. Do you remember it? I might as well say that I know what's going on. What you wrote gives me courage to face whatever there is that's coming, so what could be more appropriate than to read it for you now? Remember when you explained it to me? Obviously, I don't understand it all, but I think I get the drift:

"I believe that man must learn to live without those consolations called religious, which his own intelligence must by now have told him belong to

CHILDREN, YOUTH, AND DEATH 169

the childhood of the race. Philosophy can really give us nothing permanent to believe either; it is too rich in answers, each canceling out the rest. The quest for Meaning is foredoomed. Human life 'means' nothing. But that is not to say that it is not worth living. What does a Debussy Arabesque 'mean,' or a rainbow or a rose? A man delights in all of these, knowing himself to be no more—a wisp of music and a haze of dreams dissolving against the sun. Man has only his own two feet to stand on, his own human trinity to see him through: Reason, Courage, and Grace. And the first plus the second equals the third."

I reached the couch at last, on which I lay for some hours as though I had been clubbed, not quite to death. I wished that pound of gristle in my breast would stop its beating, as once in the course of that night I think it nearly did. The time between the last evening songs of the birds and their first cries at daybreak was a span of night without contents, blackness as stark as the lights left burning among the parlor furniture. Sometime towards its close I went to my bedroom, where from a bureau drawer I drew a small cruciform trinket on a chain. I went outside, walking down the slope of back lawn to the privet hedge, over which I hurled it as far as I could into the trees beyond. They were the sacred wood where we had so often walked, looking for the first snowdrops, listening for peepers, and in the clearings of which we had freed from drifts of dead leaves the tender heads of early violets.

I looked up through the cold air. All the stars were out. That pit of jewels, heaven, gave no answer. Among them would always be a wraith saying, "Can't I stay up a little longer?" I hear that voice in the city streets or on country roads, with my nose in a mug of cocoa, walking in the rain or standing in falling snow. "Pick one out and follow it to the ground."

How I hate this world. I would like to tear it apart with my own two hands if I could. I would like to dismantle the universe star by star, like a treeful of rotten fruit. Nor do I believe in progress. A vermin-eaten saint scratching his filth in the hope of heaven is better off than you damned in clean linen. Progress doubles our tenure in a vale of tears. Man is a mistake, to be corrected only by his abolition, which he gives promise of seeing to himself. Oh, let him pass, and leave the earth to the flowers that carpet the earth wherever he explodes his triumphs. Man is inconsolable, thanks to that eternal "Why?" when there is no Why, that question mark twisted like a fishhook in the human heart. "Let there be light," we cry, and only the dawn breaks.

. . . .

Sometime later, there was a footstep on the path and a knock on the door. It was Omar Howard, come to say good morning and to ask if I had found the Egyptian scarab ring of Carol's, which I had promised him. I had indeed, and, pressing it into his hand, received in return a volume I might find of interest—*Zen: The Answer?*

I sat paging through it for a few minutes after he had gone, sampling what would be perused at more leisure later. ". . . detached attachment . . . roll with nature . . . embrace her facts so as not to be crushed by them . . . swim with the . . ." And of course the Chinese original of that invisible wall-motto in the hospital corridor: "No fuss." On the jacket was a picture of the author, seen trimming a gardenia bush, his hobby. I boarded a train to California, in one or another of whose hanging gardens the wise man dwelt, and, bearding him there, asked whether there were any order of wisdom by which the sight of flowers being demolished could be readily borne. "Watch," I said, and tore from a branch the most perfect of his blossoms and mangled it into the dirt with my heel. Then I tore another, then another, watching studiously his expression as I ground the white blooms underfoot. . . .

These thoughts were cut short with the remainder that I must write a letter of recommendation for Omar to a prep school he was trying to get into, for which I had also promised to kick in a little tuition money, if memory served.

Time heals nothing—which should make us the better able to minister. There may be griefs beyond the reach of solace, but none worthy of the name that does not set free the springs of sympathy. Blessed are they that comfort, for they too have mourned, may be more likely the human truth. "You had a dozen years of perfection. That's a dozen more than most people get," a man had rather sharply told me one morning on the train. He was the father of one of Carol's classmates, a lumpish girl of no wiles and no ways, whose Boston mother had long since begun to embalm her dreams in alcohol. I asked him to join me sometime in a few beers and a game or two at the bowling alleys, where one often saw him hanging about alone. He agreed. Once I ran into Carol's teacher, Miss

Halsey. "Some poems are long, some are short. She was a short one," Miss Halsey had summed up, smiling, with the late-Gothic horse face which guarantees that she will never read any poems, long or short, to any children of her own. Again the throb of compassion rather than the breath of consolation: the recognition of how long, how long is the mourners' bench upon which we sit, arms linked in undeluded friendship, all of us, brief links, ourselves, in the eternal pity.

MY GRANDPA DIED TODAY
Joan Fassler (b. 1931)

This book is intended for children. The child who serves as the narrator reflects on his relationship with his grandfather, describes his grandfather's death and his own reaction to it, and shows how his life goes on even though someone he loved dearly has died.

My grandpa was very, very old. He was much, much older than me. He was much older than my mother and father. He was much older than all my aunts and uncles. He was even a little bit older than the white haired bakery-man down the block.

My grandpa taught me how to play checkers. And he read stories to me. And he helped me build my first model. And he showed me how to reach out with my bat and hit a curve ball. And he always rooted for my team.

One day, grandpa and I took a long slow walk together. Grandpa stopped to rest awhile. "David," he said, "I am getting very old now. And surely I cannot live forever." Then grandpa put his arm around my shoulders and went on talking in a soft voice. "But I am not afraid to die," he said, "because I know that you are not afraid to live." And I nodded my head in a thoughtful way, even though I did not understand what grandpa meant.

Just two days later grandpa sat down in our
big white rocking chair. And he rocked
himself for a little while. Then, very softly,
very quietly, grandpa closed his eyes.

And he stopped rocking,
And he didn't move any more.
And he didn't talk any more.
And he didn't breathe any more.
And the grownups said that grandpa died.

My mother cried and cried. And my father
cried and cried. And many people came to
our house. And they cried, too. And they
took grandpa away and buried him.

More people kept coming to our house. And
they pulled down all the window shades. And
they covered all the mirrors. And our whole
house looked as if it was going to cry. Even
the red shingles on the roof. Even the white
shutters at the windows. Even the flagstone
steps going up to the door. And everyone was
very sad.

I was sad, too. I thought about my grandpa
and about all the things we used to do
together. And, in a little while, I discovered a
funny, empty, scary, rumbly kind of feeling
at the bottom of my stomach. And some tears
streaming down my cheeks.

Somehow, I didn't feel like sitting in the
living room with all the gloomy grown-ups. So
I walked quietly into my own room, and I
took out some of my favorite toys. Then I did
two jig-saw puzzles and colored three
pictures. And I rolled a few marbles very
slowly across the floor.

The grownups didn't mind at all. They came in and smiled at me. And someone patted me gently on my head. It was almost as if they all knew that grandpa and I must have had some very special talks together.

The next day was still a very sad day at our house. Late in the afternoon, I heard a soft knock at the door. My best friend, Bobby, wanted to know if I could play ball. And again the grownups didn't seem to mind. So I left our sad, sorry house. And Bobby and I walked slowly down to the park.

Almost too soon, it was my turn at bat. I looked around and saw that the bases were loaded. Then I took a deep breath, and tried to forget about the rumbly feeling at the bottom of my stomach. I planted my feet firmly on the ground. I grasped the bat with two steady hands. I watched the ball whizz towards me. And, SMACK, I hit it high and far.

And then I ran. I ran with every bit of strength and power and speed inside my whole body.
And it was a grand slam home run!

And somehow, right there on the field, in the middle of all the cheers and shouts of joy, I could *almost* see my grandpa's face breaking into a happy smile. And that made me feel so good inside that the rumbles in my stomach disappeared.

And the solid hardness of the gound under my feet made me feel good inside, too. And the warm touch of the sun on my cheeks made me feel good inside, too.

And, it was at that very moment, that I first
began to understand why my grandpa was not
afraid to die. It was because he knew that
there would be many more hits and many
more home runs for me. It was because he
knew that I would go right on playing, and
reading, and running, and laughing, and
growing up.

Without really knowing why, I took off my
cap. I stood very still. I looked far, far away
into the clear blue sky. And I thought to
myself, "Grandpa must feel good inside, too."

Then I heard the umpire calling, "Batter-up!"
And we went on with the game.

TO HELL WITH DYING
Alice Walker (b. 1944)

"To hell with dying," my father would say, "these children want Mr.
Sweet!"

Mr. Sweet was a diabetic and an alcoholic and a guitar player and
lived down the road from us on a neglected cotton farm. My older
brothers and sisters got the most benefit from Mr. Sweet, for when they
were growing up he had quite a few years ahead of him and so was capable of being called back from the brink of death any number of
times—whenever the voice of my father reached him as he lay expiring
. . . "To hell with dying, man," my father would say, pushing the wife
away from the bedside (in tears although she knew the death was not
necessarily the last one unless Mr. Sweet really wanted it to be), "the
children want Mr. Sweet!" And they did want him, for at a signal from
Father they would come crowding around the bed and throw themselves
on the covers and whoever was the smallest at the time would kiss him all
over his wrinkled brown face and begin to tickle him so that he would
laugh all down in his stomach, and his moustache which was long and
sort of straggly, would shake like Spanish moss and was also that color.

Mr. Sweet had been ambitious as a boy, wanted to be a doctor or lawyer or sailor, only to find that black men fare better if they are not. Since he could be none of those things he turned to fishing as his only earnest career and playing the guitar as his only claim to doing anything extraordinarily well. His son, the only one that he and his wife, Miss Mary, had, was shiftless as the day is long and spent money as if he were trying to see the bottom of the mint, which Mr. Sweet would tell him was the clean brown palm of his hand. Miss Mary loved her "baby," however, and worked hard to get him the "li'l necessaries" of life, which turned out mostly to be women.

Mr. Sweet was a tall, thinnish man with thick kinky hair going dead white. He was dark brown, his eyes were very squinty and sort of bluish, and he chewed Brown Mule tobacco. He was constantly on the verge of being blind drunk, for he brewed his own liquor and was not in the least a stingy sort of man, and was always very melancholy and sad, though frequently when he was "feelin' good" he'd dance around the yard with us, usually keeling over just as my mother came to see what the commotion was.

Toward all of us children he was very kind, and had the grace to be shy with us, which is unusual in grownups. He had great respect for my mother for she never held his drunkenness against him and would let us play with him even when he was about to fall in the fireplace from drink. Although Mr. Sweet would sometimes lose complete or nearly complete control of his head and neck so that he would loll in his chair, his mind remained strangely acute and his speech not too affected. His ability to be drunk and sober at the same time made him an ideal playmate, for he was as weak as we were and we could usually best him in wrestling, all the while keeping a fairly coherent conversation going.

We never felt anything of Mr. Sweet's age when we played with him. We loved his wrinkles and would draw some on our brows to be like him, and his white hair was my special treasure and he knew it and would never come to visit us just after he had had his hair cut off at the barbershop. Once he came to our house for something, probably to see my father about fertilizer for his crops, for although he never paid the slightest attention to his crops he liked to know what things would be best to use on them if he ever did. Anyhow, he had not come with his hair since he had just had it shaved off at the barbershop. He wore a huge straw hat to keep off the sun and also to keep his head away from me. But as soon as I saw him I ran up and demanded that he take me up and kiss me, with his funny beard which smelled so strongly of tobacco. Looking forward to burying my small fingers into his woolly hair I threw away his hat only to find he had done something to his hair, that it was no longer there! I let out a squall which made my mother think that Mr. Sweet had finally dropped me in the well or something and from that day I've been wary of men in hats. However, not long after, Mr. Sweet showed up with his hair grown out and just as white and kinky and impenetrable as it ever was.

Mr. Sweet used to call me his princess, and I believed it. He made me feel pretty at five and six, and simply outrageously devastating at the blazing age of eight and a half. When he came to our house with his guitar the whole family would stop whatever they were doing to sit around him and listen to him play. He liked to play "Sweet Georgia Brown," and that was what he called me sometimes, and also he liked to play "Caldonia" and all sorts of sweet, sad, wonderful songs which he sometimes made up. It was from one of these songs that I learned that he had to marry Miss Mary when he had in fact loved somebody else (now living in Chi'-ca-go, or De-stroy, Michigan). He was not sure that Joe Lee, her "baby," was also his baby. Sometimes he would cry and that was an indication that he was about to die again. And so we would all get prepared, for we were sure to be called upon.

I was seven the first time I remember actually participating in one of Mr. Sweet's "revivals"—my parents told me I had participated before. I had been the one chosen to kiss him and tickle him long before I knew the rite of Mr. Sweet's rehabilitation. He had come to our house, it was a few years after his wife's death, and he was very sad, and also, typically, very drunk. He sat on the floor next to me and my older brother, the rest of the children were grown-up and lived elsewhere, and began to play his guitar and cry. I held his woolly head in my arms and wished I could have been old enough to have been the woman he loved so much and that I had not been lost years and years ago.

When he was leaving my mother said to us that we'd better sleep light that night for we'd probably have to go over to Mr. Sweet's before daylight. And we did. For soon after we had gone to bed one of the neighbors knocked on our door and called my father and said that Mr.

Sweet was sinking fast and if he wanted to get in a word before the crossover he'd better shake a leg and get over to Mr. Sweet's house. All the neighbors knew to come to our house if something was wrong with Mr. Sweet, but they did not know how we always managed to make him well, or at least stop him from dying, when he was often so near death. As soon as we heard the cry we got up, my brother and I and my mother and father, and put on our clothes. We hurried out of the house and down the road for we were always afraid that we might someday be too late and Mr. Sweet would get tired of dallying.

When we got to the house, a very poor shack really, we found the front room full of neighbors and relatives and someone met us at the door and said that it was all very sad that old Mr. Sweet Little (for Little was his family name although we mostly ignored it) was about to kick the bucket. My parents were advised not to take my brother and me into the "death-room" seeing we were so young and all, but we were so much more accustomed to the death-room than he that we ignored him and dashed in without giving his warning a second thought. I was almost in tears, for these deaths upset me fearfully, and the thought of how much depended on me and my brother (who was such a ham most of the time) made me very nervous.

The doctor was bending over the bed and turned back to tell us for at least the tenth time in the history of my family that alas, old Mr. Sweet Little was dying and that the children had best not see the face of implacable death (I didn't know what "implacable" was, but whatever it was, Mr. Sweet was not!). My father pushed him rather abruptly out of the way saying as he always did and very loudly for he was saying it to Mr. Sweet, "To hell with dying, man, these children want Mr. Sweet!" which was my cue to throw myself upon the bed and kiss Mr. Sweet all around the whiskers and under the eyes and around the collar of his nightshirt where he smelled so strongly of all sorts of things, mostly liniment.

I was very good at bringing him around, for as soon as I saw that he was struggling to open his eyes I knew he was going to be all right and so could finish my revival sure of success. As soon as his eyes were open he would begin to smile and that way I knew that I had surely won. Once though I got a tremendous scare for he could not open his eyes and later I learned that he had had a stroke and that one side of his face was stiff and hard to get into motion. When he began to smile I could tickle him in earnest for I was sure that nothing would get in the way of his laughter, although once he began to cough so hard that he almost threw me off his stomach, but that was when I was very small, little more than a baby, and my bushy hair had gotten in his nose.

When we were sure he would listen to us we would ask him why he was in bed and when he was coming to see us again and could we play with his guitar which more than likely would be leaning against the bed. His eyes would get all misty and he would sometimes cry out loud, but we never let it embarrass us for he knew that we loved him and that we sometimes cried too for no reason. My parents would leave the room to just the three of us; Mr. Sweet, by that time, would be propped up in bed with a number of pillows behind his head and with me sitting and lying on his shoulder and along his chest. Even when he had trouble breathing he would not ask me to get down. Looking into my eyes he would shake his white head and run a scratchy old finger all around my hairline, which was rather low down nearly to my eyebrows and for which some people said I looked like a baby monkey.

My brother was very generous in all this, he let me do all the revivaling—he had done it for years before I was born and so was glad to be able to pass it on to someone new. What he would do while I talked to Mr. Sweet was pretend to play the guitar, in fact pretend that he was a young version of Mr. Sweet, and it always made Mr. Sweet glad to think that someone wanted to be like him—of course we did not know this then, we played the thing by ear, and whatever he seemed to like, we did. We were desperately afraid that he was just going to take off one day and leave us.

It did not occur to us that we were doing anything special; we had not learned that death was final when it did come. We thought nothing of triumphing over it so many times, and in fact became a trifle contemptuous of people who let themselves be carried away. It did not occur to us that if our own father had been dying we could not have stopped it, that Mr. Sweet was the only person over whom we had power.

When Mr. Sweet was in his eighties I was a young lady studying away in a university many miles from home. I saw him whenever I went home, but he was never on the verge of dying that I could tell and I began to feel that my anxiety for his health and psychological well-being was unnecessary. By this time he not only had a moustache but a long flowing snow-white beard which I loved and combed and braided for hours. He was still a very heavy drinker and was like an old Chinese opium-user, very peaceful, fragile, gentle, and the only jarring note about him was his old steel guitar which he still played in the old sad, sweet, downhome blues way.

On Mr. Sweet's ninetieth birthday I was finishing my doctorate in Massachusetts and had been making arrangements to go home for several weeks' rest. That morning I got a telegram telling me that Mr. Sweet was dying again and could I please drop everything and come home. Of course I could. My dissertation could wait and my teachers would understand when I explained to them when I got back. I ran to the phone, called the airport, and within four hours I was speeding along the dusty road to Mr. Sweet's.

The house was more dilapidated than when I was last there, barely a shack, but it was overgrown with yellow roses which my family had planted many years ago. The air was heavy and sweet and very peaceful. I felt strange walking through the gate and up the old rickety steps. But the strangeness left me as I caught sight of the long white beard I loved so well flowing down the thin body over the familiar quilt coverlet. Mr. Sweet!

His eyes were closed tight and his hands, crossed over his stomach, were thin and delicate, no longer rough and scratchy. I remembered how always before I had run and jumped up on him just anywhere; now I knew he would not be able to support my weight. I looked around at my parents, and was surprised to see that my father and mother also looked old and frail. My father, his own hair very gray, leaned over the quietly sleeping old man who, incidentally, smelled still of wine and tobacco, and said as he'd done so many times, "To hell with dying, man! My daughter is home to see Mr. Sweet!" My brother had not been able to come as he was in the war in Asia. I bent down and gently stroked the closed eyes and gradually they began to open. The closed, wine-stained lips twitched a little, then parted in a warm, slightly embarrassed smile. Mr. Sweet could see me and he recognized me and his eyes looked very spry and twinkly for a moment. I put my head down on the pillow next to his and we just looked at each other for a long time. Then he began to trace my peculiar hairline with a thin, smooth finger. I closed my eyes when his finger halted above my ear (he used to rejoice at the dirt in my ears when I was little), his hand stayed cupped around my cheek. When I opened my eyes, sure I had reached him in time, his were closed.

Even at twenty-four how could I believe that I had failed? that Mr. Sweet was really gone? He had never gone before. But when I looked up at my parents I saw that they were holding back tears. They had loved him dearly. He was like a piece of rare and delicate china which was always being saved from breaking and which finally fell. I looked long at the old face, the wrinkled forehead, the red lips, the hands that still reached out to me. Soon I felt my father pushing something cool into my hands. It was Mr. Sweet's guitar. He had asked them months before to give it to me, he had known that even if I came next time he would not be able to respond in the old way. He did not want me to feel that my trip had been for nothing.

The old guitar! I plucked the strings, hummed "Sweet Georgia Brown." The magic of Mr. Sweet lingered still in the cool steel box. Through the window I could catch the fragrant delicate scent of tender yellow roses. The man on the high old-fashioned bed with the quilt coverlet and the flowing white beard had been my first love.

from A BOY THIRTEEN (by Jerry Irish, b. 1936)
Jeff Irish (b. 1960)

Lee Irish died in 1972 at the age of thirteen. He and his family had been traveling through Europe when he came down with acute meningitis as they toured Rome. This book is the story of his death and an account of how his parents and younger brother responded to his death. Having had another son die at the age of five, Jerry and Pat Irish have significant thoughts to share about the meaning of life and death and children. At one point in the book they include a poem written by Lee's brother Jeff a few days after Lee died. It is reproduced as he typed it on a borrowed typewriter.

A BOY THIRTEEN

He had red hair,
Was thin and tall,
One could never eat as much as he,
He hiked in the sierras,
Went back-packing and even planned
a trip for the family,
Even got me to join Boy Scouts,
Always wanted me to backpack with him,
We went to Germany,
He and I to German schools and learned German,
     went
Then it came time for our trip to Rome,
By train,
He and I couldnt wait to come back to
Germany and go sledding,
We passed through the Alps on the way
to Rome,
I looked up to him,
I twelve and HE "A BOY THIRTEEN",
He was five feet and nine inches tall,
I remember very well looking up and there
HE was with the train window down,His head
a little ways out §§§ § with the wind blowing
§ § his red hair as he watched the Alps
passing by,
He was my brother,
My only § brother,
——— §

One I could play Baseball with,
Someone I could talk to,
In Germany he had bought a camera,
A single lense reflex,
HE had alot of new things going on,
Then on Feb.6 He died.
He my only brother the one I planned to
backpack with,the guy I wanted to sled with,
the person I looked up to,the boy that
played baseball with me,the guy with a
new camera,my brother who I could talk to,the
one who could eat as no one else,my brother that
was five feet and nine inches tall,tall and thin with
red hair "THE BOY THAT WAS THIRTEEN",
He died because he happened to breath in some bacteria
that probably can only be seen under some special microscope,
I guess all I can say is §§§§ I loved him and needed him and that
I dont understand.

6. DEATH BY KILLING

MOST people die from diseases or accidents, but many people die for the simple reason that someone else kills them. Wars . . . murders . . . revolutions . . . executions . . . concentration camps . . . assassinations . . . euthanasia—the forms of death by killing are quite varied, but obviously present in every historical period and in every society.

To cite but one example, consider the United States at the beginning of the 1980s. Against a historical background of two world wars, two other wars in two decades, the assassinations of a president and two other leading political figures in the 1960s, urban riots, and numerous instances of racial violence, the United States left the decade of the 1970s, where death by killing took an almost endless number of forms: the war in Indochina . . . Kent State . . . Attica . . . the Mayaguez . . . an average of 20,000 homicides per year . . . Charles Manson . . . the "Son of Sam" murders . . . two presidential assassination attempts . . . Jim Jones . . . terrorism . . . SWAT teams . . . the execution of Gary Gilmore. . . . The list, unfortunately, could go on at considerably greater length.

As with other aspects of death, literature depicts the harsh realities of death by killing. In ancient Greece, for instance, three of the great tragedians in history used death by killing as the focal point of major dramas. In *Agamemnon* Aeschylus (c.525–456 B.C.) used murder and revenge as the theme of the play. Atreus, the father of Agamemnon, had earlier killed the children of Thyestes and served parts of their dead bodies to their father at a banquet. Agamemnon, the King of Argos, in turn killed his own daughter to appease the goddess Artemis. Then, as the climactic point of the play, Agamemnon, having returned victoriously from Troy with the slave Cassandra, was murdered by his wife Clytemnestra, who had planned the murder with her lover. Thus the entire play revolves around deaths by killing.

In *Oedipus the King* Sophocles (c.496–406 B.C.) developed the plot around the killing of Laius, the King of Thebes. Oedipus, unknowingly the son of Laius and Jocasta, met Laius at a lonely crossroads, became engaged in a quarrel and, not recognizing Laius, killed him. He later became King of Thebes himself, married Jocasta, and produced children. The play revolves around Oedipus' curse of Laius' murderer, his horrified discovery that he himself is the murderer, and the tragic consequences that discovery has for him.

In *Medea* Euripides (c.480–406 B.C.) used revenge as the play's theme, and murder as the instrument of revenge. Having earlier killed her own brother to help her husband, Jason, Medea was emotionally crushed when Jason turned her aside for a new wife. In planning her revenge Medea considered various methods of killing (fire, sword, and poison) which might be used. She finally gained revenge by killing Jason's new wife with poisoned garments and her own two sons with a sword, thus leaving Jason childless and bereaved.

More than two thousand years later and half a continent removed, another great tragedian also used death by killing as a dramatic device. For William Shakespeare (1564–1616), war, murder, and suicide are regularly repeated features of human existence which can and should be reflected in dramatic literature. Therefore, to mention several examples, he puts *Henry IV*, Part One in the context of war; tells us that Richard II, the previous king, was murdered; and, in the climactic scene of the play, has Prince Hal kill his rival Hotspur in battle. *Julius Caesar* focuses on the plot by Brutus and Cassius to kill Caesar, describes the brutal stabbing of Caesar by the band of conspirators, and then relates how even in death Caesar gains revenge through the loyalty of Mark Antony and the self-inflicted death of Brutus. *Othello* is a story of jealousy and killing in which Othello, having been falsely convinced by Iago that his wife, Desdemona, has been unfaithful, becomes intensely jealous and ends up smothering her to death; upon discovering his tragic mistake in killing a faithful wife, he kills himself. And in *Macbeth* Shakespeare weaves together a plot in which Macbeth kills Duncan, king of Scotland; tries to cover up the deed and protect his newly gained political power through the murders of the king's attendants, Banquo, and Macduff's wife and children; and is himself finally killed in battle by Macduff.

In the twentieth century a new type of literature has emerged which focuses on death by killing. In contrast to the Greek and Shakespearean tragedies, however, there is nothing fictional in the literature which has arisen out of the German and Soviet concentration camp experiences. Written by persons who survived these horrible places of torture and death, the concentration camp literature is starkly vivid and brutally realistic in its depiction of the sadistic savagery which ruled the camps and brought about the deaths of six million persons. And sometimes lost in the midst of stomach-wrenching accounts of vicious dogs, starvation, naked bodies, beatings, rapes, filth, exhaustion, disease, excrement, lice, nausea, endless roll-calls, mass shootings, and gas chambers is the frightening fact that behind this apparently disordered insanity was a ruthless logic: when human beings are forced to endure endless atrocities with no possibility of escape, they seem to become less than human and can be killed with no more thought than is given to killing any loathsome animal.

Several of the selections in this section focus on death by killing in the context of war. The *Iliad*, a generally savage portrayal of the Trojan War, provides an intricately detailed account of Hector's death at the hands of Achilles. Thomas Hardy's "The Man He Killed" is a poetical description of a curious phenomenon: individuals who might well have been friends in other times and circumstances often end up trying to kill each other in a war. Ambrose Bierce's "An Occurrence at Owl Creek Bridge" provides a graphic and imaginative account of a Confederate spy's execution during the American Civil War. "Dulce et Decorum Est," by Wilfred Owen, is a moving account of the insanity of war whose appeal is intensified through the realization that this promising young British poet was killed during the first World War. Reska Weiss, in her *Journey Through Hell*, provides an unforgettable account of the sadistic, systematic killing of Jews in German concentration camps during the second World War. And the climactic event of that war, the dropping of the atomic bomb on two Japanese cities, is portrayed in terms of its impact on individuals in *Hiroshima*, by the Pulitzer Prize-winning novelist John Hersey.

Other selections represent a literary collage whose connecting theme is death by killing. *Hamlet* provides an outstanding example of Shakespeare's frequent portrayal of death by killing in that by the end of the concluding duel between Hamlet and Laertes, every important character in the play has been killed except for Horatio and Fortinbras.

Dostoevsky's *Crime and Punishment*, representative of several great Russian novels, is a complex portrayal of a psychotic human mind and the murder first conceived in that mind. Dudley Randall, a black American poet, addresses the subject of killing in a medical setting in his poem "To The Mercy Killers." Edwin Brock, in his "Five Ways to Kill a Man," suggests satirically that the easiest way to kill a man is simply to have him live in the middle of the twentieth century. The last two selections provide vivid accounts of actual killings in recent American history. Truman Capote's *In Cold Blood* describes a multiple murder and the subsequent hanging of the two murderers in Kansas; and Edward Francisco's "Lilith's Child" is a heart-rending poetical description of a child who was beaten to death in Tennessee after having been denied food and water for days.

from the ILIAD
Homer (c.850 B.C.)

The *Iliad* and its companion piece the *Odyssey* represent the oldest extant works of Western literature. Based on the legend of the Trojan War (twelfth century B.C.), they have traditionally been attributed to a Greek poet named Homer. One of the major scenes of the *Iliad* (Book XXII) involves a battle between Achilles, son of Peleus and the central figure of the epic, and Hector, the commander of the Trojan armies. Having been humiliated earlier in the war and having had his best friend killed by the Trojans, Achilles is determined to kill Hector. The Trojan commander, in turn, is determined either to kill Achilles or die gloriously in front of Troy. The battle is viewed by the Greek gods.

While Hector stood engrossed in this inward debate, Achilles drew near him, looking like the god of War in his flashing helmet, girt for battle. Over his right shoulder he brandished the formidable ashen spear of Pelion, and the bronze on his body glowed like a blazing fire or the rising sun. Hector looked up, saw him, and began to tremble. He no longer had the heart to stand his ground; he left the gate, and ran away in terror. But the son of Peleus, counting on his speed, was after him in a flash. Light as a mountain hawk, the fastest thing on wings, when he swoops in chase of a timid dove, and shrieking close behind his quarry, darts at her time and again in his eagerness to make his kill, Achilles started off in hot pursuit; and like the dove flying before her enemy, Hector fled before him under the walls of Troy, fast as his feet would go. Passing the lookout and the windswept fig-tree and keeping some way from the wall, they sped along the cart-track, and so came to the two lovely springs that are the sources of Scamander's eddying stream. In one of these the water comes up hot; steam rises from it and hangs about like smoke above a blazing fire. But the other, even in summer, gushes up as cold as hail or freezing snow or water that has turned to ice. Close beside them, wide and beautiful, stand the troughs of stone where the wives and lovely daughters of the Trojans used to wash their glossy clothes in the peaceful days before the Achaeans came. Here the chase went by, Hector in front and Achilles after him—a good man, but with one far better at his heels. And the pace was furious. This was no ordinary race, with a sacrificial beast or a leather shield as prize. They were competing for the life of horse-taming Hector; and the pair of them circled thrice round Priam's town with flying feet, like powerful race-horses sweeping round the turning-post, all out for the splendid prize of a tripod or a woman offered at a warrior's funeral games.

They were watched by all the gods—in silence, till the Father of men and gods turned to the others with a sigh and said: "I have a warm place in my heart for this man who is being chased before my eyes round the walls of Troy. I grieve for Hector. He has burnt the thighs of many oxen in my honor, both on the rugged heights of Ida and in the lofty citadel of Troy. But now the great Achilles is pursuing him at full speed round the city of Priam. Consider, gods, and help me to decide whether we shall save his life or let a good man fall this very day to Achilles son of Peleus."

"Father!" exclaimed Athene of the Flashing Eyes. "What are you saying? Are you, the Lord of the Bright Lightning and the Black Cloud, proposing to reprieve a mortal man, whose doom has long been settled, from the pains of death? Do as you please; but do not expect the rest of us to applaud."

"Be reassured, Lady of Trito and dear Child of mine," said Zeus the Cloud-compeller. "I did not really mean to spare him. You can count on my goodwill. Act as you see fit, and act at once." With which encouragement from Zeus, Athene, who had been itching to play her part, sped down from the peaks of Olympus.

Meanwhile Achilles of the nimble feet continued his relentless chase of Hector. As a hound who has started a fawn from its mountain lair pursues it through the coombs and glades, and even when it takes cover in a thicket, runs on, picks up the scent and finds his quarry, the swift Achilles was not to be thrown off the scent by any trick of Hector's. More than once Hector made a dash for the Dardanian Gates, hoping as he slipped along under the high walls to be saved from his pursuer by the archery of those above; but Achilles, keeping always to the inner course, intercepted him every time and headed him off towards the open country. And yet he could not catch him up, just as Hector could not shake Achilles off. It was like a chase in a nightmare, when no one, pursuer or pursued, can move a limb.

You may ask, how could Hector have escaped when Death was so close at his heels? He did so only through the final intervention of Apollo, who came to him for the last time, renewed his strength and gave him speed of foot. Moreover, Achilles had been signaling to his men by movements of his head that they were not to shoot at the quarry, for fear that he might be forestalled and one of them might win renown by striking Hector with an arrow. However, when they reached the Springs for the fourth time, the Father held out his golden scales, and putting sentence of death in either pan, on one side for Achilles, on the other for horse-taming Hector, he raised the balance by the middle of the beam. The beam came down on Hector's side, spelling his doom. He was a dead man. Phoebus Apollo deserted him; and Athene, goddess of the Flashing Eyes, went up to Achilles and spoke momentous words. "Illustrious Achilles, darling of Zeus," she said, "our chance has come to go back to the ships with a glorious victory for Achaean arms. Hector will fight to the bitter end, but you and I are going to kill him. There is no escape for him now, however much the Archer-King Apollo may exert himself and grovel at the feet of his Father, aegis-bearing Zeus. Stay still now and recover your breath, while I go to Hector and persuade him to fight you."

Achilles was well pleased and did as she told him. He stood there leaning on his bronze-bladed spear, while Athene went across from him to Hector and accosted him, borrowing for her purpose the appearance and the tireless voice of Deiphobus. "My dear brother," she said to Hector, "the swift Achilles must have worn you out, chasing you at that speed round the city. Let us make a stand and face him here together."

"Deiphobus," said the great Hector of the flashing helmet, "I have always loved you far the best of all the brothers Hecabe and Priam gave me. But from now on I shall think even better of you, since you had the courage, when you saw my plight, to come outside the walls and help me, while all the rest stayed in the town."

"Dear brother," said Athene of the Flashing Eyes, "I can assure you that our father and lady mother begged and implored me to stay where I was, one after the other. My men were there and did the same—they were all in such terror of Achilles. But I was tormented by anxiety on your behalf. Let us attack him boldly and not be niggardly with spears. We shall soon find out whether Achilles is to kill the pair of us and go off with our bloodstained armor to the hollow ships, or himself be conquered by your spear." Athene's ruse succeeded and she led him forward. Hector and Achilles met.

Great Hector of the flashing helmet spoke first: "My lord Achilles, I have been chased by you three times round the great city of Priam without daring to stop and let you come near. But now I am going to run away no longer. I have made up my mind to fight you man to man and kill you or be killed. But first let us make a bargain, you with your gods for witness, I with mine—no compact could have better guarantors. If Zeus allows me to endure, and I kill you, I undertake to do no outrage to your body that custom does not sanction. All I shall do, Achilles, is to strip you of your splendid armor. Then I will give up your corpse to the Achaeans. Will you do the same for me?"

Achilles of the nimble feet looked at him grimly and replied: "Hector, you must be mad to talk to me about a pact. Lions do not come to terms with men, nor does the wolf see eye to eye with the lamb—they are enemies to the end. It is the same with you and me. Friendship between us is impossible, and there will be no truce of any kind till one of us has fallen and glutted the stubborn god of battles with his blood. So summon any courage you may have. This is the time to show your spearmanship and daring. Not that anything is going to save you now, when Pallas Athene is waiting to fell you with my spear. This moment you are going to pay the full price for all you made me suffer when your lance mowed down my friends."

With this Achilles poised and hurled his long-shadowed spear. But illustrious Hector was looking out and managed to avoid it. He crouched, with his eye on the weapon; and it flew over his head and stuck in the ground. But Pallas Athene snatched it up and brought it back to Achilles.

Hector the great captain, who had not seen this move, called across to the peerless son of Peleus: "A miss for the god-like Achilles! It seems that Zeus gave you the wrong date for my death! You were too cocksure. But then you're so glib, so clever with your tongue—trying to frighten me and drain me of my strength. Nevertheless, you will not make me run, or catch me in the back with your spear. Drive it through my breast as I charge—if you get the chance. But first you will have to dodge this one of mine. And Heaven grant that all its bronze may be buried in your flesh! This war would be an easier business for the Trojans if you, their greatest scourge, were dead."

With that he swung up his long-shadowed spear and cast. And sure enough he hit the center of Achilles' shield, but his spear rebounded from it. Hector was angry at having made so fine a throw for nothing, and he stood there discomfited, for he had no second lance. He shouted aloud to Deiphobus of the white shield, asking him for a long spear. But Deiphobus was nowhere near him; and Hector, realizing what had happened, cried: "Alas! So the gods did beckon me to my death! I thought the good Deiphobus was at my side; but he is in the town, and Athene has fooled me. Death is no longer far away; he is staring me in the face and there is no escaping him. Zeus and his Archer Son must long have been resolved on this, for all their goodwill and the help they gave me. So now I meet my doom. Let me at least sell my life dearly and have a not inglorious end, after some feat of arms that shall come to the ears of generations still unborn."

Hector had a sharp, long and weighty sword hanging down at his side. He drew this now, braced himself, and swooped like a high-flying eagle that drops to earth through the black clouds to pounce on a tender lamb or a crouching hare. Thus Hector charged, brandishing his sharp sword. Achilles sprang to meet him, inflamed with savage passion. He kept his front covered with his decorated shield; his glittering helmet with its four plates swayed as he moved his head and made the splendid golden plumes that Hephaestus had lavished on the crest dance round the top; and bright as the loveliest jewel in the sky, the Evening Star when he comes out at nightfall with the rest, the sharp point scintillated on the spear he balanced in his right hand, intent on killing Hector, and searching him for the likeliest place to reach his flesh.

Achilles saw that Hector's body was completely covered by the fine bronze armor he had taken from the great Patroclus when he killed him, except for an opening at the gullet where the collar bones lead over from the shoulders to the neck, the easiest place to kill a man. As Hector charged him, Prince Achilles drove at this spot with his lance; and the point went right through the tender flesh of Hector's neck, though the heavy bronze head did not cut his windpipe, and left him able to address his conqueror. Hector came down in the dust and the great Achilles triumphed over him. "Hector," he said, "no doubt you fancied as you stripped Patroclus that you would be safe. You never thought of me: I was too far away. You were a fool. Down by the hollow ships there was a man far better than Patroclus in reserve, the man who has brought you low. So now the dogs and birds of prey are going to maul and mangle you, while we Achaeans hold Patroclus' funeral."

"I beseech you," said Hector of the glittering helmet in a failing voice, "by your knees, by your own life and by your parents, not to throw my body to the dogs at the Achaean ships, but to take a ransom for me. My father and my lady mother will pay you bronze and gold in plenty. Give up my body to be taken home, so that the Trojans and their wives may honor me in death with the ritual of fire."

The swift Achilles scowled at him. "You cur," he said, "don't talk to me of knees or name my parents in your prayers. I only wish that I could summon up the appetite to carve and eat you raw myself, for what you have done to me. But this at least is certain, that nobody is going to keep the dogs from you, not even if the Trojans bring here and weigh out a ransom ten or twenty times your worth, and promise more besides; not if Dardanian Priam tells them to pay your weight in gold—not even so shall your lady mother lay you on a bier to mourn the son she bore, but the dogs and birds of prey shall eat you up."

Hector of the flashing helmet spoke to him once more at the point of death. "How well I know you and can read your mind!" he said. "Your heart is hard as iron—I have been wasting my breath. Nevertheless, pause before you act, in case the angry gods remember how you treated me, when your turn comes and you are brought down at the Scaean Gate in all your glory by Paris and Apollo."

Death cut Hector short and his disembodied soul took wing for the House of Hades, bewailing its lot and the youth and manhood that it left. But Prince Achilles spoke to him again though he was gone. "Die!" he said. "As for my own death, let it come when Zeus and the other deathless gods decide."

Then he withdrew his bronze spear from the corpse and laid it down. As he removed the bloodstained arms from Hector's shoulders, other Achaean warriors came running up and gathered round. They gazed in wonder at the size and marvelous good looks of Hector. And not a man of all who had collected there left him without a wound. As each went in and struck the corpse, he looked at his friends, and the jest went round: "Hector is easier to handle now than when he set the ships on fire."

After stripping Hector, the swift and excellent Achilles stood up and made a speech to the Achaeans. "My friends," he said, "Captains and Counselors of the Argives; now that the gods have let us get the better of this man, who did more damage than all the rest together, let us make an armed reconnaissance round the city and find out what the Trojans mean to do next, whether they will abandon their fortress now that their champion has fallen, or make up their minds to hold it without Hector's help. But what am I saying? How can I think of anything but the dead man who is lying by my ships unburied and unwept—Patroclus, whom I shall never forget as long as I am still among the living and can walk the earth, my own dear comrade, whom I shall remember even though the dead forget their dead, even in Hades' Halls? So come now, soldiers of Achaea, let us go back to the hollow ships carrying this corpse and singing a song of triumph: "We have won great glory. We have killed the noble Hector, who was treated like a god in Troy.'"

The next thing that Achilles did was to subject the fallen prince to shameful outrage. He slit the tendons at the back of both his feet from heel to ankle, inserted leather straps, and made them fast to his chariot, leaving the head to drag. Then he lifted the famous armor into his car, got in himself, and with a touch of his whip started the horses, who flew off with a will. Dragged behind him, Hector raised a cloud of dust, his black locks streamed on either side, and dust fell thick upon his head, so comely once, which Zeus now let his enemies defile on his own native soil.

from HAMLET (v, 2)
William Shakespeare (1564–1616)

This selection is from the final scene of the play. Laertes and Claudius, king of Denmark, have conspired to bring about Hamlet's death, Laertes to avenge the death of his father, Polonius, and Claudius to cover up his own murder of Hamlet's father. They agree to stage a duel between Hamlet and Laertes in which Laertes will have a poisoned tip on his sword. Should Laertes fail to kill Hamlet, Claudius is prepared to offer Hamlet a poisoned drink. Hamlet's mother, the queen, and Horatio, his best friend, are present at the duel.

HAMLET: Give me your pardon, sir. I have done you wrong,
But pardon 't, as you are a gentleman.
This presence knows, and you must needs have heard,
How I am punish'd with a sore distraction.
What I have done
That might your nature, honour, and exception
Roughly awake, I here proclaim was madness.
Was 't Hamlet wrong'd Laertes? Never Hamlet!
If Hamlet from himself be ta'en away,
And when he's not himself does wrong Laertes,
Then Hamlet does it not, Hamlet denies it.
Who does it, then? His madness. If 't be so,
Hamlet is of the faction that is wrong'd;
His madness is poor Hamlet's enemy.
Sir, in this audience,
Let my disclaiming from a purpos'd evil
Free me so far in your most generous thoughts,
That I have shot my arrow o'er the house
And hurt my brother.
LAERTES: I am satisfied in nature,
Whose motive, in this case, should stir me most
To my revenge; but in my terms of honour
I stand aloof, and will no reconcilement,

Till by some elder masters of known honour
I have a voice and precedent of peace,
To keep my name ungor'd. But till that time,
I do receive your offer'd love like love,
And will not wrong it.

HAMLET: I embrace it freely,
And will this brother's wager frankly play.
Give us the foils.

LAERTES: Come, one for me.

HAMLET: I'll be your foil, Laertes; in mine ignorance
Your skill shall, like a star i' th' darkest night,
Stick fiery off indeed.

LAERTES: You mock me, sir.

HAMLET: No, by this hand.

KING: Give them the foils, young Osric. Cousin Hamlet,
You know the wager?

HAMLET: Very well, my lord.
Your Grace hath laid the odds o' th' weaker side.

KING: I do not fear it, I have seen you both;
But since he is better'd, we have therefore odds.

LAERTES: This is too heavy; let me see another.

HAMLET: This likes me well. These foils have all a length? [*They prepare to fence.*]

OSRIC: Ay, my good lord.

KING: Set me the stoups of wine upon that table.
If Hamlet give the first or second hit,
Or quit in answer of the third exchange,
Let all the battlements their ordnance fire.
The King shall drink to Hamlet's better breath,
And in the cup an union shall he throw,
Richer than that which four successive kings
In Denmark's crown have worn. Give me the cups,
And let the kettle to the trumpet speak,
The trumpet to the cannoneer without,
The cannons to the heavens, the heaven to earth,
"Now the King drinks to Hamlet." Come, begin;
And you, the judges, bear a wary eye. [*Trumpets sound.*]

HAMLET: Come on, sir.

LAERTES: Come, my lord. [*They fence.*]

HAMLET: One.

LAERTES: No.

HAMLET: Judgement.

OSRIC: A hit, a very palpable hit.

LAERTES: Well; again.

KING: Stay, give me drink. Hamlet, this pearl is thine;
Here's to thy health! Give him the cup.
   [*Trumpets sound, and shot goes off within.*]

HAMLET: I'll play this bout first; set it by a while.
Come.   [*They play.*] Another hit; what say you?

LAERTES: A touch, a touch, I do confess 't.

KING: Our son shall win.

QUEEN: He's fat, and scant of breath.
Here, Hamlet, take my napkin, rub thy brows.
The Queen carouses to thy fortune, Hamlet.

HAMLET: Good madam!

KING: Gertrude, do not drink.

QUEEN: I will, my lord; I pray you, pardon me.

KING: [*Aside.*] It is the poison'd cup; it is too late.

HAMLET: I dare not drink yet, madam; by and by.

QUEEN: Come, let me wipe thy face.

LAERTES: My lord, I'll hit him now.

KING: I do not think 't.

LAERTES: [*Aside.*] And yet it is almost against my conscience.

HAMLET: Come, for the third, Laertes; you but dally.
I pray you, pass with your best violence.
I am afeard you make a wanton of me.

LAERTES: Say you so? Come on. [*They fence.*]

OSRIC: Nothing, neither way.

LAERTES: Have at you now!
   [*Laertes wounds Hamlet; then in scuffling, they change rapiers.*]

KING: Part them; they are incens'd.

HAMLET: Nay, come, again.
   [*Hamlet wounds Laertes. The Queen falls.*]

OSRIC: Look to the Queen there! Ho!

HORATIO: They bleed on both sides. How is 't, my lord!

OSRIC: How is 't, Laertes?

LAERTES: Why, as a woodcock to mine own springe, Osric;
I am justly kill'd with mine own treachery.

HAMLET: How does the Queen?

KING: She swounds to see them bleed.

QUEEN: No, no, the drink, the drink,—O my dear Hamlet,—
The drink, the drink! I am poison'd. [*Dies.*]

HAMLET: O villainy! Ho! let the door be lock'd:
Treachery! Seek it out.

LAERTES: It is here, Hamlet. Hamlet, thou art slain.
No med'cine in the world can do thee good;
In thee there is not half an hour of life;
The treacherous instrument is in thy hand,
Unbated and envenom'd: the foul practice
Hath turn'd itself on me; lo, here I lie,
Never to rise again. Thy mother's poison'd.
I can no more:—the King, the King's to blame.

HAMLET: The point envenom'd too!
Then, venom, to thy work. [*Wounds the King.*]

ALL: Treason! treason!

KING: O, yet defend me, friends; I am but hurt.

HAMLET: Here, thou incestuous, murd'rous, damned Dane,
Drink off this potion! Is thy union here?
Follow my mother! [*King dies.*]

LAERTES: He is justly serv'd;
It is a poison temper'd by himself.
Exchange forgiveness with me, noble Hamlet;
Mine and my father's death come not upon thee,
Nor thine on me! [*Dies.*]

HAMLET: Heaven make thee free of it! I follow thee.
I am dead, Horatio. Wretched queen, adieu!
You that look pale and tremble at this chance,
That are but mutes or audience to this act,
Had I but time—as this fell sergeant, Death,
Is strict in his arrest—O, I could tell you—
But let it be. Horatio, I am dead;
Thou livest; report me and my cause aright
To the unsatisfied.

HORATIO: Never believe it:
  I am more an antique Roman than a Dane;
  Here's yet some liquor left.
HAMLET: As thou 'rt a man,
  Give me the cup; let go, by heaven, I'll have 't!
  O God, Horatio, what a wounded name,
  Things standing thus unknown, shall live behind me!
  If thou didst ever hold me in thy heart,
  Absent thee from felicity a while
  And in this harsh world draw thy breath in pain
  To tell my story. [*March afar off, and shot within.*]
  What warlike noise is this?
OSRIC: Young Fortinbras, with conquest come from Poland,
  To th' ambassadors of England gives
  This warlike volley.
HAMLET: O, I die, Horatio;
  The potent poison quite o'er-crows my spirit:
  I cannot live to hear the news from England,
  But I do prophesy th' election lights
  On Fortinbras; he has my dying voice.
  So tell him, with th' occurrents, more and less,
  Which have solicited—the rest is silence. [*Dies.*]
HORATIO: Now cracks a noble heart. Good-night, sweet prince,
  And flights of angels sing thee to thy rest!

from CRIME AND PUNISHMENT
Feodor Dostoevsky (1821–1881)

As one of the great Russian novelists of the nineteenth century, Dostoevsky often wrote complex psychological studies of human motivation and behavior. In this novel the principal character is a young student named Raskolnikov. Poor, lonely, and morose, Raskolnikov borrowed money from an old woman whom he despised. He then planned and rehearsed the crime which is the focal point of the novel. That crime, described in the following selection, is marked by confusion, impulse, blundering mistakes, panic, and the unplanned murder of the old woman's sister. The double murder takes place in the old moneylender's apartment.

As before, the door opened the merest crack, and again two sharp and mistrustful eyes peered at him from the darkness. Then Raskolnikov lost his head and made what might have been a serious mistake.

Apprehensive that the old woman might be alarmed at their being alone, and without any hope that his appearance would reassure her, he took hold of the door and pulled it towards him, so that she should not be tempted to lock herself in again. Although she did not pull the door shut again at this, she did not relinquish the handle, so that he almost pulled her out on the stairs. When he saw that she was standing across the doorway in such a way that he could not pass, he advanced straight upon her, and she stood aside startled. She seemed to be trying to say something but finding it impossible, and she kept her eyes fixed on him.

"Good evening, Alëna Ivanovna," he began, as easily as possible, but his voice refused to obey him, and was broken and trembling, "I have . . . brought you . . . something . . . but hadn't we better come in here . . . to the light? . . ." And without waiting for an invitation, he passed her and went into the room. The old woman hastened after him; her tongue seemed to have been loosened.

"Good Lord! What are you doing? . . . Who are you? What do you want?"

"Excuse me, Alëna Ivanovna . . . You know me . . . Raskolnikov . . . See, I have brought the pledge I promised the other day," and he held it out to her.

The old woman threw a glance at it, but then immediately fixed her eyes on those of her uninvited guest. She looked at him attentively, ill-naturedly, and mistrustfully. A minute or so went by; he even thought he could see a glint of derision in her eyes, as if she had guessed everything. He felt that he was losing his nerve and was frightened, so frightened that he thought if she went on looking at him like that, without a word, for even half a minute longer, he would turn tail and run away.

"Why are you looking at me like that, as though you didn't recognize me?" he burst out angrily. "Do you want it, or don't you? I can take it somewhere else; it makes no difference to me."

He had not intended to say this, but it seemed to come of its own accord.

The old woman collected herself, and her visitor's resolute tone seemed to lull her mistrust.

"Why be so hasty, my friend? . . . What is it?" she asked, looking at the packet.

"A silver cigarette case; surely I told you that last time?"

She stretched out her hand.

"But what makes you so pale? And your hands are trembling. Are you ill or something?"

"Fever," he answered abruptly. "You can't help being pale . . . when you haven't anything to eat," he added, hardly able to articulate his words. His strength was failing again. But apparently the answer was plausible enough; the old woman took the packet.

"What is it?" she asked, weighing it in her hand and once again fixing her eyes on Raskolnikov.

"A thing . . . a cigarette-case . . . silver . . . look at it."

"It doesn't feel like silver. Lord, what a knot!" Trying to undo the string she turned for light towards the window (all her windows were closed, in spite of the oppressive heat), moved away from him and stood with her back to him. He unbuttoned his coat and freed the ax from the loop, but still kept it concealed, supporting it with his right hand under the garment. His arms seemed to have no strength in them; he felt them growing more and more numb and stiff with every moment. He was afraid of letting the ax slip and fall . . . His head was whirling.

"Why is it all wrapped up like this?" exclaimed the woman sharply, and turned towards him.

There was not a moment to lose. He pulled the ax out, swung it up with both hands, hardly conscious of what he was doing, and almost mechanically, without putting any force behind it, let the butt-end fall on her head. His strength seemed to have deserted him, but as soon as the ax descended it all returned to him.

The old woman was, as usual, bare-headed. Her thin fair hair, just turning grey, and thick with grease, was plaited into a rat's tail and fastened into a knot above her nape with a fragment of horn comb. Because she was so short the ax struck her full on the crown of the head. She cried out, but very feebly, and sank in a heap on the floor, still with enough strength left to raise both hands to her head. One of them still held the "pledge." Then he struck her again and yet again, with all his strength, always with the blunt side of the ax, and always on the crown of the head. Blood poured out as if from an overturned glass and the body toppled over on its back. He stepped away as it fell, and then stooped to see the face: she was dead. Her wide-open eyes looked ready to start out of their sockets, her forehead was wrinkled and her whole face convulsively distorted.

. . . .

A footstep sounded in the room where the old woman lay. He stopped and remained motionless as the dead. But all was still; he must have imagined it. The he distinctly heard a faint cry, or perhaps rather a feeble interrupted groaning, then dead silence again for a minute or two. He waited, crouching by the trunk, hardly daring to breathe; then he sprang up, seized the ax, and ran out of the room.

There in the middle of the floor, with a big bundle in her arms, stood Lizaveta, as white as a sheet, gazing in frozen horror at her murdered sister and apparently without the strength to cry out. When she saw him run in, she trembled like a leaf and her face twitched spasmodically; she raised her hand as if to cover her mouth, but no scream came and she backed slowly away from him towards the corner, with her eyes on him in a fixed stare, but still without a sound, as though she had no breath left to cry out. He flung himself forward with the ax; her lips writhed pitifully, like those of a young child when it is just beginning to be frightened and stands ready to scream, with its eyes fixed on the object of its fear. The wretched Lizaveta was so simple, brow-beaten, and utterly terrified that she did not even put up her arms to protect her face, natural and almost inevitable as the gesture would have been at this moment when the ax was brandished immediately above it. She only raised her free left hand a little and slowly stretched it out towards him as though she were trying to push him away. The blow fell on her skull, splitting it open from the top of the forehead almost to the crown of the head, and felling her instantly. Raskolnikov, completely beside himself, snatched up her bundle, threw it down again, and ran to the entrance.

. . . .

He stood still, staring, unable to believe his eyes; the door, the outer door leading to the staircase, the door at which he had rung a short time ago, and by which he had entered, was at least a hand's-breadth open; all this time it had been like that, neither locked nor bolted, all the time! The old woman had not locked it behind him, perhaps by way of precaution. But, good God, he had seen Lizaveta after that! And how could he have failed to realize that she had come from outside, and could certainly not have come through the wall?

He flung himself at the door and put up the bolt.

"But no, that's not right either! I must go, I must go „ . ."

He lifted the bolt clear, opened the door, and stood listening on the landing.

THE MAN HE KILLED
Thomas Hardy (1840–1928)

Had he and I but met
By some old ancient inn,
We should have set us down to wet
Right many a nipperkin!

But ranged as infantry,
And staring face to face,
I shot at him as he at me,
And killed him in his place.

I shot him dead because—
Because he was my foe,
Just so: my foe of course he was;
That's clear enough; although

He thought he'd 'list, perhaps,
Off-hand like—just as I;
Was out of work, had sold his traps—
No other reason why.

Yes; quaint and curious war is!
You shoot a fellow down
You'd treat if met where any bar is,
Or help to half-a-crown.

AN OCCURRENCE AT OWL CREEK BRIDGE
Ambrose Bierce (1842–1913?)

Born in Ohio, Bierce was nineteen when he joined the 9th Indiana Infantry at the beginning of the Civil War. He saw action on a dozen fronts, was severely wounded, and was a prisoner of war briefly in Alabama. His later literary works are filled with the realities of war: the pain, the broken lives, the terrible deaths. In this short story he describes the ability of the mind to "see" hours of imagined action in the instant of time it takes for a man to die by hanging. Bierce disappeared in Mexico in 1913, leaving the circumstances and timing of his death a mystery.

I

A man stood upon a railroad bridge in northern Alabama, looking down into the swift water twenty feet below. The man's hands were behind his back, the wrists bound with a cord. A rope closely encircled his neck. It was attached to a stout cross-timber above his head and the slack fell to the level of his knees. Some loose boards laid upon the sleepers supporting the metals of the railway supplied a footing for him and his executioners—two private soldiers of the Federal army, directed by a sergeant who in civil life may have been a deputy sheriff. At a short remove upon the same temporary platform was an officer in the uniform of his rank, armed. He was a captain. A sentinel at each end of the bridge stood with his rifle in the position known as "support," that is to say, vertical in front of the left shoulder, the hammer resting on the forearm thrown straight across the chest—a formal and unnatural position, enforcing an errect carriage of the body. It did not appear to be the duty of these two men to know what was occurring at the center of the bridge; they merely blockaded the two ends of the foot planking that traversed it.

Beyond one of the sentinels nobody was in sight; the railroad ran straight away into a forest for a hundred yards, then curving, was lost to view. Doubtless there was an outpost farther along. The other bank of the stream was open ground—a gentle acclivity topped with a stockade of vertical tree trunks, loopholed for rifles, with a single embrasure through which protruded the muzzle of a brass cannon commanding the bridge. Midway of the slope between the bridge and fort were the spectators—a single company of infantry in line, at "parade rest," the butts of the rifles on the ground, the barrels inclining slightly backward against the right shoulder, the hands crossed upon the stock. A lieutenant stood at the right of the line, the point of his sword upon the ground, his left hand resting upon his right. Excepting the group of four at the center of the bridge, not a man moved. The company faced the bridge, staring stonily, motionless. The sentinels, facing the banks of the stream, might have been statues to adorn the bridge. The captain stood with folded arms, silent, observing the work of his subordinates, but making no sign. Death is a dignitary who when he comes announced is to be received with formal manifestations of respect, even by those most familiar with him. In the code of military etiquette silence and fixity are forms of deference.

The man who was engaged in being hanged was apparently about thirty-five years of age. He was a civilian, if one might judge from his habit, which was that of a planter. His features were good—a straight nose, firm mouth, broad forehead, from which his long, dark hair was combed straight back, falling behind his ears to the collar of his well-fitting frock-coat. He wore a mustache and pointed beard, but no whiskers; his eyes were large and dark gray, and had a kindly expression which one would hardly have expected in one whose neck was in the hemp. Evidently this was no vulgar assassin. The liberal military code makes provision for hanging many kinds of persons, and gentlemen are not excluded.

The preparations being complete, the two private soldiers stepped aside and each drew away the plank upon which he had been standing. The sergeant turned to the captain, saluted and placed himself immediately behind that officer, who in turn moved apart one pace. These movements left the condemned man and the sergeant standing on the two ends of the same plank, which spanned three of the cross-ties of the bridge. The end upon which the civilian stood almost, but not quite, reached a fourth. This plank had been held in place by the weight of the captain; it was now held by that of the sergeant. At a signal from the former the latter would step aside, the plank would tilt and the condemned man go down between two ties. The arrangement commended itself to his judgment as simple and effective. His face had not been covered nor his eyes bandaged. He looked a moment at his "unsteadfast footing," then let his gaze wander to the swirling water of the stream racing madly beneath his feet. A piece of dancing driftwood caught his attention and his eyes followed it down the current. How slowly it appeared to move! What a sluggish stream!

He closed his eyes in order to fix his last thoughts upon his wife and children. The water, touched to gold by the early sun, the brooding mists under the banks at some distance down the stream, the fort, the soldiers, the piece of drift—all had distracted him. And now he became conscious of a new disturbance. Striking through the thought of his dear ones was a sound which he could neither ignore nor understand, a sharp, distinct, metallic percussion like the stroke of a blacksmith's hammer upon the anvil; it had the same ringing quality. He wondered what it was, and whether immeasurably distant or near by—it seemed both. Its recurrence was regular, but as slow as the tolling of a death knell. He awaited each stroke with impatience and—he knew not why—apprehension. The intervals of silence grew progressively longer; the delays became maddening. With their greater infrequency the sounds increased in strength and sharpness. They hurt his ear like the thrust of a knife; he feared he would shriek. What he heard was the ticking of his watch.

He unclosed his eyes and saw again the water below him. "If I could free my hands," he thought, "I might throw off the noose and spring into the stream. By diving I could evade the bullets and, swimming vigorously, reach the bank, take to the woods and get away home. My home, thank God, is as yet outside their lines; my wife and little ones are still beyond the invader's farthest advance."

As these thoughts, which have here to be set down in words, were flashed into the doomed man's brain rather than evolved from it the captain nodded to the sergeant. The sergeant stepped aside.

II

Peyton Farquhar was a well-to-do planter, of an old and highly respected Alabama family. Being a slave owner and like other slave owners a politician he was naturally an original secessionist and ardently devoted to the Southern cause. Circumstances of an imperious nature, which it is unnecessary to relate here, had prevented him from taking service with the gallant army that had fought the disastrous campaigns ending with the fall of Corinth, and he chafed under the inglorious restraint, longing for the release of his energies, the larger life of the soldier, the opportunity for distinction. That opportunity, he felt, would come, as it comes to all in war time. Meanwhile he did what he could. No service was too humble for him to perform in aid of the South, no adventure too perilous for him to undertake if consistent with the character of a civilian who was at heart a soldier, and who in good faith and without too much qualification assented to at least a part of the frankly villainous dictum that all is fair in love and war.

One evening while Farquhar and his wife were sitting on a rustic bench near the entrance to his grounds, a gray-clad soldier rode up to the gate and asked for a drink of water. Mrs. Farquhar was only too happy to serve him with her own white hands. While she was fetching the water her husband approached the dusty horseman and inquired eagerly for news from the front.

"The Yanks are repairing the railroads," said the man, "and are getting ready for another advance. They have reached the Owl Creek bridge, put it in order and built a stockade on the north bank. The commandant has issued an order, which is posted everywhere, declaring that any civilian caught interfering with the railroad, its bridges, tunnels or trains will be summarily hanged. I saw the order."

"How far is it to the Owl Creek bridge?" Farquhar asked.

"About thirty miles."

"Is there no force on this side the creek?"

"Only a picket post half a mile out, on the railroad, and a single sentinel at this end of the bridge."

"Suppose a man—a civilian and student of hanging—should elude the picket post and perhaps get the better of the sentinel," said Farquhar, smiling, "what could he accomplish?"

The soldier reflected. "I was there a month ago," he replied. "I observed that the flood of last winter had lodged a great quantity of driftwood against the wooden pier at this end of the bridge. It is now dry and would burn like tow."

The lady had now brought the water, which the soldier drank. He thanked her ceremoniously, bowed to her husband and rode away. An hour later, after nightfall, he repassed the plantation, going northward in the direction from which he had come. He was a Federal scout.

III

As Peyton Farquhar fell straight downward through the bridge he lost consciousness and was as one already dead. From this state he was awakened—ages later, it seemed to him—by the pain of a sharp pressure upon his throat, followed by a sense of suffocation. Keen, poignant agonies seemed to shoot from his neck downward through every fibre of his body and limbs. These pains appeared to flash along well-defined lines of ramification and to beat with an inconceivably rapid periodicity. They seemed like streams of pulsating fire heating him to an intolerable temperature. As to his head, he was conscious of nothing but a feeling of fullness—of congestion. These sensations were unaccompanied by thought. The intellectual part of his nature was already effaced; he had power only to feel, and feeling was torment. He was conscious of motion. Encompassed in a luminous cloud, of which he was now merely the fiery heart, without material substance, he swung through unthinkable arcs of oscillation, like a vast pendulum. Then all at once, with terrible suddenness, the light about him shot upward with the noise of a loud plash; a frightful roaring was in his ears, and all was cold and dark. The power of thought was restored; he knew that the rope had broken and he had fallen into the stream. There was no additional strangulation; the noose about his neck was already suffocating him and kept the water from his lungs. To die of hanging at the bottom of a river!—the idea seemed to him ludicrous. He opened his eyes in the darkness and saw above him a gleam of light, but how distant, how inaccessible! He was still sinking, for the light became fainter and fainter until it was a mere glimmer. Then it began to grow and brighten, and he knew that he was rising toward the surface—knew it with reluctance, for he was now very comfortable. "To be hanged and drowned," he thought, "that is not so bad; but I do not wish to be shot. No; I will not be shot; that is not fair."

He was not conscious of an effort, but a sharp pain in his wrist appraised him that he was trying to free his hands. He gave the struggle his attention, as an idler might observe the feat of a juggler, without interest in the outcome. What splendid effort!—what magnificent, what superhuman strength! Ah, that was a fine endeavor! Bravo! The cord fell away; his arms parted and floated upward, the hands dimly seen on each side in the growing light. He watched them with a new interest as first one and then the other pounced upon the noose at his neck. They tore it away and thrust it fiercely aside, its undulations resembling those of a water-snake. "Put it back, put it back!" He thought he shouted these words to his hands, for the undoing of the noose had been succeeded by the direst pang he had yet experienced. His neck arched horribly, his brain was on fire; his heart, which had been fluttering faintly, gave a great leap, trying to force itself out at his mouth. His whole body was racked and wrenched with an insupportable anguish! But his disobedient hands gave no heed to the command. They beat the water vigorously with quick, downward strokes, forcing him to the surface. He felt his head emerge; his eyes were blinded by the sunlight; his chest expanded convulsively, and with a supreme and crowning agony his lungs engulfed a great draught of air, which instantly he expelled in a shriek!

He was now in full possession of his physical senses. They were, indeed, preternaturally keen and alert. Something in the awful disturbance of his organic system had so exalted and refined them that they made record of things never before perceived. He felt the ripples upon his face and heard their separate sounds as they struck. He looked at the forest on the bank of the stream, saw the individual trees, the leaves and the veining of each leaf—saw the very insects upon them: the locusts, the brilliant-bodied flies, the gray spiders stretching their webs from twig to twig. He noted the prismatic colors in all the dewdrops upon a million blades of grass. The humming of the gnats that danced above the eddies of the stream, the beating of the dragon-flies' wings, the strokes of the water-spiders' legs, like oars which had lifted their boat—all these made audible music. A fish slid along beneath his eyes and he heard the rush of its body parting the water.

He had come to the surface facing down the stream; in a moment the visible world seemed to wheel slowly round, himself the pivotal point, and he saw the bridge, the fort, the soldiers upon the bridge, the captain, the sergeant, the two privates, his executioners. They were in silhouette against the blue sky. They shouted and gesticulated, pointing at him. The captain had drawn his pistol, but did not fire; the others were unarmed. Their movements were grotesque and horrible, their forms gigantic.

Suddenly he heard a sharp report and something struck the water smartly within a few inches of his head, spattering his face with spray. He heard a second report, and saw one of the sentinels with his rifle at his shoulder, a light cloud of blue smoke rising from the muzzle. The man in the water saw the eye of the man on the bridge gazing into his own through the sights of the rifle. He observed that it was a gray eye and remembered having read that gray eyes were keenest, and that all famous marksmen had them. Nevertheless, this one had missed.

A counter-swirl had caught Farquhar and turned him half round; he was again looking into the forest on the bank opposite the fort. The sound of a clear, high voice in a monotonous singsong now rang out behind him and came across the water with a distinctness that pierced and subdued all other sounds, even the beating of the ripples in his ears. Although no soldier, he had frequented camps enough to know the dread significance of that deliberate, drawling, aspirated chant; the lieutenant on shore was taking part in the morning's work. How coldly and pitilessly—with what an even, calm intonation, presaging, and enforcing tranquillity in the men—with what accurately measured intervals fell those cruel words:

"Attention, company! . . . Shoulder arms! . . . Ready! . . . Aim! . . . Fire!"

Farquhar dived—dived as deeply as he could. The water roared in his ears like the voice of Niagara, yet he heard the dulled thunder of the volley and, rising again toward the surface, met shining bits of metal, singularly flattened, oscillating slowly downward. Some of them touched him on the face and hands, then fell away, continuing their descent. One lodged between his collar and neck; it was uncomfortably warm and he snatched it out.

As he rose to the surface, gasping for breath, he saw that he had been a long time under water; he was perceptibly farther down stream—nearer to safety. The soldiers had almost finished reloading; the metal ramrods flashed all at once in the sunshine as they were drawn from the barrels, turned in the air, and thrust into their sockets. The two sentinels fired again, independently and ineffectually.

The hunted man saw all this over his shoulder; he was now swimming vigorously with the current. His brain was as energetic as his arms and legs; he thought with the rapidity of lightning.

"The officer," he reasoned, "will not make that martinet's error a second time. It is as easy to dodge a volley as a single shot. He has probably already given the command to fire at will. God help me, I cannot dodge them all!"

An appalling plash within two yards of him was followed by a loud, rushing sound, *diminuendo*, which seemed to travel back through the air to the fort and died in an explosion which stirred the very river to its deeps! A rising sheet of water curved over him, fell down upon him, blinded him, strangled him! The cannon had taken a hand in the game. As he shook his head free from the commotion of the smitten water he heard the deflected shot humming through the air ahead, and in an instant it was cracking and smashing the branches in the forest beyond.

"They will not do that again," he thought; "the next time they will use a charge of grape. I must keep my eye upon the gun; the smoke will apprise me—the report arrives too late; it lags behind the missile. That is a good gun."

Suddenly he felt himself whirled round and round—spinning like a top. The water, the banks, the forests, the now distant bridge, fort and men—all were commingled and blurred. Objects were represented by their colors only; circular horizontal streaks of color—that was all he saw. He had been caught in a vortex and was being whirled on with a velocity of advance and gyration that made him giddy and sick. In a few moments he was flung upon the gravel at the foot of the left bank of the stream—the southern bank—and behind a projecting point which concealed him from his enemies. The sudden arrest of his motion, the abrasion of one of his hands on the gravel, restored him, and he wept with delight. He dug his fingers into the sand, threw it over himself in handfuls and audibly blessed it. It looked like diamonds, rubies, emeralds; he could think of nothing beautiful which it did not resemble. The trees upon the bank were giant garden plants; he noted a definite order in their arrangement, inhaled the fragrance of their blooms. A strange, roseate light shone through the spaces among their trunks and the wind made in their branches the music of aeolian harps. He had no wish to perfect his escape—was content to remain in that enchanting spot until retaken.

A whiz and rattle of grapeshot among the branches high above his head roused him from his dream. The baffled cannoneer had fired him a random farewell. He sprang to his feet, rushed up the sloping bank, and plunged into the forest.

All that day he traveled, laying his course by the rounding sun. The forest seemed interminable; nowhere did he discover a break in it, not even a woodman's road. He had not known that he lived in so wild a region. There was something uncanny in the revelation.

By nightfall he was fatigued, footsore, famishing. The thought of his wife and children urged him on. At last he found a road which led him in what he knew to be the right direction. It was as wide and straight as a city street, yet it seemed untraveled. No fields bordered it, no dwelling anywhere. Not so much as the barking of a dog suggested human habitation. The black bodies of the trees formed a straight wall on both sides, terminating on the horizon in a point, like a diagram in a lesson in perspective. Overhead, as he looked up through this rift in the wood, shone great golden stars looking unfamiliar and grouped in strange constellations. He was sure they were arranged in some order which had a secret and malign significance. The wood on either side was full of singular noises, among which—once, twice, and again, he distinctly heard whispers in an unknown tongue.

His neck was in pain and lifting his hand to it he found it horribly swollen. He knew that it had a circle of black where the rope had bruised it. His eyes felt congested; he could no longer close them. His tongue was swollen with thirst; he relieved its fever by thrusting it forward from between his teeth into the cold air. How softly the turf had carpeted the untraveled avenue—he could no longer feel the roadway beneath his feet!

Doubtless, despite his suffering, he had fallen asleep while walking, for now he sees another scene—perhaps he has merely recovered from a delirium. He stands at the gate of his own home. All is as he left it, and all bright and beautiful in the morning sunshine. He must have traveled the entire night. As he pushes open the gate and passes up the wide white walk, he sees a flutter of female garments; his wife, looking fresh and cool and sweet, steps down from the veranda to meet him. At the bottom of the steps she stands waiting, with a smile of ineffable joy, an attitude of matchless grace and dignity. Ah, how beautiful she is! He springs forward with extended arms. As he is about to clasp her he feels a stunning blow upon the back of the neck; a blinding white light blazes all about him with a sound like the shock of a cannon—then all is darkness and silence!

Peyton Farquhar was dead; his body, with a broken neck, swung gently from side to side beneath the timbers of the Owl Creek bridge.

DULCE ET DECORUM EST
Wilfred Owen (1893–1918)

A promising young British poet, Owen was killed one week before the armistice of November 1918, as he led a group of British soldiers into battle. The final line of this poem is a quotation from the Latin poet Horace: "It is sweet and fitting to die for one's country."

Bent double, like old beggars under sacks,
Knock-kneed, coughing like hags, we cursed through sludge,
Till on the haunting flares we turned our backs,

And towards our distant rest began to trudge.
Men marched asleep. Many had lost their boots,
But limped on, blood-shod. All went lame, all blind;
Drunk with fatigue; deaf even to the hoots
Of gas-shells dropping softly behind.

Gas! GAS! Quick boys!—An ecstasy of fumbling,
Fitting the clumsy helmets just in time,
But someone still was yelling out and stumbling
And flound'ring like a man in fire or lime—
Dim through the misty panes and thick green light,
As under a green sea, I saw him drowning.
In all my dreams before my helpless sight
He plunges at me, guttering, choking, drowning.

If in some smothering dreams, you too could pace
Behind the wagon that we flung him in,
And watch the white eyes writhing in his face,
His hanging face, like a devil's sick of sin,
If you could hear, at every jolt, the blood
Come garling from the froth-corrupted lungs
Bitter as the cud
Of vile, incurable sores on innocent tongues—
My friend, you would not tell with such high zest
To children ardent for some desperate glory,
The old lie: *Dulce et decorum est*
Pro patria mori.

from JOURNEY THROUGH HELL
Reska Weiss (b. 1900)

A Hungarian Jew, Weiss lived with her husband in Ungvar and had two sons
attending a university in Budapest when the Germans occupied Hungary in 1944.
She and thousands of other Jews in Hungary were soon transported in railroad
cars to German concentration camps. Like many of the survivors of these camps,
she felt compelled to provide a record of the degradation, humiliation, disease,
suffering, despair, and deaths she experienced and witnessed during that ordeal so
that other persons could understand the savagery that ruled the camps. Often she

witnessed brutal, sadistic killings. The following passage describes one such experience in Neumark (Prussia), a camp for women. The name "Stuthofers" was a derisive term by which the Germans referred to women about to be shot (they were told they were going to be "transported to Stuthof").

One morning, as I stepped out of the sty, I ran into Halzele, who gave me a fierce blow. I fell on my back, but the blanket of snow cushioned the fall and I felt no pain. As I staggered to my feet, Halzele transfixed me with his rat-like eyes. I started to walk away, but he ordered me to stop, and I went back trembling.

"You Jewish worm," he grinned hideously, "for weeks now there has been no work for you in the fields, but there are two tents without a nurse," and he pointed to the tent of the Stuthofers. Guffawing loudly he said: "From now on you will be the nurse in there."

No one was allowed into the Stuthofers' tent. If anyone was caught visiting a mother or a sister she was never allowed to leave the tent again. The Stuthofers were seldom given food, and on the rare occasions when it was supplied it was placed on the ground in the dark in front of the tent. Then the strongest of them fetched it and distributed it.

Entering the tent from the blinding snow-whiteness, I could hardly distinguish anything in the semi-darkness, least of all the women lying on the ground. The stench was overpowering despite the airy tent. After a while my eyes became accustomed to the light, and I was completely overcome by what I saw.

I screamed in horror and shut my eyes to the sight. My knees trembled, my head began to swim, and I grasped the central tent-prop for support. It was hard to believe the women on the ground were still human beings. Their rigid bodies were skeletons, their eyes were glazed from long starvation. I had thought before that I'd seen the limit of human misery; now I knew how wrong I'd been.

For two months the Stuthofers had lain on the ground, stark naked. The meager bundles of straw on which they lay were putrid from their urine and excreta. Their frozen limbs were fetid and covered with wounds and bites to the point of bleeding, and countless lice nested in the pus. Their hair was very short indeed, but the armies of lice found a home in it. No stretch of the imagination, no power of the written word, can convey the horror of that tent. And yet . . . they were *alive* . . . they were hungry and they tore at their skeletal bodies with their emaciated hands covered in pus and dirt. They were beyond help! The S.S. guards denied them the mercy of shooting them all at once. Only three or four were called out daily to be shot. But new prisoners were quickly sent in to replace them. And so I became a nurse to these living corpses! . . .

For days I couldn't swallow even a crumb of bread. The horror I lived through watching this agony will remain with me to the end of my days. Later I saw thousands of my fellow prisoners die from rifle shots, but even that could not compare with the terrible and unspeakable ordeal of the Stuthofers.

from HIROSHIMA
John Hersey (b. 1914)

A reporter and novelist, Hersey has often pointed out the importance of novels dealing with contemporary historical events. He once said that while truth is sometimes stranger than fiction, "fiction can be stronger than truth." One of the many illustrations of this phenomenon was the bombing of Hiroshima during the second World War. Headlines reporting the deaths of approximately 100,000 Japanese simply could not have the personal, long-lasting impact that a novel could have by describing the effects of the bombing attack on the individuals who experienced it. Hersey's description of the attack, from which the following selection is taken, was published in the *New Yorker* before it appeared in book form.

The lot of Drs. Fujii, Kanda, and Machii right after the explosion—and, as these three were typical, that of the majority of the physicians and surgeons of Hiroshima—with their offices and hospitals destroyed, their equipment scattered, their own bodies incapacitated in varying degrees, explained why so many citizens who were hurt went untended and why so many who might have lived died. Of a hundred and fifty doctors in the city, sixty-five were already dead and most of the rest were wounded. Of 1,780 nurses, 1,654 were dead or too badly hurt to work. In the biggest hospital, that of the Red Cross, only six doctors out of thirty were able to function, and only ten nurses out of more than two hundred. The sole uninjured doctor on the Red Cross Hospital staff was Dr. Sasaki. After the explosion, he hurried to a storeroom to fetch bandages. This room, like everything he had seen as he ran through the hospital, was chaotic—bottles of medicines thrown off shelves and broken, salves spattered on the walls, instruments strewn everywhere. He grabbed up some bandages and an unbroken bottle of mercurochrome, hurried back to the chief surgeon, and bandaged his cuts. Then he went out into the corridor and began patching up the wounded patients and the doctors and nurses there. He blundered so without his glasses that he took a pair off the face of a wounded nurse, and although they only approximately compensated for the errors of his vision, they were better than nothing. (He was to depend on them for more than a month.)

Dr. Sasaki worked without method, taking those who were nearest him first, and he noticed soon that the corridor seemed to be getting more and more crowded. Mixed in with the abrasions and lacerations which most people in the hospital had suffered, he began to find dreadful burns. He realized then that the casualties were pouring in from outdoors. There were so many that he began to pass up the lightly wounded; he decided that all he could hope to do was to stop people from bleeding to death. Before long, patients lay and crouched on the floors of the wards and the laboratories and all the other rooms, and in the corridors, and on the stairs, and in the front hall, and under the portecochère, and on the stone front steps, and in the driveway and courtyard, and for blocks each way in the streets outside. Wounded people supported maimed people; disfigured families leaned together. Many people were vomiting. A tremendous number of schoolgirls—some of those who had been taken from their classrooms to work outdoors, clearing fire lanes—crept into the hospital. In a city of two hundred and forty-five thousand, nearly a hundred thousand people had been killed or doomed at one blow; a hundred thousand more were hurt. At least ten thousand of the wounded made their way to the best hospital in town, which was altogether unequal to such a trampling, since it had only six hundred beds, and they had all been occupied. The people in the suffocating crowd inside the hospital wept and cried, for Dr. Sasaki to hear, "*Sensei!* Doctor!," and the less seriously wounded came and pulled at his sleeve and begged him to go to the aid of the worse wounded. Tugged here and there in his stockinged feet, bewildered by the numbers, staggered by so much raw flesh, Dr. Sasaki lost all sense of profession and stopped working as a skillful surgeon and a sympathetic man; he became an automaton, mechanically wiping, daubing, winding, wiping, daubing, winding.

. . . .

By nightfall, ten thousand victims of the explosion had invaded the Red Cross hospital, and Dr. Sasaki, worn out, was moving aimlessly and dully up and down the stinking corridors with wads of bandage and bottles of mercurochrome, still wearing the glasses he had taken from the wounded nurse, binding up the worst cuts as he came to them. Other doctors were putting compresses of saline solution on the worst burns. That was all they could do. After dark, they worked by the light of the city's fire and by candles the ten remaining nurses held for them. Dr. Sasaki had not looked outside the hospital all day; the scene inside was so terrible and so compelling that it had not occurred to him to ask any questions about what had happened beyond the windows and doors. Ceilings and partitions had fallen; plaster, dust, blood, and vomit were everywhere. Patients were dying by the hundreds, but there was nobody to carry away the corpses. Some of the hospital staff distributed biscuits and rice balls, but the charnel-house smell was so strong that few were hungry. By three o'clock the next morning, after nineteen straight hours of his gruesome work, Dr. Sasaki was incapable of dressing another wound. He and some other survivors of the hospital staff got straw mats and went outdoors—thousands of patients and hundreds of dead were in the yard and on the driveway—and hurried around behind the hospital and lay down in hiding to snatch some sleep. But within an hour wounded people had found them; a complaining circle formed around them: "Doctors! Help us! How can you sleep?" Dr. Sasaki got up again and went back to work. Early in the day, he thought for the first time of his mother, at their country home in Mukairhara, thirty miles from town. He usually went home every night. He was afraid she would think he was dead.

. . . .

A comparative orderliness, at least, began to be established at the Red Cross Hospital. Dr. Sasaki, back from his rest, undertook to classify his patients (who were still scattered everywhere, even on the stairways). The staff gradually swept up the debris. Best of all, the nurses and attendants started to remove the corpses. Disposal of the dead, by decent cremation and enshrinement, is a greater moral responsibility to the Japanese than adequate care of the living. Relatives identified most of the first day's dead in and around the hospital. Beginning on the second day, whenever a patient appeared to be moribund, a piece of paper with his name on it was fastened to his clothing. The corpse detail carried the bodies to a clearing outside, placed them on pyres of wood from ruined houses, burned them, put some of the ashes in envelopes intended for exposed x-ray plates, marked the envelopes with the name of the deceased, and piled them, neatly and respectfully, in stacks in the main office. In a few days, the envelopes filled one whole side of the impromptu shrine.

TO THE MERCY KILLERS
Dudley Randall (b. 1914)

If ever mercy move you murder me,
I pray you, gentle killers, let me live.
Never conspire with death to set me free,
But let me know such life as pain can give.
Even though I be a clot, an aching clench,
A stub, a stump, a butt, a scab, a knob,
A roaring pain, a putrefying stench,
Still let me live so long as life shall throb.
Even though I be such traitor to myself
As beg to die, do not accomplice me.
Even though I seem not human, a mute shelf
Of glucose, bottled blood, machinery
To swell the lung and pump the heart—even so,
Do not put out my life. Let me still glow.

FIVE WAYS TO KILL A MAN
Edwin Brock (b. 1917)

There are many cumbersome ways to kill a man:
you can make him carry a plank of wood
to the top of a hill and nail him to it. To do this
properly you require a crowd of people
wearing sandals, a cock that crows, a cloak
to dissect, a sponge, some vinegar and one
man to hammer the nails home.

Or you can take a length of steel,
shaped and chased in a traditional way,
and attempt to pierce the metal cage he wears.
But for this you need white horses,
English trees, men with bows and arrows,
at least two flags, a prince and a
castle to hold your banquet in.

Dispensing with nobility, you may, if the wind
allows, blow gas at him. But then you need
a mile of mud sliced through with ditches,
not to mention black boots, bomb craters,
more mud, a plague of rats, a dozen songs
and some round hats made of steel.

In an age of aeroplanes, you may fly
miles above your victim and dispose of him by
pressing one small switch. All you then
require is an ocean to separate you, two
systems of government, a nation's scientists,
several factories, a psychopath and
land that no one needs for several years.

These are, as I began, cumbersome ways
to kill a man. Simpler, direct, and much more neat
is to see that he is living somewhere in the middle
of the twentieth century, and leave him there.

from IN COLD BLOOD
Truman Capote (b. 1924)

This book was intended as a contribution to a new literary form: the nonfiction
novel. Combining the talents of a reporter and a novelist, Capote investigated
and described the details of a multiple murder in Kansas, the extensive search for
the killers, and their subsequent deaths by judicial homicide. The excerpts which
follow provide an account of the murder scene by one of the first witnesses, a jail
conversation involving one of the killers, and a description of the killers' execution by hanging.

"Well, it was pretty bad. That wonderful girl—but you would never
have known her. She'd been shot in the back of the head with a shotgun

held maybe two inches away. She was lying on her side, facing the wall, and the wall was covered with blood. The bedcovers were drawn up to her shoulders. Sheriff Robinson, he pulled them back, and we saw that she was wearing a bathrobe, pajamas, socks, and slippers—like, whenever it happened, she hadn't gone to bed yet. Her hands were tied behind her, and her ankles were roped together with the kind of cord you see on Venetian blinds. Sheriff said, 'Is this Nancy Clutter?'—he'd never seen the child before. And I said, 'Yes. Yes, that's Nancy.'

"We stepped back into the hall, and looked around. All the other doors were closed. We opened one, and that turned out to be a bathroom. Something about it seemed wrong. I decided it was because of the chair—a sort of dining-room chair, that looked out of place in a bathroom. The next door—we all agreed it must be Kenyon's room. A lot of boy-stuff scattered around. And I recognized Kenyon's glasses—saw them on a bookshelf beside the bed. But the bed was empty, though it looked as if it had been slept in. So we walked to the end of the hall, the last door, and there, on her bed, that's where we found Mrs. Clutter. She'd been tied, too. But differently—with her hands in front of her, so that she looked as though she were praying—and in one hand she was holding, *gripping*, a handkerchief. Or was it Kleenex? The cord around her wrists ran down to her ankles, which were bound together, and then ran on down to the bottom of the bed, where it was tied to the footboard—a very complicated, artful piece of work. Think how long it took to do! And her lying there, scared out of her wits. Well, she was wearing some jewelry, two rings—which is one of the reasons why I've always discounted robbery as a motive—and a robe, and a white nightgown, and white socks. Her mouth had been taped with adhesive, but she'd been shot point-blank in the side of the head, and the blast—the impact—had ripped the tape loose. Her eyes were open. Wide open. As though she were still looking at the killer. Because she must have had to watch him do it—aim the gun. Nobody said anything. We were too stunned. I remember the sheriff searched around to see if he could find the discharged cartridge. But whoever had done it was much too smart and cool to have left behind any clues like that.

. . . .

. . . "About then we heard footsteps. Coming up the stairs from the basement. 'Who's that?' said the sheriff, like he was ready to shoot. And a voice said, 'It's me. Wendle.' Turned out to be Wendle Meier, the undersheriff. Seems he had come to the house and hadn't seen us, so he'd gone investigating down in the basement. The sheriff told him—and it was sort of pitiful: 'Wendle, I don't know what to make of it. There's two bodies upstairs.' 'Well,' he said, Wendle did, 'there's another one down here.' So we followed him down to the basement. Or playroom, I guess you'd call it. It wasn't dark—there were windows that let in plenty of light. Kenyon was over in a corner, lying on a couch. He was gagged with adhesive tape and bound hand and foot, like the mother—the same intricate process of the cord leading from the hands to the feet, and finally tied to an arm of the couch. Somehow he haunts me the most, Kenyon does. I think it's because he was the most recognizable, the one that looked the most like himself—even though he'd been shot in the face, directly, head-on. He was wearing a T-shirt and blue jeans, and he was barefoot—as though he'd dressed in a hurry, just put on the first thing that came to hand. His head was propped by a couple of pillows, like they'd been stuffed under him to make an easier target.

"Then the sheriff said, 'Where's this go to?' Meaning another door there in the basement. Sheriff led the way, but inside you couldn't see your hand until Mr. Ewalt found the light switch. It was a furnace room, and very warm. Around here, people just install a gas furnace and pump the gas smack out of the ground. Doesn't cost them a nickel—that's why all the houses are overheated. Well, I took one look at Mr. Clutter, and it was hard to look again. I knew plain shooting couldn't account for that much blood. And I wasn't wrong. He'd been shot, all right, the same as Kenyon—with the gun held right in front of his face. But probably he was dead before he was shot. Or, anyway, dying. Because his throat had been cut, too. He was wearing striped pajamas—nothing else. His mouth was taped; the tape had been wound plumb around his head. His ankles were tied together, but not his hands—or, rather, he'd managed, God knows how, maybe in rage or pain, to break the cord binding his hands. He was sprawled in front of the furnace. On a big cardboard box that looked as though it had been laid there specially. A mattress box. Sheriff said, 'Look here, Wendle.' What he was pointing at was a blood-stained footprint. On the mattress box. A half-sole footprint with circles—two holes in the center like a pair of eyes. Then one of us—Mr. Ewalt? I don't recall—pointed out something else. A thing I can't get out of my mind. There was a steampipe overhead, and knotted to it, dangling from it, was a piece of cord—the kind of cord the killer had used. Obviously, at some point Mr. Clutter had been tied there, strung up by his hands, and then cut down. But why? To torture him? I don't guess we'll ever know. Ever know who did it, or why, or what went on in that house that night.

. . . .

Cullivan probed, trying to gauge the depth of what he assumed would be Perry's contrition. Surely he must be experiencing a remorse sufficiently profound to summon a desire for God's mercy and forgiveness? Perry said, "Am I sorry? If that's what you mean—I'm not. I don't feel anything about it. I wish I did. But nothing about it bothers me a bit. Half an hour after it happened, Dick was making jokes and I was laughing at them. Maybe we're not human. I'm human enough to feel sorry for myself. Sorry I can't walk out of here when you walk out. But that's all." Cullivan could scarcely credit so detached an attitude; Perry was confused, mistaken, it was not possible for any man to be that devoid of conscience or compassion. Perry said, "Why? Soldiers don't lose much sleep. They murder, and get medals for doing it. The good people of Kansas want to murder me—and some hangman will be glad to get the work. It's easy to kill—a lot easier than passing a bad check. Just remember: I only knew the Clutters maybe an hour. If I'd really known them, I guess I'd feel different. I don't think I could live with myself. But the way it was, it was like picking off targets in a shooting gallery."

. . . .

Dewey had watched them die, for he had been among the twenty-odd witnesses invited to the ceremony. He had never attended an execution, and when on the midnight past he entered the cold warehouse, the scenery had surprised him: he had anticipated a setting of suitable dignity, not this bleakly lighted cavern cluttered with lumber and other debris. But the gallows itself, with its two pale nooses attached to a crossbeam, was imposing enough; and so, in an unexpected style, was the hangman, who cast a long shadow from his perch on the platform at the top of the wooden instrument's thirteen steps. The hangman, an anonymous, leathery gentleman who had been imported from Missouri for the event, for which he was paid six hundred dollars, was attired in an aged double-breasted pin-striped suit overly commodious for the narrow figure inside it—the coat came nearly to his knees; and on his head he wore a cowboy hat which, when first bought, had perhaps been bright green, but was now a weathered, sweat-stained oddity.

. . . .

The sudden rain rapped the high warehouse roof. The sound, not unlike the rat-a-tat-tat of parade drums, heralded Hickock's arrival. Accompanied by six guards and a prayer-murmuring chaplain, he entered the death place handcuffed and wearing an ugly harness of leather straps that bound his arms to his torso. At the foot of the gallows the warden read to him the official order of execution, a two-page document; and as the warden read, Hickock's eyes, enfeebled by half a decade of cell shadows, roamed the little audience until, not seeing what he sought, he asked the nearest guard, in a whisper, if any member of the Clutter family was present. When he was told no, the prisoner seemed disappointed, as though he thought the protocol surrounding this ritual of vengeance was not being properly observed.

As is customary, the warden, having finished his recitation, asked the condemned man whether he had any last statement to make. Hickock nodded. "I just want to say I hold no hard feelings. You people are sending me to a better world than this ever was"; then, as if to emphasize the point, he shook hands with the four men mainly responsible for his capture and conviction, all of whom had requested permission to attend the executions: K.B.I. Agents Roy Church, Clarence Duntz, Harold Nye, and Dewey himself. "Nice to see you," Hickock said with his most charming smile; it was as if he were greeting guests at his own funeral.

The hangman coughed—impatiently lifted his cowboy hat and settled it again, a gesture somehow reminiscent of a turkey buzzard huffing, then smoothing its neck feathers—and Hickock, nudged by an attendant, mounted the scaffold steps. "The Lord giveth, the Lord taketh away. Blessed is the name of the Lord," the chaplain intoned, as the rain sound accelerated, as the noose was fitted, and as a delicate black mask was tied round the prisoner's eyes. "May the Lord have mercy on your soul." The trap door opened, and Hickock hung for all to see a full twenty minutes before the prison doctor at last said, "I pronounce this man dead." A hearse, its blazing headlights beaded with rain, drove into the warehouse, and the body, placed on a litter and shrouded under a blanket, was carried to the hearse and out into the night.

Staring after it, Roy Church shook his head: "I never would have believed he had the guts. To take it like he did. I had him tagged a coward."

The man to whom he spoke, another detective, said, "Aw, Roy. The guy was a punk. A mean bastard. He deserved it."

Church, with thoughtful eyes, continued to shake his head.

While waiting for the second execution, a reporter and a guard conversed. The reporter said, "This your first hanging?"

"I seen Lee Andrews."

"This here's my first."

"Yeah. How'd you like it?"

The reporter pursed his lips. "Nobody in our office wanted the assignment. Me either. But it wasn't as bad as I thought it would be. Just like jumping off a diving board. Only with a rope around your neck."

"They don't feel nothing. Drop, snap, and that's it. They don't feel nothing."

"Are you sure? I was standing right close. I could hear him gasping for breath."

"Uh-huh, but he don't feel nothing. Wouldn't be humane if he did."

"Well. And I suppose they feed them a lot of pills. Sedatives."

"Hell, no. Against the rules. Here comes Smith."

"Gosh, I didn't know he was such a shrimp."

"Yeah, he's little. But so is a tarantula."

As he was brought into the warehouse, Smith recognized his old foe, Dewey; he stopped chewing a hunk of Doublemint gum he had in his mouth, and grinned and winked at Dewey, jaunty and mischievous. But after the warden asked if he had anything to say, his expression was sober. His sensitive eyes gazed gravely at the surrounding faces, swerved up to the shadowy hangman, then downward to his own manacled hands. He looked at his fingers, which were stained with ink and paint, for he'd spent his final three years on Death Row painting self-portraits and pictures of children, usually the children of inmates who supplied him with photographs of their seldom-seen progeny. "I think," he said, "it's a helluva thing to take a life in this manner. I don't believe in capital punishment, morally or legally. Maybe I had something to contribute, something—" His assurance faltered; shyness blurred his voice, lowered it to a just audible level. "It would be meaningless to apologize for what I did. Even inappropriate. But I do. I apologize."

Steps, noose, mask; but before the mask was adjusted, the prisoner spat his chewing gum into the chaplain's outstretched palm. Dewey shut his eyes; he kept them shut until he heard the thud-snap that announces a rope-broken neck. Like the majority of American law-enforcement officials, Dewey is certain that capital punishment is a deterrent to violent crime, and he felt that if ever the penalty had been earned, the present instance was it. The preceding execution had not disturbed him, he had never had much use for Hickock, who seemed to him "a small-time chiseler who got out of his depth, empty and worthless." But Smith, though he was the true murderer, aroused another response, for Perry possessed a quality, the aura of an exiled animal, a creature walking wounded, that the detective could not disregard. He remembered his first meeting with Perry in the interrogation room at Police Headquarters in Las Vegas—the dwarfish boy-man seated in the metal chair, his small booted feet not quite brushing the floor. And when Dewey now opened his eyes, that is what he saw: the same childish feet, tilted, dangling.

LILITH'S CHILD
Edward Francisco (b. 1953)

Melisha Gibson was a four-year-old girl who was beaten to death by her step-father and mother in Tennessee in 1976. Francisco, who teaches at the University of Tennessee, wrote a poem depicting this ultimate form of child abuse from the perspective of the child. The poem's title is a reminder of an ancient Jewish myth which tells of a malevolent female demon named Lilith, who without apparent cause preys on young children and threatens women in childbirth.

I had no voice before
But now
Speaking with a pale tongue
I tell of parents who give birth
To tombstones.
Parents whose faces hard and weatherbeaten
As agony
Stiffen with the venom of a kiss

For one who trusted them
As she trusted
Breathing.

Once running on pink feet
I swam breezy upon the grass
Under the clouds whiter than milk
Or the bathtub where I used to sit warmly
Counting the wrinkles
In my fingers held under water
Until mother would come unplug the drain
That swallowed all but me
Left whitely bare and shivering
Against the porcelain.

How I dreaded the swift tug
Of the brush through my hair
Sweet and wild as fieldflowers.
Yet not so much did I dread
As when in the door
He appeared, eyes glaring, marching
Me over in the furious cadence
Of his clenched heart
Until taking my arm
He would fling me breathless upon the bed
That quivered with my limbs' descent.

Then He would clap my back in cruel applause
For tricks performed by one
Who only sought to please
And so
Nailed herself to every task,
Ran up and down the stairs
Danced the cruel dance
Until one night
Hearing the ancient curse of winds
Blow fiercely from the North
I pulled the eternal blanket over shivering day
And slept.

I had not meant to sleep so long
But only wished to listen to the song
Of the bird in the egg
Outside my window.
Whose ageless voice
First rose then fell in measured echoes
To the chorus of mourning neighbors
Singing beside the grave.

And there
Standing among the shadows
I saw
Shapes of long-forgotten power rise
And heard there dreams
In which only children cried
And knew at last
That with each ritual hand of dust,
They sought to choke the final cry—
The cry of Lilith's child.

7. SUICIDE

ALBERT CAMUS, in *The Myth of Sisyphus*, declares that suicide is the only truly serious philosophical problem. He means that, in a world which often seems absurd, even the most complex problems can eventually be thought through, worked out, or coped with. But the question of life's meaning remains—as does suicide as a possible option for persons who conclude that life has lost its meaning for them. The philosophical problem is justifying that act of self-destruction.

Camus concludes that suicide is not a justifiable option—even if one believes that God does not exist and the world is absurd. An increasing number of persons, however, disagree. More than 27,000 Americans now kill themselves each year (a rate of 12.6 per 100,000), and the number of these reported suicides has increased by 25 percent over the past decade. The number of actual suicides is probably several times higher than those reported, since many acts of self-destruction are interpreted as natural deaths by physicians and surviving relatives. Most of these suicides are by males, even though women attempt suicide more often but with less success, as illustrated by the Sylvia Plath selection in this section.

The majority of suicides occur in two age categories. Men and women over the age of sixty-five, as illustrated by the Arna Bontemps story, sometimes decide to kill themselves because of poor health, economic problems, the loss of meaningful work, the deaths of spouses and close friends, and the persistent feelings of rejection and uselessness. Persons in their late teens and early twenties, as illustrated by the Shakespeare and Chikamatsu plays, sometimes decide to destroy themselves because they can't cope with the pressures placed upon them, can't compete successfully with others, can't endure a broken romance, and/or can't handle feelings of rejection and loneliness. Reported suicides in this 15–24 age category are now twice as high as ten years ago.

A number of positions can be identified regarding the morality of these self-destructive acts. Seneca, a first-century philosopher, and David Hume, an eighteenth-century philosopher, are among the persons who have concluded that suicide is morally justifiable. For Seneca, who accepted the Platonic theory of the soul's immortality, existence in this life is but a preparation for another form of existence. Accordingly, it makes no difference whether the "taking-off" for that next existence is natural or self-inflicted. What matters is living well and, when that is no longer possible, dying well. For Hume, the question of the morality of suicide hinges on a person's duties—to God, other persons, and ourselves. He reasons in *On Suicide* that this act of self-destructiveness cannot be a transgression against God because human lives, like everything in the universe, are governed by general laws of matter and motion. Since one person's death does not disrupt these laws, and since God, if God exists, has not strictly reserved the disposal of human lives for himself, anyone who wants to escape the ills of human existence can freely dispose of his own life. Suicide cannot be a transgression against other persons because when a person kills herself, she does not do harm to society but merely ceases to do good. And suicide cannot be a transgression against ourselves because no one throws away a life worth living, but only a life which is made worse than death by advanced age, infirmity, or misfortune.

Arguments against the morality of suicide have appeared in major religious traditions, as well as in philosophy. In Hinduism, for example, the nonviolent principle of *ahimsa* has brought about a general opposition to self-destruction, even though justifiable exceptions have been made for ascetics who passively accept death from starvation and for persons who kill themselves out of devotion to a deity. Buddhism has traditionally opposed suicide (the Buddha once said, "let no one destroy himself, and whosoever would destroy himself, let him be dealt with according to law"), even though allowing for at least two exceptions: the self-renunciation of a saint (*arhat*) to the point of death, and the self-destruction of an honorable person in the face of dishonor (e.g., the practice of *harakiri* in Japan). The Western monotheistic traditions—Judaism, Christianity, and Islam—have also considered suicide wrong because of the general beliefs, as argued by Augustine and Aquinas among others, that human life is a gift from God and that self-destruction is an inappropriate way of exercising stewardship over that gift.

The subject of suicide has often appeared in literature. Sophocles, Shakespeare, and a number of other writers have depicted suicide not as a major philosophical problem but simply as one of the realities of human existence. And if anything, the inclusion of suicide as a literary theme has increased in the modern period, possibly reflecting the rise in the number of suicides.

Three examples, in addition to the selections, will illustrate how suicide is handled in contemporary literature. Dorothy Parker, an American writer of poems, plays, and short stories, describes in her story "Big Blonde" the deteriorating conditions which bring about an attempted suicide. The central figure in the story, Hazel Morse, is a large, attractive woman in her middle thirties who for years has been popular with men because of her good looks. Unfortunately, her marriage was ruined by her constant complaining and her husband's constant drinking. After he left her, she spent time with a series of other men, all of whom were interested in only a transitory relationship and forced her to live a superficial life made falsely happy by heavy drinking, drugs, and parties which had little meaning for her. The possibility of killing herself became increasingly attractive—if she could just figure out a way to do it successfully. She finally decided to end her misery with an overdose of sleeping pills—only to be awakened by a friend, have her stomach pumped out, and be told, in a manner completely insensitive to the situation, to cheer up.

Yukio Mishima, a Japanese author who committed *harakiri* in 1970, describes this ritual form of suicide in his story "Patriotism." The story takes place in 1936 when Lieutenant Shinji Takeyama, the main character in the story, discovers that some of his fellow officers and friends have participated in a mutiny. Thirty-one years old, and married for less than a year, he knows that he will be placed in command of a military unit with the orders to attack his friends—and he knows he will be unable to do it. To avoid the dishonor awaiting him, he decides to disembowel himself with his sword. His wife, out of love, obedience, and honor, witnesses his ceremonial self-destruction in their home and then kills herself with a dagger.

Letters are another literary genre which, as illustrated by the Isao Matsuo selection, sometimes deals with the subject of suicide. One such letter was written several years ago by the Henry Pitney Van Dusens. Pitney, a former theological school president and internationally known church leader, was seventy-seven and had suffered a serious stroke five years earlier. Elizabeth, for years a devoted wife and partner, was eighty and almost crippled by arthritis. Together they decided, after agonizing thought, that self-inflicted death was justifiable in their case and was preferable to the painful future awaiting them. Prior to taking sleeping pills, they sent a letter to their relatives and friends which said, in part, "we hope that you will understand what we have done even though some of you will disapprove of it . . . we still feel that this is the best way and the right way to go."

The selections offer a variety of views on suicide, beginning with some of the classical arguments about the morality of the act in the writings of Plato, Seneca, and Thomas Aquinas. William Shakespeare, author of at least thirty-seven plays in English, and Chikamatsu Monzaemon, author of ninety-seven dramas in Japanese, next describe double suicides involving young lovers.

The more recent selections begin with Gustave Flaubert's graphic literary picture of Madame Bovary's suicide. Edwin Arlington Robinson, an American poet who often wrote about suicide, then depicts the suicides of a miller ("The Mill") and a rich man envied by everyone in town ("Richard Cory"). Dorothy Parker, in her favored role of satirist, writes in "Résumé" about the limitations of various self-destructive alternatives. "A Summer Tragedy," by Arna Bontemps, is a story of a double suicide reluctantly committed because life seemed to have run its course. The letter by Isao Matsuo, a young Japanese, and the novel by Sylvia Plath, a young American writer, conclude the section by providing insights into the minds and motives of two people who did kill themselves.

from PHAEDO
Plato (427–347 B.C.)

Questions about the morality of suicide are ancient. In Greece, at a time when Sophocles' plays *Oedipus the King* and *Antigone* had already depicted suicide, Plato addressed the question of whether suicide is morally permissible. In relating the final conversation between Socrates and his students, Plato interprets Socrates as having said that suicide is not a moral option because humans are not the ultimate possessors of their lives.

As he spoke, he let down his legs on to the ground, and sat thus during the rest of the talk. Then Cebes asked him, "What do you mean, Socrates, by saying, that it is not lawful for a man to do violence to himself, but that the philosopher would be willing to follow the dying?"

"Why, Cebes," he said, "have not you and Simmias heard all about such things from Philolaos, when you were his pupils?"

"Nothing clear, Socrates."

"Well truly, all I say myself is only from hearsay; however, what I happen to have heard I don't mind telling you. Indeed, it is perhaps most proper that one who is going to depart and take up his abode in that world should think about the life over there and say what sort of life we imagine it to be: for what else could one do with the time till sunset?"

"Well then, why pray do they say it is not lawful for a man to take his own life, my dear Socrates? I have already heard Philolaos myself, as you asked me just now, when he was staying in our parts, and I have heard others too, and they all said we must not do that; but I never heard anything clear about it."

"Well, go on trying," said Socrates, "and perhaps you may hear something. It might perhaps seem surprising to you if in this one thing, of all that happens to a human being, there is never any exception—if it never chances to a man amongst the other chances of his life that sometimes for some people it is better to die than to live; but it does probably seem surprising to you if those people for whom it *is* better to die may not rightly do this good to themselves, but must wait for some other benefactor."

And Cebes answered, with a light laugh. "True for ye, by Zeus!" using his native Doric.

"Indeed, put like this," said Socrates, "it would seem unreasonable; but possibly there is a grain of reason in it. At least, the tale whispered in secret about these things is that we men are in a sort of custody, and a man must not release himself or run away, which appears a great mystery to me and not easy to see through. But I do think, Cebes, it is right to say the gods are those who take care of us, and that we men are one of the gods' possessions—don't you think so?"

"Yes, I do," said Cebes.

"Then," said he, "if one of your own possessions, your slave, should kill himself, without your indicating to him that you wanted him to die, you would be angry with him, and punish him if there were any punishment?"

"Certainly," said he.

"Possibly, then, it is not unreasonable in that sense, that a man must not kill himself before God sends on him some necessity, like that which is present here now."

from EPISTULAE MORALES
Seneca (4 B.C.–A.D. 65)

A Stoic philosopher during the first century, Seneca served as the tutor of Nero and was virtually the co-ruler of the Roman empire for a number of years. In A.D. 65 he was accused of participating in a conspiracy against Nero and ordered to commit suicide. Having tried unsuccessfully to dissuade his wife from joining him in death, he and she simultaneously slashed their wrists. Earlier he had developed the following views on the morality of self-inflicted death.

You may consider that the same thing happens to us; life has carried some men with the greatest rapidity to the harbor, the harbor they were bound to reach even if they tarried on the way, while others it has fretted and harassed. To such a life, as you are aware, one should not always cling. For mere living is not a good, but living well. Accordingly, the wise man will live as long as he ought, not as long as he can. He will mark in what place, with whom, and how he is to conduct his existence, and what he is about to do. He always reflects concerning the quality, and not the quantity, of his life. As soon as there are many events in his life that give him trouble and disturb his peace of mind, he sets himself free. And this privilege is his, not only when the crisis is upon him, but as soon as Fortune seems to be playing him false; then he looks about carefully and sees whether he ought, or ought not, to end his life on that account. He holds that it makes no difference to him whether his taking-off be natural or self-inflicted, whether it comes later or earlier. He does not regard it with fear, as if it were a great loss; for no man can lose very much when but a driblet remains. It is not a question of dying earlier or later, but of dying well or ill. And dying well means escape from the danger of living ill.

That is why I regard the words of the well-known Rhodian as most unmanly. This person was thrown into a cage by his tyrant, and fed there like some wild animal. And when a certain man advised him to end his life by fasting, he replied: "A man may hope for anything while he has life." This may be true; but life is not to be purchased at any price. No matter how great or how well-assured certain rewards may be, I shall not strive to attain them at the price of a shameful confession of weakness. Shall I reflect that Fortune has all power over one who lives, rather than reflect that she has no power over one who knows how to die? There are times, nevertheless, when a man, even though certain death impends and he knows that torture is in store for him, will refrain from lending a hand to his own punishment; to himself, however, he would lend a hand. It is folly to die through fear of dying. The executioner is upon you; wait for him. Why anticipate him? Why assume the management of a cruel task that belongs to another? Do you grudge your executioner his privilege, or do you merely relieve him of his task? Socrates might have ended his life by fasting; he might have died by starvation rather than by poison. But instead of this he spent thirty days in prison awaiting death, not with the idea "everything may happen," or "so long an interval has room for many a hope" but in order that he might show himself submissive to the laws and make the last moments of Socrates an edification to his friends. What would have been more foolish than, scorning death, at the same time to be afraid of poison?

. . . .

You can find men who have gone so far as to profess wisdom and yet maintain that one should not offer violence to one's own life, and hold it accursed for a man to be the means of his own destruction; we should wait, say they, for the end decreed by nature. But one who says this does not see that he is shutting off the path to freedom. The best thing which eternal law ever ordained was that it allowed to us one entrance into life, but many exits. Must I await the cruelty either of disease or of man, when I can depart through the midst of torture, and shake off my troubles? This is the one reason why we cannot complain of life: it keeps no one against his will. Humanity is well situated, because no man is unhappy except by his own fault. Live, if you so desire; if not, you may return to the place whence you came. You have often been cupped in order to relieve headaches. You have had veins cut for the purpose of reducing your weight. If you would pierce your heart, a gaping wound is not necessary; a lancet will open the way to that great freedom, and tranquillity can be purchased at the cost of a pin-prick.

. . . .

You need not think that none but great men have had the strength to burst the bonds of human servitude; you need not believe that this cannot be done except by a Cato—Cato, who with his hand dragged forth the spirit which he had not succeeded in freeing by the sword. Nay, men of the meanest lot in life have by a mighty impulse escaped to safety, and when they were not allowed to die at their own convenience, or to suit themselves in their choice of the instruments of death, they have snatched up whatever was lying ready to hand, and by sheer strength have turned objects which were by nature harmless into weapons of their own. For example, there was lately in a training-school for wild-beast gladiators a German, who was making ready for the morning exhibition; he withdrew in order to relieve himself—the only thing which he was to do in secret and without the presence of a guard. While so engaged, he seized the stick of wood, tipped with a sponge, which was devoted to the vilest uses, and stuffed it, just as it was, down his throat; thus he blocked up his windpipe, and choked the breath from his body. That was truly to insult death! Yes, indeed; it was not a very elegant or becoming way to die; but what is more foolish than to be over-nice about dying? What a brave fellow! He surely deserved to be allowed to choose his fate! How bravely he would have wielded a sword! With what courage he would have hurled himself into the depths of the sea, or down a precipice! Cut off from resources on every hand, he yet found a way to furnish himself with death, and with a weapon for death. Hence you can understand that nothing but the will need postpone death. Let each man judge the deed of this most zealous fellow as he likes, provided we agree on this point—that the foulest death is preferable to the cleanest slavery.

from SUMMA THEOLOGICA
Thomas Aquinas (1225–1274)

Significantly influenced by the thought of Aristotle and Augustine, Aquinas was an outstanding philosopher and theologian whose influence on the Roman Catholic tradition is immeasurable. He was a prolific writer on a wide range of subjects. His *Summa Theologica*, begun in 1265 and unfinished at his death, addresses the issue of suicide in the systematic manner which characterizes the entire work. The specific question addressed is, "Whether It Is Lawful to Kill Oneself?"

We proceed thus to the Fifth Article:

Objection 1. It would seem lawful for a man to kill himself. For murder is a sin in so far as it is contrary to justice. But no man can do an injustice to himself, as is proved in *Ethic*.v.11. Therefore no man sins by killing himself.

Obj. 2. Further, It is lawful, for one who exercises public authority, to kill evildoers. Now he who exercises public authority is sometimes an evildoer. Therefore he may lawfully kill himself.

Obj. 3. Further, It is lawful for a man to suffer spontaneously a lesser danger that he may avoid a greater: Thus it is lawful for a man to cut off a decayed limb even from himself, that he may save his whole body. Now sometimes a man, by killing himself, avoids a greater evil, for an example an unhappy life, or the shame of sin. Therefore a man may kill himself.

Obj. 4. Further, Samson killed himself, as related in Judges xvi, and yet he is numbered among the saints (Heb. xi). Therefore it is lawful for a man to kill himself.

Obj. 5. Further, It is related (2 Mach. xiv.42) that a certain Razias killed himself, *choosing to die nobly rather than to fall into the hands of the wicked, and to suffer abuses unbecoming his noble birth.* Now nothing that is done nobly and bravely is unlawful. Therefore suicide is not unlawful.

On the contrary, Augustine says (*De Civ. Dei* i.20): *Hence it follows that the words "Thou shalt not kill" refer to the killing of a man; not another man; therefore, not even thyself. For he who kills himself, kills nothing else than a man.*

I answer that, It is altogether unlawful to kill oneself, for three reasons. First, because everything naturally loves itself, the result being that everything naturally keeps itself in being, and resists corruption so far as it can. Wherefore suicide is contrary to the inclination of nature, and to charity whereby every man should love himself. Hence suicide is always a mortal sin, as being contrary to the natural law and to charity.

Secondly, because every part, as such, belongs to the whole. Now every man is part of the community, and so, as such, he belongs to the community. Hence by killing himself he injures the community, as the Philosopher declares (*Ethic.* v.ii).

Thirdly, because life is God's gift to man, and is subject to His power, Who kills and makes to live. Hence whoever takes his own life, sins against God, even as he who kills another's slave, sins against that slave's master, and as he who usurps himself judgment of a matter not entrusted to him. For it belongs to God alone to pronounce sentence of death and life, according to Deut. xxxii.39, *I will kill and I will make to live.*

Reply Obj. 1. Murder is a sin, not only because it is contrary to justice, but also because it is opposed to charity which a man should have towards himself: in this respect suicide is a sin in relation to oneself. In relation to the community and to God, it is sinful, by reason also of its opposition to justice.

Reply Obj. 2. One who exercises public authority may lawfully put to death an evildoer, since he can pass judgment on him. But no man is judge of himself. Wherefore it is not lawful for one who exercises public authority to put himself to death for any sin whatever; although he may lawfully commit himself to the judgment of others.

Reply Obj. 3. Man is made master of himself through his free will; wherefore he can lawfully dispose of himself as to those matters which pertain to this life which is ruled by man's free will. But the passage from this life to another and happier one is subject not to man's free will but to the power of God. Hence it is not lawful for man to take his own life that he may pass to a happier life, nor that he may escape any unhappiness whatsoever of the present life, because the ultimate and most fearsome evil of this life is death, as the Philosopher states (*Ethic.* iii.6). Therefore to bring death upon oneself in order to escape the other afflictions of this life, is to adopt a greater evil in order to avoid a lesser. . . .

Reply Obj. 4. As Augustine says (*De Civ. Dei* i.21), *not even Samson is to be excused that he crushed himself together with his enemies under the ruins of the house, except the Holy Ghost, Who had wrought many wonders through him, had secretly commanded him to do this.* He assigns the same reason in the case of certain holy women, who at the time of persecution took their own lives, and who are commemorated by the Church.

Reply Obj. 5. It belongs to fortitude that a man does not shrink from being slain by another, for the sake of the good of virtue, and that he may avoid sin. But that a man take his own life in order to avoid penal evils has indeed an appearance of fortitude . . . yet it is not true fortitude, but rather a weakness of soul unable to bear penal evils, as the Philosopher (*Ethic.* iii.7) and Augustine (*De Civ. Dei* i.22,23) declare.

from ROMEO AND JULIET (v, 2)
William Shakespeare (1564–1616)

The subject of suicide is fairly common in Shakespeare's tragedies: Othello stabs himself, Ophelia drowns, and Hamlet seriously considers self-destruction. Perhaps the most famous Shakespearean suicide scene is the double suicide which ends the ill-fated romance of Romeo and Juliet. In the first excerpt Romeo, discovering Juliet asleep in a burial vault, believes her to be dead and drinks poison. In the second excerpt Juliet awakens, sees Romeo's dead body, and kills herself with a dagger.

ROMEO: How oft when men are at the point of death
   Have they been merry! which their keepers call
   A lightning before death: O, how may I
   Call this a lightning? O my love! my wife!
   Death, that hath suck'd the honey of thy breath,
   Hath had no power yet upon thy beauty:
   Thou art not conquer'd; beauty's ensign yet
   Is crimson in thy lips and in thy cheeks,
   And death's pale flag is not advanced there.
   Tybalt, liest thou there in thy bloody sheet?
   O, what more favor can I do to thee,
   Than with that hand that cut thy youth in twain
   To sunder his that was thine enemy?
   Forgive me, cousin! Ah, dear Juliet,
   Why art thou yet so fair? shall I believe
   That unsubstantial death is amorous,
   And that the lean abhorred monster keeps
   Thee here in dark to be his paramour?

For fear of that, I still will stay with thee;
And never from this palace of dim night
Depart again: here, here will I remain
With worms that are thy chamber-maids; O, here
Will I set up my everlasting rest,
And shake the yoke of inauspicious stars
From this world-wearied flesh. Eyes, look your last!
Arms, take your last embrace! and, lips, O you
The doors of breath, seal with a righteous kiss
A dateless bargain to engrossing death!
Come, bitter conduct, come, unsavoury guide!
Thou desperate pilot, now at once run on
The dashing rocks thy sea-sick weary bark!
Here's to my love! [*Drinks.*] O true apothecary!
Thy drugs are quick. Thus with a kiss I die. [*Dies.*]

. . . .

JULIET: What's here? a cup, closed in my true love's hand?
Poison, I see, hath been his timeless end:
O churl! drunk all, and left no friendly drop
To help me after? I will kiss thy lips;
Haply some poison yet doth hang on them,
To make me die with a restorative. [*Kisses him.*]
Thy lips are warm.
FIRST WATCHMAN: [*Within*] Lead, boy: which way?
JULIET: Yea, noise? then I'll be brief. O happy dagger!
[*Snatching Romeo's dagger.*]
This is thy sheath [*Stabs herself*]; there rust, and let me die.
[*Falls on Romeo's body, and dies.*]

from THE LOVE SUICIDES AT SONEZAKI
Chikamatsu Monzaemon (1653-1724)

In 1703 a young man named Tokubei committed suicide with Ohatsu, a
prostitute, within the grounds of the Sonezaki Shrine. Within two weeks
Chikamatsu, who had earlier been a Buddhist monk, had written a play about the
suicides, the first of several dealing with the subject of suicide, and the play was

soon performed in a puppet theater. The third scene contains some of the most famous passages in Japanese literature and provides a graphic account of the self-destructive acts known as love suicides. The often repeated *Namu Amida Butsu* ("Hail, Amida Buddha") is an invocation addressed to Amida Buddha, Lord of the Western Paradise in Shin Buddhism.

Scene III: The Journey

NARRATOR: Farewell to the world, and to the night farewell.
We who walk the road to death, to what should we be likened?
To the frost by the road that leads to the graveyard,
Vanishing with each step ahead:
This dream of a dream is sorrowful.
Ah, did you count the bell? Of the seven strokes
That mark the dawn six have sounded.
The remaining one will be the last echo
We shall hear in this life. It will echo
The bliss of annihilation.
Farewell, and not the bell alone,
We look a last time on the grass, the trees, the sky,
The clouds go by unmindful of us,
The bright Dipper is reflected in the water,
The Wife and Husband Stars inside the Milky Way.

TOKUBEI: Let's think the Bridge of Umeda
The bridge the magpies built and make a vow
That we will always be Wife and Husband Stars.

NARRATOR: "With all my heart," she says and clings to him:
So many are the tears that fall between the two,
The waters of the river must have risen.
On a teahouse balcony across the way
A party in the lamplight loudly discuss
Before they go to bed the latest gossip,
With many words about the good and bad
Of this year's crop of lovers' suicides.

TOKUBEI: How strange! but yesterday, even today,
We spoke as if such things didn't concern us.
Tomorrow we shall figure in their gossip—
Well, if they wish to sing about us, let them.

NARRATOR: This is the song that now we hear:
   "Why can't you take me for your wife?
   Although you think you don't want me . . ."
However we think, however lament,
Both our fate and the world go against us.
Never before today was there a day
Of relaxation, and untroubled night,
Instead, the tortures of an ill-starred love.
   "What did I do to deserve it?
   I never can forget you.
   You want to shake me off and go?
   I'll never let you.
   Take me with your hands and kill me
   Or I'll never let you go,"
Said the girl in tears.

TOKUBEI: Of all the many songs, that it should be that one,
This very evening, but who is it that sings?
We are those who listen; others like us
Who've gone this way have had the same ordeal.

NARRATOR: They cling to one another, weeping bitterly,
And wish, as many a lover has wished,
The night would last even a little longer.
The heartless summer night is short as ever,
And soon the cockcrows chase away their lives.

TOKUBEI: Let us die in the wood before the dawn.

NARRATOR: He takes her hands.
At Umeda Embankment, the night ravens.

TOKUBEI: Tomorrow our bodies may be their meal.

OHATSU: It's strange this year is your unlucky year
Of twenty-five, and mine of nineteen too.
That we who love should both be cursed this way
Is proof how close the ties that join us.
All the prayers that I have made for this world
To the gods and to the Buddha, I here and now
Direct to the future, and in the world to come,
May we remain together on one lotus.

NARRATOR: One hundred eight the beads her fingers tell
  On her rosary; her tears increase the sum.
  No end to her grief, but the road has an end.
  Their heart and the sky are dark, the wind intense:
  They have reached the wood of Sonezaki.

  Shall it be there, shall it be here?
  And when they brush the grass the dew which falls
  Vanishes even quicker than their lives,
  In this uncertain world a lightning flash—
  A lightning flash or was it something else?
OHATSU: Oh, I'm afraid. What was that just now?
TOKUBEI: Those were human spirits. I thought that we'd be the only ones
  to die tonight, but others have gone ahead of us. Whoever they may
  be, we'll journey together to the Mountain of Death. *Namu Amida
  Butsu. Namu Amida Butsu.*
OHATSU: How sad it is! Other souls have left the world. *Namu Amida
  Butsu.*
NARRATOR: The woman melts in helpless tears of grief.
OHATSU: To think that other people are dying tonight too! That makes
  me feel wretched.
NARRATOR: Man that he is, his tears are falling freely.
TOKUBEI: Those two spirits flying together over there—they can't be
  anyone else's! They must be ours, yours and mine!
OHATSU: Those two spirits? Are we already dead then?
TOKUBEI: Ordinarily, if we were to see a spirit we'd knot our clothes and
  howl to save our lives, but now instead we are hurrying toward our last
  moments, and soon are to live in the same place with them. You
  mustn't lose the way or mistake the road of death!
NARRATOR: They cling to each other, flesh against flesh,
  Then fall with a cry to the ground and weep.
  Their strings of tears unite like grafted branches,
  Or a pine and palm that grow from a single trunk.
  And now, where will they end their dew-like lives?
TOKUBEI: This place will do.
NARRATOR: The sash of his jacket he undoes;
  Ohatsu removes her tear-stained outer robe,

And throws it on the palm tree with whose fronds
She now might sweep away the sad world's dust.
Ohatsu takes a razor from her sleeve.

OHATSU: I had this razor ready just in case we were overtaken on the way
or got separated. I made up my mind that whatever might happen I
would not give up our plan. Oh, how happy I am that we are to die
together as we had hoped!

TOKUBEI: You make me feel so confident in our love that I am not worried even by the thought of death. And yet it would be a pity if because
of the pain that we are to suffer, people said that we looked ugly in
death. Wouldn't it be a good idea if we fastened our bodies to this
twin-trunked tree and died immaculately? Let us become an unparalleled example of a beautiful way of dying.

OHATSU: Yes, as you say.

NARRATOR: Alas! she little thought she thus would use
Her sash of powder blue. She draws it taut,
And with her razor slashes it in two.

OHATSU: My sash is divided, but you and I will never part.

NARRATOR: Face to face they sit, then twice or thrice
He ties her firmly so she will not move.

TOKUBEI: Is it tight?

OHATSU: Yes, it's very tight.

NARRATOR: She looks at him, he looks at her, they burst into tears.

BOTH: This is the end of our unfortunate lives!

TOKUBEI: No, I mustn't weep.

NARRATOR: He raises his head and joins his hands.

TOKUBEI: When I was a small child my parents died, and it was my uncle
who brought me up. I'm ashamed of myself that I am dying this way
without repaying my indebtedness to him, and that I am causing him
trouble that will last after my death. Please forgive me my sins. Now
soon I shall be seeing my parents in the other world. Father, Mother,
come welcome me there!

NARRATOR: Ohatsu also joins her hands in prayer.

OHATSU: I envy you that you will be meeting your parents in the world of
the dead. My father and mother are still alive. I wonder when I shall
meet them again. I had a letter from them this spring, but the last time
I saw them was at the beginning of autumn last year. When they get

word tomorrow in the village of my suicide, how unhappy they will be.
Mother, Father, brothers and sisters, I now say good-bye to the world.
If only my thoughts can reach you, I pray that I may be able to appear
in your dreams. Dearest Mother, beloved Father!

NARRATOR: She weeps convulsively and wails aloud.
Her lover also sheds incessant tears,
And cries out in despair, as is most natural.

OHATSU: There's no use in talking any longer. Kill me, kill me quickly!

NARRATOR: She hastens the moment of death.

TOKUBEI: I'm ready.

NARRATOR: He swiftly draws his dagger.

TOKUBEI: The moment has come. *Namu Amida. Namu Amida.*

NARRATOR: But when he tries to bring the blade against the skin
Of the woman he's loved, and held, and slept with
So many months and years, his hands begin to shake,
His eyes cloud over. He attempts to stay
His weakening resolve, but still he trembles,
And when he makes a thrust the point goes off,
Deflecting twice or thrice with flashing blade,
Until a cry tells it has reached her throat.

TOKUBEI: *Namu Amida. Namu Amida. Namu Amida Butsu.*

NARRATOR: He presses the blade ever deeper
And when he sees her weaken he falters too.
He stretches forth his arms—of all the pains
That life affords, none is as great as this.

TOKUBEI: Am I going to lag on after you? Let's draw our last breaths
together.

NARRATOR: He thrusts and twists the razor in his throat
Until it seems the handle or the blade must snap.
His eyes grow dim, and his last painful breath
With the dawn's receding tide is drawn away.
But the wind that blows through Sonezaki Wood
Transmits it, and high and low alike,
Gather to pray for them who beyond a doubt
Will in the future attain to Buddhahood.
They thus become a model of true love.

from MADAME BOVARY
Gustave Flaubert (1821–1880)

Madame Bovary was Flaubert's first book and, when published in 1857, resulted in his being prosecuted (and acquitted) for "offenses against morality and religion." The scene excerpted below occurs when Charles and Emma (Madame Bovary) have been married nine years. Simply unable to live with her transgressions and guilt, Emma has decided to kill herself with arsenic. Rather than being the quick and peaceful death she had envisioned, however, her dying is slow and agonizing—for herself, and for Charles and the other people who watch her die.

Justin returned to the kitchen. She tapped on the window. He came out.

"The key! The one for upstairs, where the . . ."

"What?"

And he stared at her, astounded by the pallor of her face, which stood out white against the blackness of the night. She seemed to him extraordinarily beautiful, majestic as an apparition from another world; without understanding what she wanted, he had a foreboding of something terrible.

But she went on quickly, in a low voice, a voice that was gentle and melting:

"I want it! Give it to me."

The wall was thin, and they could hear the clicking of forks on plates in the dining room.

She pretended she had to kill some rats that were keeping her awake nights.

"I must go ask Monsieur."

"No! Stay here!"

Then, with a casual air:

"There's no use bothering him: I'll tell him later. Come along, give me a light."

She passed into the hall off which opened the laboratory door. There against the wall hung a key marked "capharnaum."

"Justin!" called the apothecary impatiently.

"Let's go up!"

He followed her.

The key turned in the lock, and she went straight to the third shelf—so well did her memory serve her as a guide—seized the blue jar, tore out the cork, plunged in her hand, withdrew it full of white powder, and ate greedily.

"Stop!" he cried, flinging himself on her.

"Be quiet! Someone might come. . . ."

He was frantic, wanted to call out.

"Don't say a word about it: all the blame would fall on your master!"

Then she went home, suddenly at peace—almost as serene as though she had done her duty.

When Charles reached home, overwhelmed by the news of the execution, Emma had just left. He called her name, wept, fainted away, but she didn't come back. Where could she be? He sent Félicité to the pharmacist's, to the mayor's, to the dry-goods shop, to the Lion d'Or—everywhere; and whenever his anguish about her momentarily subsided he saw his reputation ruined, all their money gone, Berthe's future wrecked! What was the cause of it all . . .? Not a word! He waited until six that evening. Finally, unable to bear it any longer, and imagining that she must have gone to Rouen, he went out to the highway, followed it for a mile or so, met no one, waited a while, and returned.

She was back.

"What happened? . . . Why? . . . Tell me!"

She sat down at her desk and wrote a letter, sealed it slowly, and added the date and the hour. Then she said in a solemn tone:

"Read it tomorrow. Till then, please don't ask me a single question—not one!"

"But . . ."

"Oh, leave me alone!"

And she stretched out on her bed.

An acrid taste in her mouth woke her. She caught sight of Charles and reclosed her eyes.

She observed herself with interest, to see whether there was any pain. No—nothing yet. She heard the ticking of the clock, the sound of the fire, and Charles breathing, standing there beside her bed.

"Dying doesn't amount to much!" she thought. "I'll fall asleep, and everything will be over."

She swallowed a mouthful of water and turned to the wall.

There was still that dreadful taste of ink.

"I'm thirsty! I'm so thirsty!" she whispered.

"What's wrong with you, anyway?" said Charles, handing her a glass.

"Nothing! Open the window . . . I'm choking!"

She was seized by an attack of nausea so sudden that she scarcely had time to snatch her handkerchief from under the pillow.

"Get rid of it!" she said quickly. "Throw it out!"

He questioned her, but she made no answer. She lay very still, fearing that the slightest disturbance would make her vomit. Now she felt an icy coldness creeping up from her feet toward her heart.

"Ah! It's beginning!" she murmured.

"What did you say?"

She twisted her head from side to side in a gentle movement expressive of anguish, and kept opening her jaws as though she had something very heavy on her tongue. At eight o'clock the vomiting resumed.

Charles noticed that there was a gritty white deposit on the bottom of the basin, clinging to the porcelain.

"That's extraordinary! That's peculiar!" he kept saying.

"No!" she said loudly. "You're mistaken."

Very gently, almost caressingly, he passed his hand over her stomach. She gave a sharp scream. He drew back in fright.

She began to moan, softly at first. Her shoulders heaved in a great shudder, and she grew whiter than the sheet her clenched fingers were digging into. Her irregular pulse was almost imperceptible now.

Beads of sweat stood out on her face, which had turned blue and rigid, as though from the breath of some metallic vapor. Her teeth chattered, her dilated eyes stared about her vaguely, and her sole answer to questions was a shake of her head; two or three times she even smiled. Gradually her groans grew louder. A muffled scream escaped her; she pretended that she was feeling better and that she'd soon be getting up. But she was seized with convulsions.

"God!" she cried. "It's horrible!"

He flung himself on his knees beside her bed.

"Speak to me! What did you eat? Answer, for heaven's sake!"

And in his eyes she read a love as she had never known.

"There . . . over there . . ." she said in a faltering voice.

He darted to the secretary, broke open the seal and read aloud: "No one is to blame . . ." He stopped, passed his hand over his eyes, read it again.

"What . . . ! Help! Help!"

He could only repeat the word: "Poisoned! Poisoned!" Félicité ran to Homais, who spoke loudly as he crossed the square; Madame Lefrancois heard him at the Lion d'Or, other citizens left their beds to tell their neighbors, and all night long the village was awake.

Distracted, stammering, close to collapse, Charles walked in circles around the room. He stumbled against the furniture, tore his hair: never had the pharmacist dreamed there could be so frightful a sight.

He went back to his own house and wrote letters to Monsieur Canivet and Doctor Larivière. He couldn't concentrate, had to begin them over fifteen times. Hippolyte left for Neufchatel, and Justin spurred Bovary's horse so hard that he left it on the hill at Bois-Guillaume, foundered and all but done for.

Charles tried to consult his medical dictionary: he couldn't see; the lines danced before his eyes.

"Don't lose your head!" said the apothecary. "It's just a question of administering some powerful antidote. What poison is it?"

Charles showed him the letter. It was arsenic.

"Well then!" said Homais. "We must make an analysis."

For he knew that an analysis always had to be made in cases of poisoning.

Charles, who hadn't understood, answered with a groan:

"Do it! Do it! Save her . . . !"

And returning to her side, he sank down on the carpet and leaned his head on the edge of her bed, sobbing.

"Don't cry!" she said. "I shan't be tormenting you much longer."

"Why did you do it? What made you?"

"It was the only thing," she answered.

"Weren't you happy? Am I to blame? But I did everything I could . . . !"

"Yes . . . I know . . . You're good, you're different . . ."

She slowly passed her hand through his hair. The sweetness of her touch was more than his grief could bear. He felt his entire being give way to despair at the thought of having to lose her just when she was showing him more love than ever in the past; and he could think of nothing to do—he knew nothing, dared nothing: the need for immediate action took away the last of his presence of mind.

Emma was thinking that now she was through with all the betrayals, the infamies, the countless fierce desires that had racked her. She hated no one, now; a twilight confusion was falling over her thoughts, and of all the world's sounds she heard only the intermittent lament of this poor man beside her, gentle and indistinct, like the last echo of an ever-fainter symphony.

"Bring me my little girl," she said, raising herself on her elbow.

"You're not feeling worse, are you?" Charles asked.

"No! No!"

Berthe was carried in by the maid. Her bare feet peeped out from beneath her long nightdress; she looked serious, still half dreaming. She stared in surprise to see the room in such disorder, and she blinked her eyes, dazzled by the candles that were standing here and there on the furniture. They probably reminded her of other mornings—New Year's day or mi-carême, when she was wakened early in just this same way by candlelight and carried to her mother's bed to be given a shoeful of presents; for she asked:

"Where is it, *maman*?"

And when no one answered:

"I don't see my little shoe!"

Félicité held her over the bed, but she kept looking toward the fireplace.

"Did the nurse take it away?" she asked.

At the word "nurse," which brought back her adulteries and her calamities, Madame Bovary averted her head, as though another, stronger, poison had risen to her mouth and filled her with revulsion.

"Oh, how big your eyes are, *maman*!" cried Berthe, whom the maid had put on the bed. "How pale you are! You're sweating . . . !"

Her mother looked at her.

"I'm afraid!" cried the little girl, shrinking back.

Emma took her hand to kiss it; she struggled.

"Enough! Take her away!" cried Charles, sobbing at the foot of the bed.

The symptoms momentarily stopped; she seemed calmer; and at each insignificant word she said, each time she breathed a little more easily, his hope gained ground. When Canivet finally arrived he threw himself in his arms, weeping.

"Ah! You've come! Thank you! You're kind! But she's doing better. Here: look at her!"

His colleague was not at all of this opinion. There was no use—as he himself put it—"beating around the bush," and he prescribed an emetic, to empty the stomach completely.

Soon she was vomiting blood. Her lips pressed together more tightly. Her limbs were contorted, her body was covered with brown blotches, her pulse quivered under the doctor's fingers like a taut thread, like a harpstring about to snap.

Then she began to scream, horribly. She cursed the poison, railed against it, begged it to be quick; and with her stiffened arms she pushed away everything that Charles, in greater agony than herself, tried to make her drink. He was standing, his handkerchief to his mouth, moaning, weeping, choked by sobs and shaking all over; Félicité rushed about the room; Homais, motionless, kept sighing heavily; and Monsieur Canivet, for all his air of self-assurance, began to manifest some uneasiness:

"What the devil...! But she's purged, and since the cause is removed..."

"The effect should subside," said Homais. "It's self-evident."

"Do something to save her!" cried Bovary.

Paying no attention to the pharmacist, who was venturing the hypothesis that "this paroxysm may mark the beginning of improvement," Canivet was about the give her theriaca when there came the crack of a whip, all the windows rattled, and a post chaise drawn at breakneck speed by three mud-covered horses flashed around the corner of the market place. It was Doctor Larivière.

The sudden appearance of a god wouldn't have caused greater excitement. Bovary raised both hands, Canivet broke off his preparations, and Homais doffed his cap well before the doctor entered.

. . . .

While he was still in the doorway he frowned, catching sight of Emma's cadaverous face as she lay on her back, her mouth open. Then, seeming to listen to Canivet, he passed his forefinger back and forth beneath his nostrils, repeating:

"Yes, yes."

But his shoulders lifted in a slow shrug. Bovary noticed it; their eyes met. The sight of a grieving face was no novelty to the doctor, yet he couldn't keep a tear from dropping onto his shirt front.

He asked Canivet to step into the next room. Charles followed him.

"She's very low, isn't she? How about poultices? What else? Can't you think of something? You've saved so many lives!"

Charles put his arms around him, sagged against his chest, and looked at him anxiously and beseechingly.

"Come, my poor boy, be brave! There's nothing to be done."

And Doctor Larivière turned away.

"You're leaving?"

"I'll be back."

He pretended he had something to say to the coachman, and went out with Canivet, who was no more eager than he to watch Emma die.

The pharmacist joined them in the square. He was temperamentally incapable of staying away from celebrities, and he begged Monsieur Larivière to do him the signal honor of being his guest at lunch.

. . . .

Then the attention of the public was distracted by the appearance of Monsieur Bournisien, crossing the market with the holy oils.

Homais paid his debt to his principles by likening priests to ravens: both are attracted by the odor of the dead. Actually, he had a more personal reason for disliking the sight of a priest: a cassock made him think of a shroud, and his execration of the one owed something to his fear of the other.

Nevertheless, not flinching in the face of what he called his "mission," he returned to the Bovary house along with Canivet, whom Monsieur Larivière had urged to stay on to the end. But for his wife's protests, the pharmacist would have taken his two sons along, to inure them to life's great moments, to provide them with a lesson, an example, a momentous spectacle that they would remember later.

The bedroom, as they entered, was mournful and solemn. On the sewing table, now covered with a white napkin, were five or six small wads of cotton in a silver dish, and nearby a large crucifix between two lighted candelabra. Emma lay with her chin sunk on her breast, her eyelids unnaturally wide apart; and her poor hands picked at the sheets in the ghastly and poignant way of the dying, who seem impatient to cover themselves with their shrouds. Pale as a statue, his eyes red as coals, but no longer weeping, Charles stood facing her at the foot of the bed; the priest, on one knee, mumbled under his breath.

She slowly turned her face, and seemed overjoyed at suddenly seeing the purple stole—doubtless recognizing, in this interval of extraordinary peace, the lost ecstasy of her first mystical flights and the first visions of eternal bliss.

The priest stood up and took the crucifix; she stretched out her head like someone thirsting; and pressing her lips to the body of the God-Man, she imprinted on it, with every ounce of her failing strength, the most passionate love-kiss she had ever given. Then he recited the *Misereatur* and the *Indulgentiam*, dipped his right thumb in the oil, and began the unctions. First he anointed her eyes, once so covetous of all earthly luxuries; then her nostrils, so gluttonous of caressing breezes and amorous scents; then her mouth, so prompt to lie, so defiant in pride, so loud in lust; then her hands, that had thrilled to voluptuous contacts, and finally the soles of her feet, once so swift when she had hastened to slake her desires, and now never to walk again.

The curé wiped his fingers, threw the oil-soaked bits of cotton into the fire, and returned to the dying woman, sitting beside her and telling her that now she must unite her sufferings with Christ's and throw herself on the divine mercy.

As he ended his exhortations he tried to have her grasp a blessed candle, symbol of the celestial glories soon to surround her. Emma was too weak, and couldn't close her fingers: but for Monsieur Bournisien the candle would have fallen to the floor.

Yet she was no longer so pale, and her face was serene, as though the sacrament had cured her.

The priest didn't fail to point this out: he even explained to Bovary that the Lord sometimes prolonged people's lives when He judged it expedient for their salvation, and Charles remembered another day, when, similarly close to death, she had received communion.

"Perhaps there's hope after all," he thought.

And indeed, she looked all about her, slowly, like someone waking from a dream; then, in a distinct voice, she asked for her mirror, and she remained bowed over it for some time, until great tears flowed from her eyes. Then she threw back her head with a sigh, and sank onto the pillow.

At once her breast began to heave rapidly. Her tongue hung at full length from her mouth; her rolling eyes grew dim like the globes of two lamps about to go out; and one might have thought her dead already but for the terrifying, ever-faster movement of her ribs, which were shaken by furious gasps, as though her soul were straining violently to break its fetters. Félicité knelt before the crucifix, and even the pharmacist flexed his knees a little. Monsieur Canivet stared vaguely out into the square. Bournisien had resumed his praying, his face bowed over the edge of the bed and his long black cassock trailing out behind him into the room. Charles was on the other side, on his knees, his arms stretched out toward Emma. He had taken her hands, and was pressing them, shuddering at every beat of her heart, as at the tremors of a falling ruin. As the death-rattle grew louder, the priest speeded his prayers: they mingled with Bovary's stifled sobs, and at moments everything seemed drowned by the monotonous flow of Latin syllables that sounded like the tolling of a bell.

Suddenly from on the sidewalk came a noise of heavy wooden shoes and the scraping of a stick, and a voice rose up, a raucous voice singing:

A clear day's warmth will often move
A lass to stray in dreams of love.

Emma sat up like a galvanized corpse, her hair streaming, her eyes fixed and gaping.

To gather up the stalks of wheat
The swinging scythe keeps laying by,
Nanette goes stooping in the heat
Along the furrow where they lie.

"The blind man!" she cried.

Emma began to laugh—a horrible, frantic, desperate laugh—fancying that she saw the beggar's hideous face, a figure of terror looming up in the darkness of eternity.

The wind blew very hard that day
And snatched her petticoat away!

A spasm flung her down on the mattress. Everyone drew close. She had ceased to exist.

THE MILL
Edwin Arlington Robinson (1869–1935)

The miller's wife had waited long,
    The tea was cold, the fire was dead;
And there might yet be nothing wrong
    In how he went and what he said:
"There are no millers any more,"
    Was all that she had heard him say;
And he had lingered at the door
    So long that it seemed yesterday.

Sick with a fear that had no form
    She knew that she was there at last;
And in the mill there was a warm
    And mealy fragrance of the past.
What else there was would only seem
    To say again what he had meant;
And what was hanging from a beam
    Would not have heeded where she went.

And if she thought it followed her,
    She may have reasoned in the dark
That one way of the few there were
    Would hide her and would leave no mark:
Black water, smooth above the weir
    Like starry velvet in the night,
Though ruffled once, would soon appear
    The same as ever to the sight.

RICHARD CORY
Edwin Arlington Robinson (1869–1935)

Whenever Richard Cory went down town,
We people on the pavement looked at him:
He was a gentleman from sole to crown,
Clean favored, and imperially slim.

And he was always quietly arrayed,
And he was always human when he talked;
But still he fluttered pulses when he said,
"Good-morning," and he glittered when he walked.

And he was rich—yes, richer than a king—
And admirably schooled in every grace:
In fine, we thought that he was everything
To make us wish that we were in his place.

So on we worked, and waited for the light,
And went without the meat, and cursed the bread;
And Richard Cory, one calm summer night,
Went home and put a bullet through his head.

RÉSUMÉ
Dorothy Parker (1893–1967)

Razors pain you;
Rivers are damp;
Acids stain you;
And drugs cause cramp.
Guns aren't lawful;
Nooses give;
Gas smells awful;
You might as well live.

A SUMMER TRAGEDY
Arna Bontemps (1902-1973)

Author of poetry, essays, short stories, and novels, Bontemps ranks as one of America's leading black writers in this century. In this poignant short story he depicts the plight of an old couple who believe that life no longer holds meaning for them. Having coped with blindness, poverty, loneliness, a stroke, and the unexpected deaths of their children, Jeff and Jennie decide that death is preferable to continued living.

Old Jeff Patton, the black share farmer, fumbled with his bow tie. His fingers trembled and the high stiff collar pinched his throat. A fellow loses his hand for such vanities after thirty or forty years of simple life. Once a year, or maybe twice if there's a wedding among his kinfolks, he may spruce up; but generally fancy clothes do nothing but adorn the wall of the big room and feed the moths. That had been Jeff Patton's experience. He had not worn his stiff-bosomed shirt more than a dozen times in all his married life. His swallow-tailed coat lay on the bed beside him, freshly brushed and pressed, but it was as full of holes as the overalls in which he worked on weekdays. The moths had used it badly. Jeff twisted his mouth into a hideous toothless grimace as he contended with the obstinate bow. He stamped his good foot and decided to give up the struggle.

"Jennie," he called.

"What's that, Jeff?" His wife's shrunken voice came out of the adjoining room like an echo. It was hardly bigger than a whisper.

"I reckon you'll have to he'p me wid this heah bow tie, baby," he said meekly. "Dog if I can hitch it up."

Her answer was not strong enough to reach him, but presently the old woman came to the door, feeling her way with a stick. She had a wasted, dead-leaf appearance. Her body, as scrawny and gnarled as a string bean, seemed less than nothing in the ocean of frayed and faded petticoats that surrounded her. These hung an inch or two above the tops of her heavy unlaced shoes and showed little grotesque piles where the stockings had fallen down from her negligible legs.

"You oughta could do a heap mo' wid a thing like that'n me—beingst as you got yo' good sight."

"Looks like I oughta could," he admitted. "But ma fingers is gone democrat on me. I get all mixed up in the looking glass an' can't tell wicha way to twist the devilish thing."

Jennie sat on the side of the bed and old Jeff Patton got down on one knee while she tied the bow knot. It was a slow and painful ordeal for each of them in this position. Jeff's bones cracked, his knee ached, and it was only after a half dozen attempts that Jennie worked a semblance of a bow into the tie.

"I got to dress maself now," the old woman whispered. "These is ma old shoes an' stockings, and I ain't so much as unwrapped ma dress."

"Well, don't worry 'bout me no mo', baby," Jeff said. "That 'bout finishes me. All I gotta do now is slip on that old coat 'n ves' an' I'll be fixed to leave."

Jennie disappeared again through the dim passage into the shed room. Being blind was no handicap to her in that black hole. Jeff heard the cane placed against the wall beside the door and knew that his wife was on easy ground. He put on his coat, took a battered top hat from the bedpost and hobbled to the front door. He was ready to travel. As soon as Jennie could get on her Sunday shoes and her old black silk dress, they would start.

Outside the tiny log house, the day was warm and mellow with sunshine. A host of wasps were humming with busy excitement in the trunk of a dead sycamore. Gray squirrels were searching through the grass for hickory nuts and blue jays were in the trees, hopping from branch to branch. Pine woods stretched away to the left like a black sea. Among them were scattered scores of log houses like Jeff's, houses of black share farmers. Cows and pigs wandered freely among the trees. There was no danger of loss. Each farmer knew his own stock and knew his neighbor's as well as he knew his neighbor's children.

Down the slope to the right were the cultivated acres on which the colored folks worked. They extended to the river, more than two miles away, and they were today green with the unmade cotton crop. A tiny thread of a road, which passed directly in front of Jeff's place, ran through these green fields like a pencil mark.

Jeff, standing outside the door, with his absurd hat in his left hand, surveyed the wide scene tenderly. He had been forty-five years on these acres. He loved them with the unexplained affection that others have for the countries to which they belong.

The sun was hot on his head, his collar still pinched his throat, and the Sunday clothes were intolerably hot. Jeff transferred the hat to his right hand and began fanning with it. Suddenly the whisper that was Jennie's voice came out of the shed room.

"You can bring the car round front whilst you's waitin'," it said feebly. There was a tired pause; then it added, "I'll soon be fixed to go."

"A'right, baby," Jeff answered. "I'll get it in a minute."

But he didn't move. A thought struck him that made his mouth fall open. The mention of the car brought to his mind, with new intensity, the trip he and Jennie were about to take. Fear came into his eyes; excitement took his breath. Lord, Jesus!

"Jeff . . . O Jeff," the old woman's whisper called.

He awakened with a jolt. "Hunh, baby?"

"What you doin'?"

"Nuthin. Jes studyin'. I jes been turnin' things round'n round in ma mind."

"You could be gettin' the car," she said.

"Oh yes, right away, baby."

He started round to the shed, limping heavily on his bad leg. There were three frizzly chickens in the yard. All his other chickens had been killed or stolen recently. But the frizzly chickens had been saved somehow. That was fortunate indeed, for these curious creatures had a way of devouring "Poison" from the yard and in that way protecting against conjure and black luck and spells. But even the frizzly chickens seemed now to be in a stupor. Jeff thought they had some ailment; he expected all three of them to die shortly.

The shed in which the old T-model Ford stood was only a grass roof held up by four corner poles. It had been built by tremulous hands at a time when the little rattletrap car had been regarded as a peculiar treasure. And, miraculously, despite wind and downpour it still stood.

Jeff adjusted the crank and put his weight upon it. The engine came to life with a sputter and bang that rattled the old car from radiator to taillight. Jeff hopped into the seat and put his foot on the accelerator. The sputtering and banging increased. The rattling became more violent.

That was good. It was good banging, good sputtering and rattling, and it meant that the aged car was still in running condition. She could be depended on for this trip.

Again Jeff's thought halted as if paralyzed. The suggestion of the trip fell into the machinery of his mind like a wrench. He felt dazed and weak. He swung the car out into the yard, made a half turn and drove around to the front door. When he took his hands off the wheel, he noticed that he was trembling violently. He cut off the motor and climbed to the ground to wait for Jennie.

A few minutes later she was at the window, her voice rattling against the pane like a broken shutter.

"I'm ready, Jeff."

He did not answer, but limped into the house and took her by the arm. He led her slowly through the big room, down the step and across the yard.

"You reckon I'd oughta lock the do'?" he asked softly.

They stopped and Jennie weighed the question. Finally she shook her head.

"Ne' mind the do'," she said. "I don't see no cause to lock up things."

"You right," Jeff agreed. "No cause to lock up."

Jeff opened the door and helped his wife into the car. A quick shudder passed over him. Jesus! Again he trembled.

"How come you shaking so?" Jennie whispered.

"I don't know," he said.

"You mus' be scairt, Jeff."

"No, baby, I ain't scairt."

He slammed the door after her and went around to crank up again. The motor started easily. Jeff wished that it had not been so responsive. He would have liked a few more minutes in which to turn things around in his head. As it was, with Jennie chiding him about being afraid, he had to keep going. He swung the car into the little pencil-mark road and started off toward the river, driving very slowly, very cautiously.

Chugging across the green countryside, the small battered Ford seemed tiny indeed. Jeff felt a familiar excitement, a thrill, as they came down the first slope to the immense levels on which the cotton was growing. He could not help reflecting that the crops were good. He knew what that meant, too; he had made forty-five of them with his own hands. It was true that he had worn out nearly a dozen mules, but that was the fault of old man Stevenson, the owner of the land. Major Stevenson had the odd notion that one mule was all a share farmer needed to work a thirty-acre plot. It was an expensive notion, the way it killed mules from overwork, but the old man held to it. Jeff thought it killed a good many share farmers as well as mules, but he had no sympathy for them. He had always been strong, and he had been taught to have no patience with weakness in men. Women or children might be tolerated if they were puny, but a weak man was a curse. Of course, his own children——

Jeff's thought halted there. He and Jennie never mentioned their dead children any more. And naturally he did not wish to dwell upon them in his mind. Before he knew it, some remark would slip out of his mouth and that would make Jennie feel blue. Perhaps she would cry. A woman like Jennie could not easily throw off the grief that comes from losing five grown children within two years. Even Jeff was still staggered by the blow. His memory had not been much good recently. He frequently talked to himself. And, although he had kept it a secret, he knew that his courage had left him. He was terrified by the least unfamiliar sound at night. He was reluctant to venture far from home in the daytime. And that habit of trembling when he felt fearful was now far beyond his control. Sometimes he became afraid and trembled without knowing what had frightened him. The feeling would just come over him like a chill.

The car rattled slowly over the dusty road. Jennie sat erect and silent, with a little absurd hat pinned to her hair. Her useless eyes seemed very large, very white in their deep sockets. Suddenly Jeff heard her voice, and he inclined his head to catch the words.

"Is we passed Delia Moore's house yet?" she asked.

"Not yet," he said.

"You must be drivin' might slow, Jeff."

"We might just as well take our time, baby."

There was a pause. A little puff of steam was coming out of the radiator of the car. Heat wavered above the hood. Delia Moore's house was nearly half a mile away. After a moment Jennie spoke again.

"You ain't really scairt, is you, Jeff?"

"Nah, baby, I ain't scairt."

"You know how we agreed—we gotta keep on goin'."

Jewels of perspiration appeared on Jeff's forehead. His eyes rounded, blinked, became fixed on the road.

"I don't know," he said with a shiver. "I reckon it's the only thing to do."

Hm."

A flock of guinea fowls, pecking in the road, were scattered by the passing car. Some of them took to their wings; others hid under bushes. A blue jay, swaying on a leafy twig, was annoying a roadside squirrel. Jeff held an even speed till he came near Delia's place. Then he slowed down noticeably.

Delia's house was really no house at all, but an abandoned store building converted into a dwelling. It sat near a crossroads, beneath a single black cedar tree. There Delia, a cattish old creature of Jennie's age, lived alone. She had been there more years than anybody could remember, and long ago had won the disfavor of such women as Jennie. For in her young days Delia had been gayer, yellower, and saucier than seemed proper in those parts. Her ways with menfolks had been dark and suspicious. And the fact that she had had as many husbands as children did not help her reputation.

"Yonder's old Delia," Jeff said as they passed.

"What she doin'?"

"Jes sittin' in the do'," he said.

"She see us?"

"Hm," Jeff said. "Musta did."

That relieved Jennie. It strengthened her to know that her old enemy had seen her pass in her best clothes. That would give the old she-devil something to chew her gums and fret about, Jennie thought. Wouldn't she have a fit if she didn't find out? Old evil Delia! This would be just the thing for her. It would pay her back for being so evil. It would also pay her, Jennie thought, for the way she used to grin at Jeff—long ago when her teeth were good.

The road became smooth and red, and Jeff could tell by the smell of the air that they were nearing the river. He could see the rise where the road turned and ran along parallel to the stream. The car chugged on monotonously. After a long silent spell, Jennie leaned against Jeff and spoke.

"How many bale o' cotton you think we got standin'?" she said.

Jeff wrinkled his forehead as he calculated.

"'Bout twenty-five, I reckon."

"How many you make las' year?"

"Twenty-eight," he said. "How come you ask that?"

"I's jes thinking'," Jennie said quietly.

"It don't make a speck o' difference though," Jeff reflected. "If we get much or if we get little, we still gonna be in debt to old man Stevenson when he gets through counting up agin us. It's took us a long time to learn that."

Jennie was not listening to these words. She had fallen into a trance-like meditation. Her lips twitched. She chewed her gums and rubbed her gnarled hands nervously. Suddenly she leaned forward, buried her face in the nervous hands and burst into tears. She cried aloud in a dry cracked voice that suggested the rattle of fodder on dead stalks. She cried aloud like a child, for she had never learned to suppress a genuine sob. Her slight old frame shook heavily and seemed hardly able to sustain such violent grief.

"What's the matter, baby?" Jeff asked awkwardly. "Why you cryin' like that?"

"I's jes thinking'," she said.

"So you the one what's scairt now, hunh?"

"I ain't scairt, Jeff. I's jes thinking' 'bout leavin' eve'thing like this—eve-thing we been used to. It's right sad-like."

Jeff did not answer, and presently Jennie buried her face again and cried.

The sun was almost overhead. It beat down furiously on the dusty wagon-path road, on the parched roadside grass and the tiny battered car. Jeff's hands, gripping the wheel, became wet with perspiration; his forehead sparkled. Jeff's lips parted. His mouth shaped a hideous grimace. His face suggested the face of a man being burned. But the torture passed and his expression softened again.

"You mustn't cry, baby," he said to his wife. "We gotta be strong. We can't break down."

Jennie waited a few seconds, then said, "You reckon we oughta do it, Jeff? You reckon we oughta go 'head an' do it, really?"

Jeff's voice choked; his eyes blurred. He was terrified to hear Jennie say the thing that had been in his mind all morning. She had egged him on when he had wanted more than anything in the world to wait, to reconsider, to think things over a little longer. Now she was getting cold feet. Actually there was no need of thinking the question through again. It would only end in making the same painful decision once more. Jeff knew that. There was no need of fooling around longer.

"We jes as well to do like we planned," he said. "They ain't nothin' else for us now—it's the bes' thing."

Jeff thought of the handicaps, the near impossibility, of making another crop with his leg bothering him more and more each week. Then there was always the chance that he would have another stroke, like the one that had made him lame. Another one might kill him. The least it could do would be to leave him helpless. Jeff gasped—Lord, Jesus! He could not bear to think of being helpless, like a baby, on Jennie's hands. Frail, blind Jennie.

The little pounding motor of the car worked harder and harder. The puff of steam from the cracked radiator became larger. Jeff realized that they were climbing a little rise. A moment later the road turned abruptly and he looked down upon the face of the river.

"Jeff."

"Hunh?"

"Is that the water I hear?"

"Hm. Tha's it."

"Well, which way you goin' now?"

"Down this-a way," he said. "The road runs 'long 'side o' the water a lil piece."

She waited a while calmly. Then she said, "Drive faster."

"A'right, baby," Jeff said.

The water roared in the bed of the river. It was fifty or sixty feet below the level of the road. Between the road and the water there was a long smooth slope, sharply inclined. The slope was dry, the clay hardened by prolonged summer heat. The water below, roaring in a narrow channel, was noisy and wild.

"Jeff."

"Hunh?"

"How far you goin'?"

"Jes a lil piece down the road."

"You ain't scairt, is you, Jeff?"

"Nah, baby," he said trembling. "I ain't scairt."

"Remember how we planned it, Jeff. We gotta do it like we said. Brave-like."

"Hm."

Jeff's brain darkened. Things suddenly seemed unreal, like figures in a dream. Thoughts swam in his mind foolishly, hysterically, like little blind fish in a pool within a dense cave. They rushed, crossed one another, jostled, collided, retreated and rushed again. Jeff soon became dizzy. He shuddered violently and turned to his wife.

"Jennie, I can't do it. I can't." His voice broke pitifully.

She did not appear to be listening. All the grief had gone from her face. She sat erect, her unseeing eyes wide open, strained and frightful. Her glossy black skin had become dull. She seemed as thin, as sharp and bony, as a starved bird. Now, having suffered and endured the sadness of tearing herself away from beloved things, she showed no anguish. She was absorbed with her own thoughts, and she didn't even hear Jeff's voice shouting in her ear.

Jeff said nothing more. For an instant there was light in his cavernous brain. The great chamber was, for less than a second, peopled by characters he knew and loved. They were simple, healthy creatures, and they behaved in a manner that he could understand. They had quality. But since he had already taken leave of them long ago, the remembrance did not break his heart again. Young Jeff Patton was among them, the Jeff Patton of fifty years ago who went down to New Orleans with a crowd of country boys to the Mardi Gras doings. The gay young crowd, boys with candy-striped shirts and rouged-brown girls in noisy silks, was like a picture in his head. Yet it did not make him sad. On that very trip Slim Burns had killed Joe Beasley—the crowd had been broken up. Since then Jeff Patton's world had been the Greenbriar Plantation. If there had been other Mardi Gras carnivals, he had not heard of them. Since then there had been no time; the years had fallen on him like waves. Now he was old, worn out. Another paralytic stroke (like the one he had already suffered) would put him on his back for keeps. In that condition, with a frail blind woman to look after him, he would be worse off than if he were dead.

Suddenly Jeff's hands became steady. He actually felt brave. He slowed down the motor of the car and carefully pulled off the road. Below, the water of the stream boomed, a soft thunder in the deep channel. Jeff ran the car onto the clay slope, pointed it directly toward the stream and put his foot heavily on the accelerator. The little car leaped furiously down the steep incline toward the water. The movement was nearly as swift and direct as a fall. The two old black folks, sitting quietly side by side, showed no excitement. In another instant the car hit the water and dropped immediately out of sight.

A little later it lodged in the mud of a shallow place. One wheel of the crushed and upturned little Ford became visible above the rushing water.

THE LAST LETTER
Isao Matsuo (1921–1944)

In 1281 the Japanese islands were saved from a Mongol invasion by a great typhoon which destroyed most of the Mongol ships. Believing the storm to be a sign of divine protection, the Japanese called the storm *Kamikaze* ("the Divine Wind"). In 1944 the Japanese again prepared to defend themselves against a foreign invasion, this time hoping that they would be saved by another Kamikaze—the Special Attack Force established for suicidal missions against American ships. The following letter was written by a young Japanese in the 701st Air Group before he took off on his last mission.

28 October 1944

Dear Parents:

Please congratulate me. I have been given a splendid opportunity to die. This is my last day. The destiny of our homeland hinges on the decisive battle in the seas to the south where I shall fall like a blossom from a radiant cherry tree.

I shall be a shield for His Majesty and die cleanly along with my squadron leader and other friends. I wish that I could be born seven times, each time to smite the enemy.

How I appreciate this chance to die like a man! I am grateful from the depths of my heart to the parents who have reared me with their constant prayers and tender love. And I am grateful as well to my squadron leader and superior officers who have looked after me as if I were their own son and given me such careful training.

Thank you, my parents, for the twenty-three years during which you have cared for me and inspired me. I hope that my present deed will in some small way repay what you have done for me. Think well of me and know that your Isao died for our country. This is my last wish, and there is nothing else that I desire.

I shall return in spirit and look forward to your visit at the Yasukuni Shrine. Please take good care of yourselves.

How glorious is the Special Attack Corps' Giretsu Unit whose *Suisei* bombers will attack the enemy. Our goal is to dive against the aircraft carriers of the enemy. Movie cameramen have been here to take our pictures. It is possible that you may see us in newsreels at the theater.

We are sixteen warriors manning the bombers. May our death be as sudden and clean as the shattering of crystal.

Written at Manila on the eve of our sortie.

Isao

Soaring into the sky of the southern seas, it is our glorious mission to die as the shields of His Majesty. Cherry blossoms glisten as they open and fall.

from THE BELL JAR
Sylvia Plath (1933-1963)

This is the only novel written by Plath, a promising but frustrated young American poet who found the world to be a bad dream. It is a thinly disguised autobiographical account of events which occurred in her life during six months of 1953. It begins with her on the verge of a successful career in New York and ends with her leaving a mental hospital after going through a living nightmare of despair, suffering, psychotherapy, electroshock therapy, and several suicide attempts. Her thoughts about suicide and her early unsuccessful attempts to kill herself, as described in the excerpts below, are portents of her suicide by gassing years later in London.

I rolled onto my back again and made my voice casual. "If you were going to kill yourself, how would you do it?"

Cal seemed pleased. "I've often thought of that. I'd blow my brains out with a gun."

I was disappointed. It was just like a man to do it with a gun. A fat chance I had of laying my hands on a gun. And even if I did, I wouldn't have a clue as to what part of me to shoot at.

I'd already read in the papers about people who'd tried to shoot themselves, only they ended up shooting an important nerve and getting paralyzed or blasting their face off, but being saved, by surgeons and a sort of miracle, from dying outright.

The risks of a gun seemed great.

"What kind of a gun?"

"My father's shotgun. He keeps it loaded. I'd just have to walk into his study one day and," Cal pointed a finger to his temple and made a comical, screwed-up face, "click!" He widened his pale gray eyes and looked at me.

"Does your father happen to live near Boston?" I asked idly.

"Nope, in Clacton-on-Sea. He's English."

Jody and Mark ran up hand-in-hand, dripping and shaking off water drops like two loving puppies. I thought there would be too many people, so I stood up and pretended to yawn.

"I guess I'll go for a swim."

Being with Jody and Mark and Cal was beginning to weigh on my nerves, like a dull wooden block on the strings of a piano. I was afraid that at any moment my control would snap, and I would start babbling about how I couldn't read and couldn't write and how I must be just about the only person who had stayed awake for a solid month without dropping dead of exhaustion.

A smoke seemed to be going up from my nerves like the smoke from the grills and the sun-saturated road. The whole landscape—beach and headland and sea and rock—quavered in front of my eyes like a stage backcloth.

I wondered at what point in space the silly, sham blue of the sky turned black.

"You swim too, Cal."

Jody gave Cal a playful little push.

"Ohhh." Cal hid his face in the towel. "It's too cold."

I started to walk toward the water.

Somehow, in the broad, shadowless light of noon, the water looked amiable and welcoming.

I thought drowning must be the kindest way to die, and burning the worst. Some of those babies in the jars that Buddy Willard showed me had gills, he said. They went through a stage where they were just like fish.

A little, rubbishy wavelet, full of candy wrappers and orange peel and seaweed, folded over my foot.

I heard the sand thud behind me, and Cal came up.

"Let's swim to that rock out there." I pointed at it.

"Are your crazy? That's a mile out."

"What are you?" I said. "Chicken?"

Cal took me by the elbow and jostled me into the water. When we were waist high, he pushed me under. I surfaced, splashing, my eyes seared with salt. Underneath, the water was green and semi-opaque as a hunk of quartz.

I started to swim, a modified dogpaddle, keeping my face toward the rock. Cal did a slow crawl. After a while he put his head up and treaded water.

"Can't make it." He was panting heavily.

"Okay, You go back."

I thought I would swim out until I was too tired to swim back. As I paddled on, my heartbeat boomed like a dull motor in my ears.

I am I am I am.

That morning I had tried to hang myself.

I had taken the silk cord of my mother's yellow bathrobe as soon as she left for work, and, in the amber shade of the bedroom, fashioned it into a knot that slipped up and down on itself. It took me a long time to do this, because I was poor at knots and had no idea how to make a proper one.

Then I hunted around for a place to attach the rope.

The trouble was, our house had the wrong kind of ceilings. The ceilings were low, white, and smoothly plastered, without a light fixture or a wood beam in sight. I thought with longing of the house my grandmother had before she sold it to come and live with us, and then with my Aunt Libby.

My grandmother's house was built in the fine, nineteenth-century style, with lofty rooms and sturdy chandelier brackets and high closets with stout rails across them, and an attic where nobody ever went, full of trunks and parrot cages and dressmakers' dummies and overhead beams thick as a ship's timbers.

But it was an old house, and she'd sold it, and I didn't know anybody else with a house like that.

After a discouraging time of walking about with the silk cord dangling from my neck like a yellow cat's tail and finding no place to fasten it, I sat on the edge of my mother's bed and tried pulling the cord tight.

But each time I would get the cord so tight I could feel a rushing in my ears and a flush of blood in my face, my hands would weaken and let go, and I would be all right again.

Then I saw that my body had all sorts of little tricks, such as making my hands go limp at the crucial second, which would save it, time and again, whereas if I had the whole say, I would be dead in a flash.

I would simply have to ambush it with whatever sense I had left, or it would trap me in its stupid cage for fifty years without any sense at all. And when people found out my mind had gone, as they would have to, sooner or later, in spite of my mother's guarded tongue, they would persuade her to put me into an asylum where I could be cured.

Only my case was incurable.

. . . .

Cal had turned around and was swimming in.

As I watched, he dragged himself slowly out of the neck-deep sea. Against the khaki-colored sand and the green shore wavelets, his body was bisected for a moment, like a white worm. Then it crawled completely out of the green and onto the khaki and lost itself among dozens and dozens of other worms that were wriggling or just lolling about between the sea and the sky.

I paddled my hands in the water and kicked my feet. The egg-shaped rock didn't seem to be any nearer than it had been when Cal and I had looked at it from the shore.

Then I saw it would be pointless to swim as far as the rock, because my body would take that excuse to climb out and lie in the sun, gathering strength to swim back.

The only thing to do was to drown myself then and there.

So I stopped.

I brought my hands to my breast, ducked my head, and dived, using my hands to push the water aside. The water pressed in on my eardrums and on my heart. I fanned myself down, but before I knew where I was, the water had spat me up into the sun, the world was sparkling all about me like blue and green and yellow semi-precious stones.

I dashed the water from my eyes.

I was panting, as after a strenuous exertion, but floating, without effort.

I dived, and dived again, and each time popped up like a cork.

The gray rock mocked me, bobbing on the water easy as a lifebuoy.

I knew when I was beaten.

I turned back.

. . . .

I knew just how to go about it.

The minute the car tires crunched off down the drive and the sound of the motor faded, I jumped out of bed and hurried into my white blouse and green figured skirt and black raincoat. The raincoat felt damp still, from the day before, but that would soon cease to matter.

I went downstairs and picked up a pale blue envelope from the dining room table and scrawled on the back, in large painstaking letters: *I am going for a long walk.*

I propped the message where my mother would see it the minute she came in.

Then I laughed.

I had forgotten the most important thing.

I ran upstairs and dragged a chair into my mother's closet. Then I climbed up and reached for the small green strongbox on the top shelf. I could have torn the metal cover off with my bare hands, the lock was so feeble, but I wanted to do things in a calm, orderly way.

I pulled out my mother's upper right-hand bureau drawer and slipped the blue jewelry box from its hiding place under the scented Irish linen handkerchiefs. I unpinned the little key from the dark velvet. Then I unlocked the stongbox and took out the bottle of new pills. There were more than I had hoped.

There were at least fifty.

If I had waited until my mother doled them out to me, night by night, it would have taken me fifty nights to save up enough. And in fifty nights, college would have opened, and my brother would have come back from Germany, and it would be too late.

I pinned the key back in the jewelry box among the clutter of inexpensive chains and rings, put the jewelry box back in the drawer under the handkerchiefs, returned the strongbox to the closet shelf and set the chair on the rug in the exact spot I had dragged it from.

Then I went downstairs and into the kitchen. I turned on the tap and poured myself a tall glass of water. Then I took the glass of water and the bottle of pills and went down into the cellar.

A dim, undersea light filtered through the slits of the cellar windows. Behind the oil burner, a dark gap showed in the wall at about shoulder height and ran back under the breezeway, out of sight. The breezeway had been added to the house after the cellar was dug, and built out over this secret, earth-bottomed crevice.

A few old, rotting fireplace logs blocked the hole mouth. I shoved them back a bit. Then I set the glass of water and the bottle of pills side by side on the flat surface of one of the logs and started to heave myself up.

It took me a good while to heft my body into the gap, but at last, after many tries, I managed it, and crouched at the mouth of the darkness, like a troll.

The earth seemed friendly under my bare feet, but cold. I wondered how long it had been since this particular square of soil had seen the sun.

Then, one after the other, I lugged the heavy, dust-covered logs across the hole mouth. The dark felt thick as velvet. I reached for the glass and bottle, and carefully, on my knees, with bent head, crawled to the farthest wall.

Cobwebs touched my face with the softness of moths. Wrapping my black coat round me like my own sweet shadow, I unscrewed the bottle of pills and started taking them swiftly, between gulps of water, one by one by one.

At first nothing happened, but as I approached the bottom of the bottle, red and blue lights began to flash before my eyes. The bottle slid from my fingers and I lay down.

The silence drew off, baring the pebbles and shells and all the tatty wreckage of my life. Then, at the rim of vision, it gathered itself, and in one sweeping tide, rushed me to sleep.

8. FUNERAL AND BURIAL CUSTOMS

BEOWULF, generally dated around 750, is the oldest extant poem in a modern European language. Written by an unknown poet during the Anglo-Saxon period of English history, the epic poem tells of the legendary efforts by Beowulf, Danish king for fifty years, to protect the people of Denmark and Sweden from monsters and dragons. Combining a mixture of mythological and Christian elements, the poem graphically describes Beowulf's killing of Grendel, a cannibalistic monster, and Grendel's revenge-seeking mother. Then, the years having taken their toll on Beowulf's strength, he is once again called into battle, this time against a dragon. Although he and a companion slay the dragon, Beowulf is mortally wounded and dies after communicating his wish for a stately barrow—"Beowulf's Barrow"—to be constructed overlooking the sea.

Beowulf's people responded to his death in two ways. First, they engaged in ritual acts which celebrated his great life and allowed them to grieve over their great loss. They praised his daring, sang about his deeds of prowess, called him the best among kings—and cried over their loss, chanted a dirge of woe, and wondered how they would get along without him. Second, they carried out his wish regarding the disposal of his body. After having burned his body on a funeral pyre (surrounded with helmets, shields, and coats of mail), they buried his ashes along with bracelets, rings, and other treasures appropriate for a king. Then they worked for ten days to construct a magnificent barrow which could be seen for a great distance by seafaring men.

As illustrated by this poem, the death of a person necessitates several decisions on the part of individuals who survive the death. One of these decisions involves a postmortem service. When death occurs, there is a human need for some kind of service or ritual act which will give official recognition that a life has come to an end, a family and/or a community circle has become smaller, and some persons in the community face the difficult task of rebuilding their lives after having suffered a significant personal loss. The precise form of this official recognition of death differs from one culture to another, from one historical period to another, and frequently from one ethnic or religious group to another. But barring extreme situations sometimes produced by war, epidemic, or natural disaster, the majority of persons who die in any society have their deaths marked by some kind of communal service that recognizes both the significance of the life now terminated and the importance of the lives which must now confront a future fractured by death.

Until the latter part of the nineteenth century, the event of death was usually recognized in our society in an unpretentious manner. When a member of a family died, the surviving members of the family generally assumed several necessary tasks: they cleaned and dressed the corpse, built a casket (or hired a local carpenter or cabinetmaker to build one), contacted a clergyman about a graveside service, carried the casket to the churchyard or local cemetery in a farm wagon (or sometimes a hearse secured from the local livery stable), dug a grave (sometimes with the help of a local sexton), and covered the body with dirt after a service of committal. In the small towns and farming communities of rural America, certain parts of this family-organized, family-centered ritual of officially recognizing a death continued well into the current century.

Substantial changes in this tradition have taken place over the past hundred years as the country has become more urbanized. Changes have occurred in the type of service, the procedures employed in preparation for the service, the place used for the service, and the persons in charge of the service. The service has changed from a brief service of committal at the graveside (sometimes preceded by religious rituals) to a longer, more formal service usually involving religious symbols, music, a eulogy, and the dead body often present in an open casket. The key element in the changed format of the service has been the discovery and development of modern procedures of embalming, which preserve the body for a period of days and thus make possible the viewing of the dead body at the service. The persons responsible for arranging and managing the funeral service, preserving the dead body, and providing the place for most services are funeral directors and their staffs, a segment of the business community which did not even exist until rather late in the nineteenth century.

Of course, as illustrated by Sandra Scoppettone's *Trying Hard to Hear You*, the dead body at a funeral does not have to be placed in an open casket, nor do the survivors have to opt for a traditional funeral. Many funeral directors allow, and some even encourage, departures in funeral ritual when the changes seem beneficial for the survivors.

An alternative to the funeral is a memorial service held without the dead body. Often chosen by members of memorial societies, a memorial service can be held at any time after a person dies and, because the dead body is not a constraining factor, often is held a few days after the body has been buried, cremated, or entombed. As illustrated by the Eric Lund story, memorial services are often characterized by an informality not usually found at funerals.

Another decision necessitated by death involves the disposal of the dead body. Beowulf's body was burned and then covered with a mound of earth and stones. Had he lived and died in twentieth-century America—and had he not made a request regarding the disposal of his body—his body would probably have been embalmed, restored to a pleasing appearance with cosmetics, placed in a casket, made available for viewing by his survivors, and then interred in the earth.

If, however, Beowulf lived in twentieth-century America and made a request regarding the disposal of his body once dead, he would have a number of alternatives. (1) He could choose immediate burial, in which case his surviving friends would need to obtain a death certificate and burial permit, and place his body in some kind of burial container prior to interring it in the ground. (2) He could choose immediate cremation, in which case his friends would need to obtain a death certificate and cremation permit, place the body in a simple casket or body bag, and transport it to a crematory. (3) He could choose to donate his body to a medical school, although, as Doris Lund discovered, this choice can sometimes be difficult to carry out if advance arrangements have not been made. (4) He could choose to donate specific organs prior to being cremated, or embalmed and interred. (5) He could choose to be buried or cremated after a funeral service. (6) He could choose to be entombed after a funeral—or before or after a memorial service—in which case his body would be placed in a mausoleum crypt rather than in a grave. (7) He could choose, if he wanted to try to defeat death, to have his dead body frozen, in which case he would need to have made the expensive arrangements for the purchase and maintenance of a cryonics capsule.

The selections reflect the diverse ways in which a person's death can be officially recognized, as well as a number of the alternatives for disposing of a dead body. The excerpt from the *Iliad* shows some of the practices of ancient Greece: a funeral pyre, the construction of a barrow, athletic contests for lessening the survivors' grief—and the brutal possibilities for abusing a dead enemy's body. Benjamin Franklin's satirical piece reflects critically on the effusive eulogies sometimes heard at funerals. Thomas Hardy's poem reflects in a humorous way on the commonness of a gravesite. Robert Louis Stevenson, in contrast, shows how deeply felt epitaphs can give a gravesite special significance. William Carlos Williams shows how a poem can both reflect and criticize conventional practices of handling a dead body.

The remaining prose selections focus on a number of practices connected with death. Thomas Wolfe depicts a scene in a funeral home and highlights the vulnerability of survivors as they select a casket and make arrangements for a funeral. John Steinbeck shows that unusual circumstances sometimes compel survivors to repeat the practices of an earlier period: cleaning and dressing the body for burial, digging a simple grave, holding a simple service. Margaret Craven describes a quite different way of disposing of dead bodies by placing them in tree boxes. Still another way of disposing of the dead, that of a cremation ground, is described vividly by R. K. Narayan, a contemporary novelist from India. Albert Camus depicts a vigil or wake held in a nursing home prior to a funeral. Doris Lund describes the difficulties she encountered in trying to donate Eric's body to a medical school—and then suggests one way of "outwitting the system." And Sandra Scoppettone concludes the section by contrasting a traditional funeral with one consisting of a closed casket, rock music, and audience participation.

from THE ILIAD
Homer (c.850 B.C.)

Book XXIII of this epic work contains a description of some of the funeral and burial customs observed when an important person died in ancient Greece. Patroclus, the squire and close friend of Achilles, has been killed by Hector.

Patroclus' body, having been fought over by the Achaeans and the Trojans, is retrieved from the field of battle by the Achaeans and returned to their ships. After killing Hector, Achilles returns to take charge of the ceremonies that will reflect the devotion and respect he had for his friend.

While the city of Troy gave itself up to lamentation, the Achaeans withdrew to the Hellespont, and when they reached the ships, dispersed to their several vessels. Only the battle-loving Myrmidons were not dismissed. Achilles kept his followers with him and addressed them. "Myrmidons," he said, "lovers of the fast horse, my trusty band; we will not unyoke our horses from their chariots yet, but mounted as we are, will drive them past Patroclus and mourn for him as a dead man should be mourned. Then, when we have wept and found some solace in our tears, we will unharness them and all have supper here."

The Myrmidons with one accord broke into lamentation. Achilles led the way, and the mourning company drove their long-maned horses three times round the dead, while Thetis stirred them all to weep without restraint. The sands were moistened and their warlike panoply was bedewed with tears, fit tribute to so great a panic-maker. And now the son of Peleus, laying his man-killing hands on his comrade's breast, led them in the melancholy dirge: "Rejoice, Patroclus, even in the Halls of Hades. I am keeping all the promises I made you.I have dragged Hector's body here, for the dogs to eat it raw; and at your pyre I am going to cut the throats of a dozen of the highborn youths of Troy, to vent my anger at your death."

. . . .

Meanwhile King Agamemnon sent mules and men from every part of the encampment to fetch wood.

. . . .

Having stacked this huge supply of wood all round the site, they sat down and waited there in a body. Achilles then gave orders for his war-loving Myrmidons to put on their bronze and for every charioteer to yoke his horses. They hurried off and got into their armor, and the fighting men and drivers mounted their cars. The horse led off, and after them came a mass of infantry one could not count. In the middle of the procession Patroclus was carried by his own men, who had covered his body with the locks of hair they had cut off and cast upon it. Behind them Prince Achilles supported the head, as the chief mourner, who was dispatching his highborn comrade to the Halls of Hades.

When they came to the place appointed for them by Achilles, they put Patroclus down and quickly built him a noble pile of wood. But now a fresh idea occurred to the swift and excellent Achilles. Stepping back from the pyre, he cut off from his head an auburn lock he had allowed to grow ever since its dedication to the River Spercheus.

. . . .

As he spoke, he put the lock in the hands of his beloved comrade. His gesture moved the whole gathering to further tears, and sunset would have found them still lamenting, if Achilles had not had a sudden thought. He went up to Agamemnon and said: "My lord Atreides, you are the man to whom the troops will listen. Of course they can mourn as much as they wish; but for the moment I ask you to dismiss them from the pyre and tell them to prepare their midday meal. We that are the chief mourners will see to everything here, though I should like the Achaean commanders to remain."

On hearing what Achilles wished, Agamemnon King of Men dismissed the troops to their trim ships; but the chief mourners stayed where they were and piled up wood. They made a pyre a hundred feet in length and breadth, and with sorrowful hearts laid the corpse on top. At the foot of the pyre they flayed and prepared many well-fed sheep and shambling cattle with crooked horns. The great-hearted Achilles, taking fat from all of them, covered the corpse with it from head to foot, and then piled the flayed carcasses round Patroclus. To these he added some two-handled jars of honey and oil, leaning them against the bier; and in his zeal he cast on the pyre four high-necked horses, groaning aloud as he did so. The dead lord had kept nine dogs as pets. Achilles slit the throats of two and threw them on the pyre. Then he went on to do an evil thing—he put a dozen brave men, the sons of noble Trojans, to the sword, and set the pyre alight so that the pitiless flames might feed on them. This done, he gave a groan and spoke once more to his beloved friend: "All hail from me, Patroclus, in the very Halls of Hades! I am keeping all the promises I made you. Twelve gallant Trojans, sons of noblemen, will be consumed by the same fire as you. For Hector son of Priam I have other plans—I will not give him to the flames, I will throw him to the dogs to eat."

But in spite of this threat from Achilles the dogs were not given access to the corpse of Hector. Day and night, Zeus' Daughter Aphrodite kept them off, and she anointed him with ambrosial oil of roses, so that Achilles should not lacerate him when he dragged him to and fro. Moreover, Phoebus Apollo caused a dark cloud to sink from the sky to the ground and settle on the corpse, covering the whole area in which it lay, so that the heat of the sun getting at this side and that should not wither the skin on his sinews and his limbs too soon.

. . . .

At the time when the Morning Star comes up to herald a new day on earth, and in his wake Dawn spreads her saffron mantle over the sea, the fire sank low, the flames expired, and the Winds set out for home across the Thracian Sea, where the roaring waves ran high. Achilles was exhausted. Turning from the pyre he sank to the ground and instantly fell fast asleep. But the other chieftains, who had joined King Agamemnon, would not let him be, and the whole party now approached him. Roused by their voices and footsteps, he sat up and told them what he wanted done. "My lord Atreides," he said, "and you other leaders of the united Achaeans; make it your first task to put out with sparkling wine whatever portions of the pyre the flames have reached. Then we must collect my lord Patroclus' bones, being careful to distinguish them, though that will not be difficult, as he lay in the center of the pyre, separated from the rest, who were burnt on the verge of it, horses and men together. We will put the bones in a golden vase and seal it with a double layer of fat, against the time when I myself shall have vanished in the world below. As for his barrow, I do not ask you to construct a very large one, something that is seemly but no more. Later you can build a big and high one, you Achaeans that are left in the well-found ships when I am gone."

They went about the business as the swift son of Peleus had directed. First they put out with sparkling wine all parts of the funeral pyre in which the flames had done their work and the ash had fallen deep. Then, with tears on their cheeks, they collected the white bones of their gentle comrade in a golden vase, closed it with a double seal of fat, laid it in his hut and covered it with a soft linen shroud. Next they designed his barrow by laying down a ring of stone revetments round the pyre. Then they fetched earth and piled it up inside.

When the troops had built the monument, they made as if to go. But Achilles stopped them and told them all to sit down in a wide ring where the sports were to be held. For these he brought out prizes from the ships—cauldrons and tripods; horses, mules, and sturdy cattle; grey iron and women in their girdled gowns.

A RECEIPT TO MAKE A NEW ENGLAND FUNERAL ELEGY
Benjamin Franklin (1706–1790)

In 1721 a weekly newspaper called the *New England Courant* began in Boston. Among its features were satirical pieces written by Franklin, then a teenager, under the pseudonym "Silence Dogood." In the following selection Franklin satirizes the pompous eulogies he often heard at funerals and graveside services.

For the Title of your Elegy. Of these you may have enough ready made to your Hands; but if you should chuse to make it your self, you must be sure not to omit the Words *Aetatis Suae* [of his age], which will Beautify it exceedingly.

For the Subject of your Elegy. Take one of your Neighbors who has lately departed this Life; it is no great matter at what Age the Party dy'd, but it will be best if he went away suddenly, being *Kill'd, Drown'd,* or *Froze to Death.*

Having chose the person, take all his Virtues, Excellencies, &c., and if he have not enough, you may borrow some to make up a sufficient Quantity: To these add his last Words, dying Expressions, &c., if they are to be had; mix all these together, and be sure you *strain* them well. Then season all with a Handful or two of Melancholly Expressions, such as *Dreadful, Deadly, cruel cold Death, unhappy Fate, weeping Eyes,* &c. have mixed all these Ingredients well, put them into the empty Scull of some young *Harvard*; (but, in Case you have ne'er a One at Hand, you may use your own); there let them Ferment for the Space of a Fortnight, and by that Time they will be incorporated into a Body, which take out, and having prepared a sufficient Quantity of double Rhimes, such as, *Power, Flower; Quiver, Shiver; Grieve us, Leave us; tell you, excel you; Expeditions, Physicians; Fatigue him, Intrigue him;* &c., you must spread all upon Paper, and if you can procure a Scrap of Latin to put at

the End, it will garnish it mightily; then having affixed your Name at the
Bottom, with a *Maestus Composuit* [a mourner composed], you will have
an Excellent Elegy.

N.B. This Receipt will serve when a Female is the Subject of your
Elegy, provided you borrow a greater Quantity of Virtues, Excellencies,
&c.

Silence Dogood

"AH, ARE YOU DIGGING ON MY GRAVE?"
Thomas Hardy (1840–1928)

"Ah, are you digging on my grave
    My beloved one?—planting rue?"
—"No: yesterday he went to wed
One of the brightest wealth has bred,
'It cannot hurt her now,' he said,
    'That I should not be true.'"

"Then who is digging on my grave?
    My nearest, dearest kin?"
—"Ah, no: they sit and think, 'What use!
What good will planting flowers produce?
No tendance of her mound can loose
    Her spirit from Death's gin.'"

"But someone digs upon my grave?
    My enemy?—prodding sly?"
—"Nay: when she heard you had passed the Gate
That shuts on all flesh soon or late,
She thought you no more worth her hate,
    And cares not where you lie."

"Then, who is digging on my grave?
    Say—since I have not guessed!"
—"O it is I, my mistress dear,
Your little dog, who still lives near,
And much I hope my movements here
    Have not disturbed your rest?"

"Ah, yes! *You* dig upon my grave. . . .
        Why flashed it not on me
That one true heart was left behind!
What feeling do we ever find
To equal among human kind
        A dog's fidelity!"

"Mistress, I dug upon your grave
        To bury a bone, in case
I should be hungry near this spot
When passing on my daily trot.
I am sorry, but I quite forgot
        It was your resting-place."

MY WIFE
Robert Louis Stevenson (1850–1894)

When Stevenson died in Samoa, he was buried on the top of Mount Vailima.
When his wife died, she was buried beside him. Marking the burial site are two
bronze tablets with two epitaphs: one of them being the closing stanza of "My
Wife" and the other being the epitaph he wrote for himself, entitled "Requiem."

Trusty, dusky, vivid, true,
With eyes of gold and bramble-dew,
        Steel-true and blade-straight,
The great Artificer
        Made my mate.

Honor, anger, valor, fire;
A love that life could never tire,
        Death quench, or evil stir,
The mighty Master
        Gave to her.

Teacher, tender, comrade, wife
A fellow farer true through life,
        Heart-whole and soul-free,
The august Father
        Gave to me.

REQUIEM
Robert Louis Stevenson (1850–1894)

Under the wide and starry sky
Dig the grave and let me lie.
Glad did I live and gladly die,
    And I laid me down with a will.

This be the verse you grave for me:
Here he lies where he longed to be;
Home is the sailor, home from sea,
    And the hunter home from the hill.

TRACT
William Carlos Williams (1883–1963)

I will teach you my townspeople
how to perform a funeral—
for you have it over a troop
of artists—
unless one should scour the world—
you have the ground sense necessary.

See! the hearse leads.
I begin with a design for a hearse.
For Christ's sake not black—
nor white either—and not polished!
Let it be weathered—like a farm wagon—
with gilt wheels (this could be
applied fresh at small expense)
or no wheels at all:
a rough dray to drag over the ground.

Knock the glass out!
My God—glass, my townspeople!
For what purpose? Is it for the dead
to look out or for us to see
how well he is housed or to see

the flowers or the lack of them—
or what?
To keep the rain and snow from him?
He will have a heavier rain soon:
pebbles and dirt and what not.
Let there be no glass—
and no upholstery! phew!
and no little brass rollers
and small easy wheels on the bottom—
my townspeople what are you thinking of!

A rough plain hearse then
with gilt wheels and no top at all.
On this the coffin lies
by its own weight.

       No wreaths please—
especially no hot-house flowers.
Some common memento is better,
something he prized and is known by:
his old clothes—a few books perhaps—
God knows what! You realize
how we are about these things,
my townspeople—
something will be found—anything—
even flowers if he had come to that.
So much for the hearse.

For heaven's sake though see to the driver!
Take off the silk hat! In fact
that's no place at all for him
up there unceremoniously
dragging our friend out of his own dignity!
Bring him down—bring him down!
Low and inconspicuous! I'd not have him ride
on the wagon at all—damn him—
the undertaker's understrapper!
Let him hold the reins
and walk at the side
and inconspicuously too!

Then briefly as to yourselves:
Walk behind—as they do in France,
seventh class, or if you ride
Hell take curtains: Go with some show
of inconvenience; sit openly—
to the weather as to grief.
Or do you think you can shut grief in?
What—from us? We who have perhaps
nothing to lose? Share with us
share with us—it will be money
in your pockets.

    Go now
I think you are ready.

from LOOK HOMEWARD, ANGEL
Thomas Wolfe (1900–1938)

A novelist and short-story writer, Wolfe frequently used his own experiences as the basis of his fiction. In *Look Homeward, Angel*, published in 1929, he described his early years in North Carolina through the character of Eugene Gant. Like Wolfe, Gant grew up in a divided family, was lonely, and was especially close to his older brother, Ben. When Ben died, Eugene, along with his stuttering brother, Luke, assumed the responsibility of going to the funeral home to select a casket.

 The brothers slept heavily until past noon. Then they went out again to see Horse Hines. They found him with his legs comfortably disposed on the desk of his dark little office, with its odor of weeping ferns, and incense, and old carnations.

 He got up quickly as they entered, with a starchy crackle of his hard boiled shirt, and a solemn rustle of his black garments. Then he began to speak to them in a hushed voice, bending forward slightly.

 How like Death this man is (thought Eugene). He thought of the awful mysteries of burial—the dark ghoul-ritual, the obscene communion with the dead, touched with some black and foul witch-magic. Where is the can in which they throw the parts? There is a restaurant near here. Then he took the cold phthisic hand, freckled on its back, that the man extended, with a sense of having touched something embalmed. The undertaker's manner had changed since the morning: it had become official, professional. He was the alert marshal of their grief, the efficient master-of-ceremonies. Subtly he made them feel there was an order and decorum in death: a ritual of mourning that must be observed. They were impressed.

"We thought we'd like to s-s-s-see you f-f-f-first, Mr. Hines, about the c-c-c-c-casket," Luke whispered nervously. "We're going to ask your advice. We want you to help us find something appropriate."

Horse Hines nodded with grave approval. Then he led them softly back, into a large room with polished waxen floors where, amid a rich dead smell of wood and velvet, upon wheeled trestles, the splendid coffins lay in their proud menace.

"Now," said Horse Hines quietly, "I know the family doesn't want anything cheap."

"No, sir!" said the sailor positively. "We want the b-b-b-best you have."

"I take a personal interest in this funeral," said Horse Hines with gentle emotion. "I have known the Gant and Pentland families for thirty years or more. I have had business dealings with your father for nigh on to twenty years."

"And I w-w-want you to know, Mr. Hines, that the f-f-f-family appreciates the interest you're taking in this," said the sailor very earnestly.

He likes this, Eugene thought. The affection of the world. He must have it.

"Your father," continued Horse Hines, "is one of the oldest and most respected business men in the community. And the Pentland family is one of the wealthiest and most prominent."

Eugene was touched with a moment's glow of pride.

"You don't want anything shoddy," said Horse Hines. "I know that. What you get ought to be in good taste and have dignity. Am I right?"

Luke nodded emphatically.

"That's the way we feel about it, Mr. Hines. We want the best you have. We're not pinching p-p-p-pennines where Ben's concerned," he said proudly.

"Well, then," said Horse Hines, "I'll give you my honest opinion. I could give you this one cheap," he placed his hand upon one of the caskets, "but I don't think it's what you want. Of course," he said, "it's good at the price. It's worth the money. It'll give you service, don't worry. You'll get value out of it—"

Now there's an idea, thought Eugene.

"They're all good, Luke. I haven't got a bad piece of stock in the place. But—"

"We want something b-b-b-better," said Luke earnestly. He turned to Eugene. "Don't you think so, 'Gene?"

"Yes," said Eugene.

"Well," said Horse Hines, "I could sell you this one," he indicated the most sumptuous casket in the room. "They don't come better than that, Luke. That's the top. She's worth every dollar I ask for her."

"All right," said Luke. "You're the judge. If that's the best you've g-g-g-got, we'll take it."

No, no! thought Eugene. You mustn't interrupt. Let him go on.

"But," said Horse Hines relentlessly, "there's no need for you to take that one, either. What you're after, Luke, is dignity and simplicity. Is that right?"

"Yes," said the sailor meekly, "I guess you're right at that, Mr. Hines."

Now we'll have it, thought Eugene. This man takes joy in his work.

"Well, then," said Horse Hines decisively, "I was going to suggest to you boys that you take this one." He put his hand affectionately upon a handsome casket at his side.

"This is neither too plain nor too fancy. It's simple and in good taste. Silver handles, you see—silver plate here for the name. You can't go wrong on this one. It's a good buy. She'll give you value for every dollar you put into it."

They walked around the coffin, starring at it critically.

After a moment, Luke said nervously:

"How--wh--wh--wh-what's the price of this one?"

"That sells for $450," said Horse Hines. "But," he added, after a moment's dark reflection. "I'll tell you what I'll do. Your father and I are old friends. Out of respect for the family, I'll let you have it at cost—$375."

"What do you say, 'Gene?" the sailor asked. "Does it look all right to you?"

Do your Christmas shopping early.

"Yes," said Eugene, "let's take it. I wish there were another color. I don't like black," he added. "Haven't you got any other color?"

Horse Hines stared at him a moment.

"Black *is* the color," he said.

Then, after a moment's silence, he went on:

"Would you boys care to see the body?"

"Yes," they said.

He led them on tiptoe down the aisle of the coffins, and opened a door to a room behind. It was dark. They entered and stood with caught breath. Horse Hines switched on a light and closed the door.

Ben, clad in his best suit of clothes, a neat one of dark gray-black, lay in rigid tranquillity upon a table. His hands, cold and white, with clean dry nails, withered a little like an old apple, were crossed loosely on his stomach. He had been closely shaved: he was immaculately groomed. The rigid head was thrust sharply upward, with a ghastly counterfeit of a smile: there was a little gum of wax at the nostrils, and a waxen lacing between the cold firm lips. The mouth was tight, somewhat bulging. It looked fuller than it ever had looked before.

There was a faint indefinably cloying odor.

The sailor looked with superstition, nervously, with puckered forehead. Then he whispered to Eugene:

"I g-g-guess that's Ben, all right."

Because, Eugene thought, it is not Ben, and we are lost. He looked at the cold bright carrion, that bungling semblance which had not even the power of a good wax-work to suggest its image. Nothing of Ben could be buried here. In this poor stuffed crow, with its pathetic barbering, and its neat buttons, nothing of the owner had been left. All that was there was the tailoring of Horse Hines, who now stood by, watchfully, hungry for their praise.

No, this is not Ben (Eugene thought). No trace of him is left in this deserted shell. It bears no mark of him. Where has he gone? Is this his bright particular flesh, made in his image, given life by his unique gesture, by his one soul? No, he is gone from that bright flesh. This thing is one with all carrion; it will be mixed with the earth again. Ben? Where? O lost!

The sailor, looking, said:

"That b-b-b-boy sure suffered." Suddenly, turning his face away into his hand, he sobbed briefly and painfully, his confused stammering life drawn out of its sprawl into a moment of hard grief.

Eugene wept, not because he saw Ben there, but because Ben had gone, and because he remembered all the tumult and the pain.

"It is over now," said Horse Hines gently. "He is at peace."

"By God, Mr. Hines," said the sailor earnestly, as he wiped his eyes on his jacket, "that was one g-g-g-great boy."

Horse Hines looked raptly at the cold strange face.

"A fine boy," he murmured as his fish-eye fell tenderly on his work. "And I have tried to do him justice."

They were silent for a moment, looking.

"You've d-d-done a fine job," said the sailor. "I've got to hand it to you. What do you say, 'Gene?"

"Yes," said Eugene, in a small choking voice. "Yes."

"He's a b-b-b-bit p-p-p-pale, don't you think?" the sailor stammered, barely conscious of what he was saying.

"Just a moment!" said Horse Hines quickly, lifting a finger. Briskly he took a stick of rouge from his pocket, stepped forward, and deftly, swiftly, sketched upon the dead gray cheeks a ghastly rose-hued mockery of life and health.

"There!" he said, with deep satisfaction; and, rouge-stick in hand, head critically cocked, like a painter before his canvas, he stepped back into the terrible staring prison of their horror.

"There are artists, boys, in every profession." Horse Hines continued in a moment, with quiet pride, "and though I do say it myself, Luke, I'm proud of my work on this job. Look at him!" he exclaimed with sudden energy, and a bit of color in his gray face. "Did you ever see anything more natural in your life?"

Eugene turned upon the man a grim and purple stare, noting with pity, with a sort of tenderness, as the dogs of laughter tugged at his straining throat, the earnestness and pride in the long horse-face.

"Look at it!" said Horse Hines again in slow wonder. "I'll never beat that again! Not if I live to be a million! That's art, boys!"

from THE GRAPES OF WRATH
John Steinbeck (1902–1968)

This Pulitzer Prize-winning novel describes the plight of the Joad family during the Depression. Forced to leave their farm in Oklahoma because of severe drought conditions, they head west for the fertile fields of California and along the way team up with the Wilsons from Kansas. A crisis occurs when Grandpa Joad has a stroke. Casy, a former minister traveling with them, is called into duty, and the family has to have a simple funeral and burial necessitated by their severe shortage of cash and distance from home.

Granma hopped about like a chicken. "Pray," she said. "Pray, you. Pray, I tell ya." Sairy tried to hold her back. "Pray, goddamn you!" Granma cried.

Casy looked up at her for a moment. The rasping breath came louder and more unevenly. "Our father who art in Heaven, hallowed be Thy name—"

"Glory!" shouted Granma.

"Thy kingdom come, Thy will be done—on earth—as it is in Heaven."

"Amen."

A long gasping sigh came from the open mouth, and then a crying release of air.

"Give us this day—our daily bread—and forgive us—" The breathing had stopped. Casy looked down into Grampa's eyes and they were clear and deep and penetrating, and there was a knowing serene look in them.

"Hallelujah!" said Granma. "Go on."

"Amen," said Casy.

Granma was still then. And outside the tent all the noise had stopped. A car whished by on the highway. Casy still knelt on the floor beside the mattress. The people outside were listening, standing quietly intent on the sounds of dying. Sairy took Granma by the arm and led her outside, and Granma moved with dignity and held her head high. She walked for the family and held her head straight for the family. Sairy took her to a mattress lying on the ground and sat her down on it. And Granma looked straight ahead, proudly, for she was on show now. The tent was still, and at last Casy spread the tent flaps with his hands and stepped out.

Pa asked softly, "What was it?"

"Stroke," said Casy. "A good quick stroke."

Life began to move again. The sun touched the horizon and flattened over it. And along the highway there came a long line of huge freight trucks with red sides. They rumbled along, putting a little earthquake in the ground, and the standing exhaust pipes sputtered blue smoke from the Diesel oil. One man drove each truck, and his relief man slept in a bunk high up against the ceiling. But the trucks never stopped; they thundered day and night and the ground shook under their heavy march.

The family became a unit. Pa squatted down on the ground, and Uncle John beside him. Pa was the head of the family. Ma stood behind him. Noah and Tom and Al squatted, and the preacher sat down, and then reclined on his elbow. Connie and Rose of Sharon walked at a distance. Now Ruthie and Winfield, clattering up with a bucket of water held between them, felt the change, and they slowed up and set down the bucket and moved quitely to stand with Ma.

Granma sat proudly, coldly, until the group was formed, until no one looked at her, and then she lay down and covered her face with her arm. The red sun set and left a shining twilight on the land, so that faces were bright in the evening and eyes shone in reflection of the sky. The evening picked up light where it could.

Pa said, "It was in Mr. Wilson's tent."

Uncle John nodded. "He loaned his tent."

"Fine friendly folks," Pa said softly.

Wilson stood by his broken car, and Sairy had gone to the mattress to sit beside Granma, but Sairy was careful not to touch her.

Pa called, "Mr. Wilson!" The man scuffed near and squatted down, and Sairy came and stood beside him. Pa said, "We're thankful to you folks."

"We're proud to help," said Wilson.

"We're beholden to you," said Pa.

"There's no beholden in a time of dying," said Wilson, and Sairy echoed him, "Never no beholden."

Al said, "I'll fix your car—me an' Tom will." And Al looked proud that he could return the family's obligation.

"We could use some help." Wilson admitted the retiring of the obligation.

Pa said, "We got to figger what to do. They's laws. You got to report a death, an' when you do that, they either take forty dollars for the undertaker or they take him for a pauper."

Uncle John broke in, "We never did have no paupers."

Tom said, "Maybe we got to learn. We never got booted off no land before, neither."

"We done it clean," said Pa. "There can't no blame be laid on us. We never took nothin' we couldn' pay; we never suffered no man's charity. When Tom here got in trouble we could hold up our heads. He only done what any man would a done."

"Then what'll we do?" Uncle John asked.

"We go in like the law says an' they'll come out for him. We on'y got a hundred an' fifty dollars. They take forty to bury Grampa an' we won't get to California—or else they'll bury him a pauper." The men stirred restively, and they studied the darkening ground in front of their knees.

Pa said softly, "Grampa buried his pa with his own hand, done it in dignity, an' shaped the grave nice with his own shovel. That was a time when a man had the right to be buried by his own son an' a son had the right to bury his own father."

"The law says different now," said Uncle John.

"Sometimes the law can't be foller'd no way," said Pa. "Not in decency, anyways. They's lots a times you can't. When Floyd was loose an' goin' wild, law said we got to give him up—an' nobody give him up. Sometimes a fella got to sift the law. I'm sayin' now I got the right to bury my own pa. Anybody got somepin to say?"

The preacher rose high on his elbow. "Law changes," he said, "but 'got to's' go on. You got the right to do what you got to do."

Pa turned to Uncle John. "It's your right too, John. You got any word against?"

"No word against," said Uncle John. "On'y it's like hidin' him in the night. Grampa's way was t'come out a-shootin'."

Pa said ashamedly, "We can't do like Grampa done. We got to get to California 'for our money gives out."

Tom broke in, "Sometimes fellas workin' dig up a man an' then they raise hell an' figger he been killed. The gov'ment's got more interest in a dead man than a live one. They'll go hell-scrapin' tryin' to fin' out who he was and how he died. I offer we put a note of writin' in a bottle an' lay it with Grampa, tell' who he is an' how he died, an' why he's buried here."

Pa nodded agreement. "Tha's good. Wrote out in a nice han'. Be not so lonesome too, knowin' his name is there with 'im, not jus' a old fella lonesome underground. Any more stuff to say?" The circle was silent.

Pa turned his head to Ma. "You'll lay 'im out?"

"I'll lay 'im out," said Ma. "But who's to get supper?"

Sairy Wilson said, "I'll get supper. You go right ahead. Me an' that big girl of yourn."

"We sure thank you," said Ma. "Noah, you get into them kegs an' bring out some nice pork. Salt won't be deep in it yet, but it'll be right nice eatin'."

"We got a half sack a potatoes," said Sairy.

Ma said, "Gimme two half-dollars." Pa dug in his pocket and gave her the silver. She found the basin, filled it full of water, and went into the tent. It was nearly dark in there. Sairy came in and lighted a candle and stuck it upright on a box and then she went out. For a moment Ma looked down at the dead old man. And then in pity she tore a strip from her own apron and tied up his jaw. She straightened his limbs, folded his hands over his chest. She held his eyelids down and laid a silver piece on each one. She buttoned his shirt and washed his face.

Sairy looked in, saying, "Can I give you any help?"

Ma looked slowly up. "Come in," she said. "I like to talk to ya."

"That's a good big girl you got," said Sairy. "She's right in peelin' potatoes. What can I do to help?"

"I was gonna wash Grampa all over," said Ma, "but he got no other clo'es to put on. An' 'course your quilt's spoilt. Can't never get the smell a death from a quilt. I seen a dog growl an' shake at a mattress my ma died on, an' that was two years later. We'll wrop 'im in your quilt. We'll make it up to you. We got a quilt for you."

Sairy said, "You shouldn' talk like that. We're proud to help. I ain't felt so—safe in a long time. People needs—to help."

Ma nodded. "They do," she said. She looked long into the old whiskery face, with its bound jaw and silver eyes shining in the candle-light. "He ain't gonna look natural. We'll wrop him up."

"The ol' lady took it good."

"Why, she's so old," said Ma, "maybe she don't even rightly know what happened. Maybe she won't really know for quite a while. Besides, us folks takes a pride holdin' in. My pa used to say, 'Anybody can break down. It takes a man not to.' We always try to hold in.'' She folded the quilt neatly about Grampa's legs and around his shoulders. She brought the corner of the quilt over his head like a cowl and pulled it down over his face. Sairy handed her half-a-dozen big safety pins, and she pinned the quilt neatly and tightly about the long package. And at last she stood up. "It won't be a bad burying," she said. "We got a preacher to see him in, an' his folks is all aroun'." Suddenly she swayed a little, and Sairy went to her and steadied her. "It's sleep—" Ma said in a shamed tone. "No, I'm awright. We been so busy gettin' ready, you see."

"Come out in the air," Sairy said.

"Yeah, I'm all done here." Sairy blew out the candles and the two went out.

A bright fire burned in the bottom of the little gulch. And Tom, with sticks and wire, had made supports from which two kettles hung and bubbled furiously, and good steam poured out under the lids. Rose of Sharon knelt on the ground out of range of the burning heat, and she had a long spoon in her hand. She saw Ma come out of the tent, and she stood up and went to her.

"Ma," she said. "I got to ask."

"Scared again?" Ma asked. "Why, you can't get through nine months without sorrow."

"But will it—hurt the baby?"

Ma said, "They used to be a sayin', 'A chile born outa sorrow'll be a happy chile.' Isn't that so, Mis' Wilson?"

"I heard it like that," said Sairy. "An' I heard the other: 'Born outa too much joy'll be a doleful boy.'"

"I'm all jumpy inside," said Rose of Sharon.

"Well, we ain't none of us jumpin' for fun," said Ma. "You jes' keep watchin' the pots."

On the edge of the ring of firelight the men had gathered. For tools they had a shovel and a mattock. Pa marked out the ground—eight feet long and three feet wide. The work went on in relays. Pa chopped the earth with the mattock and then Uncle John shoveled it out. Al chopped and Tom shoveled, Noah chopped and Connie shoveled. And the hole drove down, for the work never diminished in speed. The shovels of dirt flew out of the hole in quick spurts. When Tom was shoulder deep in the rectangular pit, he said, "How deep, Pa?"

"Good an' deep. A couple feet more. You get out now, Tom, and get that paper wrote."

Tom boosted himself out of the hole and Noah took his place. Tom went to Ma, where she tended the fire. "We got any paper an' pen, Ma?"

Ma shook her head slowly, "No-o. That's one thing we didn' bring." She looked toward Sairy. And the little woman walked quickly to her tent. She brought back a Bible and a half pencil. "Here," she said. "They's a clear page in front. Use that an' tear it out." She handed book and pencil to Tom.

Tom sat down in the firelight. He squinted his eyes in concentration, and at last wrote slowly and carefully on the end paper in big clear letters: "This here is William James Joad, dyed of a stroke, old old man. His fokes bured him becaws they got no money to pay for funerls. Nobody kilt him. Jus a stroke and he dyed." He stopped. "Ma, listen to this here." He read it slowly to her.

"Why, that soun's nice," she said. "Can't you stick on somepin from Scripture so it'll be religious? Open up an' git a-sayin' somepin outa Scripture."

"Got to be short," said Tom. "I ain't got much room lef' on the page."

Sairy said, "How 'about 'God have mercy on his soul'?"

"No," said Tom. "Sounds too much like he was hung. I'll copy somepin." He turned the pages and read, mumbling his lips, saying the words under his breath. "Here's a good short one," he said. "'An' Lot said unto them, Oh, not so, my Lord.'"

"Don't mean nothin'," said Ma. "Long's you're gonna put one down, it might's well mean somepin."

Sairy said, "Turn to Psalms, over further. You kin always get somepin outa Psalms."

Tom flipped the pages and looked down the verses. "Now here *is* one," he said. "This here's a nice one, just blowed full a religion: 'Blessed is he whose transgression is forgiven, whose sin is covered.' How's that?"

"That's real nice," said Ma. "Put that one in."

Tom wrote it carefully. Ma rinsed and wiped a fruit jar and Tom screwed the lid down tight on it. "Maybe the preacher ought to wrote it," he said.

Ma said, "No, the preacher wan't no kin." She took the jar from him and went into the dark tent. She unpinned the covering and slipped the fruit jar in under the cold hands and pinned the comforter tight again. And then she went back to the fire.

The men came from the grave, their faces shining with perspiration. "Awright," said Pa. He and John and Noah and Al went into the tent, and they came out carrying the long, pinned bundle between them. They carried it to the grave. Pa leaped into the hole and received the bundle in his arms and laid it gently down. Uncle John put out a hand and helped Pa out of the hole. Pa asked, "How about Granma?"

"I'll see," Ma said. She walked to the mattress and looked down at the old woman for a moment. Then she went back to the grave. "Sleepin'," she said. "Maybe she'd hold it against me, but I ain't a-gonna wake her up. She's tar'd."

Pa said, "Where at's the preacher? We oughta have a prayer."

Tom said, "I seen him walkin' down the road. He don't like to pray no more."

"Don't like to pray?"

"No," said Tom. "He ain't a preacher no more. He figgers it ain't right to fool people actin' like a preacher when he ain't a preacher. I bet he went away so nobody wouldn' ast him."

Casy had come quietly near, and he heard Tom speaking. "I didn' run away," he said. "I'll he'p you folks, but I won't fool ya."

Pa said, "Won't you say a few words? Ain't none of our folks ever been buried without a few words."

"I'll say 'em," said the preacher.

Connie led Rose of Sharon to the graveside, she reluctant. "You got to," Connie said. "It ain't decent not to. It'll jus' be a little."

The firelight fell on the grouped people, showing their faces and their eyes, dwindling on their dark clothes. All the hats were off now. The light danced, jerking over the people.

Casy said, "It'll be a short one." He bowed his head, and the others followed his lead. Casy said solemnly, "This here ol' man jus' lived a life an' jus' died out of it. I don't know whether he was good or bad, but that don't matter much. He was alive, an' that's what matters. An' now he's dead, an' that don't matter. Heard a fella tell a poem one time, an' he says 'All that lives is holy.' Got to thinkin', an' purty soon it means more than the words says. An' I wouldn' pray for a ol' fella that's dead. He's awright. He got a job to do, but it's all laid out for 'im an' there's on'y one way to do it. But us, we got a job to do, an' they's a thousan' ways, an' we don' know which one to take. An' if I was to pray, it'd be for the folks that don' know which way to turn. Grampa here, he got the easy straight. An' now cover 'im up and let 'im get to his work." He raised his head.

Pa said, "Amen," and the others muttered, "A-men." Then Pa took the shovel, half filled it with dirt, and spread it gently into the black hole. He handed the shovel to Uncle John, and John dropped in a shovelful. Then the shovel went from hand to hand until every man had his turn. When all had taken their duty and their right, Pa attacked the mound of loose dirt and hurriedly filled the hole. The women moved back to the fire to see to supper. Ruthie and Winfield watched, absorbed.

Ruthie said solemnly, "Grampa's down under there." And Winfield looked at her with horrified eyes. And then he ran away to the fire and sat on the ground and sobbed to himself.

from I HEARD THE OWL CALL MY NAME
Margaret Craven (b. 1902)

In attempting to minister to the Indians at the village of Kingcome, Mark Brian gradually builds a relationship of trust with them. They finally trust him enough to share a serious problem involving the bodies of dead members of the tribe. The selection describes the traditional manner in which these Indians disposed of their dead.

When they were seated there was a long silence, as the old watched Mark intently and soberly. It was not the drinking that had brought them here. It was not even the loss of the young. It was something that led back into the deepest beliefs of the tribe, and Mark sensed it and waited.

T. P. spoke for them.

"We have come about the ancient burial ground," he said. "Except for the weesa-bedó, it has not been used for many years."

"And you want the body of the weesa-bedó moved to the new graveyard. Is that it, T. P.?"

"No—he is well where he is. In the early days we buried our dead in a square box and we placed the box about a third of the way up a large tree, and we cut off the limbs below the box so the animals could not reach it, and later, other boxes were hauled up by ropes and each family had its own burial tree."

"I have seen them."

"Later we cut down a large tree ten feet from the ground and on its stump we built a house, and in the house we placed ten boxes and sometimes more."

"I have seen them also."

"But now many boxes have fallen from the trees and other trees have fallen on the grave houses built on the stumps. The bones of our ancestors lie scattered on the ground, and the old totems and the carvings are broken and beyond repair."

"If this disturbs you," Mark said, choosing his words carefully, "we can build a large communal grave and in it we can place all the boxes and the broken carvings. And if you wish in the morning I will go with you and the older men to start the clearing."

The old people rose.

"It is well," T. P. said. "I will stop by for you in the morning."

The next day the fine weather holding, Mark went with the elder men of the tribe, and what had seemed so reasonable a project became suddenly huge and macabre.

The little path that led to the ancient burial ground was overgrown. When they had cut their way through it, they saw that the year's windfall had been severe and that the old grave houses and the boxes that had fallen from the trees were covered with brush and branches.

For five days the men of the tribe worked at the clearing, and when this was done, Jim and other younger men went up the huge spruce trees with ropes to lower the grave boxes that were still intact. Where any box had fallen and touched the ground, only bones were left, but where the boxes had remained in the air, the bodies were partially mummified, the wrists still holding the copper bracelets, green now and paper-thin; and beside the heads were ancient water vessels placed there in case the soul of the dead thirsted on his journey.

When the huge grave was dug and ready, forty boxes were placed in it, and all the broken bones and bits of ancient grave posts and carvings. The men who had done the work buried also the clothes they had worn. Then on a sunny, clear morning, Mark held a brief service and the grave was covered. When it was over, he saw relief in the eyes of the old, and again T. P. spoke for them.

"At last a man has come to us who has seen to it that our dead can rest in peace."

from GRATEFUL TO LIFE AND DEATH
R. K. Narayan (b.1906)

Born in a village close to Madras, Narayan often uses southern Indian villages as the scenes of this novels. In the novel excerpted below, he depicts a professor's life at a boys' school. At one point the wife of the narrator comes down with typhoid and dies after a long period of illness. The selection describes the practice of cremation in a contemporary Indian village.

I looked at the patient. She had grown a shade whiter, and breathed noisily. There were drops of perspiration on her forehead. I touched it, and found it very cold. "Doctor, the temperature is coming down."

"Yes, yes, I knew it would . . ." he said, biting his nails. Nothing seemed to be right anywhere. "Doctor . . . tell me . . ."

"For heaven's sake, don't ask questions," he said. He felt the pulse; drew aside the blanket and ran his fingers over her abdomen which appeared slightly distended. He tapped it gently, and said: "Run to the car and fetch the other bag please, which you will find in the back seat. . . ."

The doctor opened it. "Hot water, hot water, please." He poured turpentine into the boiling water, and applied fomentations to her abdomen. He took out a hypodermic syringe, heated the needle, and pushed it into her arm: at the pressure of the needle she winced. "Perhaps it hurts her," I muttered. The doctor looked at me without an answer. He continued the fomentation.

An hour later, he drew up the blanket and packed his bag. I stood and watched in silence. All through this, he wouldn't speak a word to me. I stood like a statue. The only movement the patient showed was the heaving of her bosom. The whole house was silent. The doctor held his bag in one hand, patted my back and pursed his lips. My throat had gone dry and smarted. I croaked through this dryness: "Don't you have to remain, doctor?" He shook his head: "What can we do? We have done our best. . . ." He stood looking at the floor for a few moments, heaved a sigh, patted my back once again, and whispered: "You may expect a change in about two and a half hours." He turned and walked off. I stood stock still, listening to his shoe creaks going away, the starting of his car; after the car had gone, a stony silence closed in on the house, punctuated by the stentorian breathing, which appeared to me the creaking of the hinges of a prison gate, opening at the command of a soul going into freedom.

Here is an extract from my diary: The child has been cajoled to sleep in the next house. The cook has been sent there to keep her company. Two hours past midnight. We have all exhausted ourselves, so a deep quiet has descended on us (moreover a great restraint is being observed by all of us for the sake of the child in the next house, whom we don't wish to scare). Susila lies there under the window, laid out on the floor. For there is the law that, the body, even if it is an Emperor's must rest only on the floor, on Mother Earth.

We squat on the bare floor around her, her father, mother, and I. We mutter, talk among ourselves, and wail between convulsions of grief; but our bodies are worn out with fatigue. An unearthly chill makes our teeth chatter as we gaze on the inert form and talk about it. Gradually, unknown to ourselves, we recline against the wall and sink into sleep. The dawn finds us all huddled on the cold floor.

The first thing we do is to send for the priests and the bearers. . . . And then the child's voice is heard in the next house. She is persuaded to have her milk there, dress, and go out with a boy in the house, who promises to keep her engaged and out of our way for at least four hours. She is surprised at the extraordinary enthusiasm with which people are sending her out today. I catch a glimpse of her as she passes on the road in front of our house, wearing her green velvet coat, bright and sparkling.

Neighbors, relations, and friends arrive, tears and lamentations, more tears and lamentations, and more and more of it. The priest roams over the house, asking for one thing or other for performing the rites. . . . The corpse-bearers, grim and sub-human, have arrived with their equipment—bamboo and coir ropes. Near the front step they raise a small fire with cinders and faggots—this is the fire which is to follow us to the cremation ground.

A bamboo stretcher is ready on the ground in front of the house. Some friends are hanging about with red eyes. I am blind, dumb, and dazed.

The parting moment has come. The bearers, after brief and curt preliminaries, walk in, lift her casually without fuss, as if she were an empty sack or a box, lay her on the stretcher, and tie her up with ropes. Her face looks at the sky, bright with the saffron touched on her face, and the vermilion on the forehead, and a string of jasmine somewhere about her head.

The downward curve of her lips gives her face a repressed smile. . . . Everyone gathers a handful of rice and puts it between her lips—our last offering.

They shoulder the stretcher. I'm given a pot containing the fire and we march out, down our street, Ellamman Street. Passers-by stand and look for a while. But every face looks blurred to me. The heat of the sun is intense. We cut across the sands, ford the river at Nallappa's Grove, and on to the other bank of the river, and enter the cremation ground by a small door on its southern wall.

The sun is beating down mercilessly, but I don't feel it. I feel nothing, and see nothing. All sensations are blurred and vague.

They find it necessary to put down the stretcher a couple of times on the roadside. Half a dozen flies are dotting her face. Passers-by stand and look on sadly at the smiling face. A madman living in Ellamman Street comes by, looks at her face and breaks down, and follows us on, muttering vile and obscure curses on fate and its ways.

Stretcher on the ground. A deep grove of tamarind trees and mangoes, full of shade and quiet—an extremely tranquil place. Two or three smouldering pyres are ranged about, and bamboos and coirs lie scattered, and another funeral group is at the other end of this grove. "This is a sort of cloakroom, a place where you leave your body behind," I reflect as we sit down and wait. Somebody appears carrying a large notebook, and writes down name, age, and disease; collects a fee, issues a receipt, and goes away.

The half a dozen flies are still having their ride. After weeks, I see her face in daylight, in the open, and note the devastation of the weeks of fever—this shrivelling heat has baked her face into a peculiar tinge of pale yellow. The purple cotton saree which I bought her on another day is wound round her and going to burn with her.

The priest and the carriers are ceaselessly shouting for someone or other. Basket after basket of dry cowdung fuel is brought and dumped. . . . Lively discussion over prices and quality goes on. The trappings of trade do not leave us even here. Some hairy man sits under a tree and asks for alms. I am unable to do anything, but quietly watch in numbness. . . . I'm an imbecile, incapable of doing anything or answering any questions. I'm incapable of doing anything except what our priest orders me to do. Presently I go over, plunge in the river, return, and perform a great many rites and mutter a lot of things which the priest asks me to repeat.

They build up a pyre, place her on it, cover her up with layers of fuel. . . . Leaving only the face and a part of her chest out, four layers deep down. I pour ghee on and drop the fire.

We are on our homeward march, a silent and benumbed gang. As we cross Nallappa's Grove once again, I cannot resist the impulse to turn and look back. Flames appear over the wall. . . . It leaves a curiously dull pain at heart. There are no more surprises and shocks in life, so that I watch the flame without agitation. For me the greatest reality is this and nothing else. . . . Nothing else will worry or interest me in life hereafter.

from THE STRANGER
Albert Camus (1913–1960)

Novelist, playwright, and existentialist philosopher, Camus was awarded the Nobel Prize in Literature in 1957 and was killed in an automobile accident three years later. *The Stranger* was his first novel and remains his best-known work. In it Camus depicts the inexplicable events which occur in the life of an ordinary man living in Algiers. The novel begins with word of his mother's death and the subsequent vigil as the body lies in state until the funeral.

Mother died today. Or, maybe, yesterday; I can't be sure. The telegram from the Home says: YOUR MOTHER PASSED AWAY. FUNERAL TOMORROW.

DEEP SYMPATHY. Which leaves the matter doubtful; it could have been yesterday.

The Home for Aged Persons is at Marengo, some fifty miles from Algiers. With the two-o'clock bus I should get there well before nightfall. Then I can spend the night there, keeping the usual vigil beside the body, and be back here by tomorrow evening. I have fixed up with my employer for two days' leave; obviously, under the circumstances, he couldn't refuse. Still, I had an idea he looked annoyed, and I said, without thinking: "Sorry, sir, but it's not my fault, you know."

Afterwards it struck me I needn't have said that. I had no reason to excuse myself; it was up to him to express his sympathy and so forth. Probably he will do so the day after tomorrow, when he sees me in black. For the present, it's almost as if Mother weren't really dead. The funeral will bring it home to me, put an official seal on it, so to speak. . . .

. . . .

The Home is a little over a mile from the village. I went there on foot. I asked to be allowed to see Mother at once, but the doorkeeper told me I must see the warden first. He wasn't free, and I had to wait a bit. The doorkeeper chatted with me while I waited; then he led me to the office. The warden was a very small man, with gray hair, and a Legion of Honor rosette in his buttonhole. He gave me a long look with his watery blue eyes. Then we shook hands, and he held mine so long that I began to feel embarrassed. After that he consulted a register on his table, and said:

"Madame Meursault entered the Home three years ago. She had no private means and depended entirely on you."

I had a feeling he was blaming me for something, and started to explain. But he cut me short.

"There's no need to excuse yourself, my boy. I've looked up the record and obviously you weren't in a position to see that she was properly cared for. She needed someone to be with her all the time, and young men in jobs like yours don't get too much pay. In any case, she was much happier in the Home."

I said, "Yes, sir; I'm sure of that."

Then he added: "She had good friends here, you know, old folks like herself, and one gets on better with people of one's own generation. You're much too young; you couldn't have been much of a companion to her."

That was so. When we lived together, Mother was always watching me, but we hardly ever talked. During her first few weeks at the Home she used to cry a good deal. But that was only because she hadn't settled down. After a month or two she'd have cried if she'd been told to leave the Home. Because this, too, would have been a wrench. That was why, during the last year, I seldom went to see her. Also, it would have meant losing my Sunday—not to mention the trouble of going to the bus, getting my ticket, and spending two hours on the journey each way.

The warden went on talking, but I didn't pay much attention. Finally he said:

"Now, I suppose you'd like to see your mother?"

I rose without replying, and he led the way to the door. As we were going down the stairs he explained:

"I've had the body moved to our little mortuary—so as not to upset the other old people, you understand. Every time there's a death here, they're in a nervous state for two or three days. Which means, of course, extra work and worry for our staff."

We crossed a courtyard where there were a number of old men, talking amongst themselves in little groups. They fell silent as we came up with them. Then, behind our backs, the chattering began again. Their voices reminded me of parakeets in a cage, only the sound wasn't quite so shrill. The warden stopped outside the entrance of a small, low building.

"So here I leave you, Monsieur Mersault. If you want me for anything, you'll find me in my office. We propose to have the funeral tomorrow morning. That will enable you to spend the night beside your mother's coffin, as no doubt you would wish to do. Just one more thing; I gathered from your mother's friends that she wished to be buried with the rites of the Church. I've made arrangements for this; but I thought I should let you know."

I thanked him. So far as I knew, my mother, though not a professed atheist, had never given a thought to religion in her life.

I entered the mortuary. It was a bright, spotlessly clean room, with whitewashed walls and a big skylight. The furniture consisted of some chairs and trestles. Two of the latter stood open in the center of the room and the coffin rested on them. The lid was in place, but the screws had been given only a few turns and their nickeled heads stuck out above the wood, which was stained dark walnut. An Arab woman—a nurse, I supposed—was sitting beside the bier; she was wearing a blue smock and had a rather gaudy scarf wound round her hair.

Just then the keeper came up behind me. He'd evidently been running, as he was a little out of breath.

"We put the lid on, but I was told to unscrew it when you came, so that you could see her."

While he was going up to the coffin I told him not to trouble.

"Eh? What's that?" he exclaimed. "You don't want me to . . . ?"

"No," I said.

He put back the screwdriver in his pocket and stared at me. I realized then that I shouldn't have said, "No," and it made me rather embarrassed. After eying me for some moments he asked:

"Why not?" But he didn't sound reproachful; he simply wanted to know.

"Well, really I couldn't say," I answered.

He began twiddling his white mustache; then, without looking at me, said gently:

"I understand."

He was a pleasant-looking man, with blue eyes and ruddy cheeks. He drew up a chair for me near the coffin, and seated himself just behind. The nurse got up and moved toward the door. As she was going by, the keeper whispered in my ear:

"It's a tumor she has, poor thing."

I looked at her more carefully and I noticed that she had a bandage round her head, just below her eyes. It lay quite flat across the bridge of her nose, and one saw hardly anything of her face except that strip of whiteness.

As soon as she had gone, the keeper rose.

"Now I'll leave you to yourself."

I don't know whether I made some gesture, but instead of going he halted behind my chair. The sensation of someone posted at my back made me uncomfortable. The sun was getting low and the whole room was flooded with a pleasant, mellow light. Two hornets were buzzing overhead, against the skylight. I was so sleepy I could hardly keep my eyes open. Without looking around, I asked the keeper how long he'd been at the Home. "Five years." The answer came so pat that one could have thought he'd been expecting my question.

That started him off, and he became quite chatty. If anyone had told him ten years ago that he'd end his days as doorkeeper at a home at Marengo, he'd never have believed it. He was sixty-four, he said, and hailed from Paris.

When he said that, I broke in. "Ah, you don't come from here?"

I remembered then that, before taking me to the warden, he'd told me something about Mother. He had said she'd have to be buried mighty quickly because of the heat in these parts, especially down in the plain. "At Paris they keep the body for three days, sometimes four." After that he had mentioned that he'd spent the best part of his life in Paris, and could never manage to forget it. "Here," he had said, "things have to go with a rush, like. You've hardly time to get used to the idea that someone's dead, before you're hauled off to the funeral." "That's enough," his wife had put in. "You didn't ought to say such things to the poor young gentleman." The old fellow had blushed and begun to apologize. I told him it was quite all right. As a matter of fact, I found it rather interesting, what he'd been telling me; I hadn't thought of that before. . . .

. . . .

After a while he started talking again.

"You know, your mother's friends will be coming soon, to keep vigil with you beside the body. We always have a 'vigil' here, when anyone dies. I'd better go and get some chairs and a pot of black coffee."

The glare off the white walls was making my eyes smart, and I asked him if he couldn't turn off one of the lamps. "Nothing doing," he said. They'd arranged the lights like that; either one had them all on or none at all. After that I didn't pay much more attention to him. He went out, brought some chairs, and set them out round the coffin. On one he placed a coffeepot and ten or a dozen cups. Then he sat down facing me, on the far side of Mother. The nurse was at the other end of the room, with her back to me. I couldn't see what she was doing, but by the way her arms moved I guessed that she was knitting. I was feeling very comfortable; the coffee had warmed me up, and through the open door came scents of flowers and breaths of cool night air. I think I dozed off for a while.

I was wakened by an odd rustling in my ears. After having had my eyes closed, I had a feeling that the light had grown even stronger than before. There wasn't a trace of shadow anywhere, and every object, each curve or angle, seemed to score its outline on one's eyes. The old people, Mother's friends, were coming in. I counted ten in all, gliding almost soundlessly through the bleak white glare. None of the chairs creaked when they sat down. Never in my life had I seen anyone so clearly as I saw these people; not a detail of their clothes or features escaped me. And yet I couldn't hear them, and it was hard to believe they really existed.

Nearly all the women wore aprons, and the strings drawn tight round their waists made their big stomachs bulge still more. I'd never yet noticed what big paunches old women usually have. Most of the men, however, were as thin as rakes, and they all carried sticks. What struck me most about their faces was that one couldn't see their eyes, only a dull glow in a sort of nest of wrinkles.

On sitting down, they looked at me, and wagged their heads awkwardly, their lips sucked in between their toothless gums. I couldn't decide if they were greeting me and trying to say something, or if it was due to some infirmity of age. I inclined to think that they were greeting me, after their fashion, but it had a queer effect, seeing all those old fellows grouped round the keeper, solemnly eying me and dandling their heads from side to side. For a moment I had an absurd impression that they had come to sit in judgment on me.

A few minutes later one of the women started weeping. She was in the second row and I couldn't see her face because of another woman in front. At regular intervals she emitted a little choking sob; one had a feeling she would never stop. The others didn't seem to notice. They sat in silence, slumped in their chairs, staring at the coffin or at their walking sticks or any object just in front of them, and never took their eyes off it. And still the woman sobbed. I was rather surprised, as I didn't know who she was. I wanted her to stop crying, but dared not speak to her. After a while the keeper bent toward her and whispered in her ear; but she merely shook her head, mumbled something I couldn't catch, and went on sobbing as steadily as before.

The keeper got up and moved his chair beside mine. At first he kept silent; then, without looking at me, he explained.

"She was devoted to your mother. She says your mother was her only friend in the world, and now she's all alone."

I had nothing to say, and the silence lasted quite a while. Presently the woman's sighs and sobs became less frequent, and, after blowing her nose and snuffling for some minutes, she, too, fell silent.

I'd ceased feeling sleepy, but I was very tired and my legs were aching badly. And now I realized that the silence of these people was telling on my nerves. The only sound was a rather queer one; it came only now and then, and at first I was puzzled by it. However, after listening attentively, I guessed what it was; the old men were sucking at the insides of their cheeks, and this caused the odd, wheezing noises that had mystified me. They were so much absorbed in their thoughts that they didn't know what they were up to. I even had an impression that the dead body in their midst meant nothing at all to them. But now I suspect that I was mistaken about this.

We all drank the coffee, which the keeper handed round. After that, I can't remember much; somehow the night went by. I can recall only one moment; I had opened my eyes and I saw the old men sleeping hunched up on their chairs, with one exception. Resting his chin on his hands clasped round his stick, he was staring hard at me, as if he had been waiting for me to wake. Then I fell asleep again. I woke up after a bit, because the ache in my legs had developed into a sort of cramp.

There was a glimmer of dawn above the skylight. A minute or two later one of the old men woke up and coughed repeatedly. He spat into a big check handkershief, and each time he spat it sounded as if he were retching. This woke the others, and the keeper told them it was time to make a move. They all got up at once. Their faces were ashen gray after the long, uneasy vigil. To my surprise each of them shook hands with me, as though this night together, in which we hadn't exchanged a word, had created a kind of intimacy between us.

from ERIC
Doris Lund (b. 1919)

Eric died in a hospital after struggling valiantly against leukemia for four years. His mother and other survivors were then confronted with the necessity of making a number of postmortem decisions. Among these decisions was the decision of what kind of service to have to celebrate Eric's life, and the decision of what to do with his dead body.

Dr. Dowling called me the next morning. "What are you going to do about disposing of Eric's body?"

"Can we give him to a medical school—or something like that?"

"It's not easy," said Dr. Dowling thoughtfully. "*We* can't take him because we'd be accused of body-snatching. I think maybe I can help you, though. Let me give you the name of a doctor across the street at Cornell. Tell him I said to call."

"First, tell me how *you* feel about it," I said, knowing how much Dr. Dowling had cared about Eric.

His answer was quick. "The bodies you get in medical school are pretty bad. I'd have been honored to work on a beautiful body like Eric's."

All right. Let's go. Sidney had been listening. He agreed.

The next morning I sat up in bed next to the telephone and tried to give away my son's body. I looked first for signs of revulsion or horror in myself. There were none. He had given himself to science long ago, that part of him that was becoming less and less important. As his athlete's body finally failed, Eric—the essential Eric—had retreated to his skull. His eyes held all his life those last few days. His face had a purity and stark beauty that constantly reminded me of someone else. But who?

Later, when I went to Spain and saw Goya's etchings, and the face of El Greco's Christ on the cross, I saw the Eric of those last days. Still later, among photographs of the survivors of the Andes air crash who had cannibalized to survive, I saw—in the face of a young, near-starved youth—again, Eric. When we are reduced to the last essence of what is valuable in man, do we become more and more alike, as the newborn are alike? In the hospital where Eric was born, a nurse had brought out a tiny infant to demonstrate "The Bath" to a class of new mothers. "Whose baby is this?" she asked, before unwrapping it and putting it in the soapy little tub. There were about eleven of us sitting around in our wrappers or flannel bathrobes. Six hands went up! Mine almost did. I am ashamed and amused about that moment to this day. The baby was a girl! Now I think that the very old or the dying may be like the very new—less personalized, less stylish and defined. They are vessels that hold the deeply common experience.

It is not easy to give away a body. I called the number Dr. Dowling had given me. Four times. The doctor's secretary seemed embarrassed.

Finally I was put through to the doctor himself. He was cautiously grateful. But the problems seemed to be legion. Forms. Red tape. And we would have to hire a hearse to take the body over to Cornell.

"But it's just across the street!"

I have since heard of other instances where people were successful in donating a body to scientific research in some hospitals in New York. But at that time and that place there seemed to be no legal way to transport a body several hundred yards across York Avenue between 68th and 69th streets. I was too tired to go into all the reasons why, but I did protest. "I thought all you medical schools needed bodies." (I'd just read an article in the *New York Times* the week before entitled "The Grave Shortage of Bodies.")

"That's true," said the doctor seriously. "But of course we can't look too interested. In any case, you'd have to claim the body again after we'd used it and have a funeral home furnish a casket and——"

"Casket!" Ye gods! What for? For what would be left of Eric then? Odds and ends. What was left of Eric now but the beauty of his spirit, the memory of his laugh, his wicked humor, his open-eyed honesty? You can't tell me I have to put up with this. I thanked the man for talking to me and said we'd have to think of something else.

I decided to talk to Susan, who usually knows about things. "You know," I said, "we've shot our savings these past few years. Mark's going to have to drop out of Yale next year to earn money, and he already owes them three thousand dollars for loans. And Lisa needs a new piano. She's been trying to play Bach and Chopin on that barroom upright in the basement that has half the keys sticking. Now they tell me we've got to have a casket and the works for Eric. Even with cremation. What's it going to cost?"

"No way you can get out for less than a thousand dollars, Doris," Susan said.

So for a thousand dollars I could buy a casket to get Eric taken to the crematorium; then eventually Eric's ashes would be delivered to my doorstep in a small wooden box with "Eric Lund" on the cover. "Sign here, please," the messenger would say. What if I wasn't home? What if Lisa answered the door?

I called Dr. Dowling. "I'm not getting very far." I explained the difficulties. "So it looks like no matter what we do, we've got to buy Eric a revolting, candy-box casket. Eric would absolutely hate that. It's phony, it's useless, it's wasteful!"

"You can let the city claim the body."

"Then what?"

"He goes to potter's field."

Suddenly it sounded beautiful. Potter's field! Where the poor, lost, bottom-of-the-ladder people go. Eric belonged with them. He would have cared for them if he had lived. He was no rich kid from the suburbs. He belonged to the city where he'd loved MaryLou, where they'd ridden their bicycles, walked the avenues holding hands—where he'd loved so many other people, too.

When we were all together I asked each member of the family what they thought of letting the city claim Eric's body, of sending him to potter's field, with love?

MaryLou said, "As long as I can go, too, what do I care?"

Susan thought Eric would have loved the joke of outwitting the system.

Sidney, struggling with tears, laughed and said, "Well, the human body is about ninety-seven percent water and twenty cents' worth of other ingredients—even with inflation. So why not?"

Meredith and Jim thought it was a good, practical idea.

Mark said, "I'll go along. I'll go to potter's field, too—only I'm not ready just yet."

"But how do you feel, Mommy?" Lisa asked.

"Oh, I guess the only thing I really would have wanted is a funeral pyre with beautiful flames soaring seventy-five feet in the air. And maybe a parade with lots of music and flags and everybody in town, especially the little boys he played with—and maybe *Aida's* elephants and all the animals from Noah's Ark, too—marching down the main street right by Eric's bonfire."

"Pollution, Mommy!" said Lisa, my child of the seventies. "Bonfires make too much smoke. No. This is better. Give Eric back to the earth. We should send him to potter's field. Then he'll be recycled."

So it was settled. Eric went to potter's field. We're all going to potter's field, if we can manage it. It's the family plot. And now when somebody asks me where Eric is buried, I just say, "In the family plot."

There was a memorial service in the church by the river. It's the same church where Eric had started out to be head counselor in the boys' camp the summer before he died. Each of us wrote something for Eric, and the minister, who was Eric's friend, read our words. The pews were nearly full, and there were many small boys among the soccer teammates, college boys and girls, old family friends and relatives.

Afterward a great many people came back to the house. Then it was over. Hard to believe, but it was really over.

from TRYING HARD TO HEAR YOU
Sandra Scoppettone (b. 1936)

This novel is written for teenagers and depicts the difficulty of encountering persons who differ from an accepted norm. It tells the story of one summer in the life of Camilla Crawford, a summer spent working, dating, and rehearsing for a play. Toward the end of the summer she discovers that Jeff, her best friend, and Phil, her new boy friend, are homosexuals. The boys are immediately ridiculed and ostracized. One girl, Penny, accepts a bet to get Phil drunk and convert him into a heterosexual. The two of them die in a car wreck. The excerpt describes their quite different funeral services.

There was no cast party that night, and two days later we went to the funerals. Phil's was eleven in the morning and Penny's was at one that afternoon. Everyone but Eben and Bruce came to Phil's funeral.

I had never been to a funeral before but I'd seen them in movies and on television so I knew pretty much what to expect. Mother was there but she said she didn't expect Rachel or me to sit with her. All the kids sat together in our various groups. None of us had been asked to be pall-bearers because the Chrysties really didn't know any of us. I'd asked Jeff if he wanted me to sit with him but he said he'd rather sit alone. He looked awful. I don't think he'd slept since it happened and he was thinner than I'd ever seen him.

The casket was, of course, at the front of the church. And it was open. I was surprised about that because I had heard all kinds of rumors that both of them had been terribly disfigured.

Mr. and Mrs. Chrystie and Phil's brother sat in front on the right-hand side. There were two much older people next to them and I assumed they were Phil's grandparents. They were both crying a lot but not as much as Mrs. Chrystie. Or at least not as loud. Mr. Chrystie didn't seem to be crying at all. I remembered what Phil had told me about his father not liking him too much and I wondered if he wasn't crying because he didn't care or because he was doing the old male thing of being a stoic. I decided it was the second.

Then the hymns stopped and the eulogy began. I have to confess I really didn't hear a word of it. Oh, maybe a word here and there, but I wasn't actually listening. My mind was on the casket. It wasn't that I was afraid . . . I don't think. I mean what's to be afraid of? When people are dead they're dead. They can't hurt you. And yet it *was* fear I was feeling. There was no mistaking that crawly dampness on the back of my neck or the heavy pounding my heart was doing. It may have been my first experience with death but it certainly wasn't my first with fear. I couldn't figure out what was making me feel that way until I noticed that people were getting up and going to the casket. Then I knew. It was simply the thought of looking at Phil. Here I was, sixteen years old, and I had never seen a dead person. What if I fainted? Or threw up or something? But that was silly—why should that happen? What was it about looking at dead people that might make you do that? They were just lying there like they were sleeping, weren't they?

"Camilla?"

I felt a tug at my arm. It was Janet who was sitting next to me.

"C'mon . . . we have to go look at Phil."

"Why?" I asked.

"Because we have to," Mary El said, leaning across Janet. "Move."

I was on the aisle. "Why do we *have* to?"

"Oh, don't start," Janet said. "If you're not going to look, at least move so we can go up."

So that's what I did. I stood up and stepped out into the aisle and let them go past.

"Gross," Mary El whispered as she passed me.

Was it? Or was it gross to go and stare at him? I really didn't know. I stood in the aisle a few seconds, watching the people file past the casket, and then I decided that to make a decision about it I had to go up. There would be lots more funerals in my lifetime and if I was going to have a point of view about them, I should experience at least one the way everybody else did.

Slowly I walked down the aisle. When I got to the casket I stopped, took two more steps, and looked in. As I had expected, his eyes were closed and his hands were folded across his chest. I had seen enough movies to know that would be his position. But movies are one thing, and real life . . . real death is another. There was rouge on his cheeks and his lips were colored and he looked like he was made of wax. It was awful. That body lying there in the blue-lined coffin was no more Phil than I was. I turned away quickly and started back up the aisle. Before I had even gotten to my seat I had made my decision. Never, never again would I look at a dead person if I had a choice. There was no point. It certainly did nothing for the person who was dead and served no purpose for the person who was looking, as far as I could figure. It was just some terrible old custom that people followed without thinking about it. I made up my mind right there and then to leave instructions that I was to have a closed casket. *I was to have a closed casket.* The words bounced around my head like a tennis ball gone wild. Someday *I* was going to die. It was the first time I had ever *really* thought about my own death.

Not that up until this point I had thought I was immortal or anything. It was just that I hadn't thought about it at all. But now, sitting in this church with Phil lying in his casket, there was no way I couldn't think about it. If it could happen to him and Penny so suddenly, it could happen to me. It was a terrible thought and one I wanted to push aside. I guess that's called not facing reality. And the reality was that even if I didn't die suddenly or die young, someday I *was* going to die. I began to feel like I couldn't breathe. I knew from listening to my mother talk about patients with other analysts that I was having an anxiety attack. I guess knowing that helped a bit because soon my breathing was okay.

Okay, I said to myself, so someday I was going to die. I was no different from anyone else in that regard. There was no reason to dwell on it, make myself sick about it. It was a fact and there was nothing I could do about it. The important thing was to live . . . and to live the best way I knew how. I couldn't do anything about my death but I could do something about my life, and that's what I would concentrate on: getting the most out of life that I possibly could without hurting anyone else's life. I felt better.

Everyone was rising. The pallbearers were picking up the casket and leaving the church. Phil's family followed the casket out and then we all left.

The service at the cemetery was short. The minister said a prayer and then the casket was lowered into the grave. Everybody cried a lot, including me, and then it was over. We all got back into our cars and headed for the church where Penny's funeral was being held.

Hers was altogether different from Phil's. While his was what you might call traditional, Penny's was kind of offbeat. For instance, at Phil's they played hymns and at Penny's they had a friend of the Lademans' playing the score from *Jesus Christ Superstar*, which was some of Penny's favorite music. A lot of older people were commenting on it, saying it was shocking and dreadful and stuff like that, but I thought it was neat. I mean, what did hymns have to do with Penny? The second thing that was different was that Penny's casket was closed. I thought it was because the rumors I had heard were true but later I learned that the Lademans didn't believe in open caskets. The third thing that was different was the service. Byron Krausse, the minister, was very different from any other minister on the North Fork. He was very young and he had a full reddish beard. He started the service by saying that he didn't know Penny too well and rather than say a lot of ordinary things about her it was his wish, as well as her family's, to have anyone who wanted to, come up and say something about Penny. There was a lot of buzzing and clucking of tongues from some of the older people, and then I saw Sam walking up to the front. He cleared his throat and pushed his hair out of his eyes.

"Once when Penny and I were walking on the beach we found a sea gull with a broken leg. Penny took the sea gull home and put a splint on his leg and took care of him for a whole month. When he was better she let him go. She cried for a whole day because she'd grown to love that bird, whom she called Joshua. I probably would have kept him but Penny thought more about the bird's feelings than her own. That's the way she was."

Then Sam went back to his seat. Janet went up next.

Her voice cracked slightly as she began to talk. "Whenever I was depressed Penny could make me laugh. She always had a funny story to tell and, if she knew you were upset, even when she was herself, she concentrated on making *you* laugh."

One by one the kids went up. I was really surprised when Maura walked to the front.

"I didn't know Penny too well but, well, she very much wanted the part of Reno Sweeney that I got this summer. For a long time I thought she hated me, and maybe she did, but about two weeks ago she came up to me after a rehearsal and said: 'Maura, I gotta tell ya . . . you're really good. I'm not sure I could've done it.' That meant more to me than if the biggest producer on Broadway had said I was good. And all I could think was that if things had been reversed I don't know if I would have had the guts to say it to her. I think she was a super person."

By now everyone was crying. None of us had known that Penny had said that to Maura and it showed us a side of her we hadn't known.

Finally, I went up. "After listening to everything that everyone else has said I'm really sorry I didn't know Penny a lot better. What I knew I liked but it makes me realize that there's a whole lot more to people than we know. Penny made me laugh too and sometimes she made me mad and sometimes I just didn't know what to make of her, but basically I think she was a good person and made the most of her life and that's what's most important. I'll miss her a lot."

There were three or four people after me and then Byron Krausse said a short prayer. When that was over the pallbearers, who consisted of Sam, Walt, Eben, Penny's brother, and two men, led the procession out of the church.

After the service at the cemetery we all went to the Sweet Shop. All except Jeff, who went home I guess. We all agreed that when we died we wanted to have a funeral like Penny's. Sam said he wanted to be cremated and Walt said he wanted to be frozen. Mary El said she couldn't stand to think about it and couldn't we talk about something else.

"You can talk all you want about something else," Janet said, "but it's going to happen to you too someday. This we know."

"Well, it's gross to go on and on about it."

"No it isn't. It's dumb not to face it," I said.

"You face it if you want to, Camilla. I'm going to put it out of my mind."

"Are you going to put Phil and Penny out of your mind, too?"

"Well, no, but I'm not going to dwell on them either," Mary El said.

"I, for one," Janet said, "will never forget them."

"I didn't mean I'd forget them. I just mean I don't want to dwell on

them forever. I don't see what good it'll do anybody to keep thinking . . ."

I interrupted. "You don't want to face that they're dead. Well, the fact
is that they are. We're never going to see either of them again and we
can't run away from that."

Nobody said anything then and one by one we made excuses and left
for our various destinations. I went home and stayed in my room for the
rest of the afternoon, listening to music and thinking about Penny and
Phil and the pleasure each of them had given me. I guess you could say it
was my own memorial. That night I went off to do the show.

9. BEREAVEMENT

LITERARY accounts of bereavement appear in a variety of genres. Poems, short stories, essays, biographies, novels, and letters are all used by writers to convey certain aspects of the process of grief. Elegies stand out among these literary forms because they are a particular type of poetry that concentrates on expressing a poet's emotional reactions to another person's death. While literary works in various genres do on occasion deal with the subject of bereavement, elegies are written for the primary purpose of conveying a poet's loss and suffering brought about by death.

Most elegies are written in response to a particular person's death. Walt Whitman's "When Lilacs Last in the Dooryard Bloomed," for instance, was written in response to the assassination of President Lincoln. Among these elegies, three are generally regarded as the greatest elegies in English literature: Milton's "Lycidas," Shelley's *Adonais*, and Tennyson's *In Memoriam*. Each of these works mourns a young man of great talent who died before realizing his potential, and each of them expresses some of the characteristic features of the process of grief.

John Milton's "Lycidas," an outstanding example of English lyrical poetry, was written in 1637 as a response to the death of Edward King, who drowned in the Irish Sea earlier that year. Milton and King had been friends at Cambridge and had shared several common interests, including a love of poetry. The loss that Milton experienced is demonstrated a number of times in the poem as he reflects on their common love of nature, their enjoyment of music, and their hope for fame. At one point he expresses anger and remorse that his friend, who along with himself had shunned the more frivolous aspects of student life, had been on the verge of a promising career when along came "the blind Fury with the abhorred shears" and severed "the thin-spun life." Toward the poem's end, Milton voices his religious belief that prolonged sadness is unnecessary because his friend "is not dead," but alive in another realm where joy, love, and singing God's glory prevail.

Adonais was written by Shelley shortly after John Keats died from tuberculosis in 1821. Having given Keats financial assistance even though they were not close friends, Shelley was moved to write this long pastoral poem as a way of celebrating Keats' productive but abbreviated life and responding to some of Keat's critics. Charging that Keats' critics caused his death—and at one point calling forth "the curse of Cain" upon Keats' most severe critic—Shelley tempers his anger with lavish praise for the young poet who has been able to cultivate the senses and portray the manifold forms of beauty. In the context of portraying a procession of mourners by the dead poet, he predicts that Keats will have "a remembered name" because of his accomplishments—and those who mourn his death will find that "grief returns with the revolving year." The elegy concludes with a declaration that Keats lives on— "'tis Death is dead, not he"—and a remarkably prophetic description of Shelley's own death the following year.

Tennyson's *In Memoriam*, much more than the elegies of Milton and Shelley, represents a grief-stricken autobiography in poetical form. Arthur Hallam, his best friend and fiancé to his sister, died unexpectedly in 1833. The loss of his friend threw Tennyson into a prolonged period of confusion, depression, and loneliness which could be relieved only by using poetry as an emotional outlet: "for the unquiet heart and brain, / a use in measured language lies / . . . like dull narcotics, numbing pain." The result of his bereavement was a series of elegies written over a period of seventeen years until they were finally published under a single title in 1850. In this composite elegy, he writes about the recurring emotional pain of remembering his friend ("A hand that can be clasped no more"), the difficulty of living without him ("How dare we keep our Christmas-eve"), and yet the necessity of continuing the struggle to live ("Be cheerful-minded, talk and treat/of all things ev'n as he were by"). The last part of the poem to be written—as Tennyson finally reestablished a meaningful life in his friend's absence—contains an affirmation of faith in immortal life and in God's love: "I trust he lives in thee, and there/I find him worthier to be loved."

As demonstrated by these elegies, the process of grief consists of a series of emotional and physiological responses to the death of an emotionally significant person. The intensity and duration of the grief process is influenced by a number of factors. If the death is accidental, unexpected, or involves a young person, the process of grief will be more intense and prolonged than it would be if the death had been anticipated because of a prolonged illness or an advanced age. If the death involves a relative or friend with whom there are intimate emotional ties, as in the case of Hallam and Tennyson, the process of grief will be more intense and prolonged than if the person who died were a distant relative, a casual friend (e.g., Keats and Shelley), or a business colleague. If a bereaved person cannot accept the finality of the loss and/or blocks the expression of normal emotional responses to death, the process of grief will be more problematic and prolonged than in cases where the death is accepted as a permanent loss and the grief work necessitated by that loss is allowed to run its proper course.

For bereaved persons who respond normally to the death of a loved one, grief work entails a process of releasing the emotional tension brought about by the death. The process—something like the gradual release of a tightened spring—generally goes through three phases. The *initial phase* lasts for several weeks after the death occurs and involves a number of emotional and physiological responses to the death. The bereaved person commonly experiences shock and disbelief if the death was unexpected, and often goes through a period of denial followed by confusion and general disorganization because of the discrepancy between external events (the death, the funeral, etc.) and an internal awareness of what these events mean. Associated with this emotional turmoil are physiological changes such as shortness of breath, increased glandular activity, gastrointestinal problems, and loss of muscular power.

The *second phase* of normal bereavement begins several weeks after the death and continues for a number of months. The intensity and duration of this phase depend, in part, on the variables mentioned earlier. Emotional and behavioral characteristics of this period include the expression of anger, jealousy, and resentment (directed at the person now dead, the unfairness of the death, or persons still alive); the recurring experience of loss and loneliness, especially on holidays or dates of mutual importance; the ongoing search to find some meaning in the death; the manifestation of guilt over things done wrong during the lifetime of the person now dead, as well as over things which could have been done to enhance that life; and the experience of depression over the loss which sometimes is combined with anxiety regarding the future. With the passage of time—generally six to twelve months—most of these responses to death subside, and the pieces of an individual's life-puzzle are sufficiently together again to go on living in a normal manner.

At approximately the end of the first year of bereavement, a *third phase* of grief work takes over. At this point the emotional spring tightened by the death of a loved one has been sufficiently released that recovery and reestablishment can take place. New friends are made, old friends can discuss previously forbidden topics, and new experiences are once again enjoyable. Feelings of loss and loneliness return at specific dates on the "anniversary cycle," but in general life goes on with an increased sense of self-confidence and control.*

For bereaved persons who are unable to accept the finality of the death and get on with their grief work, the emotional tension is intensified rather than released. Abnormal responses to death often include initial, unrealistic demonstrations of emotional strength and well-being followed by a variety of artificial coping mechanisms (regression, increased alcohol consumption, increased drug use) which delay or inhibit the expression of normal emotions during a time of bereavement. The result of this abnormal emotional condition is, if prolonged, long-term psychophysiological damage which can take a number of forms: headaches, insomnia, symptom identification with the person now dead, alcoholism, drug addiction, and ulcers.

Some of the selections reflect quite divergent responses to death. The excerpt from the *Iliad* shows the manifest sorrow and lamentations of the citizens of Troy after Hector was killed, and the author of the Paiute poem states that everything in his life became worthless after his son died. The short piece by Chuang Tzu, in contrast, indicates that this Chinese Taoist philosopher saw no need for prolonged sorrow after his wife died, and Macbeth's speech clearly reveals that he was too involved in preparing for a military battle to express grief over his wife's death.

Other selections reveal several aspects of the grief process. Poe's

* Ira O. Glick, Robert S. Weiss, and C. Murray Parkes, *The First Year of Bereavement* (New York: Wiley, 1974).

"Annabel Lee" shows the tendency to idealize a dead person by accentuating her virtues and forgetting any vices she may have had. Tennyson's "Break, Break, Break" demonstrates the acute loss (of a friend's hand, a friend's voice, a day shared together) experienced by some survivors of death. "Song," by Christina Rossetti, attempts to minimize the sad necessity of the grief process, but this view is countered by Anton Chekhov's short story and Amy Lowell's poem, both of which provide poignant pictures of the loss and loneliness experienced by persons left behind by death. The excerpt from James Agee's novel focuses on the shock and confusion initially experienced by survivors of a death, while the excerpts from the books by C. S. Lewis and John Gunther provide outstanding first-person accounts of the joys and sorrows which fill the mind as a loved one is remembered.

The remaining selections provide a major contrast in perspective. Edna St. Vincent Millay's "Dirge Without Music" is unparalleled in conveying an unmitigated anger at the tragic losses brought about by death, while E. E. Cummings' "nobody loses all the time" is equally unparalleled in looking at death and bereavement in a humorous vein.

from the ILIAD
Homer (c.850 B.C.)

A remarkable scene occurs in Book XXIV of this work. Priam, king of Troy and father of Hector, goes to Achilles, kisses his hands, and offers a ransom to get his dead son's body back. Achilles, suddenly moved by compassion and empathy, agrees to release Hector's body and also agrees to refrain from further fighting for the twelve days Priam says the Trojans will need to mourn for Hector and bury his body. Priam then transports his dead son's body in a wagon to Troy, where his daughter Cassandra and others wait in bereavement.

Cassandra, beautiful as Golden Aphrodite, was the first among the men and girdled womenfolk of Troy to recognize them as they came. She had climbed to the top of Pergamus and from that point she saw her father standing in the chariot with the herald, his town-crier. She saw Hector too, lying on a bier in the mule-cart. She gave a scream and cried for all the town to hear: "Trojans and women of Troy, you used to welcome Hector when he came home safe from battle. He was the darling of every soul in the town. Come out and see him now."

Cassandra's cries plunged the whole town in grief, and soon there was not a man or woman left in Troy. They met the King with Hector's body at no great distance from the gates. His loving wife and lady mother fell upon the well-built wagon, to be the first to pluck their hair for him and touch his head. They were surrounded by a wailing throng. Indeed the townsfolk would have stayed there by the gates and wept for Hector all day long till sunset, if the old man, who was still in the chariot, had not commanded them to make way for the mules and told them they could mourn for Hector later to their hearts' content, when he had got him home. The people, thus admonished, fell back on either side and made a passage for the cart, leaving the family to bring Hector to the palace.

Once there, they laid him on a wooden bed and brought in musicians to lead in the laments and sing the melancholy dirges while the women wailed in chorus. White-armed Andromache, holding the head of Hector killer of men between her hands, gave them the first lament:

"Husband, you were too young to die and leave me widowed in our home. Your son, the boy that we unhappy parents brought into the world, is but a little baby. And I have no hope that he will grow into a man: Troy will come tumbling down before that can ever be. For you, her guardian, have perished, you that watched over her and kept her loyal wives and little babies safe. They will be carried off soon in the hollow ships, and I with them. And you, my child, will go with me to labor somewhere at a menial task under a heartless master's eye; or some Achaean will seize you by the arm and hurl you from the walls to a cruel death, venting his wrath on you because Hector killed a brother of his own, maybe, or else his father or a son. Yes, when he met Hector's hands, many an Achaean bit the dust of this wide world; for your father was by no means kindly in the heat of battle. And that is why the whole of Troy is wailing for him now. Ah, Hector, you have brought utter desolation to your parents. But who will mourn you as I shall? Mine is the bitterest regret of all, because you did not die in bed and stretching out your arms to me give me some tender word that I might have treasured in my tears by night and day."

Such was Andromache's lament; and the women joined her. Next, Hecabe took up for them the impassioned dirge: "Hector, dearest to me of all my sons, the gods loved you well while you were with me in the world; and now that Destiny has struck you down they have not forgotten you.

Swift-foot Achilles took other sons of mine, and sent them over the barren seas for sale in Samos or in Imbros or in smoke-capped Lemnos. And he took your life with his long blade of bronze; but though he dragged you many times round the barrow of the friend you killed (not that he brought Patroclus back to life by that), you have come home to me fresh as the morning dew and are laid out in the palace like one whom Apollo of the Silver Bow has visited and put to death with gentle darts."

Her words and sobs stirred all the women to unbridled grief. But Helen followed now and led them in a third lament: "Hector, I loved you far the best of all my Trojan brothers. Prince Paris brought me here and married me (I wish I had perished first), but in all the nineteen years since I came away and left my own country, it is from you that I have never heard a single harsh or spiteful word. Others in the house insulted me—your brothers, your sisters, your brothers' wealthy wives, even your mother, though your father could not be more gentle with me if he were my own. But you protested every time and stopped them, out of the kindness of your heart, in your own courteous way. So these tears of sorrow that I shed are both for you and for my miserable self. No one else is left in the wide realm of Troy to treat me gently and befriend me. They shudder at me as I pass." Thus Helen through her tears; and the countless multitude wailed with her.

from the CHUANG TZU
Chuang Tzu (c.399–295 B.C.)

A contemporary of Mencius, the great Confucian philosopher, Chuang Tzu was a major philosopher in the Taoist tradition of China. He was convinced that the Tao ("the way") represents an endless process of change and that life—in nature and in the human community—is characterized by continual change and transformation. Death is but a part of this ongoing process of change, as indicated by his response to his wife's death.

Chuang Tzu's wife died and Hui Tzu went to offer his condolence. He found Chuang Tzu squatting on the ground and singing, beating on an earthen bowl. He said, "Someone has lived with you, raised children for you, and now she has aged and died. Is it not enough that you should not shed any tear? But now you sing and beat the bowl. Is this not too much?"

"No," replied Chuang Tzu. "When she died, how could I help being affected? But as I think the matter over, I realize that originally she had no life; and not only no life, she had no form; not only no form, she had no material force. In the limbo of existence and non-existence, there was transformation and the material force was evolved. The material force was transformed to be form, form was transformed to become life, and now birth has transformed to become death. This is like the rotation of the four seasons, spring, summer, fall, and winter. Now she lies asleep in the great house (the universe). For me to go about weeping and wailing would be to show my ignorance of destiny. Therefore I desist.

from MACBETH (v, 8)
William Shakespeare (1564–1616)

The last act of this play takes place years after Macbeth and his wife conspired to kill Duncan, king of Scotland. Lady Macbeth, unable to live with her guilt, experienced serious mental problems prior to her death. Macbeth learns of her death as he prepares for a final battle against Macduff.

MACBETH: She should have died hereafter;
There would have been a time for such a word.
To-morrow, and to-morrow, and to-morrow,
Creeps in this petty pace from day to day
To the last syllable of recorded time,
And all our yesterdays have lighted fools
The way to dusty death. Out, out, brief candle!
Life's but a walking shadow, a poor player
That struts and frets his hour upon the stage
And then is heard no more: it is a tale
Told by an idiot, full of sound and fury,
Signifying nothing.

LAMENT OF A YOUNG MAN FOR HIS SON
Paiute poem (n.d.)

Son, my son!
I will go up to the mountain
And there I will light a fire
To the feet of my son's spirit,
And there I will lament him;
Saying,
O my son,
What is life to me, now you are departed?

Son, my son,
In the deep earth
We softly laid thee
In a chief's robe,
In a warrior's gear.
Surely there,
In the spirit land
Thy deeds attend thee!
Surely,
The corn comes to the ear again!
But I, here,
I am the stalk that the seed-gatherers
Descrying empty, afar, left standing.
Son, my son!
What is my life to me, now you are departed?

ANNABEL LEE
Edgar Allan Poe (1809–1849)

Poe married his cousin, Virginia Clemm, in 1835. Within a decade, they both knew she would die from tuberculosis. This poem, the last one that he wrote, is an idealized picture of her. It was first published two days after his death.

It was many and many a year ago,
    In a kingdom by the sea,
That a maiden there lived whom you may know
    By the name of Annabel Lee;
And this maiden she lived with no other thought
    Than to love and be loved by me.

I was a child and she was a child,
    In this kingdom by the sea,
But we loved with a love that was more than love—
    I and my Annabel Lee;
With a love that the winged seraphs of heaven
    Coveted her and me.

And this was the reason that, long ago,
    In this kingdom by the sea,
A wind blew out of a cloud, chilling
    My beautiful Annabel Lee;
So that her highborn kinsmen came
    And bore her away from me,
To shut her up in a sepulcher
    In this kingdom by the sea.

The angels, not half so happy in heaven,
    Went envying her and me—
Yes! that was the reason (as all men know,
    In this kingdom by the sea)
That the wind came out of the cloud by night,
    Chilling and killing my Annabel Lee.

But our love it was stronger by far than the love
    Of those who were older than we,
    Of many far wiser than we;
And neither the angels in heaven above,
    Nor the demons down under the sea,
Can ever dissever my soul from the soul
    Of the beautiful Annabel Lee;

For the moon never beams, without bringing me dreams
    Of the beautiful Annabel Lee;
And the stars never rise, but I feel the bright eyes
    Of the beautiful Annabel Lee;
And so, all the night-tide, I lie down by the side
Of my darling—my darling—my life and my bride,
    In the sepulcher there by the sea,
    In her tomb by the sounding sea.

BREAK, BREAK, BREAK
Alfred, Lord Tennyson (1809–1892)

As mentioned in the introduction to this section, Arthur Hallam's death had an immeasurable effect on Tennyson's life and poetry. Long before he wrote *In Memoriam*, he expressed his grief over his closest friend's death in this poem. The poem depicts the rocky coast of Somersetshire, viewed from the hill on which Hallam was buried.

Break, break, break,
    On thy cold gray stones, O Sea!
And I would that my tongue could utter
    The thoughts that arise in me.

O well for the fisherman's boy,
    That he shouts with his sister at play!
O well for the sailor lad,
    That he sings in his boat on the bay!

And the stately ships go on
    To their haven under the hill;
But O for the touch of a vanished hand,
    And the sound of a voice that is still!

Break, break, break,
    At the foot of thy crags, O Sea!
But the tender grace of a day that is dead
    Will never come back to me.

SONG
Christina Rossetti (1830–1894)

When I am dead, my dearest,
    Sing no sad songs for me;
Plant thou no roses at my head,
    Nor shady cypress tree.
Be the green grass above me
      With showers and dewdrops wet;
      And if thou wilt, remember,
      And if thou wilt, forget.

I shall not see the shadows,
    I shall not feel the rain;
I shall not hear the nightingale
    Sing on as if in pain.
And dreaming through the twilight
      That doth not rise nor set,
      Haply I may remember,
      And haply may forget.

HEARTACHE
Anton Chekhov (1860–1904)

A playwright and author of numerous short stories, Chekhov ranks as one of the outstanding writers of nineteenth-century Russia. In this short story, written in 1886, he provides a moving description of the loneliness which often hits the survivors of death. Apparently without family or friends to share his anguish, the cabdriver in the story demonstrates an urgent need for someone—anyone—to listen to him pour out the details of his son's recent death.

To whom shall I tell my sorrow?
Evening twilight. Thick flakes of wet snow were circling lazily round the newly lighted street lamps, settling in thin soft layers on rooftops, on the horses' backs, and on people's shoulders and caps. The cabdriver Iona Potapov was white as a ghost, and bent double as much as any human body can be bent double, sitting very still on his box. Even if a whole snowdrift had fallen on him, he would have found no need to shake it off.

The little mare, too, was white, and quite motionless. Her immobility, and the fact that she was all sharp angles and sticklike legs, gave her a resemblance to one of those gingerbread horses which can be bought for a kopeck. No doubt the mare was plunged in deep thought. So would you be if you were torn from the plow, snatched away from familiar, gray surroundings, and thrown into a whirlpool of monstrous illuminations, ceaseless uproar, and people scrambling hither and thither.

For a long while neither Iona nor the little mare had made the slightest motion. They had driven out of the stableyard before dinner, and so far not a single fare had come to them. The evening mist fell over the city. The pale glow of the street lamps grew brighter, more intense, as the street noises grew louder.

Iona heard someone saying: "Driver—you, there!—take me to Vyborg District!"

Iona started, and through his snow-laden eyelashes he made out an officer wearing a military overcoat with a hood.

"Vyborg!" the officer repeated. "Are you asleep, eh? Get on with it—Vyborg!"

To show he had heard, Iona pulled at the reins, sending whole layers of snow flying from the horse's back and from his own shoulders. The officer sat down in the sleigh. The driver clucked with his tongue, stretched out his neck like a swan, rose in his seat, and more from habit than necessity, he flourished his whip. The little horse also stretched her neck, crooked her sticklike legs, and started off irresolutely. . . .

"Where are you going, you fool!" Iona was being assailed with shouts from some massive, dark object wavering to and fro in front of him. "Where the devil are you going? Stay on the right side of the road!"

"You don't know how to drive! Stay on the right side!" the officer shouted angrily.

A coachman driving a private carriage was swearing at him, and a pedestrian, running across the road and brushing his shoulder against the mare's nose, glanced up at him and shook the snow from his sleeve. Iona shifted about on the box, as though sitting on needles, thrust out his elbows, rolled his eyes like a madman, as though he did not understand where he was or what he was doing there.

"They're all scoundrels," the officer laughed. "All trying to shove into you, or fall under your horse. Quite a conspiracy!"

The driver turned towards the officer, his lips moving. He appeared about to say something, but the only sound coming from him was a hoarse wheezing cough.

"What is it?" the officer asked.

Iona's lips twitched into a smile, and he strained his throat and croaked: "My son, sir. He died this week."

"Hm, what did he die of?"

Iona turned his whole body round to face his fare.

"Who knows? They say it was fever. . . . He was in the hospital only three days, and then he died. It was God's will!"

"Get over, damn you!" came a sudden shout out of the darkness. "Have you gone blind, you old idiot? Keep your eyes skinned!"

"Keep going," the officer said. "This way we won't get there till tomorrow morning. Put the whip to her!"

Once more the driver stretched his neck, rose in his seat, and with heavy grace flourished the whip. Several times he turned to watch his fare, but the officer's eyes were closed and apparently he was in no mood to listen. And then, letting off the passenger in the Vyborg District, the driver stopped by a tavern, and again he remained motionless, doubled up on his box. And again the wet snow splashed him and his mare with its white paint. An hour passed, and then another.

Then three young men came loudly pounding the sidewalk in galoshes, quarreling furiously among themselves. Two were tall and slender, the third was a small hunchback.

"Driver, to the Police Bridge!" the hunchback shouted in a cracked voice. "The three of us for twenty kopecks!"

Iona tugged at the reins and smacked his lips. Twenty kopecks was not a fair price, but he did not care any more. Whether it was a ruble or five kopecks no longer mattered, so long as he had a fare. The young men, jostling and cursing one another, came up to the sleigh, and all three of them tried to jump onto the seat, and then they began to argue about which two should sit down, and who should be the one to stand up. After a long, fantastic, and ill-natured argument they decided that the hunchback would have to stand, because he was the shortest.

"Let's go!" cried the hunchback in his cracked voice, taking his place and breathing down Iona's neck. "Get going! Eh, brother, what a funny cap you're wearing. You won't find a worse one anywhere in St. Petersburg!"

"Hee-hee-hee," Iona giggled. "Yes, it's a funny cap."

"Then get a move on! Are you going to crawl along all this time at the same pace? Do you want to get it in the neck?"

"My head's splitting!" said one of the tall ones. "Yesterday at the Dukmassovs', I drank all of four bottles of cognac with Vaska."

"I don't know why you have to tell lies," the other tall one said angrily. "You lie like a swine!"

"May God strike me dead if I am not telling the truth!"

"A flea coughs the truth, too."

"Hee-hee-hee," Iona giggled. "What a lot of merry gentlemen. . . ."

"Pfui!" the hunchback exclaimed indignantly. "Damn you for an old idiot! Will you get a move on, or won't you? Is that how to drive? Use the whip, dammit! Go on, you old devil, give it to her!"

Iona could feel at his back the hunchback's wriggling body, and the tremble in the voice. He heard the insults which were being hurled at him, he saw the people in the street, and little by little the feeling of loneliness was lifted from his heart. The hunchback went on swearing until he choked on an elaborate six-story-high oath, and then was overcome with a fit of coughing. The tall ones began to talk about a certain Nadezhda Petrovna. Iona looked round at them. He waited until there was a short pause in the conversation, and then he turned again and murmured: "My son died—he died this week. . . ."

"We all die," sighed the hunchback, wiping his lips after his fit of coughing. "Keep going, eh? Gentlemen, we simply can't go any further like this. We'll never get there!"

"Give him a bit of encouragement. Hit him in the neck!"

"Did you hear that, old pest? You'll get it in the neck all right. One shouldn't stand on ceremony with people like you—one might just as well walk. Do you hear me, you old snake? I don't suppose you care a tinker's damn about what we are saying."

Then Iona heard rather than felt a thud on the nape of his neck.

"Hee-hee-hee," he laughed. "Such merry gentlemen! God bless them!"

"Driver, are you married?" one of the tall men asked.

"Me, am I married? Hee-hee-hee. You're all such merry gentlemen. There's only one wife left to me now—the damp earth. Hee-ho-ho. The grave, that's what's left for me. My son is dead, and I'm alive. Strange how death comes by the wrong door. It didn't come for me, it came for my son. . . ."

Iona turned round to tell them how his son died, but at that moment the hunchback gave a little sigh of relief and announced that, thank God, they had come to the end of the journey. Having received his twenty kopecks, Iona gazed after the revelers for a long time, even after they had vanished through a dark gateway. Once more he was alone, once more silence fell on him. The grief he had kept at bay for a brief while now returned to wrench his heart with still greater force. With an expression of anxiety and torment, he gazed at the crowds hurrying along both sides of the street, wondering whether there was anyone among those thousands of people who would listen to him. But the crowds hurried past, paying no attention to him or to his grief. His grief was vast, boundless. If his heart could break, and the grief could pour out of it, it would flow over the whole world; but no one would see it. It had found a hiding place invisible to all: even in broad daylight, even if you held a candle to it, you wouldn't see it.

There was a doorman carrying some kind of sack, and Iona decided to talk to him.

"What time is it, my dear fellow?" he asked.

"Ten o'clock. What the devil are you standing there for? Get a move on!"

Iona drove along the street a bit. His body was bent, and he was surrendering to his grief. He felt it was useless to turn to people for help, but in less than five minutes he had straightened himself up, shaking his head as though he felt a sharp pang of pain, and then he pulled at the reins. He could bear it no longer.

"Back to the stables," he thought. "Back to the stables."

The little mare, as though she read his thoughts, started off at a trot.

An hour and a half later Iona was sitting by a large dirty stove. On the stove, on the floor, on benches, men were snoring. The air was noisome, suffocating. Iona found himself gazing at the sleeping people. He scratched himself, and he was sorry he had come back so early.

"I haven't earned enough even for the hay," he thought. "There's grief for you. But a man who knows his work, and has a full belly, and a well-fed horse besides, he's at peace with the world all his days."

From one of the corners a young driver rose, grunting sleepily as he reached for the water bucket.

"You thirsty?" Iona asked him.

"Reckon so."

"Well, it's a good thing to be thirsty, but as for me, brother, my son is dead. Did you hear me? This week, at the hospital. . . . Such a lot of trouble!"

Iona looked to see whether the words were producing any effect, but saw none—the young man had covered up his face and was asleep again. The old man sighed and scratched himself. Just as the young man wanted to drink, so he wanted to talk. Soon it would be a week since his son died, and still no one had let him talk about it properly. He would have to tell it slowly, very carefully. He would tell them how his son fell ill, how he suffered, what he said before he died, how he died. He would have to describe the funeral, and how he went to the hospital to collect his son's clothes. His daughter Anissya was still in the country. He wanted to talk about her, too. Yes, there was so much to talk about. And the listener would have to gasp and sigh and bewail the fate of the dead man. And maybe it would be better to talk about it to women. Even though women are so foolish, you can bring the tears to their eyes with a few words.

"Now I'll go and look at my horse," Iona thought to himself. "There's always time for sleep—nothing there to be afraid of."

He threw on his coat and went down to the stable to look after her, thinking about such things as hay, oats, and the weather. Alone, he dared not let his mind dwell on his son. He could talk about him to anyone, but alone, thinking about him, conjuring up his living presence, no—no, that was too painful for words.

"Filling your belly, eh?" he said, seeing the mare's shining eyes. "Well, eat up! We haven't earned enough for oats, but we can eat hay. Oh, I'm too old to be driving. My son should be driving, not me. He was a real cabdriver, and he should be alive now. . . ."

Iona was silent for a moment, and then he went on: "That's how it is, old girl. My son, Kuzma Ionich, is no more. He died on us. Now let's say you had a foal, and you were the foal's mother, and suddenly, let's say, the same little foal departed this life. You'd be sorry, eh?"

The little mare munched and listened and breathed on his hands.

Surrendering to his grief, Iona told her the whole story.

PATTERNS
Amy Lowell (1874–1925)

I walk down the garden-paths,
And all the daffodils
Are blowing, and the bright blue squills.
I walk down the patterned garden-paths
In my stiff, brocaded gown.
With my powdered hair and jeweled fan,
I too am a rare
Pattern. As I wander down
The garden-paths.
My dress is richly figured,
And the train
Makes a pink and silver stain
On the gravel, and the thrift
Of the borders.
Just a plate of current fashion,
Tripping by in high-heeled, ribboned shoes.
Not a softness anywhere about me,
Only whalebone and brocade.
And I sink on a seat in the shade
Of a lime-tree. For my passion
Wars against the stiff brocade.
The daffodils and squills
Flutter in the breeze
As they please.
And I weep;
For the lime-tree is in blossom
And one small flower has dropped upon my bosom.

And the plashing of waterdrops
In the marble fountain
Comes down the garden-paths.
The dripping never stops.
Underneath my stiffened gown
Is the softness of a woman bathing in a marble basin,
A basin in the midst of hedges grown

So thick, she cannot see her lover hiding,
But she guesses he is near,
And the sliding of the water
Seems the stroking of a dear
Hand upon her.
What is Summer in a fine brocaded gown!
I should like to see it lying in a heap upon the ground.
All the pink and silver crumpled up on the ground.

I would be the pink and silver as I ran along the paths,
And he would stumble after,
Bewildered by my laughter.
I should see the sun flashing from his sword hilt and the buckles on his
    shoes.
I would choose
To lead him in a maze along the patterned paths,
A bright and laughing maze for my heavy-booted lover.
Till he caught me in the shade,
And the buttons of his waistcoat bruised my body as he clasped me
Aching, melting, unafraid.
With the shadows of the leaves and the sundrops,
And the plopping of the waterdrops,
All about us in the open afternoon—
I am very like to swoon
With the weight of this brocade,
For the sun sifts through the shade.

Underneath the fallen blossom
In my bosom,
Is a letter I have hid.
It was brought to me this morning by a rider from the Duke.
"Madam, we regret to inform you that Lord Hartwell
Died in action Thursday se'nnight."
As I read it in the white, morning sunlight,
The letters squirmed like snakes.
"Any answer, Madam," said my footman.
"No," I told him.
"See that the messenger takes some refreshment.
No, no answer."

And I walked into the garden,
Up and down the patterned paths,
In my stiff, correct brocade.
The blue and yellow flowers stood up proudly in the sun,
Each one.
I stood upright too,
Held rigid to the pattern
By the stiffness of my gown.
Up and down I walked,
Up and down.

In a month he would have been my husband.
In a month, here, underneath this lime,
We would have broke the pattern;
He for me, and I for him,
He as Colonel, I as Lady,
On this shady seat.
He had a whim
That sunlight carried blessing.
And I answered, "It shall be as you have said."
Now he is dead.

In Summer and in Winter I shall walk
Up and down
The patterned garden-paths
In my stiff, brocaded gown.
The squills and daffodils
Will give place to pillared roses, and to asters, and to snow.
I shall go
Up and down
In my gown.
Gorgeously arrayed,
Boned and stayed.
And the softness of my body will be guarded from embrace
By each button, hook, and lace.
For the man who should loose me is dead,
Fighting with the Duke in Flanders,
In a pattern called a war.
Christ! What are patterns for?

DIRGE WITHOUT MUSIC
Edna St. Vincent Millay (1892-1950)

I am not resigned to the shutting away of loving hearts in the hard
    ground.
So it is, and so it will be, for so it has been time out of mind:
Into the darkness they go, the wise and the lovely. Crowned
With lilies and with laurel they go; but I am not resigned.

Lovers and thinkers, into the earth with you,
Be one with the dull, the indiscriminate dust.
A fragment of what you felt, of what you knew,
A formula, a phrase remains—but the best is lost.

The answers quick and keen, the honest look, the laughter, the love—
They are gone. They are gone to feed the roses. Elegant and curled
Is the blossom. Fragrant is the blossom. I know. But I do not approve.
More precious was the light in your eyes than all the roses of the world.

Down, down, down into the darkness of the grave
Gently they go, the beautiful, the tender, the kind;
Quietly they go, the intelligent, the witty, the brave.
I know. But I do not approve. And I am not resigned.

NOBODY LOSES ALL THE TIME
E. E. Cummings (1894-1962)

nobody loses all the time

i had an uncle named
Sol who was a born failure and
nearly everybody said he should have gone
into vaudeville perhaps because my Uncle Sol could
sing McCann He Was A Diver on Xmas Eve like Hell Itself which
may or may not account for the fact that my Uncle

Sol indulged in that possibly most inexcusable
of all to use a highfalootin phrase
luxuries that is or to
wit farming and be
it needlessly
added

my Uncle Sol's farm
failed because the chickens
ate the vegetables so
my Uncle Sol had a
chicken farm till the
skunks ate the chickens when

my Uncle Sol
had a skunk farm but
the skunks caught cold and
died and so
my Uncle Sol imitated the
skunks in a subtle manner

or by drowning himself in the watertank
but somebody who'd given my Uncle Sol a Victor
Victrola and records while he lived presented to
him upon the auspicious occasion of his decease a
scrumptious not to mention splendiferous funeral with
tall boys in black gloves and flowers and everything and

i remember we all cried like the Missouri
when my Uncle Sol's coffin lurched because
somebody pressed a button
(and down went
my Uncle
Sol

and started a worm farm)

from A DEATH IN THE FAMILY
James Agee (1910–1955)

Mary, the wife and mother of the family, received a telephone call informing her that Jay had been in a serious car accident. Her brother Andrew went to the scene of the accident to see how serious it was. She and Aunt Hannah wait anxiously for Andrew to call and then, as time passes, gradually suspect that Jay has been killed in the accident. At last Andrew returns to the house as the bearer of the tragic news.

Andrew did not bother to knock, but opened the door and closed it quietly behind him and, seeing their moving shadows near the kitchen threshold, walked quickly down the hall. They could not see his face in the dark hallway but by his tight, set way of walking, they were virtually sure. They were all but blocking his way. Instead of going into the hall to meet him, they drew aside to let him into the kitchen. He did not hesitate with their own moment's hesitation but came straight on, his mouth a straight line and his eyes like splintered glass, and without saying a word he put his arms around his aunt so tightly that she gasped, and lifted her from the floor. "Mary," Hannah whispered, close to his ear; he looked; there she stood waiting, her eyes, her face, like that of an astounded child which might be pleading. Oh, don't hit me; and before he could speak he heard her say, thinly and gently, "He's dead, Andrew, isn't he?" and he could not speak, but nodded, and he became aware that he was holding his aunt's feet off the floor and virtually breaking her bones, and his sister said, in the same small and unearthly voice, "He was dead when you got there"; and again he nodded; and then he set Hannah down carefully on her feet and, turning to his sister, took her by her shoulders and said, more loudly than he had expected, "He was instantly killed," and he kissed her upon the mouth and they embraced, and without tears but with great violence he sobbed twice, his cheek against hers, while he stared downwards through her loose hair at her humbled back and at the changeful blinking of the linoleum; then, feeling her become heavy against him, said, "Here, Mary," catching her across the shoulders and helping her to a chair, just as she, losing strength in her knees, gasped, "I've got to sit down," and looked timidly towards her aunt, who at the same moment saying, in a broken voice, "Sit down, Mary," was at her other side, her arm around her waist and her face as bleached and shocking as a skull. She put an arm tightly around each of them and felt gratitude and pleasure, in the firmness and warmth of their moving bodies, and they walked three abreast (like bosom friends, it occurred to her, the three Musketeers) to the nearest chair; and she could see Andrew twist it towards her with his outstretched left hand, and between them, slowly, they let her down into it, and then she could see only her aunt's face, leaning deep above her, very large and very close, the eyes at once intense and tearful behind their heavy lenses, the strong mouth loose and soft, the whole face terrible in love and grief, naked and undisciplined as she had never seen it before.

"Let Papa know and Mama," she whispered. "I promised."

"I will," Hannah, starting for the hall.

"Walter's bringing them straight up," Andrew said. "They know by now." He brought another chair. "Sit down, Aunt Hannah." She sat and took both Mary's hands in her own, on Mary's knees, and realized that Mary was squeezing her hands with all her strength, and as strongly as she was able. She replied in kind to this constantly shifting, almost writhing pressure.

"Sit with us, Andrew," Mary said, a little more loudly; he was already bringing a third chair and now he sat, and put his hands upon theirs, and, feeling the convulsing of her hands, thought, Christ, it's as if she were in labor. *And she is.* Thus they sat in silence a few moments while he thought: now I've got to tell them how it happened. In God's name, how can I begin!

"I want whiskey," Mary said, in a small, cold voice, and tried to get up.

"I'll get it," Andrew said, standing.

"You don't know where it is," she said, continuing to put aside their hands even after they were withdrawn. She got up and they stood as if respectfully aside and she walked between them and went into the hall; they heard her rummaging in the closet, and looked at each other. "She needs it," Hannah said.

He nodded. He had been surprised, because of Jay, that there was whiskey in the house; and he was sick with self-disgust to have thought of it. "We all do," he said.

Without looking at them Mary went to the kitchen closet and brought a thick tumbler to the table. The bottle was almost full. She poured the tumbler full while they watched her, feeling they must not interfere, and took a deep gulp and choked on it, and swallowed most of it.

"Dilute it," Hannah said, slapping her hard between the shoulders and drying her lips and her chin with a dish towel. "It's much too strong, that way."

"I will," Mary croaked, and cleared her throat, "I will," she said more clearly.

"Just sit down, Mary," Andrew and Hannah said at the same moment, and Andrew brought her a glass of water and Hannah helped her to her chair.

"I'm going to have some, too," Andrew said.

"Goodness, do!" said Mary.

"Let me fix us a good strong toddy," Hannah said. "It'll help you to sleep."

"I don't want to sleep," Mary said; she sipped at her whiskey and took plenty of the water. "I've got to learn how it happened."

"Aunt Hannah," Andrew asked quietly, motioning towards the bottle. "Please."

While he broke ice and brought glasses and a pitcher of water, none of them spoke; Mary sat in a distorted kind of helplessness at once meek and curiously sullen, waiting. Months later, seeing a horse which had fallen in the street, Andrew was to remember her; and he was to remember it wasn't drunkenness, either. It was just the flat of the hand of Death.

"Let me pour my own," Mary said. "Because," she added with deliberation while she poured, "I want it just as strong as I can stand it." She tasted the dark drink, added a little more whiskey, tasted again, and put the bottle aside. Hannah watched her with acute concern, thinking, if she gets drunk tonight, and if her mother sees her drunk, she'll half die of shame, and thinking, nonsense. It's the most sensible thing she could do.

"Drink it very slowly, Mary," Andrew said gently. "You aren't used to it."

"I'll take care," Mary said.

"It's just the thing for shock," Hannah said.

Andrew poured two small straight drinks and gave one to his aunt; they drank them off quickly and took water, and he prepared two pale highballs.

"Now, Andrew, I want to hear all about it," Mary said.

He looked at Hannah.

"Mary," he said. "Mama and Papa'll be here any minute. You'd just have to hear it all over again. I'll tell you, of course, if you prefer, right away but—could you wait?"

But even as he was speaking she was nodding, and Hannah was saying, "Yes, child," as all three thought of the confusions and repetitions which were, at best, inevitable. Now after a moment Mary said, "Anyway, you say he didn't have to suffer. *Instantly*, you said."

He nodded, and said, "Mary, I saw him—at Roberts'. There was just one mark on his body."

She looked at him. "His head."

"Right at the exact point of the chin, a small bruise. A cut so small—they can close it with one stitch. And a little blue bruise on his lower lip. It wasn't even swollen."

"That's all," she said.

"All," Hannah said.

"That's all," Andrew said. "The doctor said it was concussion of the brain. It was instantaneous."

She was silent; he felt that she must be doubting it. Christ, he thought furiously, at least she could be spared *that!*

"He can't have suffered, Mary, not even for a fraction of second. Mary, I saw his face. There wasn't a glimmer of pain in it. Only—a kind of surprise. Startled."

Still she said nothing. I've got to make her sure of it, he thought. How in heaven's name can I make it clearer? If necessary, I'll get hold of the doctor and make him tell her hims. . . .

"He never knew he was dying," she said. "Not a minute, not one moment, to know, 'my life is ending.'"

Hannah put a quick hand to her shoulder; Andrew dropped to his knees before her; took her hands and said, most earnestly, "Mary, in God's name be thankful he didn't! That's a hideous thing for a man in the prime of life to have to know. He wasn't a *Christian*, you know," he blurted it fiercely. "He didn't have to make his peace with God. He was a man, with a wife and two children, and I'd say that sparing him *that* horrible knowledge was the one thing we can thank God for!" And he added, in a desperate voice, "I'm so terribly sorry I said that, Mary!"

But Hannah, who had been gently saying, "He's right, Mary, he's right, be thankful for that," now told him quietly, "It's all right, Andrew"; and Mary, whose eyes fixed upon his, had shown increasing shock and terror, now said tenderly, "Don't mind, dear. Don't be sorry. I understand. You're right."

"That venomous thing I said about Christians," Andrew said after a moment. "I can never forgive myself, Mary."

"Don't grieve over it, Andrew. Don't. Please. Look at me, please." He looked at her. "It's true I was thinking as I was bound to as a Christian, but I was forgetting we're human, and you set me right and I'm thankful. You're right. Jay wasn't—a religious man, in that sense, and to realize could have only been—as you said for him. Probably as much so, even if he were religious." She looked at him quietly. "So just please know I'm not hurt or angry. I needed to realize what you told me and I thank God for it."

from A GRIEF OBSERVED
C. S. Lewis (1898–1963)

For many years a professor at Oxford, Lewis later held an endowed chair in Medieval and Renaissance Literature at Cambridge. He was a prolific writer: books of adult fiction, books on theology, essays, children's books, poems, and letters on a variety of subjects. When his wife died, he decided—partially for therapeutic reasons—to record his thoughts and emotional responses to her death. The result is an extraordinary, firsthand account of the process of grief.

No one ever told me that grief felt so like fear. I am not afraid, but the sensation is like being afraid. The same fluttering in the stomach, the same restlessness, the yawning. I keep on swallowing.

At other times it feels like being mildly drunk, or concussed. There is a sort of invisible blanket between the world and me. I find it hard to take in what anyone says. Or perhaps, hard to want to take it in. It is so uninteresting. Yet I want the others to be about me. I dread the moments when the house is empty. If only they would talk to one another and not to me.

There are moments, most unexpectedly, when something inside me tries to assure me that I don't really mind so much, not so very much, after all. Love is not the whole of a man's life. I was happy before I ever met H. I've plenty of what are called "resources." People get over these things. Come, I shan't do so badly. One is ashamed to listen to this voice but it seems for a little to be making out a good case. Then comes a sudden jab of red-hot memory and all this "commonsense" vanishes like an ant in the mouth of a furnace.

On the rebound one passes into tears and pathos. Maudlin tears. I almost prefer the moments of agony. These are at least clean and honest. But the bath of self-pity, the wallow, the loathsome sticky-sweet pleasure of indulging it—that disgusts me. And even while I'm doing it I know it leads me to misrepresent H. herself. Give that mood its head and in a few minutes I shall have substituted for the real woman a mere doll to be blubbered over. Thank God the memory of her is still too strong (will it always be too strong?) to let me get away with it.

For H. wasn't like that at all. Her mind was lithe and quick and muscular as a leopard. Passion, tenderness, and pain were all equally unable to disarm it. It scented the first whiff of cant or slush; then sprang, and knocked you over before you knew what was happening. How many bubbles of mine she pricked! I soon learned not to talk rot to her unless I did it for the sheer pleasure—and there's another red-hot jab—of being exposed and laughed at. I was never less silly than as H's lover.

And no one ever told me about the laziness of grief. Except at my job—where the machine seems to run on much as usual—I loathe the slightest effort. Not only writing but even reading a letter is too much. Even shaving. What does it matter now whether my cheek is rough or smooth? They say an unhappy man wants distractions—something to take him out of himself. Only as a dog-tired man wants an extra blanket on a cold night; he'd rather lie there shivering than get up and find one. It's easy to see why the lonely become untidy; finally, dirty and disgusting.

. . . .

I think I am beginning to understand why grief feels like suspense. It comes from the frustration of so many impulses that had become habitual. Thought after thought, feeling after feeling, action after action, had H. for their object. Now their target is gone. I keep on through habit fitting an arrow to the string; then I remember and have to lay the bow down. So many roads lead thought to H. I set out on one of them. But now there's an impassable frontier-post across it. So many roads once; now so many *culs de sac*.

For a good wife contains so many persons in herself. What was H. not to me? She was my daughter and my mother, my pupil and my teacher, my subject and my sovereign; and always, holding all these in solution, my trusty comrade, friend, shipmate, fellow-soldier. My mistress; but at the same time all that any man friend (and I have good ones) has ever been to me. Perhaps more. If we had never fallen in love we should have none the less been always together, and created a scandal. That's what I meant when I once praised her for her "masculine virtues." But she soon put a stop to that by asking how I'd like to be praised for my feminine ones. It was a good *riposte*, dear. Yet there was something of the Amazon, something of Penthesileia and Camilla. And you, as well as I, were glad it should be there. You were glad I should recognize it.

. . . .

And then one or other dies. And we think of this as love cut short; like a dance stopped in mid-career or a flower with its head unluckily snapped off—something truncated and therefore, lacking its due shape. I wonder. If, as I can't help suspecting, the dead also feel the pains of separation (and this may be one of their purgatorial sufferings), then for both lovers, and for all pairs of lovers without exception, bereavement is a universal and integral part of our experience of love. It follows marriage as normally as marriage follows courtship or as autumn follows summer. It is not a truncation of the process but one of its phases; not the interruption of the dance, but the next figure. We are "taken out of ourselves" by the loved one while she is here. Then comes the tragic figure of the dance in which we must learn to be still taken out of ourselves though the bodily presence is withdrawn, to love the very Her, and not fall back to loving our past, or our memory, or our sorrow, or our relief from sorrow, or our own love.

. . . .

Getting over it so soon? But the words are ambiguous. To say the patient is getting over it after an operation for appendicitis is one thing; after he's had his leg off it is quite another. After that operation either the wounded stump heals or the man dies. If it heals, the fierce, continuous pain will stop. Presently he'll get back his strength and be able to stump about on his wooden leg. He has "got over it." But he will probably have recurrent pains in the stump all his life, and perhaps pretty bad ones; and he will always be a one-legged man. There will be hardly any moment when he forgets it. Bathing, dressing, sitting down and getting up again, even lying in bed, will all be different. His whole way of life will be changed. All sorts of pleasures and activities that he once took for granted will have to be simply written off. Duties too. At present I am learning to get about on crutches. Perhaps I shall presently be given a wooden leg. But I shall never be a biped again.

. . . .

This is the fourth—and the last—empty MS. book I can find in the house; at least nearly empty, for there are some pages of very ancient arithmetic at the end by J. I resolve to let this limit my jottings. I *will not* start buying books for the purpose. In so far as this record was a defense against total collapse, a safety valve, it has done some good. The other end I had in view turns out to have been based on a misunderstanding. I thought I could describe a *state;* make a map of sorrow. Sorrow, however, turns out to be not a state but a process. It needs not a map but a history, and if I don't stop writing that history at some quite arbitrary point, there's no reason why I should ever stop. There is something new to be chronicled every day. Grief is like a long valley, a winding valley where any bend may reveal a totally new landscape. As I've already noted, not every bend does. Sometimes the surprise is the opposite one; you are presented with exactly the same sort of country you thought you had left behind miles ago. That is when you wonder whether the valley isn't a circular trench. But it isn't. There are partial recurrences, but the sequence doesn't repeat.

from DEATH BE NOT PROUD (John Gunther)
Frances Gunther

Johnny Gunther died when he was seventeen. His father, because of contractual obligations as a writer, had frequently been out of the country on research trips during Johnny's teen-age years. His mother, Frances, had spent more time with him during those years and, after his death, recorded her thoughts about her son and her own grief in an addendum to the book.

Death always brings one suddenly face to face with life. Nothing, not even the birth of one's child, brings one so close to life as his death.

Johnny lay dying of a brain tumor for fifteen months. He was in his seventeenth year. I never kissed him good night without wondering whether I should see him alive in the morning. I greeted him each morning as though he were newly born to me, a re-gift of God. Each day he lived was a blessed day of grace.

The impending death of one's child raises many questions in one's mind and heart and soul. It raises all the infinite questions, each answer ending in another question. What is the meaning of life? What are the relations between things: life and death? the individual and the family? the family and society? marriage and divorce? the individual and the state? medicine and research? science and politics and religion? man, men, and God?

All these questions came up in one way or another, and Johnny and I talked about them, in one way or another, as he was dying for fifteen months. He wasn't just dying, of course. He was living and dying and being reborn all at the same time each day. How we loved each day. "It's been another wonderful day, Mother!" he'd say, as I knelt to kiss him good night.

There are many complex and erudite answers to all these questions, which men have thought about for many thousands of years, and about which they have written many thousands of books.

Yet at the end of them all, when one has put away all the books, and all the words, when one is alone with oneself, when one is alone with God, what is left in one's heart? Just this:

I wish we had loved Johnny more.

. . . .

My grief, I find, is not desolation or rebellion at universal law or deity. I find grief to be much simpler and sadder. Contemplating the Eternal Deity and His Universal Laws leaves me grave but dry-eyed. But a sunny fast wind along the Sound, good sailing weather, a new light boat, will shake me to tears: how Johnny would have loved this boat, this wind, this sunny day!

All the things he loved tear at my heart because he is no longer here on earth to enjoy them. All the things he loved! An open fire with a broiling steak, a pancake tossed in the air, fresh nectarines, black-red cherries—the science columns in the papers and magazines, the fascinating new technical developments—the Berkshire music festival coming in over the air, as we lay in the moonlight on our wide open beach, listening—how he loved all these! . . .

Today, when I see parents impatient or tired or bored with their children, I wish I could say to them, But they are alive, think of the wonder of that! They may be a care and a burden, but think, they are alive! You can touch them—what a miracle! You don't have to hold back sudden tears when you see just a headline about the Yale–Harvard game because you know your boy will never see the Yale–Harvard game, never see the house in Paris he was born in, never bring home his girl, and you will not hand down your jewels to his bride and will have no grandchildren to play with and spoil. Your sons and daughters are alive. Think of that—not dead but alive! Exult and sing.

10. PERSPECTIVES ON IMMORTALITY

QUESTIONS about immortality are ancient. Whenever humans have come to realize the pervasiveness of death, they have wondered if death is a necessary condition of human existence—or if there is some possibility of not having to die. Gilgamesh is a paradigm case in that when his friend Enkidu died, Gilgamesh set out on a dangerous adventure in the hope of discovering the secret of immortality in this life. Whenever humans have come to realize that death is an inherent feature of their lives—all who live, die—they have wondered if death is not only inevitable but also final. Does death represent individual annihilation, or is there some kind of life after death? If there is life after death, what kind of life is it and how does it come about?

The earliest recorded perspectives on immortality after *The Epic of Gilgamesh* contained beliefs in life after death, but the varied descriptions of that life suggest that it is impersonal, joyless, and considerably inferior to human existence. Life goes on, but it is hardly anything to get excited about. In ancient Egypt, for instance, immortality was believed to involve a continuance of the body, but the process of mummification was usually reserved for the pharoahs and other affluent persons; and anyone embarking on a journey to the land of the dead first had to survive a formidable process of judgment. In ancient Greece the *Iliad* and the *Odyssey* depicted immortality as bloodless and bodiless shadows wandering around Hades as pale images of the vibrant persons they had once been. The ancient Hebrews believed that the dead exist in a lower world known as Sheol, a land of no return, no memory, and no communication with God. And at approximately the same time in India, the *Rig-Veda* described life after death as a dispersal to the elements (the body to the earth, the eye to the sun, the breath to the wind), a form of immortality which could not compare to the enjoyable lives of the Indo-Aryans who produced the document.

In the West, perspectives on immortality began to change significantly during the fifth and fourth centuries B.C. The move away from earlier ideas about bloodless phantoms began with the pre-Socratic Greek philosophers, but was most clearly articulated in the dialogues of Plato. Rather than positing some kind of gloomy postmortem existence in Hades, Plato argued that at death the soul (*psyche*) is liberated from its bodily prison and escapes to another, perfect realm of existence. Operating with a dualistic view of human nature, Plato believed the soul to be pre-existent, eternal, immutable, separate from the body, and the locus of intelligence and personal identity. Whereas the body is finite, corporeal, and subject to death, the soul is unlimited, immaterial, and undying. The clear implication of this position is that postmortem existence is preferable to earthy existence limited by the physical body. Persons wise enough to understand the soul's immortality, according to Plato, "make dying their profession" and actually "look forward to death all their lives."

A very different perspective on immortality developed in Greece several decades after Plato's death. Epicurus, significantly influenced by the earlier materialism of Democritus, rejected Plato's theory about the immortality of the soul. Rather than conceiving of the soul as incorporeal and eternal, Epicurus was convinced that the soul is composed of atoms. The only difference between the body and the soul is that the soul's atoms differ in size, weight, and shape from those of the body. At death, the insignificance of these differences is clear in that both body and soul perish. Since there is no postmortem existence of any kind, the practical implication of this position is to concentrate on getting the most enjoyment out of life.

In contrast to the body-soul dualism of the Greeks, the Hebrew tradition conceived of humans as psychosomatic units. Rather than being an imprisoned soul, a person was regarded as an animated body (*nefesh*) whose "state of aliveness" was evidenced by breathing. Death represents the cessation of the body's breathing and thus the draining away of its aliveness—"like water spilt on the ground, which cannot be gathered up again" (2 Samuel 14:14).

As to the possibilities of a postmortem existence, three positions developed over the years. Some Jews, having accepted the bleak classical view of Sheol as a kingdom of shadows, came to emphasize a kind of social immortality through the continuing existence of the corporate personality: even though death ends an individual's life, the family and the nation of Israel continue indefinitely. Other Jews, especially the Pharisees beginning around the fourth century B.C., began to believe in the resurrection of the body. As the Hebrew people had risen from bondage in Babylonia and been reconstituted as a unit, so the Pharisees argued that at some future time dead bodies would be restored to life by God and appear in God's presence for judgment. And other Jews who came under strong Greek influence beginning in the second century B.C. moved away from the classical Hebrew view of human nature and accepted the classical Greek position regarding the soul's immortality.

With the advent of Christianity, another perspective on immortality developed in the West. Jesus assumed some kind of continuing personal existence after death (see Mark 12:18–27) and spoke in general terms of a future resurrection and judgment of the dead. Paul followed him by developing a Christian perspective on immortality in a letter to the Corinthians, first by reporting a series of visions of the resurrected Christ and then by explaining what the resurrection of the dead means. Rather than referring to disembodied souls or revivified corpses, he declared that resurrection of the dead means a continuing personal existence of "the spiritual body" (*soma pneumatikon*). Whereas flesh and bones will not be restored after death, the spiritual body—or person—will be transformed by God "in the twinkling of an eye" and continue to live "in glory."

In the East, classical perspectives on immortality developed in Hinduism and Buddhism. By the end of the Vedic period (c.450 B.C.), the developing tradition of Hinduism accepted the basic features of the theory of reincarnation. Central to this theory is the belief that human existence consists of an endless cycle of births and deaths known as *samsara*. Rather than having a single birth and death as set parameters, human existence is conceived as an endlessly turning wheel involving numerous births and deaths. Individual human bodies come and go, but a limitless number of souls (*jivas*) exist eternally. Ultimately identical with the power of the universe, Brahman-Atman, these *jivas* are connected with individual human (and nonhuman) bodies in various realms of existence. The particular realm of existence for a *jiva* is determined by the Law of Karma and is a direct consequence of the way former lives of the *jiva* have been conducted. The implication of this theory is that when human bodies die, most *jivas* are recycled by being attached to other human bodies or other vehicles of incarnation. Only those *jivas* that attain liberation (*moksha*) are released from the cycle of births and deaths and escape to be in union with Brahman-Atman.

The Buddhist tradition, while accepting many of the features of the theory of reincarnation as it developed in Hinduism, has revised the theory in significant ways and prefers to speak of rebirth rather than reincarnation. Rather than accepting the idea of *jivas* which exist eternally and immutably, Buddhism offers a theory known as the no-soul doctrine (*anatta*). Human lives, like the entirety of existence, are transient, continually changing, and subject to suffering and evil. Each human life is composed of five psychophysical factors known as *skandhas*: the physical body, perception, feeling, reason, and the stream of consciousness. At death, these factors disintegrate. But there remains a "stream of life"—not an unchanging soul, but a certain character disposition—which is reborn in another human organism. This stream of life impresses itself on a series of human beings—something like a flame being transmitted to a series of candles—for an indefinite number of lifetimes until it is finally extinguished in the state of eternal bliss and peacefulness known as nirvana.

Like the other aspects of death, immortality has often been a subject of literature. There are, in addition to the selections in this section, several classic literary treatments of life after death. *The Egyptian Book of the Dead*, generally dated around 1800 B.C., was written on long papyrus rolls and used as a guidebook for persons about to die. It contains intriguing accounts of a process of judgment after death: the embodied soul appears before forty-two judges and Osiris, the final judge; recites a list of wrong deeds it has not committed in its earthly life; and then has its heart weighed against a feather to determine whether it will enter the land of Osiris or be devoured by animals. The *Aeneid*, written by Virgil (70–19 B.C.) and modeled after the Homeric epics, is the Roman national epic that tells of Aeneas' legendary trip from Troy to Italy. In Book VI Aeneas, accompanied by a female prophet, descends to Hades, where his dead father explains the Pythagorean theory of reincarnation: souls, after finishing a thousand-year cycle in Hades, revisit the earth and are born again in new bodies. *The Divine Comedy*, by

Dante (1265–1321), is an intricately developed poetical picture of life after death, compartmentalized into the spheres of hell, purgatory, and heaven. Using these medieval Christian categories for the realms of immortality, Dante indicates that persons entering hell face eternal damnation, those in purgatory are to be purified before entering heaven, and those in heaven enjoy the presence of God for eternity. *The Tibetan Book of the Dead* has a long, mysterious history. Its teachings apparently existed as oral traditions for centuries; were put into written form during the eighth century; and then, after being long kept secret, were published early in this century. Used as a guidebook for the dying, the book describes in minute detail the *Bardo* state of embodied consciousness which exists between death and rebirth.

Immortality continues to be used as a subject in twentieth-century literature. Three examples, in addition to the selections, will illustrate its varied treatment in poems, plays, and novels. D. H. Lawrence's "Ship of Death" is an imaginative poetical picture of embodied souls after death. Some souls are unable to depart for the goal of oblivion because they have no ship to carry them across the sea; other souls, having built ships, make the long journey until they finally reach the goal of peace, silence, and oblivion. *Our Town*, the Pulitzer Prize-winning play by Thornton Wilder, depicts the world of the dead in a cemetery scene in the third act. The dead are presented as emotionless bodies who could return to live among people, but prefer to concentrate on the future because they know that people have a critical lack of understanding of the way the universe operates. Amos Tutuola's *The Palm-Wine Drinkard*, previously excerpted in the section on personification, is a fascinating novel which repeatedly explores the subject of immortality. One of his more intriguing folk tales gives a detailed description of the embodied lives which continue to exist in a location called "the deads' town."

Quite different from these literary pieces is a new kind of literature whose entire focus is on the subject of immortality. Three examples from the recent literature of parapsychology will illustrate the diversity of this literature and indicate the interest parapsychologists have in moving beyond the boundaries of creative literature to demonstrate a scientific basis for believing in life after death. *Twenty Cases Suggestive of Reincarnation*, by Ian Stevenson, is one of several books in which he uses cross-cultural case studies to present a plausible argument for the prenatal and postmortem existence of a psychical entity or soul. *At the Hour of Death*, by Karlis Osis and Erlendur Haraldsson, is a cross-cultural study of the experiences of dying persons which concludes, based on dying patient's apparitions and out-of-body experiences, that there is postmortem survival of a spiritual body. And *Life After Life*, by Raymond Moody, is a study of persons who have had temporary death experiences and now relate the remarkable features of their "journeys" beyond this life.

Several of the selections represent classical perspectives on immortality. The excerpt from *The Epic of Gilgamesh* describes his quest for a deathless life. The selection from the *Iliad* depicts the Homeric view of shadows roaming around in Hades. The passage from the Book of Job reflects the classical Hebrew view of Sheol, but is equally important because of the basic question it raises about continuing personal life after death. Differences among Greek philosophers regarding the immortality of the soul are evidenced by the writings of Plato and Epicurus. The classical Hindu understanding of reincarnation is given poetic expression in the dialogue presented in the *Bhagavad Gita*. And the earliest Christian interpretation of a resurrected spiritual body is presented in one of Paul's letters.

The more recent selections provide equally diverse views regarding life after death. "Heaven and Hell," an Eskimo poem of uncertain origin, describes three postmortem sites somewhat along the lines of heaven, purgatory, and hell. *Faust*, Goethe's famous work, describes a wager made to get an indefinite extension on earthly life—at the risk of eternal life. Tennyson's "Crossing the Bar" and Browning's "Prospice" provide poetic expressions of the general belief that the postmortem future will be all right because God—Tennyson's "Pilot"—will take care of it. "Laura," by the Burmese-born English writer H. H. Munro (Saki), and *The Prophet*, by the Lebanese-born Kahlil Gibran, suggest a direct continuation of life after death, with Munro giving a fascinating interpretation of reincarnation as the mechanism of continuation. Another perspective is presented in Narayan's *Grateful to Life and Death*, with an apparition as the focal point.

The remaining selections reveal ongoing differences in perspectives on immortality—and leave unanswered questions. For James Kidd, the question is whether the existence of an immortal soul is scientifically demonstrable. For C. S. Lewis, the question is whether any of the available theories about immortality are intellectually sound. For Dylan Thomas, who thought his father was near death as he wrote, the question is the ultimate meaning of "that good night" when one can resist death no longer.

from *THE EPIC OF GILGAMESH*
Anonymous (c.2300 B.C.)

This ancient mythological account says that when his friend Enkidu died, Gilgamesh was forced to confront the fact of human mortality. If his friend died, surely that same fate awaited him as well. In an effort to avoid having to die, he set out on a desperate venture to discover the secret of immortality in this life. He failed, of course, because he found out that there are inherent limits to human existence—the necessity of sleep, the necessity of death—beyond which one cannot go.

Bitterly Gilgamesh wept for his friend Enkidu; he wandered over the wilderness as a hunter, he roamed over the plains; in his bitterness he cried, "How can I rest, how can I be at peace? Despair is in my heart. What my brother is now, that shall I be when I am dead. Because I am afraid of death I will go as best I can to find Utnapishtim whom they call the Faraway, for he has entered the assembly of the gods." So Gilgamesh traveled over the wilderness, he wandered over the grasslands, a long journey, in search of Utnapishtim, whom the gods took after the deluge; and they set him to live in the land of Dilmun, in the garden of the sun; and to him alone of men they gave everlasting life.

At night when he came to the mountain passes Gilgamesh prayed: "In these mountain passes long ago I saw lions, I was afraid and I lifted my eyes to the moon; I prayed and my prayers went up to the gods, so now, O moon god Sin, protect me." When he had prayed he lay down to sleep, until he was woken from out of a dream. He saw the lions round him glorying in life; then he took his ax in his hand, he drew his sword from his belt, and he fell upon them like an arrow from the string, and struck and destroyed and scattered them.

So at length Gilgamesh came to Mashu, the great mountains about which he had heard many things, which guard the rising and the setting sun. Its twin peaks are as high as the wall of heaven and its paps reach down to the underworld. At its gate the Scorpions stand guard, half man and half dragon; their glory is terrifying, their stare strikes death into men, their shimmering halo sweeps the mountains that guard the rising sun. When Gilgamesh saw them he shielded his eyes for the length of a moment only; then he took courage and approached. When they saw him so undismayed the Man-Scorpion called to his mate, "This one who comes to us now is flesh of the gods." The mate of the Man-Scorpion answered, "Two thirds is god but one third is man."

Then he called to the man Gilgamesh, he called to the child of the gods: "Why have you come so great a journey; for what have you traveled so far, crossing the dangerous waters; tell me the reason for your coming?" Gilgamesh answered, "For Enkidu; I loved him dearly, together we endured all kinds of hardships; on his account I have come, for the common lot of man has taken him. I have wept for him day and night, I would not give up his body for burial, I thought my friend would come back because of my weeping. Since he went, my life is nothing; that is why I have traveled here in search of Utnapishtim my father; for men say he has entered the assembly of the gods, and has found everlasting life. I have a desire to question him concerning the living and the dead." The Man-Scorpion opened his mouth and said, speaking to Gilgamesh, "No man born of woman has done what you have asked, no mortal man has gone into the mountain; the length of it is twelve leagues of darkness; in it there is no light, but the heart is oppressed with darkness. From the rising of the sun to the setting of the sun there is no light." Gilgamesh said, "Although I should go in sorrow and in pain, with sighing and with weeping, still I must go. Open the gate of the mountain." And the Man-Scorpion said, "Go, Gilgamesh, I permit you to pass through the mountain of Mashu and through the high ranges; may your feet carry you safely home. The gate of the mountain is open."

When Gilgamesh heard this he did as the Man-Scorpion had said, he followed the sun's road to his rising, through the mountain. When he had gone one league the darkness became thick around him, for there was no light, he could see nothing ahead and nothing behind him. After two leagues the darkness was thick and there was no light, he could see nothing ahead and nothing behind him. . . . After nine leagues he felt the north wind on his face, but the darkness was thick and there was no light, he could see nothing ahead and nothing behind him. After ten leagues the end was near. After eleven leagues the dawn light appeared. At the end of twelve leagues the sun streamed out.

There was the garden of the gods; all round him stood bushes bearing gems. Seeing it he went down at once, for there was fruit of carnelian with the vine hanging from it, beautiful to look at; lapis lazuli leaves hung thick with fruit, sweet to see. For thorns and thistles there were haematite and rare stones, agate, and pearls from out of the sea. While Gilgamesh walked in the garden by the edge of the sea Shamash saw him, and he saw that he was dressed in the skins of animals and ate their flesh. He was distressed, and he spoke and said, "No mortal man has gone this way before, nor will, as long as the winds drive over the sea." And to Gilgamesh he said, "You will never find the life for which you are searching." Gilgamesh said to glorious Shamesh, "Now that I have toiled and strayed so far over the wilderness, am I to sleep, and let the earth cover my head for ever? Let my eyes see the sun until they are dazzled with looking. Although I am no better than a dead man, still let me see the light of the sun."

Beside the sea she lives, the woman of the vine, the maker of wine; Siduri sits in the garden at the edge of the sea, with the golden bowl and the golden vats that the gods gave her. She is covered with a veil; and where she sits she sees Gilgamesh coming towards her, wearing skins, the flesh of the gods in his body, but despair in his heart, and his face like the face of one who has made a long journey. She looked, and as she scanned the distance she said in her own heart, "Surely this is some felon; where is he going now?" And she barred her gate against him with the cross-bar and shot home the bolt. But Gilgamesh, hearing the sound of the bolt, threw up his head and lodged his foot in the gate; he called to her, "Young woman, maker of wine, why do you bolt your door; what did you see that made you bar your gate? I will break in your door and burst in your gate, for I am Gilgamesh who seized and killed the Bull of Heaven, I killed the watchman of the cedar forest, I overthrew Humbaba who lived in the forest, and I killed the lions in the passes of the mountain."

Then Siduri said to him, "If you are that Gilgamesh who seized and killed the Bull of Heaven, who killed the watchman of the cedar forest, who overthrew Humbaba that lived in the forest, and killed the lions in the passes of the mountain, why are your cheeks so starved and why is your face so drawn? Why is despair in your heart and your face like the face of one who has made a long journey? Yes, why is your face burned from heat and cold, and why do you come here wandering over the pastures in search of the wind?"

Gilgamesh answered her, "And why should not my cheeks be starved and my face drawn? Despair is in my heart and my face is the face of one who has made a long journey, it was burned with heat and with cold. Why should I not wander over the pastures in search of the wind? My friend, my younger brother, he who hunted the wild ass of the wilderness and the panther of the plains, my friend, my younger brother who seized and killed the Bull of Heaven and overthrew Humbaba in the cedar forest, my friend who was very dear to me and who endured dangers beside me, Enkidu my brother, whom I loved, the end of mortality has overtaken him. I wept for him seven days and nights till the worm fastened on him. Because of my brother I am afraid of death, because of my brother I stray through the wilderness and cannot rest. But now, young woman, maker of wine, since I have seen your face do not let me see the face of death which I dread so much."

She answered, "Gilgamesh, where are you hurrying to? You will never find that life for which you are looking. When the gods created man they allotted to him death, but life they retained in their own keeping. As for you, Gilgamesh, fill your belly with good things; day and night, night and day, dance and be merry, feast and rejoice. Let your clothes be fresh, bathe yourself in water, cherish the little child that holds your hand, and make your wife happy in your embrace; for this too is the lot of man."

But Gilgamesh said to Siduri, the young woman, "How can I be silent, how can I rest, when Enkidu whom I love is dust, and I too shall die and be laid in the earth. You live by the seashore and look into the heart of it; young woman, tell me now, which is the way to Utnapishtim, the son of Ubara-Tutu? What directions are there for the passage; give me, oh, give me directions. I will cross the Ocean if it is possible; if it is not I will wander still farther in the wilderness." The wine-maker said to him, "Gilgamesh, there is no crossing the Ocean; whoever has come, since the days of old, has not been able to pass that sea. The Sun in his glory crosses the Ocean, but who beside Shamash has ever crossed it? The place and the passage are difficult, and the waters of death are deep which flow between. Gilgamesh, how will you cross the Ocean? When you come to the waters of death what will you do? But Gilgamesh, down in the woods you will find Urshanabi, the ferryman of Utnapishtim; with him are the holy things, the things of stone. He is fashioning the serpent prow of the boat. Look at him well, and if it is possible, perhaps you will cross the waters with him; but if it is not possible, then you must go back."

When Gilgamesh heard this he was seized with anger. He took his ax in his hand, and his dagger from his belt. He crept forward and he fell on them like a javelin. Then he went into the forest and sat down. Urshanabi saw the dagger flash and heard the ax, and he beat his head, for Gilgamesh had shattered the tackle of the boat in his rage. Urshanabi said to him, "Tell me, what is your name? I am Urshanabi, the ferryman of Utnapishtim the Faraway." He replied to him, "Gilgamesh is my name, I am from Uruk, from the house of Anu." Then Urshanabi said to him, "Why are your cheeks so starved and your face drawn? Why is despair in your heart and your face like the face of one who has made a long journey; yes, why is your face burned with heat and with cold, and why do you come here wandering over the pastures in search of the wind?"

Gilgamesh said to him, "Why should not my cheeks be starved and my face drawn? Despair is in my heart, and my face is the face of one who has made a long journey. I was burned with heat and with cold. Why should I not wander over the pastures? My friend, my younger brother who seized and killed the Bull of Heaven, and overthrew Humbaba in the cedar forest, my friend who was very dear to me, and who endured dangers beside me, Enkidu my brother whom I loved, the end of mortality has overtaken him. I wept for him seven days and nights till the worm fastened on him. Because of my brother I am afraid of death, because of my brother I stray through the wilderness. His fate lies heavy upon me. How can I be silent, how can I rest? He is dust and I too shall die and be laid in the earth for ever. I am afraid of death, therefore, Urshanabi, tell me which is the road to Utnapishtim? If it is possible I will cross the waters of death; if not I will wander still farther through the wilderness."

Urshanabi said to him, "Gilgamesh, your own hands have prevented you from crossing the Ocean; when you destroyed the tackle of the boat you destroyed its safety." Then the two of them talked it over and Gilgamesh said, "Why are you so angry with me, Urshanabi, for you yourself cross the sea by day and night, at all seasons you cross it." "Gilgamesh, those things you destroyed, their property is to carry me over the water, to prevent the waters of death from touching me. It was for this reason that I preserved them, but you have destroyed them, and the *urnu* snakes with them. But now, go into the forest, Gilgamesh; with your ax cut poles, one hundred and twenty, cut them sixty cubits long, paint them with bitumen, set on them ferrules and bring them back."

When Gilgamesh heard this he went into the forest, he cuts poles one hundred and twenty; he cut them sixty cubits long, he painted them with bitumen, he set on them ferrules, and he brought them to Urshanabi. Then they boarded the boat, Gilgamesh and Urshanabi together, launching it out on the waves of Ocean. For three days they ran on as it were a journey of a month and fifteen days, and at last Urshanabi brought the boat to the waters of death. Then Urshanabi said to Gilgamesh, "Press on, take a pole and thrust it in, but do not let your hands touch the waters. Gilgamesh, take a second pole, take a third, take a fourth pole. Now, Gilgamesh, take a fifth, take a sixth and seventh pole. Gilgamesh, take an eighth, and ninth, a tenth pole. Gilgamesh, take an eleventh, take a twelfth pole." After one hundred and twenty thrusts Gilgamesh had used the last pole. Then he stripped himself, he held up his arms for a mast and his covering for a sail, So Urshanabi the ferryman brought Gilgamesh to Utnapishtim, whom they call the Faraway, who lives in Dilmun at the place of the sun's transit, eastward of the mountain. To him alone of men the gods had given everlasting life.

Now Utnapishtim, where he lay at ease, looked into the distance and he said in his heart, musing to himself, "Why does the boat sail here without tackle and mast; why are the sacred stones destroyed, and why does the master not sail the boat? That man who comes is none of mine; where I look I see a man whose body is covered with skins of beasts. Who is this who walks up the shore behind Urshanabi, for surely he is no man of mine?" So Utnapishtim looked at him and said, "What is your name, you who come here wearing the skins of beasts, with your cheeks starved and your face drawn? Where are you hurrying to now? For what reason have you made this great journey, crossing the seas whose passage is difficult? Tell me the reason for your coming."

He replied, "Gilgamesh is my name. I am from Uruk, from the house of Anu." Then Utnapishtim said to him, "If you are Gilgamesh, why are your cheeks so starved and your face drawn? Why is despair in your heart and your face like the face of one who has made a long journey? Yes, why is your face burned with heat and cold; and why do you come here, wandering over the wilderness in search of the wind?"

Gilgamesh said to him, "Why should not my cheeks be starved and my face drawn? Despair is in my heart and my face is the face of one who has made a long journey. It was burned with heat and with cold. Why should I not wander over the pastures? My friend, my younger brother who seized and killed the Bull of Heaven and overthrew Humbaba in the cedar forest, my friend who was very dear to me and endured dangers beside me, Enkidu, my brother whom I loved, the end of mortality has overtaken him. I wept for him seven days and nights till the worm fastened on him. Because of my brother I am afraid of death; because of my brother I stray through the wilderness. His fate lies heavy upon me. How can I be silent, how can I rest? He is dust and I shall die also and be laid in the earth for ever."

Again Gilgamesh said, speaking to Utnapishtim, "It is to see Utnapishtim whom we call the Faraway that I have come this journey. For this I have wandered over the world, I have crossed many difficult ranges, I have crossed the seas, I have wearied myself with traveling; my joints are aching, and I have lost acquaintance with sleep which is sweet. My clothes were worn out before I came to the house of Siduri. I have killed the bear and hyena, the lion and panther, the tiger, the stag and the ibex, all sorts of wild game and the small creatures of the pastures. I ate their flesh and I wore their skins; and that was how I came to the gate of the young woman, the maker of wine, who barred her gate of pitch and bitumen against me. But from her I had news of the journey; so then I came to Urshanabi the ferryman, and with him I crossed over the waters of death. Oh, father Utnapishtim, you who have entered the assembly of the gods, I wish to question you concerning the living and the dead, how shall I find the life for which I am searching?"

Utnapishtim said, "There is no permanence. Do we build a house to stand for ever, do we seal a contract to hold for all time? Do brothers divide an inheritance to keep for ever, does the flood-time of rivers endure? It is only the nymph of the dragon-fly who sheds her larva and sees the sun in his glory. From the days of old there is no permanence. The sleeping and the dead, how alike they are, they are like a painted death. What is there between the master and the servant when both have fulfilled their doom? When the Anunnaki, the judges, come together, and Mammetun the mother of destinies, together they decree the fates of men. Life and death they allot but the day of death they do not disclose."

from the ILIAD
Homer (c.850 B.C.)

Book XXIII provides insights into the pre-Socratic Greek view of immortality. Death was regarded as a terrible fate—far worse than slavery—and the dead were believed to become bloodless and bodiless shadows wandering aimlessly in the underworld known as Hades. In the excerpt below, Achilles, exhausted from his battle with Hector, has just gone to sleep when the ghost of his dead friend Patroclus appears to him.

It halted by his head and said to him: "You are asleep: you have forgotten me, Achilles. You neglect me now that I am dead; you never did so when I was alive. Bury me instantly and let me pass the Gates of Hades. I am kept out by the disembodied spirits of the dead, who have not let me cross the River and join them, but have left me to pace up and down forlorn on this side of the Gaping Gates. And give me that hand, I beseech you; for once you have passed me through the flames I shall never come back again from Hades. Never again on earth will you and I sit down together, out of earshot of our men, to lay our plans. For I have been engulfed by the dreadful fate that must have been my lot at birth; and it is your destiny too, most worshipful Achilles, to perish under the walls of the rich town of Troy. And now, one more request. Do not let them bury my bones apart from yours, Achilles. Let them lie together, just as you and I grew up together in your house, after Menoetius brought me there from Opus as a child because I had had the misfortune to commit homicide and kill Amphidamas' boy by accident in a childish quarrel over a game of knuckle-bones. The knightly Peleus welcomed me to his palace and brought me up with loving care. And he appointed me your squire. So let one urn, the golden vase your lady Mother gave you, hold our bones."

"Dear heart," said the swift Achilles, "what need was there for you to come and ask me to attend to all these things? Of course I will see to everything and do exactly as you wish. But now come nearer to me, so that we may hold each other in our arms, if only for a moment, and draw cold comfort from our tears."

With that, Achilles held out his arms to clasp the spirit, but in vain. It vanished like a wisp of smoke and went gibbering underground. Achilles leapt up in amazement. He beat his hands together and in his desolation cried: "Ah then, it is true that something of us does survive even in the Halls of Hades, but with no intellect at all, only the ghost and semblance of a man; for all night long the ghost of poor Patroclus (and it looked exactly like him) has been standing at my side, weeping and wailing, and telling me of all the things I ought to do."

JOB 14:7–17 (RSV)
Anonymous (c.560 B.C.)

For there is hope for a tree,
    if it be cut down, that it will sprout again,
    and that its shoots will not cease.
Though its root grow old in the earth,
    and its stump die in the ground,
yet at the scent of water it will bud
    and put forth branches like a young plant.
But man dies, and is laid low;
    man breathes his last, and where is he?
As waters fail from a lake,
    and a river wastes away and dries up,
so man lies down and rises not again;
    till the heavens are no more he will not awake,
    or be roused out of his sleep.
Oh that thou wouldest hide me in Sheol,
    that thou wouldest conceal me until thy wrath be past,
    that thou wouldest appoint me a set time, and remember me!
If a man die, shall he live again?
    All the days of my service I would wait,
    till my release should come.
Thou wouldest call, and I would answer thee;
    thou wouldest long for the work of thy hands.
For then thou wouldest number my steps,
    thou wouldest not keep watch over my sin;
my transgression would be sealed up in a bag,
    and thou wouldest cover my iniquity.

from PHAEDO
Plato (427–347 B.C.)

In his account of Socrates' last conversation, Plato raised the possibility that the soul does not perish when the body dies. Because both Socrates and Plato operated with a dualistic theory of human nature, they believed that death was an event of liberation in which the soul was set free from its bodily prison to migrate to another realm of existence. Socrates explored this possibility with some of his students just prior to his death.

"Very well," said he, "I will try to convince you better than I did my judges. I believe, my dear Simmias and Cebes, that I shall pass over first of all to other gods, both wise and good, secondly to dead men better than those in this world; and if I did not think so, I should do wrong in not objecting to death; but, believing this, be assured that I hope I shall find myself in the company of good men, although I would not maintain it for certain; but that I shall pass over to gods who are very good masters, be assured that if I would maintain for certain anything else of the kind, I would with certainty maintain this. Then for these reasons, so far from objecting, I have good hopes that something remains for the dead, as has been the belief from time immemorial, and something much better for the good than for the bad."

. . . .

"Then," said Socrates, "if this is true, my comrade, there is great hope that when I arrive where I am traveling, there if anywhere I shall sufficiently possess that for which all our study has been pursued in this past life. So the journey which has been commanded for me is made with good hope, and the same for any other man who believes he has got his mind purified, as I may call it."

"Certainly," replied Simmias.

"And is not purification really that which has been mentioned so often in our discussion, to separate as far as possible the soul from the body, and to accustom it to collect itself together out of the body in every part, and to dwell alone by itself as far as it can, both at this present and in the future, being freed from the body as if from a prison?"

"By all means," said he.

"Then is not this called death—a freeing and separation of soul from body?"

"Not a doubt of that," said he.

"But to set it free, as we say, is the chief endeavor of those who rightly love wisdom, nay of those alone, and the very care and practice of the philosophers is nothing but the freeing and separation of soul from body, don't you think so?"

"It appears to be so."

"Then, as I said at first, it would be absurd for a man preparing himself in his life to be as near as possible to death, so to live, and then when death came, to object?"

. . . .

When Socrates had thus finished, Cebes took up the word: "Socrates," he said, "on the whole I think you speak well; but that about the soul is a thing which people find very hard to believe. They fear that when it parts from the body it is nowhere any more; but on the day when a man dies, as it parts from the body, and goes out like a breath or a whiff of smoke, it is dispersed and flies away and is gone and is nowhere any more. If it existed anywhere, gathered together by itself, and rid of these evils which you have just described, there would be great and good hope, Socrates, that what you say is true; but this very thing needs no small reassurance and faith, that the soul exists when the man dies, and that it has some power and sense."

"Quite true," said Socrates, "quite true, Cebes; well, what are we to do? Shall we discuss this very question, whether such a thing is likely or not?"

"For my part," said Cebes, "I should very much like to know what your opinion is about it."

Then Socrates answered, "I think no one who heard us now could say, not even a composer of comedies, that I am babbling nonsense and talking about things I have nothing to do with! So if you like, we must make a full enquiry.

"Let us enquire whether the souls of dead men really exist in the house of Hades or not. Well, there is the very ancient legend which we remember, that they are continually arriving there from this world, and further that they come back here and are born again from the dead. If that is true, and the living are born again from the dead, must not our souls exist there? For they could not be born again if they did not exist; and this would be sufficient proof that it is true, if it should be really shown that the living are born from the dead and from nowhere else. But if this be not true, we must take some other line."

from LETTER TO MENOECEUS
Epicurus (341–270 B.C.)

In contrast to Plato, Epicurus believed the world and everything in it to be composed of atoms. The human soul differs from the body only in the sense that it is made up of round, fiery atoms located in the chest. When death occurs, both body and soul perish. There is therefore, as he indicated in one of his letters, no reason to raise questions about immortality.

Become accustomed to the belief that death is nothing to us. For all good and evil consists in sensation, but death is deprivation of sensation. And therefore a right understanding that death is nothing to us makes the mortality of life enjoyable, not because it adds to it an infinite span of time, but because it takes away the craving for immortality. For there is nothing terrible in life for the man who has truly comprehended that there is nothing terrible in not living. So that the man speaks but idly who says that he fears death not because it will be painful when it comes, but because it is painful in anticipation. For that which gives no trouble when it comes, is but an empty pain in anticipation. So death, the most terrifying of ills, is nothing to us, since so long as we exist death is not with us; but when death comes, then we do not exist. It does not then concern either the living or the dead, since for the former it is not, and the latter are no more.

from the BHAGAVAD GITA
Anonymous (200 B.C.–A.D. 200)

This long epic poem, inserted into the longer *Mahabharata* at its most dramatic point, is the best known and loved literary work in India. Written and revised over a long period of time, the *Gita* is a dialogue between the god Krishna and prince Arjuna. The setting for the conversation is a field of battle. Arjuna, seeing that some of his relatives and friends are in the opposing army, lays down his weapons and says he would rather be killed than kill them. Krishna, serving as Arjuna's charioteer, responds (in chapter II) by declaring that man's essential self or soul is not subject to death because it is eternal: it "slays not, is not slain."

Arjuna said:

4. "How shall I in battle against Bhisma,
   And Drona, O Slayer of Madhu,
   Fight with arrows,
   Who are both worthy of reverence, Slayer of Enemies?

5. "For not slaying my revered elders of great dignity
   'Twere better to eat alms-food, even, in this world;
   But having slain my elders who seek their ends, right in this world
   I should eat food smeared with blood.

6. "And we know not which of the two were better for us,
   Whether we should conquer, or they should conquer us;
   What very ones having slain we wish not to live,
   They are arrayed in front of us, Dhrtarastra's men.

7. "My very being afflicted with the taint of weak compassion,
   I ask Thee, my mind bewildered as to the right:
   Which were better, that tell me definitely;
   I am Thy pupil, teach me that have come to Thee (for
   instruction).

8. "For I see not what would dispel my
   Grief, the witherer of the senses,
   If I attained on earth rivalless, prosperous
   Kingship, and even the overlordship of the gods."

. . . .

The Blessed One said:

11. "Thou hast mourned those who should not be mourned,
    And (yet) thou speakest words about wisdom!
    Dead and living men
    The (truly) learned do not mourn.

12. "But not in any respect was I (ever) not,
    Nor thou, nor these kings;
    And not at all shall we ever come not to be,
    All of us, henceforward.

13. "As to the embodied (soul) in this body
    Come childhood, youth, old age,

So the coming to another body;
    The wise man is not confused herein.

14. "But contacts with matter, son of Kunti,
    Cause cold and heat, pleasure and pain;
  They come and go, and are impermanent;
    Put up with them, son of Bharata!

15. "For whom these (contacts) do not cause to waver,
    The man, O bull of men,
  To whom pain and pleasure are alike, the wise,
    He is fit for immortality.

16. "Of what is not, no coming to be occurs;
    No coming not to be occurs of what is;
  But the dividing-line of both is seen,
    Of these two, by those who see the truth.

17. "But know that that is indestructible,
    By which this all is pervaded;
  Destruction of this imperishable one
    No one can cause.

18. "These bodies come to an end,
    It is declared, of the eternal embodied (soul),
  Which is indestructible and unfathomable.
    Therefore fight, son of Bharata!

19. "Who believes him a slayer,
    And who thinks him slain,
  Both these understand not:
    He slays not, is not slain.

20. "He is not born, nor does he ever die;
    Nor, having come to be, will he ever more come not to be.
  Unborn, eternal, everlasting, this ancient one
    Is not slain when the body is slain.

21. "Who knows as indestructible and eternal
    This unborn, imperishable one,
  That man, son of Prtha, how
    Can he slay or cause to slay—whom?

22. "As leaving aside worn-out garments
    A man takes other, new ones,
    So leaving aside worn-out bodies
        To other, new ones goes the embodied (soul).

23. "Swords cut him not,
      Fire burns him not,
      Water wets him not,
        Wind dries him not.

24. "Not to be cut is he, not to be burnt is he,
      Not to be wet nor yet dried;
    Eternal, omnipresent, fixed,
      Immovable, everlasting is he.

25. "Unmanifest he, unthinkable he,
      Unchangeable he is declared to be;
    Therefore knowing him thus
      Thou shouldst not mourn him.

26. "Moreover, even if constantly born
      Or constantly dying thou considerest him,
    Even so, great-armed one, thou
      Shouldst not mourn him.

27. "For to one that is born death is certain,
      And birth is certain for one that has died;
    Therefore, the thing being unavoidable,
      Thou shouldst not mourn."

1 CORINTHIANS 15:1-8, 35-57 (RSV)
Paul (A.D. c.55)

Now I would remind you, brethren, in what terms I preached to you the gospel, which you received, in which you stand, by which you are saved, if you hold it fast—unless you believed in vain.

For I delivered to you as of first importance what I also received, that Christ died for our sins in accordance with the scriptures, that he was buried, that he was raised on the third day in accordance with the scriptures, and that he appeared to Cephas, then to the twelve. Then he appeared to more than five hundred brethren at one time, most of whom are still alive, though some have fallen asleep. Then he appeared to James, then to all the apostles. Last of all, as to one untimely born, he appeared also to me.

. . . .

But some one will ask, "How are the dead raised? With what kind of body do they come?" You foolish man! What you sow does not come to life unless it dies. And what you sow is not the body which is to be, but a bare kernel, perhaps of wheat or of some other grain. But God gives it a body as he has chosen, and to each kind of seed its own body. For not all flesh is alike, but there is one kind for men, another for animals, another for birds, and another for fish. There are celestial bodies and there are terrestrial bodies; but the glory of the celestial is one, and the glory of the terrestrial is another. There is one glory of the sun, and another glory of the moon, and another glory of the stars; for star differs from star in glory.

So is it with the resurrection of the dead. What is sown is perishable, what is raised is imperishable. It is sown in dishonor, it is raised in glory. It is sown in weakness, it is raised in power. It is sown a physical body, it is raised a spiritual body. If there is a physical body, there is also a spiritual body. Thus it is written, "The first man Adam became a living being"; the last Adam became a life-giving spirit. But it is not the spiritual which is first but the physical, and then the spiritual. The first man was from the earth, a man of dust; the second man is from heaven. As was the man of dust, so are those who are of the dust; and as is the man of heaven, so are those who are of heaven. Just as we have borne the image of the man of dust, we shall also bear the image of the man of heaven. I tell you this, brethren: flesh and blood cannot inherit the kingdom of God, nor does the perishable inherit the imperishable.

Lo! I tell you a mystery. We shall not all sleep, but we shall all be changed, in a moment, in the twinkling of an eye, at the last trumpet. For the trumpet will sound, and the dead will be raised imperishable, and we shall be changed. For this perishable nature must put on the imperishable, and this mortal nature must put on immortality. When the perishable puts on the imperishable, and the mortal puts on immortality, then shall come to pass the saying that is written:

"Death is swallowed up in victory."
"O death, where is thy victory?
O death, where is thy sting?"
The sting of death is sin, and the power of sin is the law. But thanks be to God, who gives us the victory through our Lord Jesus Christ.

HEAVEN AND HELL
Eskimo poem (n.d.)

And when we die at last,
we really know very little about what happens then.
But people who dream
have often seen the dead appear to them
just as they were in life.
Therefore we believe life does not end here on earth.

We have heard of three places where men go after death:
There is the Land of the Sky, a good place
where there is no sorrow and fear.
There have been wise men who went there
and came back to tell us about it:
They saw people playing ball, happy people
who did nothing but laugh and amuse themselves.
What we see from down here in the form of stars
are the lighted windows of the villages of the dead
in the Land of the Sky.

Then there are other worlds of the dead underground:
Way down deep is a place just like here
except on earth you starve
and down there they live in plenty.
The caribou graze in great herds
and there are endless plains
with juicy berries that are nice to eat.
Down there too, everything
is happiness and fun for the dead.

But there is another place, the Land of the Miserable,
right under the surface of the earth we walk on.
There go all the lazy men who were poor hunters,
and all women who refused to be tattooed,
not caring to suffer a little to become beautiful.
They had no life in them when they lived
so now after death they must squat on their haunches
with hanging heads, bad-tempered and silent,
and live in hunger and idleness
because they wasted their lives.
Only when a butterfly comes flying by
do they lift their heads
(as young birds open pink mouths uselessly after a gnat)
and when they snap at it, a puff of dust
comes out of their dry throats.

from FAUST
Johann Wolfgang von Goethe (1749–1832)

The legend of Faust—a man willing to sell his soul to Satan in exchange for
superhuman knowledge and power—has its roots in sixteenth-century Germany.
Of the several versions of the legend, two stand out as important literary pieces.
Doctor Faustus, written by Christopher Marlowe in 1588, depicts Faust making a
pact with Mephistophilis for a period of twenty-four years, then being carried off
to hell. Goethe's *Faust*, in contrast, presents a pact between Faust and Mephis-
topheles for an indefinite period of time—with an eternal reversal of roles a continual possibility.

MEPHISTO: Stop playing with your melancholy
    That, like a vulture, ravages your breast;
    The worst of company still cures this folly,
    For you are human with the rest.
    Yet that is surely not to say
    That you should join the herd you hate.
    I'm not one of the great
    But if you want to make your way
    Through the world with me united,

I should surely be delighted
To be yours, as of now,
Your companion, if you allow;
And if you like the way I behave,
I shall be your servant, or your slave.

FAUST: And in return, what do you hope to take?

MEPHISTO: There's so much time—so why insist?

FAUST: No, no! The Devil is an egoist
And would not just for heaven's sake
Turn into a philanthropist.
Make your conditions very clear;
Where such a servant lives, danger is near.

MEPHISTO: *Here* you shall be the master, I be bond,
And at your nod I'll work incessantly;
But when we meet again *beyond*,
Then you shall do the same for me.

FAUST: Of the beyond I have no thought;
When you reduce this world to nought,
The other one may have its turn.
My joys come from this earth, and there,
That sun has burnt on my despair:
Once I have left those, I don't care:
What happens is of no concern.
I do not even wish to hear
Whether beyond they hate and love,
And whether in that other sphere
One realm's below and one above.

MEPHISTO: So minded, dare it cheerfully.
Commit yourself and you shall see
My arts with joy. I'll give you more
Than any man has seen before.

FAUST: What would you, wretched Devil, offer?
Was ever a man's spirit in its noble striving
Grasped by your like, devilish scoffer?
But have you food that is not satisfying,
Red gold that rolls off without rest,
Quicksilver-like, over your skin—

A game in which no man can win—
A girl who, lying at my breast,
Ogles already to entice my neighbor,
And honor—that perhaps seems best—
Though like a comet it will turn to vapor?
Show me fruit that, before we pluck them, rot,
And trees whose foliage every day makes new!

MEPHISTO: Such a commission scares me not,
With such things I can wait on you.
But, worthy friend, the time comes when we would
Recline in peace and feast on something good.

FAUST: If ever I recline, calmed, on a bed of sloth,
You may destroy me then and there.
If ever flattering you should wile me
That in myself I find delight,
If with enjoyment you beguile me,
Then break on me, eternal night!
This bet I offer.

MEPHISTO: I accept it.

FAUST: Right.
If to the moment I should say:
Abide, you are so fair—
Put me in fetters on that day,
I *wish* to perish then, I swear.
Then let the death bell ever toll,
Your service done, you shall be free,
The clock may stop, the hand may fall,
As time comes to an end for me.

CROSSING THE BAR
Alfred, Lord Tennyson (1808–1892)

This poem "came in a moment" to Tennyson two years before his death. Later, a few days before he died, he asked his son to see that the poem was placed last in all editions of his poetry.

Sunset and evening star,
    And one clear call for me!
And may there be no moaning of the bar,
    When I put out to sea,

But such a tide as moving seems asleep,
    Too full for sound and foam,
When that which drew from out the boundless deep
    Turns again home.

Twilight and evening bell,
    And after that the dark!
And may there be no sadness of farewell,
    When I embark;

For though from out our bourn of time and place
    The flood may bear me far,
I hope to see my Pilot face to face
    When I have crossed the bar.

PROSPICE
Robert Browning (1812–1889)

This poem—the Latin title means "Look Forward!"—was written in 1861, a few months after Elizabeth Barrett Browning died. It expresses his attitude toward death and his belief that he and his wife will eventually be reunited.

Fear death?—to feel the fog in my throat,
    The mist in my face,
When the snows begin, and the blasts denote
    I am nearing the place,
The power of the night, the press of the storm,
    The post of the foe;

Where he stands, the Arch Fear in a visible form,
    Yet the strong man must go;
For the journey is done and the summit attained,
    And the barriers fall,
Though a battle's to fight ere the guerdon be gained
    The reward of it all.
I was ever a fighter, so—one fight more,
    The best and the last!
I would hate that death bandaged my eyes, and forbore,
    And bade me creep past.
No! let me taste the whole of it, fare like my peers,
    The heroes of old,
Bear the brunt, in a minute pay glad life's arrears
    Of pain, darkness, and cold.
For sudden the worst turns the best to the brave,
    The black minute's at end,
And the elements' rage, the fiend-voices that rave,
    Shall dwindle, shall blend,
Shall change, shall become first a peace out of pain,
    Then a light, then thy breast,
O thou soul of my soul! I shall clasp thee again,
    And with God be the rest!

LAURA
Saki (H. H. Munro 1870–1916)

With very little formal education, Munro became an excellent writer of short stories and novels. Using the pen name Saki, he often wrote stories with abrupt endings. Such is the case with this story about reincarnation. Munro was killed in action in the first World War.

"You are not really dying, are you?" asked Amanda.

"I have the doctor's permission to live till Tuesday," said Laura.

"But today is Saturday; this is serious!" gasped Amanda.

"I don't know about it being serious; it is certainly Saturday," said Laura.

"Death is always serious," said Amanda.

"I never said I was going to die. I am presumably going to leave off being Laura, but I shall go on being something. An animal of some kind, I suppose. You see, when one hasn't been very good in the life one has just lived, one reincarnates in some lower organism. And I haven't been very good, when one comes to think of it. I've been petty and mean and vindictive and all that sort of thing when circumstances have seemed to warrant it."

"Circumstances never warrant that sort of thing," said Amanda hastily.

"If you don't mind my saying so," observed Laura, "Egbert is a circumstance that would warrant any amount of that sort of thing. You're married to him—that's different; you've sworn to love, honor, and endure him: I haven't."

"I don't see what's wrong with Egbert," protested Amanda.

"Oh, I daresay the wrongness has been on my part," admitted Laura dispassionately; "he has merely been the extenuating circumstance. He made a thin, peevish kind of fuss, for instance, when I took the collie puppies from the farm out for a run the other day."

"They chased his young broods of speckled Sussex and drove two sitting hens off their nests, besides running all over the flower beds. You know how devoted he is to his poultry and garden."

"Anyhow, he needn't have gone on about it for the entire evening and then have said, 'Let's say no more about it' just when I was beginning to enjoy the discussion. That's where one of my petty vindictive revenges came in," added Laura with an unrepentant chuckle; "I turned the entire family of speckled Sussex into his seedling shed the day after the puppy episode."

"How could you?" exclaimed Amanda.

"It came quite easy," said Laura; "two of the hens pretended to be laying at the time, but I was firm."

"And we thought it was an accident!"

"You see," resumed Laura, "I really *have* some grounds for supposing that my next incarnation will be in a lower organism. I shall be an animal of some kind. On the other hand, I haven't been a bad sort in my way, so I think I may count on being a nice animal, something elegant and lively, with a love of fun. An otter, perhaps."

"I can't imagine you as an otter," said Amanda.

"Well, I don't suppose you can imagine me as an angel, if it comes to that," said Laura.

Amanda was silent. She couldn't.

"Personally I think an otter life would be rather enjoyable," continued Laura; "salmon to eat all the year round, and the satisfaction of being able to fetch the trout in their own homes without having to wait for hours till they condescend to rise to the fly you've been dangling before them; and an elegant svelte figure ——"

"Think of the otter hounds," interposed Amanda; "how dreadful to be hunted and harried and finally worried to death!"

"Rather fun with half the neighborhood looking on, and anyhow not worse than this Saturday-to-Tuesday business of dying by inches; and then I should go into something else. If I had been a moderately good otter, I suppose I should get back into human shape of some sort; probably something rather primitive—a little brown, unclothed Nubian boy, I should think."

"I wish you would be serious," sighed Amanda; "you really ought to be if you're only going to live till Tuesday."

As a matter of fact, Laura died on Monday.

"So dreadfully upsetting," Amanda complained to her uncle-in-law, Sir Lulworth Quayne. "I've asked quite a lot of people down for golf and fishing, and the rhododendrons are just looking their best."

"Laura always was inconsiderate," said Sir Lulworth; "she was born during Goodwood week, with an Ambassador staying in the house who hated babies."

"She had the maddest kind of ideas," said Amanda; "do you know if there was any insanity in her family?"

"Insanity? No, I never heard of any. Her father lives in West Kensington, but I believe he's sane on all other subjects."

"She had an idea that she was going to be reincarnated as an otter," said Amanda.

"One meets with those ideas of reincarnation so frequently, even in the West," said Sir Lulworth, "that one can hardly set them down as being mad. And Laura was such an unaccountable person in this life that I should not like to lay down definite rules as to what she might be doing in an afterstate."

"You think she really might have passed into some animal form?" asked Amanda. She was one of those who shape their opinions rather readily from the standpoint of those around them.

Just then Egbert entered the breakfast room, wearing an air of bereavement that Laura's demise would have been insufficient, in itself, to account for.

"Four of my speckled Sussex have been killed," he exclaimed; "the very four that were to go to the show on Friday. One of them was dragged away and eaten right in the middle of that new carnation bed that I've been to such trouble and expense over. My best flower bed and my best fowls singled out for destruction; it almost seems as if the brute that did the deed had special knowledge how to be as devastating as possible in a short space of time."

"Was it a fox, do you think?" asked Amanda.

"Sounds more like a polecat," said Sir Lulworth.

"No," said Egbert, "there were marks of webbed feet all over the place, and we followed the tracks down to the stream at the bottom of the garden; evidently an otter."

Amanda looked quickly and furtively across at Sir Lulworth.

Egbert was too agitated to eat any breakfast, and went out to superintend the strengthening of the poultry-yard defenses.

"I think she might at least have waited till the funeral was over," said Amanda in a scandalized voice.

"It's her own funeral, you know," said Sir Lulworth; "it's a nice point in etiquette how far one ought to show respect to one's own mortal remains."

Disregard for mortuary convention was carried to further lengths next day; during the absence of the family at the funeral ceremony the remaining survivors of the speckled Sussex were massacred. The marauder's line of retreat seemed to have embraced most of the flower beds on the lawn, but the strawberry beds in the lower garden had also suffered.

"I shall get the otter hounds to come here at the earliest possible moment," said Egbert savagely.

"On no account! You can't dream of such a thing!" exclaimed Amanda. "I mean, it wouldn't do, so soon after a funeral in the house."

"It's a case of necessity," said Egbert; "once an otter takes to that sort of thing, it won't stop."

"Perhaps it will go elsewhere now that there are no more fowls left," suggested Amanda.

"One would think you wanted to shield the beast," said Egbert.

"There's been so little water in the stream lately," objected Amanda; "it seems hardly sporting to hunt an animal when it has so little chance of taking refuge anywhere."

"Good gracious!" fumed Egbert, "I'm not thinking about sport. I want to have the animal killed as soon as possible."

Even Amanda's opposition weakened when, during church time on the following Sunday, the otter made its way into the house, raided half a salmon from the larder and worried it into scaly fragments on the Persian rug in Egbert's studio.

"We shall have it hiding under our beds and biting pieces out of our feet before long," said Egbert, and from what Amanda knew of this particular otter she felt that the possibility was not a remote one.

On the evening preceding the day fixed for the hunt Amanda spent a solitary hour walking by the banks of the stream making what she imagined to be hound noises. It was charitably supposed by those who overheard her performance that she was practicing for farmyard imitations at the forthcoming village entertainment.

It was her friend and neighbor, Aurora Burret, who brought her news of the day's sport.

"Pity you weren't out; we had quite a good day. We found it at once, in the pool just below your garden."

"Did you—kill?" asked Amanda.

"Rather. A fine she-otter. Your husband got rather badly bitten in trying to 'tail it.' Poor beast, I felt quite sorry for it, it had such a human look in its eyes when it was killed. You'll call me silly, but do you know who the look reminded me of? My dear woman, what is the matter?"

When Amanda had recovered to a certain extent from her attack of nervous prostration, Egbert took her to the Nile Valley to recuperate. Change of scene speedily brought about the desired recovery of health and mental balance. The escapades of an adventurous otter in search of a variation of diet were viewed in their proper light. Amanda's normally placid temperament reasserted itself. Even a hurricane of shouted curses, coming from her husband's dressing room, in her husband's voice, but hardly in his usual vocabulary, failed to disturb her serenity as she made a leisurely toilet one evening in a Cairo hotel.

"What is the matter? What has happened?" she asked in amused curiosity.

"The little beast has thrown all my clean shirts into the bath! Wait till I catch you, you little ——"

"What little beast?" asked Amanda, supressing a desire to laugh; Egbert's language was so hopelessly inadequate to express his outraged feelings.

"A little beast of a naked brown Nubian boy," spluttered Egbert.

And now Amanda is seriously ill.

from THE PROPHET
Kahlil Gibran (1883–1931)

Then Almitra spoke, saying, We would ask now of Death.
And he said:
You would know the secret of death.
But how shall you find it unless you seek it in the heart of life?
The owl whose night-bound eyes are blind unto the day cannot unveil the mystery of light.
If you would indeed behold the spirit of death, open your heart wide unto the body of light.
For life and death are one, even as the river and the sea are one.

In the depth of your hopes and desires lies your silent knowledge of the beyond;
And like seeds dreaming beneath the snow your heart dreams of spring.
Trust the dreams, for in them is hidden the gate to eternity.
Your fear of death is but the trembling of the shepherd when he stands before the king whose hand is to be laid upon him in honor.
Is the shepherd not joyful beneath his trembling, that he shall wear the mark of the king?
Yet is he not more mindful of his trembling?

For what is it to die but to stand naked in the wind and to melt into the sun?

And what is it to cease breathing, but to free the breath from its restless tides, that it may rise and expand and seek God unencumbered?

Only when you drink from the river of silence shall you indeed sing.

And when you have reached the mountain top, then you shall begin to climb.

And when the earth shall claim your limbs, then shall you truly dance.

from A GRIEF OBSERVED
C. S. Lewis (1898–1963)

In his intensely personal reflections on the process of grief, Lewis raises some of the philosophical questions about immortality. If there is some kind of personal life after death, he wants to know precisely what that means in terms of his dead wife's continued existence. The answers to his questions do not come easily—nor are they finally satisfying.

What pitiable cant to say "She will live forever in my memory!" *Live?* That is exactly what she won't do. You might as well think like the old Egyptians that you can keep the dead by embalming them. Will nothing persuade us that they are gone? What's left? A corpse, a memory, and (in some versions) a ghost. All mockeries or horrors. Three more ways of spelling the word *dead.* It was H. I loved. As if I wanted to fall in love with my memory of her, an image in my own mind! It would be a sort of incest.

. . . .

But there are other difficulties. "Where is she now?" That is, *in what place* is she *at the present time.* But if H. is not a body—and the body I loved is certainly no longer she—she is in no place at all. And "the present time" is a date or point in our time series. It is as if she were on a journey without me and I said, looking at my watch, "I wonder is she at Euston now." But unless she is proceeding at sixty seconds a minute along this same time-line that all we living people travel by, what does *now* mean? If the dead are not in time, or not in our sort of time, is there any clear difference, when we speak of them, between *was* and *is* and *will be?*

Kind people have said to me "She is with God." In one sense that is most certain. She is, like God, incomprehensible and unimaginable.

But I find that this question, however important it may be in itself, is not after all very important in relation to grief. Suppose that the earthly lives she and I shared for a few years are in reality only the basis for, or prelude to, or earthly appearance of, two unimaginable, supercosmic, eternal somethings. Those somethings could be pictured as spheres or globes. Where the plane of Nature cuts through them—that is, in earthly life—they appear as two circles (circles are slices of spheres). Two circles that touched. But those two circles, above all the point at which they touched, are the very thing I am mourning for, homesick for, famished for. You tell me "she goes on." But my heart and body are crying out, come back, come back. Be a circle, touching my circle on the plane of Nature. But I know this is impossible. I know that the thing I want is exactly the thing I can never get. The old life, the jokes, the drinks, the arguments, the love-making, the tiny, heartbreaking commonplace. On any view whatever, to say "H. is dead," is to say "All that is gone." It is a part of the past. And the past is the past and that is what time means, and time itself is one more name for death, and Heaven itself is a state where "the former things have passed away."

Talk to me about the truth of religion and I'll listen gladly. Talk to me about the duty of religion and I'll listen submissively. But don't come talking to me about the consolations of religion or I shall suspect that you don't understand.

from GRATEFUL TO LIFE AND DEATH
R. K. Narayan (b. 1906)

Apparitions are a perennial subject of literature. Ghosts, spirits, and communications with the dead are found in numerous plays, short stories, and novels representing different cultures and time periods. Narayan's novel, with its setting in southern India, describes the death and cremation of the narrator's wife. It concludes with a dramatic portrayal of the narrator's encounter with an apparition he believes to be his wife.

I was walking down our lone street late at night, enveloped in the fragrance of the jasmine and rose garland, slung on my arm. "For whom am I carrying this jasmine home?" I asked myself. Susila would treasure a garland for two whole days, cutting up and sticking masses of it in her hair morning and evening. "Carrying a garland to a lonely house—a dreadful job," I told myself.

I fumbled with the key in the dark, opened the door and switched on the light. I hung up the garland on a nail and kicked up the roll of bedding. The fragrance permeated the whole house. I sprinkled a little water on the flowers to keep them fresh, put out the light and lay down to sleep.

The garland hung by the nail right over my head. The few drops of water which I sprinkled on the flowers seemed to have quickened in them a new life. Their essences came forth into the dark night as I lay in bed, bringing a new vigor with them. The atmosphere became surcharged with strange spiritual forces. Their delicate aroma filled every particle of the air, and as I let my mind float in the ecstasy, gradually perceptions and senses deepened. Oblivion crept over me like a cloud. The past, present, and the future welded into one.

I had been thinking of the day's activities and meetings and associations. But they seemed to have no place now. I checked my mind. Bits of memory came floating—a gesture of Brown's, the toy house in the dentist's front room, Rangappa with a garland, and the ring of many speeches and voices—all this was gently overwhelmed and swept aside, till one's mind became clean and bare and a mere chamber of fragrance. It was a superb, noble intoxication. And I had no choice but to let my mind and memories drown in it. I softly called "Susila! Susila, my wife . . ." with all my being. It sounded as if it were a hypnotic melody. "My wife . . . my wife, my wife. . . ." My mind trembled with this rhythm, I forgot myself and my own existence. I fell into a drowse, whispering, "My wife, wife." How long? How could I say? When I opened my eyes again she was sitting on my bed looking at me with an extraordinary smile in her eyes.

"Susila! Susila!" I cried. "You here!" "Yes, I'm here, have always been here." I sat up leaning on my pillow. "Why do you disturb yourself?" she asked.

"I am making a place for you," I said, edging away a little. I looked her up and down and said: "How well you look!" Her complexion had a golden glow, her eyes sparked with a new light, her saree shimmered with blue interwoven with "light" as she had termed it. . . "How beautiful!" I said looking at it. "Yes, I always wear this when I come to you. I know you like it very much," she said. I gazed on her face. There was an overwhelming fragrance of jasmine surrounding her. "Still jasmine-scented!" I commented.

"Oh wait," I said and got up. I picked up the garland from the nail and returned to bed. I held it to her "For you as ever. I somehow feared you wouldn't take it. . . ." She received it with a smile, cut off a piece of it and stuck it in a curve on the back of her head. She turned her head and asked: "Is this all right?"

"Wonderful," I said, smelling it.

A cock crew. The first purple of the dawn came through our window, and faintly touched the walls of our room. "Dawn!" she whispered and rose to her feet.

We stood at the window, gazing on a slender, red streak over the eastern rim of the earth. A cool breeze lapped our faces. The boundaries of our personalities suddenly dissolved. It was a moment of rare, immutable joy—a moment for which one feels grateful to Life and Death.

THE KIDD WILL
James Kidd (1879–1950)

The subject of immortality fascinated an Arizona miner named James Kidd. He believed it might be possible to prove the soul's immortality, perhaps by photographing the soul as it left a dead body. He disappeared in 1949 and was declared legally dead the following year. Several years later bank auditors discovered Kidd's handwritten will and approximately $300,000 which was finally given to the American Society for Psychical Research for the purpose of coming up with a "scientific proof" of the soul's immortality.

> Phoenix Arizona
> Jan 2.nd 1946
> this is my first and only will
> and is dated the second day in
> January 1946. I have no. heir's
> have not been married in my life,
> an after all my funeral expenses
> have been paid and $100. one hundred
> dollars to some preacher of the
> gospital to say fare well at my
> grave sell all my property which
> is all in cash and stocks with
> E F Hutton Co Phoenix some in
> safety box, and have this balance
> money to go in a research or some
> scientific proof of a soul of the
> human body which leaves at death
> I think in time their can be a
> Photograph of soul leaving the
> human at death,
>   James Kidd
>
> (dated 2nd
> January 1946)

some cash in Valley bank some in Bank America LA Cal

DO NOT GO GENTLE INTO THAT GOOD NIGHT
Dylan Thomas (1914–1953)

Do not go gentle into that good night,
Old age should burn and rave at close of day;
Rage, rage against the dying of the light.

Though wise men at their end know dark is right,
Because their words had forked no lightning they
Do not go gentle into that good night.

Good men, the last wave by, crying how bright
Their frail deeds might have danced in a green bay,
Rage, rage against the dying of the light.

Wild men who caught and sang the sun in flight,
And learn, too late, they grieved it on its way,
Do not go gentle into that good night.

Grave men, near death, who see with blinding sight
Blind eyes could blaze like meteors and be gay,
Rage, rage against the dying of the light.

And you, my father, there on the sad height,
Curse, bless, me now with your fierce tears, I pray.
Do not go gentle into that good night.
Rage, rage against the dying of the light.

11. DEATH AS A LITERARY SUBJECT

DEATH is a perennial subject of literature. It appears in the literature of significantly different cultures and transcends the differences between historical periods. Its richness and diversity as a subject permits writers to range the gamut from the highly theoretical to the very practical, from the fictional to the factual, and from the generally applicable to the intensely personal. Whatever the genre of literature—poetry, short stories, essays, biographies, novels, journals, letters—death appears repeatedly to stimulate the minds and appeal to the emotions of readers, regardless of their ages.

Because of its magnitude and variability as a literary subject, death cannot be restricted to certain categories or heuristic divisions. While the preceding sections of this book explore certain aspects of the subject of death, the sectional units are intended to be prismatic rather than constraining. Some of the thematic sections could include works placed in other sections. The section on bereavement, for instance, could include Mary Lavin's "Story of the Widow's Son"; Walt Whitman's "The Carol of Death"; several of the items in the section on children, youth, and death; and excerpts from the novels of John Steinbeck, R. K. Narayan, Albert Camus, Sandra Scoppettone, and Doris Lund. Likewise, some of the literary pieces include several of the aspects of the subject of death. Homer's *Iliad*, James Agee's *A Death in the Family*, John Gunther's *Death Be Not Proud*, and Margaret Craven's *I Heard the Owl Call My Name* all offer rich, wide-ranging treatments of the subject of death.

To supplement these other works, this final section contains one literary interpretation of death in its entirety. *The Death of Ivan Ilych*, an extended short story by Leo Tolstoy, is the most comprehensive literary treatment of death available. Tolstoy is generally known for his novels, with *War and Peace* (1869) and *Anna Karenina* (1877) being his crowning achievements as a novelist. He did, however, also write a number of stories, with *The Death of Ivan Ilych* (1886) clearly being the outstanding one.

Tolstoy's story is unmatched for the purposes of teaching death as a literary subject and learning to appreciate the prismatic aspects of death in literature. It offers a single, continuous presentation of one man's dying and death, and along the way covers the majority of the topics presented in this book. The *inevitability* of death is frequently mentioned in the story—by Ivan; by his butler's assistant, Gerasim; and by his friend Peter Ivanovich when he sees Ivan's dead body ("that might . . . , at any time, happen to me"). Death is *personified* in an unusual series of *It* passages ("*It* would come and stand before him and look at him. . . ."). The *personal views* of Ivan occur repeatedly as he thinks about his pain, denies he is dying, becomes angry at others' health and the insensitivity of the doctors, remarks about his increasing isolation from others, acknowledges his continual despair ("blacker than night"), affirms the importance of Gerasim's love and truthfulness, and shows acute awareness that his life is "inexorably waning but not yet extinguished." The *death scene*, having been anticipated throughout the story, is described in the last chapter. As to *youth and death*, Ivan's daughter and son are markedly different in their responses to his dying, as well as in their bereavement after his death. The *funeral and burial customs* of nineteenth-century Russia are described in some detail, with interesting information regarding the procedures used to keep unembalmed bodies around for a limited time ("Peter Ivanovich found the fresh air particularly pleasant after the smell of incense, the dead body, and carbolic acid"). The story shows how *bereavement* affects persons differently, with Gerasim taking the death calmly, Ivan's son crying ashamedly, and Ivan's wife and daughter only playing out expected roles. The subject of *immortality* appears frequently, with Ivan raising questions about what happens after death, having what seems to be an out-of-body experience, and finally experiencing light and joy as he died.

THE DEATH OF IVAN ILYCH
Leo Tolstoy (1828–1910)

CHAPTER I

During an interval in the Melvinski trial in the large building of the Law Courts the members and public prosecutor met in Ivan Egorovich

Shebek's private room, where the conversation turned on the celebrated Krasovski case. Fëdor Vasilievich warmly maintained that it was not subject to their jurisdiction, Ivan Egorovich maintained the contrary, while Peter Ivanovich, not having entered into the discussion at the start, took no part in it but loked through the *Gazette* which had just been handed in.

"Gentlemen," he said, "Ivan Ilych has died!"

"You don't say so!"

"Here, read it yourself," replied Peter Ivanovich, handing Fëdor Vasilievich the paper still damp from the press. Surrounded by a black border were the words: "Praskovya Fëdorovna Golovina, with profound sorrow, informs relatives and friends of the demise of her beloved husband Ivan Ilych Golovin, Member of the Court of Justice, which occurred on February the 4th of this year 1882. The funeral will take place on Friday at one o'clock in the afternoon."

Ivan Ilych had been a colleague of the gentlemen present and was liked by them all. He had been ill for some weeks with an illness said to be incurable. His post had been kept open for him, but there had been conjectures that in case of his death Alexeev might receive his appointment, and that either Vinnikov or Shtabel would succeed Alexeev. So on receiving the news of Ivan Ilych's death the first thought of each of the gentlemen in that private room was of the changes and promotions it might occasion among themselves or their acquaintances.

"I shall be sure to get Shtabel's place or Vinnikov's," thought Fëdor Vasilievich. "I was promised that long ago, and the promotion means an extra eight hundred rubles a year for me besides the allowance."

"Now I must apply for my brother-in-law's transfer from Kaluga," thought Peter Ivanovich. "My wife will be very glad, and then she won't be able to say that I never do anything for her relations."

"I thought he would never leave his bed again," said Peter Ivanovich aloud. "It's very sad."

"But what really was the matter with him?"

"The doctors couldn't say—at least they could, but each of them said something different. When last I saw him I thought he was getting better."

"And I haven't been to see him since the holidays. I always meant to go."

"Had he any property?"

"I think his wife had a little—but something quite trifling."

"We shall have to go to see her, but they live so terribly far away."

"Far away from you, you mean. Everything's far away from your place."

"You see, he never can forgive my living on the other side of the river," said Peter Ivanovich, smiling at Shebek. Then, still talking of the distances between different parts of the city, they returned to the Court.

Besides considerations as to the possible transfers and promotions likely to result from Ivan Ilych's death, the mere fact of the death of a near acquaintance aroused, as usual, in all who heard of it the complacent feeling that, "it is he who is dead and not I."

Each one thought or felt, "Well, he's dead but I'm alive!" But the more intimate of Ivan Ilych's acquaintances, his so-called friends, could not help thinking also that they would now have to fulfill the very tiresome demands of propriety by attending the funeral service and paying a visit of condolence to the widow.

Fëdor Vasilievich and Peter Ivanovich had been his nearest acquaintances. Peter Ivanovich had studied law with Ivan Ilych and had considered himself to be under obligations to him.

Having told his wife at dinner-time of Ivan Ilych's death, and of his conjecture that it might be possible to get her brother transferred to their circuit, Peter Ivanovich sacrificed his usual nap, put on his evening clothes, and drove to Ivan Ilych's house.

At the entrance stood a carriage and two cabs. Leaning against the wall in the hall downstairs near the cloak-stand was a coffin-lid covered with cloth of gold, ornamented with gold cord and tassels, that had been polished up with metal powder. Two ladies in black were taking off their fur cloaks. Peter Ivanovich recognized one of them as Ivan Ilych's sister, but the other was a stranger to him. His colleague Schwartz was just coming downstairs, but on seeing Peter Ivanovich enter he stopped and winked at him, as if to say: "Ivan Ilych has made a mess of things—not like you and me."

Schwartz's face with his Piccadilly whiskers and his slim figure in evening dress, had as usual an air of elegant solemnity which contrasted with the playfulness of his character and had a special piquancy here, or so it seemed to Peter Ivanovich.

Peter Ivanovich allowed the ladies to precede him and slowly followed them upstairs. Schwartz did not come down but remained where he was, and Peter Ivanovich understood that he wanted to arrange where they should play bridge that evening. The ladies went upstairs to the widow's room, and Schwartz with seriously compressed lips but a playful look in his eyes, indicated by a twist of his eyebrows the room to the right where the body lay.

Peter Ivanovich, like everyone else on such occasions, entered feeling uncertain what he would have to do. All he knew was that at such times it is always safe to cross oneself. But he was not quite sure whether one should make obeisances while doing so. He therefore adopted a middle course. On entering the room he began crossing himself and made a slight movement resembling a bow. At the same time, as far as the motion of his head and arm allowed, he surveyed the room. Two young men—apparently nephews, one of whom was a high-school pupil—were leaving the room, crossing themselves as they did so. An old woman was standing motionless, and a lady with strangely arched eyebrows was saying something to her in a whisper. A vigorous, resolute Church Reader, in a frock-coat, was reading something in a loud voice with an expression that precluded any contradiction. The butler's assistant, Gerasim, stepping lightly in front of Peter Ivanovich, was strewing something on the floor. Noticing this, Peter Ivanovich was immediately aware of a faint odor of a decomposing body.

The last time he had called on Ivan Ilych, Peter Ivanovich had seen Gerasim in the study. Ivan Ilych had been particularly fond of him and he was performing the duty of a sick nurse.

Peter Ivanovich continued to make the sign of the cross slightly inclining his head in an intermediate direction between the coffin, the Reader, and the icons on the table in a corner of the room. Afterwards, when it seemed to him that this movement of his arm in crossing himself had gone on too long, he stopped and began to look at the corpse.

The dead man lay, as dead men always lie, in a specially heavy way, his rigid limbs sunk in the soft cushions of the coffin, with the head forever bowed on the pillow. His yellow waxen brow with bald patches over his sunken temples was thrust up in the way peculiar to the dead, the protruding nose seeming to press on the upper lip. He was much changed and had grown even thinner since Peter Ivanovich had last seen him, but, as is always the case with the dead, his face was handsomer and above all more dignified than when he was alive. The expression on the face said that what was necessary had been accomplished, and accomplished rightly. Besides this there was in that expression a reproach and a warning to the living. This warning seemed to Peter Ivanovich out of place, or at least not applicable to him. He felt a certain discomfort and so he hurriedly crossed himself once more and turned and went out of the door—too hurriedly and too regardless of propriety, as he himself was aware.

Schwartz was waiting for him in the adjoining room with legs spread wide apart and both hands toying with his top-hat behind his back. The mere sight of that playful, well-groomed, and elegant figure refreshed Peter Ivanovich. He felt that Schwartz was above all these happenings and would not surrender to any depressing influences. His very look said that this incident of a church service for Ivan Ilych could not be a sufficient reason for infringing the order of the session—in other words, that it would certainly not prevent his unwrapping a new pack of cards and shuffling them that evening while a footman placed four fresh candles on the table: in fact, there was no reason for supposing that this incident would hinder their spending the evening agreeably. Indeed he said this in a whisper as Peter Ivanovich passed him, proposing that they should meet for a game at Fëdor Vasilievich's. But apparently Peter Ivanovich was not destined to play bridge that evening. Praskovya Fëdorovna (a short, fat woman who despite all efforts to the contrary had continued to broaden steadily from her shoulders downwards and who had the same extraordinarily arched eyebrows as the lady who had been standing by the coffin), dressed all in black, her head covered with lace, came out of her own room with some other ladies, conducted them to the room where the dead body lay, and said: "The service will begin immediately. Please go in."

Schwartz, making an indefinite bow, stood still, evidently neither accepting nor declining this invitation. Praskovya Fëdorovna, recognizing Peter Ivanovich, sighed, went close up to him, took his hand, and said: "I know you were a true friend to Ivan Ilych . . ." and looked at him awaiting some suitable response. And Peter Ivanovich knew that, just as it had been the right thing to cross himself in that room, so what he had to do here was to press her hand, sigh, and say, "Believe me . . ." So he did all this and as he did it felt that the desired result had been achieved: that both he and she were touched.

"Come with me. I want to speak to you before it begins," said the widow. "Give me your arm."

Peter Ivanovich gave her his arm and they went to the inner rooms, passing Schwartz, who winked at Peter Ivanovich compassionately.

"That does for our bridge! Don't object if we find another player. Perhaps you can cut in when you do escape," said his playful look.

Peter Ivanovich sighed still more deeply and despondently, and Praskovya Fëdorovna pressed his arm gratefully. When they reached the drawing-room, upholstered in pink cretonne and lighted by a dim lamp, they sat down at the table—she on a sofa and Peter Ivanovich on a low pouffe, the springs of which yielded spasmodically under his weight. Praskovya Fëdorovna had been on the point of warning him to take another seat, but felt that such a warning was out of keeping with her present condition and so changed her mind. As he sat down on the pouffe Peter Ivanovich recalled how Ivan Ilych had arranged this room and had consulted him regarding this pink cretonne with green leaves. The whole room was full of furniture and knickknacks, and on her way to the sofa the lace of the widow's black shawl caught on the carved edge of the table. Peter Ivanovich rose to detach it, and the springs of the pouffe, relieved of his weight, rose also and gave him a push. The widow began detaching her shawl herself, and Peter Ivanovich again sat down, suppressing the rebellious springs of the pouffe under him. But the widow had not quite freed herself and Peter Ivanovich got up again, and again the pouffe rebelled and even creaked. When this was all over she took out a clean cambric handkerchief and began to weep. The episode with the shawl and the struggle with the pouffe had cooled Peter Ivanovich's emotions and he sat there with a sullen look on his face. This awkward situation was interrupted by Sokolov, Ivan Ilych's butler, who came to report that the plot in the cemetery that Praskovya Fëdorovna had chosen would cost two hundred rubles. She stopped weeping and, looking at Peter Ivanovich with the air of a victim, remarked in French that it was very hard for her. Peter Ivanovich made a silent gesture signifying his full conviction that it must indeed be so.

"Please smoke," she said in a magnanimous yet crushed voice, and turned to discuss with Sokolov the price of the plot for the grave.

Peter Ivanovich while lighting his cigarette heard her inquiring very circumstantially into the prices of different plots in the cemetery and finally decide which she would take. When that was done she gave instructions about engaging the choir. Sokolov then left the room.

"I look after everything myself," she told Peter Ivanovich, shifting the albums that lay on the table; and noticing that the table was endangered by his cigarette-ash, she immediately passed him an ash-tray, saying as she did so: "I consider it an affectation to say that my grief prevents my attending to practical affairs. On the contrary, if anything can—I won't say console me, but—distract me, it is seeing to everything concerning him." She again took out her handkerchief as if preparing to cry, but suddenly, as if mastering her feeling, she shook herself and began to speak calmly. "But there is something I want to talk to you about."

Peter Ivanovich bowed, keeping control of the springs of the pouffe, which immediately began quivering under him.

"He suffered terribly the last few days."

"Did he?" said Peter Ivanovich.

"Oh, terribly! He screamed unceasingly, not for minutes but for hours. For the last three days he screamed incessantly. It was unendurable. I cannot understand how I bore it; you could hear him three rooms off. Oh, what I have suffered!"

"Is it possible that he was conscious all that time?" asked Peter Ivanovich.

"Yes," she whispered. "To the last moment. He took leave of us a quarter of an hour before he died, and asked us to take Volodya away."

The thought of the sufferings of this man he had known so intimately, first as a merry little boy, then as a school-mate, and later as a grown-up colleague, suddenly struck Peter Ivanovich with horror, despite an unpleasant consciousness of his own and this woman's dissimulation. He again saw that brow, and that nose pressing down on the lip, and felt afraid for himself.

"Three days of frightful suffering and then death! Why, that might suddenly, at any time, happen to me," he thought, and for a moment felt terrified. But—he did not himself know how—the customary reflection at once occurred to him that this had happened to Ivan Ilych and not to him, and that it should not and could not happen to him, and that to think that it could would be yielding to depression which he ought not to do, as Schwartz's expression plainly showed. After which reflection Peter Ivanovich felt reassured, and began to ask with interest about the details of Ivan Ilych's death, as though death was an accident natural to Ivan Ilych but certainly not to himself.

After many details of the really dreadful physical sufferings Ivan Ilych had endured (which details he learnt only from the effect those sufferings had produced on Praskovya Fëdorovna's nerves) the widow apparently found it necessary to get to business.

"Oh, Peter Ivanovich, how hard it is! How terribly, terribly hard!" and she again began to weep.

Peter Ivanovich sighed and waited for her to finish blowing her nose. When she had done so he said, "Believe me . . ." and she again began talking and brought out what was evidently her chief concern with him—namely, to question him as to how she could obtain a grant of money from the government on the occasion of her husband's death. She made it appear that she was asking Peter Ivanovich's advice about her pension, but he soon saw that she already knew about that to the minutest detail, more even than he did himself. She knew how much could be got out of the government in consequence of her husband's death, but wanted to find out whether she could not possibly extract something more. Peter Ivanovich tried to think of some means of doing so, but after reflecting for a while and, out of propriety, condemning the government for its niggardliness, he said he thought that nothing more could be got. Then she sighed and evidently began to devise means of getting rid of her visitor. Noticing this, he put out his cigarette, rose, pressed her hand, and went out into the anteroom.

In the dining-room where the clock stood that Ivan Ilych had liked so much and had bought at an antique shop, Peter Ivanovich met a priest and a few acquaintances who had come to attend the service, and he recognized Ivan Ilych's daughter, a handsome young woman. She was in black and her slim figure appeared slimmer than ever. She had a gloomy, determined, almost angry expression, and bowed to Peter Ivanovich as though he were in some way to blame. Behind her, with the same offended look, stood a wealthy young man, an examining magistrate, whom Peter Ivanovich also knew and who was her fiancé, as he had heard. He bowed mournfully to them and was about to pass into the death-chamber, when from under the stairs appeared the figure of Ivan Ilych's schoolboy son, who was extremely like his father. He seemed a little Ivan Ilych, such as Peter Ivanovich remembered when they studied law together. His tear-stained eyes had in them the look that is seen in the eyes of boys of thirteen or fourteen who are not pure-minded. When he saw Peter Ivanovich he scowled morosely and shame-facedly. Peter Ivanovich nodded to him and entered the death-chamber. The service began: candles, groans, incense, tears, and sobs. Peter Ivanovich stood looking gloomily down at his feet. He did not look once at the dead man, did not yield to any depressing influence, and was one of the first to leave the room. There was no one in the anteroom, but Gerasim darted out of the dead man's room, rummaged with his strong hands among the fur coats to find Peter Ivanovich's and helped him on with it.

"Well, friend Gerasim," said Peter Ivanovich, so as to say something. "It's a sad affair, isn't it?"

"It's God's will. We shall all come to it some day," said Gerasim, displaying his teeth—the even, white teeth of a healthy peasant—and, like a man in the thick of urgent work, he briskly opened the front door, called the coachman, helped Peter Ivanovich into the sledge, and sprang back to the porch as if in readiness for what he had to do next.

Peter Ivanovich found the fresh air particularly pleasant after the smell of incense, the dead body, and carbolic acid.

"Where to, sir?" asked the coachman.

"It's not too late even now. . . . I'll call around on Fëdor Vasilievich."

He accordingly drove there and found them just finishing the first rubber, so that it was quite convenient for him to cut in.

CHAPTER II

Ivan Ilych's life had been most simple and most ordinary and therefore most terrible.

He had been a member of the Court of Justice, and died at the age of forty-five. His father had been an official who, after serving in various ministries and departments of Petersburg, had made the sort of career which brings men to positions from which by reason of their long service they cannot be dismissed, though they are obviously unfit to hold any responsible position, and for whom therefore posts are specially created, which though fictitious carry salaries of from six to ten thousand rubles that are not fictitious, and in receipt of which they live on to a great age.

Such was the Privy Councilor and superfluous member of various superfluous institutions, Ilya Epimovich Golovin.

He had three sons, of whom Ivan Ilych was the second. The eldest son was following in his father's footsteps only in another department, and was already approaching that stage in the service at which a similar sinecure would be reached. The third son was a failure. He had ruined his prospects in a number of positions and was now serving in the railway department. His father and brothers, and still more their wives, not merely disliked meeting him, but avoided remembering his existence unless compelled to do so. His sister had married Baron Greff, a Petersburg official of her father's type. Ivan Ilych was *le phénix de la famille* as people said. He was neither as cold and formal as his elder brother nor as wild as the younger, but was a happy mean between them—an intelligent, polished, lively, and agreeable man. He had studied with his younger brother at the School of Law, but the latter had failed to complete the course and was expelled when he was in the fifth class. Ivan Ilych finished the course well. Even when he was at the School of Law he was just what he remained for the rest of his life: a capable, cheerful, good-natured, and sociable man, though strict in the fulfillment of what he considered to be his duty: and he considered his duty to be what was so considered by those in authority. Neither as a boy nor as a man was he a toady, but from early youth was by nature attracted to people of high station as a fly is drawn to the light, assimilating their ways and views of life and establishing friendly relations with them. All the enthusiasms of childhood and youth passed without leaving much trace on him; he succumbed to sensuality, to vanity, and latterly among the highest classes to liberalism, but always within limits which his instinct unfailingly indicated to him as correct.

At school he had done things which had formerly seemed to him very horrid and made him feel disgusted with himself when he did them; but when later on he saw that such actions were done by people of good position and that they did not regard them as wrong, he was able not exactly to regard them as right, but to forget about them entirely or not be at all troubled at remembering them.

Having graduated from the School of Law and qualified for the tenth rank of the civil service, and having received money from his father for his equipment, Ivan Ilych ordered himself clothes at Scharmer's, the fashionable tailor, hung a medallion inscribed *respice finem* on his watch chain, took leave of his professor and the prince who was patron of the school, had a farewell dinner with his comrades at Donon's first-class restaurant, and with his new and fashionable portmanteau, linen, clothes, shaving and other toilet appliances, and a traveling rug, all purchased at the best shops, he set off for one of the provinces where, through his father's influence, he had been attached to the governor as an official for special service.

In the province Ivan Ilych soon arranged as easy and agreeable a position for himself as he had had at the School of Law. He performed his official tasks, made his career, and at the same time amused himself pleasantly and decorously. Occasionally he paid official visits to country districts, where he behaved with dignity both to his superiors and inferiors, and performed the duties entrusted to him, which related chiefly to the sectarians, with an exactness and incorruptible honesty of which he could not but feel proud.

In official matters, despite his youth and taste for frivolous gaiety, he was exceedingly reserved, punctilious, and even severe; but in society he was often amusing and witty, and always good-natured, correct in his manner, and *bon enfant*, as the governor and his wife—with whom he was like one of the family—used to say of him.

In the provinces he had an affair with a lady who made advances to the elegant young lawyer, and there was also a milliner; and there were carousals with aides-de-camp who visited the district, and after-supper visits to a certain outlying street of doubtful reputation; and there was too some obsequiousness to his chief and even to his chief's wife, but all this was done with such a tone of good breeding that no hard names could be applied to it. It all came under the heading of the French saying: "*Il faut que jeunesse se passe*" ["Youth must have its fling"]. It was all done with clean hands, in clean linen, with French phrases, and above all among people of the best society and consequently with the approval of people of rank.

So Ivan Ilych served for five years and then came a change in his official life. The new and reformed judicial institutions were introduced, and new men were needed. Ivan Ilych became such a new man. He was offered the post of examining magistrate, and he accepted it though the post was in another province and obliged him to give up the connections he had formed and to make new ones. His friends met to give him a send-off; they had a group photograph taken and presented him with a silver cigarette case, and he set off to his new post.

As examining magistrate Ivan Ilych was just as *comme il faut* and decorous a man, inspiring general respect and capable of separating his official duties from his private life, as he had been when acting as an official on special service. His duties now as examining magistrate were far more interesting and attractive than before. In his former position it had been pleasant to wear an undress uniform made by Scharmer, and to pass through the crowd of petitioners and officials who were timorously awaiting an audience with the governor, and who envied him as with free and easy gait he went straight into his chief's private room to have a cup of tea and a cigarette with him. But not many people had been directly dependent on him—only police officials and the sectarians when he went on special missions—and he liked to treat them politely, almost as comrades, as if he were letting them feel that he who had the power to crush them was treating them in this simple, friendly way. There were then but few such people. But now, as an examining magistrate, Ivan Ilych felt that everyone without exception, even the most important and self-satisfied, was in his power, and that he need only write a few words on a sheet of paper with a certain heading, and this or that important, self-satisfied person would be brought before him in the role of an accused person or a witness, and if he did not choose to allow him to sit down, would have to stand before him and answer his questions. Ivan Ilych never abused his power; he tried on the contrary to soften its expression, but the consciousness of it and of the possibility of softening its effect, supplied the chief interest and attraction of his office. In his work itself, especially in his examinations, he very soon acquired a method of eliminating all considerations irrelevant to the legal aspect of the case, and reducing even the most complicated case to a form in which it would be presented on paper only in its externals, completely excluding his personal opinion of the matter, while above all observing every prescribed formality. The work was new and Ivan Ilych was one of the first men to apply the new Code of 1864.

On taking up the post of examining magistrate in a new town, he made new acquaintances and connections, placed himself on a new footing, and assumed a somewhat different tone. He took up an attitude of rather dignified aloofness towards the provincial authorities, but picked out the best circle of legal gentlemen and wealthy gentry living in the town and assumed a tone of slight dissatisfaction with the government, of moderate liberalism, and of enlightened citizenship. At the same time, without at all altering the elegance of his toilet, he ceased shaving his chin and allowed his beard to grow as it pleased.

Ivan Ilych settled down very pleasantly in this new town. The society there, which inclined towards opposition to the governor, was friendly, his salary was larger, and he began to play *vint*, which he found added not a little to the pleasure of life, for he had a capacity for cards, played good-humoredly, and calculated rapidly and astutely, so that he usually won.

After living there for two years he met his future wife, Praskovya Fëdorovna Mikhel, who was the most attractive, clever, and brilliant girl of the set in which he moved, and among other amusements and relaxations from his labors as examining magistrate, Ivan Ilych established light and playful relations with her.

While he had been an official on special service he had been accustomed to dance, but now as an examining magistrate it was exceptional for him to do so. If he danced now, he did it as if to show that though he served under the reformed order of things, and had reached the fifth official rank, yet when it came to dancing he could do it better than most people. So at the end of an evening he sometimes danced with Praskovya Fëdorovna, and it was chiefly during these dances that he captivated her. She fell in love with him. Ivan Ilych had at first no definite intention of marrying, but when the girl fell in love with him he said to himself: "Really, why shouldn't I marry?"

Praskovya Fëdorovna came of a good family, was not bad looking, and had some little property. Ivan Ilych might have aspired to a more brilliant match, but even this was good. He had his salary, and she, he hoped, would have an equal income. She was well connected, and was a sweet, pretty, and thoroughly correct young woman. To say that Ivan Ilych married because he fell in love with Praskovya Fëdorovna and found that she sympathized with his view of life would be as incorrect as to say that he married because his social circle approved of the match. He was swayed by both these considerations: the marriage gave him personal satisfaction, and at the same time it was considered the right thing by the most highly placed of his associates.

So Ivan Ilych got married.

The preparations for marriage and the beginning of married life, with its conjugal caresses, the new furniture, new crockery, and new linen, were very pleasant until his wife became pregnant—so that Ivan Ilych had begun to think that marriage would not impair the easy, agreeable, gay, and always decorous character of his life, approved of by society and regarded by himself as natural, but would even improve it. But from the first months of his wife's pregnancy, something new, unpleasant, depressing, and unseemly and from which there was no way of escape, unexpectedly showed itself.

His wife, without any reason—*de gaiete de coeur* as Ivan Ilych expressed it to himself—began to disturb the pleasure and propriety of their life. She began to be jealous without any cause, expected him to devote his whole attention to her, found fault with everything, and made coarse and ill-mannered scenes.

At first Ivan Ilych hoped to escape from the unpleasantness of this state of affairs by the same easy and decorous relation to life that had served him heretofore: he tried to ignore his wife's disagreeable moods, continued to live in his usual easy and pleasant way, invited friends to his house for a game of cards, and also tried going out to his club or spending his evenings with friends. But one day his wife began upbraiding him so vigorously, using such coarse words, and continued to abuse him every time he did not fulfill her demands, so resolutely and with such evident determination not to give way till he submitted—that is, till he stayed at home and was bored just as she was—that he became alarmed. He now realized that matrimony—at any rate with Praskovya Fëdorovna—was not always conducive to the pleasure and amenities of life, but on the contrary often infringed both comfort and propriety, that he must therefore entrench himself against such infringement. And Ivan Ilych began to seek for means of doing so. His official duties were the one thing that imposed upon Praskovya Fëdorovna, and by means of his official work and the duties attached to it he began struggling with his wife to secure his own independence.

With the birth of their child, the attempts to feed it and the various failures in doing so, and with the real and imaginary illnesses of mother and child, in which Ivan Ilych's sympathy was demanded but about which he understood nothing, the need of securing for himself an existence outside his family life became still more imperative.

As his wife grew more irritable and exacting and Ivan Ilych transferred the center of gravity of his life more and more to his official work, so did he grow to like his work better and became more ambitious than before.

Very soon, within a year of his wedding, Ivan Ilych had realized that marriage, though it may add some comforts to life, is in fact a very intricate and difficult affair towards which in order to perform one's duty, that is, to lead a decorous life approved of by society, one must adopt a definite attitude just as towards one's official duties.

And Ivan Ilych evolved such an attitude towards married life. He only required of it those conveniences—dinner at home, housewife, and bed—which it could give him, and above all that propriety of external forms required by public opinion. For the rest he looked for light-hearted pleasure and propriety, and was very thankful when he found them, but if he met with antagonism and querulousness he at once retired into his separate fenced-off world of official duties, where he found satisfaction.

Ivan Ilych was esteemed a good official, and after three years was made Assistant Public Prosecutor. His new duties, their importance, the possibility of indicting and imprisoning anyone he chose, the publicity his speeches received, and the success he had in all these things, made his work still more attractive.

More children came. His wife became more and more querulous and ill-tempered, but the attitude Ivan Ilych had adopted towards his home life rendered him almost impervious to her grumbling.

After seven years' service in that town he was transferred to another province as Public Prosecutor. They moved, but were short of money and his wife did not like the place they moved to. Though the salary was higher the cost of living was greater, besides which two of their children died and family life became still more unpleasant for him.

Praskovya Fëdorovna blamed her husband for every inconvenience they encountered in their new home. Most of the conversations between husband and wife, especially as to the children's education, led to topics which recalled former disputes, and those disputes were apt to flare up again at any moment. There remained only those rare periods of amorousness which still came to them at times but did not last long. These were islets at which they anchored for a while and then again set out upon that ocean of veiled hostility which showed itself in their aloofness from one another. This aloofness might have grieved Ivan Ilych had he considered that it ought not to exist, but he now regarded the position as normal, and even made it the goal at which he aimed in family life. His aim was to free himself more and more from those unpleasantnesses and to give them a semblance of harmlessness and propriety. He attained this by spending less and less time with his family, and when obliged to be at home he tried to safeguard his position by the presence of outsiders. The chief thing however was that he had his official duties. The whole interest of his life now centered in the official world and that interest absorbed him. The consciousness of his power, being able to ruin anybody he wished to ruin, the importance, even the external dignity of his entry into court, or meetings with his subordinates, his success with superiors and inferiors, and above all his masterly handling of cases, of which he was conscious—all this gave him pleasure and filled his life, together with chats with his colleagues, dinners, and bridge. So that on the whole Ivan Ilych's life continued to flow as he considered it should do—pleasantly and properly.

So things continued for another seven years. His eldest daughter was already sixteen, another child had died, and only one son was left, a schoolboy and a subject of dissension. Ivan Ilych wanted to put him in the School of Law, but to spite him Praskovya Fëdorovna entered him at the High School. The daughter had been educated at home and had turned out well: the boy did not learn badly either.

CHAPTER III

So Ivan Ilych lived for seventeen years after his marriage. He was already a Public Prosecutor of long standing, and had declined several proposed transfers while awaiting a more desirable post, when an unanticipated and unpleasant occurrence quite upset the peaceful course of his life. He was expecting to be offered the post of presiding judge in a university town, but Happe somehow came to the front and obtained the appointment instead. Ivan Ilych became irritable, reproached Happe, and quarreled both with him and with his immediate superiors—who became colder to him and again passed him over when other appointments were made.

This was in 1880, the hardest year of Ivan Ilych's life. It was then that it became evident on the one hand that his salary was insufficient for them to live on, and on the other that he had been forgotten, and not only this, but that what was for him the greatest and most cruel injustice appeared to others a quite ordinary occurrence. Even his father did not consider it his duty to help him. Ivan Ilych felt himself abandoned by everyone, and that they regarded his position with a salary of 3,500 rubles as quite normal and even fortunate. He alone knew that with the consciousness of the injustices done him, with his wife's incessant nagging, and with the debts he had contracted by living beyond his means, his position was far from normal.

In order to save money that summer he obtained leave of absence and went with his wife to live in the country at her brother's place.

In the country, without his work, he experienced *ennui* for the first time in his life, and not only *ennui* but intolerable depression, and he decided that it was impossible to go on living like that, and that it was necessary to take energetic measures.

Having passed a sleepless night pacing up and down the veranda, he decided to go to Petersburg and bestir himself, in order to punish those who had failed to appreciate him and to get transferred to another ministry.

Next day, despite many protests from his wife and her brother, he started for Petersburg with the sole object of obtaining a post with a salary of five thousand rubles a year. He was no longer bent on any particular department, or tendency, or kind of activity. All he now wanted was an appointment to another post with a salary of five thousand rubles, either in the administration, in the banks, with the railways, in one of the Empress Marya's Institutions, or even in the customs—but it had to carry with it a salary of five thousand rubles and be in a ministry other than that in which they had failed to appreciate him.

And this quest of Ivan Ilych's was crowned with remarkable and unexpected success. At Kursk an acquaintance of his, F. I. Ilyin, got into the first-class carriage, sat down beside Ivan Ilych, and told him of a telegram just received by the Governor of Kursk announcing that a change

was about to take place in the ministry: Peter Ivanovich was to be super-
seded by Ivan Semënovich.

The proposed change, apart from its significance for Russia, had a special significance for Ivan Ilych, because by bringing forward a new man,
Peter Petrovich, and consequently his friend Zachar Ivanovich, it was
highly favorable for Ivan Ilych, since Zachar Ivanovich was a friend and
colleague of his.

In Moscow this news was confirmed, and on reaching Petersburg Ivan
Ilych found Zachar Ivanovich and received a definite promise of an appointment in his former Department of Justice.

A week later he telegraphed to his wife: "Zachar in Miller's place. I
shall receive appointment on presentation of report."

Thanks to this change of personnel, Ivan Ilych had unexpectedly obtained an appointment in his former ministry which placed him two
stages above his former colleagues besides giving him 5,000 rubles salary
and 3,500 rubles for expenses connected with his removal. All his ill-
humor toward his former enemies and the whole department vanished, and
Ivan Ilych was completely happy.

He returned to the country more cheerful and contented than he had
been for a long time. Praskovya Fëdorovna also cheered up and a truce
was arranged between them. Ivan Ilych told of how he had been feted by
everybody in Petersburg, how all those who had been his enemies were
put to shame and now fawned on him, how envious they were of his appointment, and how much everybody in Petersburg had liked him.

Praskovya Fëdorovna listened to all this and appeared to believe it.
She did not contradict anything, but only made plans for their life in the
town to which they were going. Ivan Ilych saw with delight that these
plans were his plans, that he and his wife agreed, and that, after a stumble, his life was regaining its due and natural character of pleasant
lightheartedness and decorum.

Ivan Ilych had come back for a short time only, for he had to take up
his new duties on the 10th of September. Moreover, he needed time to
settle into the new place, to move all his belongings from the province,
and to buy and order many additional things: in a word, to make such
arrangements as he had resolved on, which were almost exactly what
Praskovya Fëdorovna too had decided on.

Now that everything had happened so fortunately, and that he and his wife were at one in their aims and moreover saw so little of one another, they got on together better than they had done since the first years of marriage. Ivan Ilych had thought of taking his family away with him at once, but the insistence of his wife's brother and her sister-in-law, who had suddenly become particularly amiable and friendly to him and his family, induced him to depart alone.

So he departed, and the cheerful state of mind induced by his success and by the harmony between his wife and himself, the one intensifying the other, did not leave him. He found a delightful house, just the thing both he and his wife had dreamt of. Spacious, lofty reception rooms in the old style, a convenient and dignified study, rooms for his wife and daughter, a study for his son—it might have been specially built for them. Ivan Ilych himself superintended the arrangements, chose the wallpapers, supplemented the furniture (preferably with antiques which he considered particularly *comme il faut*), and supervised the upholstering. Everything progressed and progressed and approached the ideal he had set himself: even when things were only half completed they exceeded his expectations. He saw what a refined and elegant character, free from vulgarity, it would all have when it was ready. On falling asleep he pictured to himself how the reception-room would look. Looking at the yet unfinished drawing-room he could see the fireplace, the screen, the whatnot, the little chairs dotted here and there, the dishes and plates on the walls, and the bronzes, as they would be when everything was in place. He was pleased by the thought of how his wife and daughter, who shared his taste in this matter, would be impressed by it. They were certainly not expecting as much. He had been particularly successful in finding, and buying cheaply, antiques which gave a particularly aristocratic character to the whole place. But in his letters he intentionally understated everything in order to be able to surprise them. All this so absorbed him that his new duties—though he liked his official work—interested him less than he had expected. Sometimes he even had moments of absentmindedness during the Court Sessions, and would consider whether he should have straight or curved cornices for his curtains. He was so interested in it all that he often did things himself, rearranging the furniture, or rehanging the curtains. Once when mounting a step-ladder to show the upholsterer, who did not understand, how he wanted the hanging draped, he made a false step and slipped, but being a strong and agile man he clung on and only knocked his side against the knob of the window frame. The bruised place was painful but the pain soon passed, and he felt particularly bright and well just then. He wrote: "I feel fifteen years younger." He thought he would have everything ready by September, but it dragged on till mid-October. But the result was charming not only in his eyes but to everyone who saw it.

In reality it was just what is usually seen in the houses of people of moderate means who want to appear rich, and therefore succeed only in resembling others like themselves: there were damasks, dark wood, plants, rugs, and dull and polished bronzes—all the things people of a certain class have in order to resemble other people of that class. His house was so like the others that it would never have been noticed, but to him it all seemed to be quite exceptional. He was very happy when he met his family at the station and brought them to the newly furnished house all lit up, where a footman in a white tie opened the door into the hall decorated with plants, and when they went on into the drawing-room and the study uttering exclamations of delight. He conducted them everywhere, drank in their praises eagerly, and beamed with pleasure. At tea that evening, when Praskovya Fëdorovna among other things asked him about his fall, he laughed, and showed them how he had gone flying and had frightened the upholsterer.

"It's a good thing I'm a bit of an athlete. Another man might have been killed, but I merely knocked myself, just here; it hurts when it's touched, but it's passing off already—it's only a bruise."

So they began living in their new home—in which, as always happens, when they got thoroughly settled in they found they were just one room short—and with the increased income, which as always was just a little (some five hundred rubles) too little, but it was all very nice.

Things went particularly well at first, before everything was finally arranged and while something had still to be done: this thing bought, that thing ordered, another thing moved, and something else adjusted. Though there were some disputes between husband and wife, they were both so well satisfied and had so much to do that it all passed off without any serious quarrels. When nothing was left to arrange it became rather dull and something seemed to be lacking, but they were then making acquaintances, forming habits, and life was growing fuller.

Ivan Ilych spent his mornings at the law court and came home to dinner, and at first he was generally in a good humor, though he occasionally became irritable just on account of his house. (Every spot on the tablecloth or the upholstery, and every broken window-blind string, irritated him. He had devoted so much trouble to arranging it all that every disturbance of it distressed him.) But on the whole his life ran its course as he believed life should do: easily, pleasantly, and decorously.

He got up at nine, drank his coffee, read the paper, and then put on his undress uniform and went to the law courts. There the harness in which he worked had already been stretched to fit him and he donned it without a hitch: petitioners, inquiries at the chancery, the chancery itself, and the sittings public and administrative. In all this the thing was to exclude everything fresh and vital, which always disturbs the regular course of official business, and to admit only official relations with people, and then only on official grounds. A man would come, for instance, wanting some information. Ivan Ilych, as one in whose sphere the matter did not lie, would have nothing to do with him: but if the man had some business with him in his official capacity, something that could be expressed on officially stamped paper, he would do everything, positively everything he could within the limits of such relations, and in doing so would maintain the semblance of friendly human relations, that is, would observe the courtesies of life. As soon as the official relations ended, so did everything else. Ivan Ilych possessed this capacity to separate his real life from the official side of affairs and not mix the two, in the highest degree, and by long practice and natural aptitude had brought it to such a pitch that sometimes, in the manner of a virtuoso, he would even allow himself to let the human and official relations mingle. He let himself do this just because he felt that he could at any time he chose resume the strictly official attitude again and drop the human relation. And he did it all easily, pleasantly, correctly, and even artistically. In the intervals between the sessions he smoked, drank tea, chatted a little about politics, a little about general topics, a little about cards, but most of all about official appointments. Tired, but with the feelings of a virtuoso—one of the first violins who has played his part in an orchestra with precision—he would return home to find that his wife and daughter had been out paying calls, or had a visitor, and that his son had been to school, had done his homework with his tutor, and was duly learning what is taught at High Schools. Everything was as it should be. After dinner, if they had no visitors, Ivan Ilych sometimes read a book that was being much discussed at the time, and in the evening settled down to work, that is, read official papers, compared the depositions of witnesses, and noted paragraphs of the Code applying to them. This was neither dull nor amusing. It was dull when he might have been playing bridge, but if no bridge was available it was at any rate better than doing nothing or sitting with his wife. Ivan Ilych's chief pleasure was giving little dinners to which he invited men and women of good social position, and just as his drawing-room resembled all other drawing-rooms so did his enjoyable little parties resemble all other such parties.

Once they even gave a dance. Ivan Ilych enjoyed it and everything went off well, except that it led to a violent quarrel with his wife about the cakes and sweets. Praskovya Fëdorovna had made her own plans, but Ivan Ilych insisted on getting everything from an expensive confectioner and ordered too many cakes, and the quarrel occurred because some of those cakes were left over and the confectioner's bill came to forty-five rubles. It was a great and disagreeable quarrel. Praskovya Fëdorovna called him "a fool and an imbecile," and he clutched at his head and made angry allusions to divorce.

But the dance itself had been enjoyable. The best people were there, and Ivan Ilych had danced with Princess Trufonova, a sister of the distinguished founder of the Society "Bear my Burden."

The pleasures connected with his work were pleasures of ambition; his social pleasures were those of vanity; but Ivan Ilych's greatest pleasure was playing bridge. He acknowledged that whatever disagreeable incident happened in his life, the pleasure that beamed like a ray of light above everything else was to sit down to bridge with good players, not noisy partners, and of course to four-handed bridge (with five players it was annoying to have to stand out, though one pretended not to mind), to play a clever and serious game (when the cards allowed it), and then to have supper and drink a glass of wine. After a game of bridge, especially if he had won a little (to win a large sum was unpleasant), Ivan Ilych went to bed in specially good humor.

So they lived. They formed a circle of acquaintances among the best people and were visited by people of importance and by young folk. In their views as to their acquaintances, husband, wife, and daughter were entirely agreed, and tacitly and unanimously kept at arm's length and shook off the various shabby friends and relations who, with much show of affection, gushed into the drawing-room with its Japanese plates on the wall. Soon these shabby friends ceased to obtrude themselves and only the best people remained in the Golovins' set.

Young men made up to Lisa, and Petrishchev, an examining magistrate and Dmitri Ivanovich Petrishchev's son and sole heir, began to be so attentive to her that Ivan Ilych had already spoken to Praskovya Fëdorovna about it, and considered whether they should not arrange a party for them or get up some private theatricals.

So they lived, and all went well, without change, and life flowed pleasantly.

CHAPTER IV

They were all in good health. It could not be called ill health if Ivan Ilych sometimes said that he had a queer taste in his mouth and felt some discomfort in his left side.

But this discomfort increased and, though not exactly painful, grew into a sense of pressure in his side accompanied by ill humor. And his irritability became worse and worse and began to mar the agreeable, easy, and correct life that had established itself in the Golovin family. Quarrels between husband and wife became more and more frequent, and soon the ease and amenity disappeared and even the decorum was barely maintained. Scenes again became frequent, and very few of those islets remained on which husband and wife could meet without an explosion. Praskovya Fëdorovna now had good reason to say that her husband's temper was trying. With characteristic exaggeration she said he had always had a dreadful temper, and that it had needed all her good nature to put up with it for twenty years. It was true that now the quarrels were started by him. His bursts of temper always came just before dinner, often just as he began to eat his soup. Sometimes he noticed that a plate or dish was chipped, or the food was not right, or his son put his elbow on the table, or his daughter's hair was not done as he liked it, and for all this he blamed Praskovya Fëdorovna. At first she retorted and said disagreeable things to him, but once or twice he fell into such a rage at the beginning of dinner that she realized it was due to some physical derangement brought on by taking food, and so she restrained herself and did not answer, but only hurried to get the dinner over. She regarded this self-restraint as highly praiseworthy. Having come to the conclusion that her husband had a dreadful temper and made her life miserable, she began to feel sorry for herself, and the more she pitied herself the more she hated her husband. She began to wish he would die; yet she did not want him to die because then his salary would cease. And this irritated her against him still more. She considered herself dreadfully unhappy just because not even his death could save her, and though she concealed her exasperation, that hidden exasperation of hers increased his irritation also.

After one scene in which Ivan Ilych had been particularly unfair and after which he had said in explanation that he certainly was irritable but that it was due to his not being well, she said that if he was ill it should be attended to, and insisted on his going to see a celebrated doctor.

He went. Everything took place as he had expected and as it always does. There was the usual waiting and the important air assumed by the doctor, with which he was so familiar (resembling that which he himself assumed in court), and the sounding and listening, and the questions which called for answers that were forgone conclusions and were evidently unnecessary, and the look of importance which implied that "if only you put yourself in our hands we will arrange everything—we know indubitably how it has to be done, always in the same way for everybody alike." It was all just as it was in the law courts. The doctor put on just the same air towards him as he himself put on towards an accused person.

The doctor said that so-and-so indicated that there was so-and-so inside the patient, but if the investigation of so-and-so did not confirm this, then he must assume that and that. If he assumed that and that, then . . . and so on. To Ivan Ilych only one question was important: was his case serious or not? But the doctor ignored that inappropriate question. From his point of view it was not the one under consideration, the real question was to decide between a floating kidney, chronic catarrh, or appendicitis. It was not a question of Ivan Ilych's life or death, but one between a floating kidney and appendicitis. And that question the doctor solved brilliantly, as it seemed to Ivan Ilych, in favor of the appendix, with the reservation that should an examination of the urine give fresh indications the matter would be reconsidered. All this was just what Ivan Ilych had himself brilliantly accomplished a thousand times in dealing with men on trial. The doctor summed up just as brilliantly, looking over his spectacles triumphantly and even gaily at the accused. From the doctor's summing up Ivan Ilych concluded that things were bad, but that for the doctor, and perhaps for everybody else, it was a matter of indifference, though for him it was bad. And this conclusion struck him painfully, arousing in him a great feeling of pity for himself and of bitterness towards the doctor's indifference to a matter of such importance.

He said nothing of this, but rose, placed the doctor's fee on the table, and remarked with a sigh: "We sick people probably often put inappropriate questions. But tell me, in general, is this complaint dangerous, or not? . . ."

The doctor looked at him sternly over his spectacles with one eye, as if to say: "Prisoner, if you will not keep to the questions put to you, I shall be obliged to have you removed from the court."

"I have already told you what I consider necessary and proper. The analysis may show something more." And the doctor bowed.

Ivan Ilych went out slowly, seated himself disconsolately in his sledge, and drove home. All the way home he was going over what the doctor had said, trying to translate those complicated, obscure, scientific phrases into plain language and find in them an answer to the question: "Is my condition bad? Is it very bad? Or is there as yet nothing much wrong?" And it seemed to him that the meaning of what the doctor had said was that it was very bad. Everything in the streets seemed depressing. The cabmen, the houses, the passers-by, and the shops, were dismal. His ache, this dull gnawing ache that never ceased for a moment, seemed to have acquired a new and more serious significance from the doctor's dubious remarks. Ivan Ilych now watched it with a new and oppressive feeling.

He reached home and began to tell his wife about it. She listened, but in the middle of his account his daughter came in with her hat on, ready to go out with her mother. She sat down reluctantly to listen to this tedious story, but could not stand it long, and her mother too did not hear him to the end.

"Well, I am very glad," she said. "Mind now to take your medicine regularly. Give me the prescription and I'll send Gerasim to the chemist's." And she went to get ready to go out.

While she was in the room Ivan Ilych had hardly taken time to breathe, but he sighed deeply when she left it.

"Well," he thought, "perhaps it isn't so bad after all."

He began taking his medicine and following the doctor's directions, which had been altered after the examination of the urine. But then it happened that there was a contradiction between the indications drawn from the examination of the urine and the symptoms that showed themselves. It turned out that what was happening differed from what the doctor had told him, and that he had either forgotten, or blundered, or hidden something from him. He could not, however, be blamed for that, and Ivan Ilych still obeyed his orders implicitly and at first derived some comfort from doing so.

From the time of his visit to the doctor, Ivan Ilych's chief occupation was the exact fulfillment of the doctor's instructions regarding hygiene and the taking of medicine, and the observation of his pain and his excretions. His chief interests came to be people's ailments and people's health. When sickness, deaths, or recoveries were mentioned in his presence, especially when the illness resembled his own, he listened with agitation which he tried to hide, asked questions, and applied what he heard to his own case.

The pain did not grow less, but Ivan Ilych made efforts to force himself to think that he was better. And he could do this so long as nothing agitated him. But as soon as he had any unpleasantness with his wife, any lack of success in his official work, or held bad cards at bridge, he was at once acutely sensible of his disease. He had formerly borne such mischances, hoping soon to adjust what was wrong, to master it and attain success, or make a grand slam. But now every mischance upset him and plunged him into despair. He would say to himself: "There now, just as I was beginning to get better and the medicine had begun to take effect, comes this accursed misfortune, or unpleasantness . . ." And he was furious with the mishap, or with the people who were causing the unpleasantness and killing him, for he felt that this fury was killing him but could not restrain it. One would have thought that it should have been clear to him that this exasperation with circumstances and people aggravated his illness, and that he ought therefore to ignore unpleasant occurrences. But he drew the very opposite conclusion: he said that he needed peace, and he watched for everything that might disturb it and became irritable at the slightest infringement of it. His condition was rendered worse by the fact that he read medical books and consulted doctors. The progress of his disease was so gradual that he could deceive himself when comparing one day with another—the difference was so slight. But when he consulted the doctors it seemed to him that he was getting worse, and even very rapidly. Yet despite this he was continually consulting them.

That month he went to see another celebrity, who told him almost the same as the first had done but put his questions rather differently, and the interview with this celebrity only increased Ivan Ilych's doubts and fears. A friend of a friend of his, a very good doctor, diagnosed his illness again quite differently from the others, and though he predicted recovery, his questions and suppositions bewildered Ivan Ilych still more and increased his doubts. A homoeopathist diagnosed the disease in yet another way, and prescribed medicine which Ivan Ilych took secretly for a week. But after a week, not feeling any improvement and having lost confidence both in the former doctor's treatment and in this one's, he became still more despondent. One day a lady acquaintance mentioned a cure effected by a wonder-working icon. Ivan Ilych caught himself listening attentively and beginning to believe that it had occurred. This incident alarmed him. "Has my mind really weakened to such an extent?" he asked himself. "Nonsense! It's all rubbish. I mustn't give way to nervous fears but having chosen a doctor must keep strictly to his treatment. That is what I will do. Now it's all settled. I won't think about it, but will follow the treatment seriously till summer, and then we shall see. From now there must be no more of this wavering!" This was easy to say but impossible to carry out. The pain in his side oppressed him and seemed to grow worse and more incessant, while the taste in his mouth grew stranger and stranger. It seemed to him that his breath had a disgusting smell, and he was conscious of a loss of appetite and strength. There was no deceiving himself: something terrible, new, and more important than anything before in his life, was taking place within him of which he alone was aware. Those about him did not understand or would not understand it, but thought everything in the world was going on as usual. That tormented Ivan Ilych more than anything. He saw that his household, especially his wife and daughter who were in a perfect whirl of visiting, did not understand anything of it and were annoyed that he was so depressed and so exacting, as if he were to blame for it. Though they tried to disguise it he saw that he was an obstacle in their path, and that his wife had adopted a definite line in regard to his illness and kept to it regardless of anything he said or did. Her attitude was this: "You know," she would say to her friends, "Ivan Ilych can't do as other people do, and keep to the treatment prescribed for him. One day he'll take his drops and keep strictly to his diet and go to bed in good time, but the next day unless I watch him he'll suddenly forget his medicine, eat sturgeon—which is forbidden—and sit up playing cards till one o'clock in the morning."

"Oh, come, when was that?" Ivan Ilych would ask in vexation. "Only once at Peter Ivanovich's."

"And yesterday with Shebek."

"Well, even if I hadn't stayed up, this pain would have kept me awake."

"Be that as it may you'll never get well like that, but will always make us wretched."

Praskovya Fëdorovna's attitude to Ivan Ilych's illness, as she expressed it both to others and to him, was that it was his own fault and was another of the annoyances he caused her. Ivan Ilych felt that this opinion escaped her involuntarily—but that did not make it easier for him.

At the law courts too, Ivan Ilych noticed, or thought he noticed, a strange attitude towards himself. It sometimes seemed to him that people were watching him inquisitively as a man whose place might soon be vacant. Then again, his friends would suddenly begin to chaff him in a friendly way about his low spirits, as if the awful, horrible, and unheard-of thing that was going on within him, incessantly gnawing at him and irresistibly drawing him away, was a very agreeable subject for jests. Schwartz in particular irritated him by his jocularity, vivacity, and savoir-faire, which reminded him of what he himself had been ten years ago.

Friends came to make up a set and they sat down to cards. They dealt, bending the new cards to soften them, and he sorted the diamonds in his hand and found he had seven. His partner said "No trumps" and supported him with two diamonds. What more could be wished for? It ought to be jolly and lively. They would make a grand slam. But suddenly Ivan

Ilych was conscious of that gnawing pain, that taste in his mouth, and it seemed ridiculous that in such circumstances he should be pleased to make a grand slam.

He looked at his partner Mikhail Mikhaylovich, who rapped the table with his strong hand and instead of snatching up the tricks pushed the cards courteously and indulgently towards Ivan Ilych that he might have the pleasure of gathering them up without the trouble of stretching out his hand for them. "Does he think I am too weak to stretch out my arm?" thought Ivan Ilych, and forgetting what he was doing he over-trumped his partner, missing the grand slam by three tricks. And what was most awful of all was that he saw how upset Mikhail Mikhaylovich was about it but did not himself care. And it was dreadful to realize why he did not care.

They all saw that he was suffering, and said: "We can stop if you are tired. Take a rest." Lie down? No, he was not at all tired, and he finished the rubber. All were gloomy and silent. Ivan Ilych felt that he had diffused this gloom over them and could not dispel it. They had supper and went away, and Ivan Ilych was left alone with the consciousness that his life was poisoned and was poisoning the lives of others, and that this poison did not weaken but penetrated more and more deeply into his whole being.

With this consciousness, and with physical pain besides the terror, he must go to bed, often to lie awake the greater part of the night. Next morning he had to get up again, dress, go to the law courts, speak, and write; or if he did not go out, spend at home those twenty-four hours a day each of which was a torture. And he had to live thus all alone on the brink of an abyss, with no one who understood or pitied him.

CHAPTER V

So one month passed and then another. Just before the New Year his brother-in-law came to town and stayed at their house. Ivan Ilych was at the law courts and Praskovya Fëdorovna had gone shopping. When Ivan Ilych came home and entered his study he found his brother-in-law there—a healthy, florid man—unpacking his portmanteau himself. He raised his head on hearing Ivan Ilych's footsteps and looked up at him for a moment without a word. That stare told Ivan Ilych everything. His brother-in-law opened his mouth to utter an exclamation of surprise but checked himself, and that action confirmed it all.

"I have changed, eh?"

"Yes, there is a change."

And after that, try as he would to get his brother-in-law to return to the subject of his looks, the latter would say nothing about it. Praskovya Fëdorovna came home and her brother went out to her. Ivan Ilych locked the door and began to examine himself in the glass, first full face, then in profile. He took up a portrait of himself taken with his wife, and compared it with what he saw in the glass. The change in him was immense. Then he bared his arms to the elbow, looked at them, drew the sleeves down again, sat down on an ottoman, and grew blacker than night.

"No, no, this won't do!" he said to himself, and jumped up, went to the table, took up some law papers and began to read them, but could not continue. He unlocked the door and went into the reception-room. The door leading to the drawing-room was shut. He approached it on tiptoe and listened.

"No, you are exaggerating!" Praskovya Fëdorovna was saying.

"Exaggerating! Don't you see it? Why, he's a dead man! Look at his eyes—there's no light in them. But what is it that is wrong with him?"

"No one knows. Nikolaevich [that was another doctor] said something, but I don't know what. And Leshchetitsky [this was the celebrated specialist] said quite the contrary . . ."

Ivan Ilych walked away, went to his own room, lay down, and began musing: "The kidney, a floating kidney." He recalled all the doctors had told him of how it detached itself and swayed about. And by an effort of imagination he tried to catch that kidney and arrest it and support it. So little was needed for this, it seemed to him. "No, I'll go to see Peter Ivanovich again." [That was the friend whose friend was a doctor.] He rang, ordered the carriage, and got ready to go.

"Where are you going, Jean?" asked his wife, with a specially sad and exceptionally kind look.

This exceptionally kind look irritated him. He looked morosely at her.

"I must go to see Peter Ivanovich."

He went to see Peter Ivanovich, and together they went to see his friend, the doctor. He was in, and Ivan Ilych had a long talk with him.

Reviewing the anatomical and physiological details of what in the doctor's opinion was going on inside him, he understood it all.

There was something, a small thing, in the vermiform appendix. It might all come right. Only stimulate the energy of one organ and check the activity of another, then absorption would take place and everything would come right. He got home rather late for dinner, ate his dinner, and conversed cheerfully, but could not for a long time bring himself to go back to work in his room. At last, however, he went to his study and did what was necessary, but the consciousness that he had put something aside—an important, intimate matter which he would revert to when his work was done—never left him. When he had finished his work he remembered that this intimate matter was the thought of his vermiform appendix. But he did not give himself up to it, and went to the drawing-room for tea. There were callers there, including the examining magistrate who was a desirable match for his daughter, and they were conversing, playing the piano, and singing. Ivan Ilych, as Praskovya Fëdorovna remarked, spent the evening more cheerfully than usual, but he never for a moment forgot that he had postponed the important matter of the appendix. At eleven o'clock he said good-night and went to his bedroom. Since his illness he had slept alone in a small room next to his study. He undressed and took up a novel by Zola, but instead of reading it he fell into thought, and in his imagination that desired improvement in the vermiform appendix occurred. There was the absorption and evacuation and the re-establishment of normal activity. "Yes, that's it!" he said to himself. "One need only assist nature, that's all." He remembered his medicine, rose, took it, and lay down on his back watching for the beneficent action of the medicine and for it to lessen the pain. "I need only take it regularly and avoid all injurious influences. I am already feeling better, much better." He began touching his side: it was not painful to the touch. "There, I really don't feel it. It's much better already." He put out the light and turned on his side. . . . "The appendix is getting better, absorption is occurring." Suddenly he felt the old, familiar, dull, gnawing pain, stubborn and serious. There was the same familiar loathsome taste in his mouth. His heart sank and he felt dazed. "My God! My God!" he muttered. "Again, again! And it will never cease." And suddenly the matter presented itself in a quite different aspect. "Vermiform appendix! Kidney!" he said to himself. "It's not a question of appendix or kidney, but of life and . . . death. Yes, life was there and now it is going, going and I cannot stop it. Yes. Why deceive myself? Isn't it obvious to everyone but me that I'm dying, and that it's only a question of weeks, days . . . it may happen this moment. There was light and now there is darkness. I was here and now I'm going there! Where?" A chill came over him, his breathing ceased, and he felt only the throbbing of his heart.

"When I am not, what will there be? There will be nothing. Then where shall I be when I am no more? Can this be dying? No, I don't want to!" He jumped up and tried to light the candle, felt for it with trembling hands, dropped candle and candlestick on the floor, and fell back on his pillow.

"What's the use? It makes no difference," he said to himself, staring with wide-open eyes into the darkness. "Death. Yes, death. And none of them know or wish to know it, and they have no pity for me. Now they are playing." (He heard through the door the distant sound of a song and its accompaniment.) "It's all the same to them, but they will die too! Fools! I first, and they later, but it will be the same for them. And now they are merry . . . the beasts!"

Anger choked him and he was agonizingly, unbearably miserable. "It is impossible that all men have been doomed to suffer this awful horror!" He raised himself.

"Something must be wrong. I must calm myself—must think it all over from the beginning." And he again began thinking. "Yes, the beginning of my illness: I knocked my side, but I was still quite well that day and the next. It hurt a little, then rather more. I saw the doctors, then followed despondency and anguish, more doctors, and I drew nearer to the abyss. My strength grew less and I kept coming nearer and nearer, and now I have wasted away and there is no light in my eyes. I think of the appendix—but this is death! I think of mending the appendix, and all the while here is death! Can it really be death?" Again terror seized him and he gasped for breath. He leant down and began feeling for the matches, pressing with his elbow on the stand beside the bed. It was in his way and hurt him, he grew furious with it, pressed on it still harder, and upset it. Breathless and in despair he fell on his back, expecting death to come immediately.

Meanwhile the visitors were leaving. Praskovya Fëdorovna was seeing them off. She heard something fall and came in.

"What has happened?"

"Nothing. I knocked it over accidentally."

She went out and returned with a candle. He lay there panting heavily, like a man who has run a thousand yards, and stared upwards at her with a fixed look.

"What is it, Jean?"

"No . . . o . . . thing. I upset it." ("Why speak of it? She won't understand," he thought.)

And in truth she did not understand. She picked up the stand, lit his candle, and hurried away to see another visitor off. When she came back he still lay on his back, looking upwards.

"What is it? Do you feel worse?"

"Yes."

She shook her head and sat down.

"Do you know, Jean, I think we must ask Leshchetitsky to come and see you here."

This meant calling in the famous specialist, regardless of expense. He smiled malignantly and said "No." She remained a little longer and then went up to him and kissed his forehead.

While she was kissing him he hated her from the bottom of his soul and with difficulty refrained from pushing her away.

"Good-night. Please God you'll sleep."

"Yes."

CHAPTER VI

Ivan Ilych saw that he was dying, and he was in continual despair.

In the depth of his heart he knew he was dying, but not only was he not accustomed to the thought, he simply did not and could not grasp it.

The syllogism he had learnt from Kiezewetter's Logic: "Caius is a man, men are mortal, therefore Caius is mortal," had always seemed to him correct as applied to Caius, but certainly not as applied to himself. That Caius—man in the abstract—was mortal, was perfectly correct, but he was not Caius, not an abstract man, but a creature quite, quite separate from all others. He had been little Vanya, with a mamma and a papa; with Mitya and Volodya, with the toys, a coachman and a nurse, afterwards with Katenka and with all the joys, griefs, and delights of childhood, boyhood, and youth. What did Caius know of the smell of that striped leather ball Vanya had been so fond of? Had Caius kissed his mother's hand like that, and did the silk of her dress rustle so for Caius?

Had he rioted like that at school when the pastry was bad? Had Caius been in love like that? Could Caius preside at a session as he did? "Caius really was mortal, and it was right for him to die; but for me, little Vanya, Ivan Ilych, with all my thoughts and emotions, it's altogether a different matter. It cannot be that I ought to die. That would be too terrible."

Such was his feeling.

"If I had to die like Caius I should have known it was so. An inner voice would have told me so, but there was nothing of the sort in me and I and all my friends felt that our case was quite different from that of Caius. And now here it is!" he said to himself. "It can't be. It's impossible! But here it is. How is this? How is one to understand it?"

He could not understand it, and tried to drive this false, incorrect, morbid thought away and to replace it by other proper and healthy thoughts. But that thought, and not the thought only but the reality itself, seemed to come and confront him.

And to replace that thought he called up a succession of others, hoping to find in them some support. He tried to get back into the former current of thoughts that had once screened the thought of death from him. But strange to say, all that had formerly shut off, hidden, and destroyed, his consciousness of death, no longer had that effect. Ivan Ilych now spent most of his time in attempting to reestablish that old current. He would say to himself: "I will take up my duties again—after all I used to live by them." And banishing all doubts he would go to the law courts, enter into conversation with his colleagues, and sit carelessly as was his wont, scanning the crowd with a thoughtful look and leaning both his emaciated arms on the arms of his oak chair; bending over as usual to a colleague and drawing his papers nearer he would interchange whispers with him, and then suddenly raising his eyes and sitting erect would pronounce certain words and open the proceedings. But suddenly in the midst of those proceedings the pain in his side, regardless of the stage the proceedings had reached, would begin its own gnawing work. Ivan Ilych would turn his attention to it and try to drive the thought of it away, but without success. *It* would come and stand before him and look at him, and he would be petrified and the light would die out of his eyes, and he would again begin asking himself whether *It* alone was true. And his colleagues and subordinates would see with surprise and distress that he, the brilliant and subtle judge, was becoming confused and making mistakes. He would shake himself, try to pull himself together, manage somehow to bring the sitting to a close, and return home with the sorrowful consciousness that his judicial labors could not as formerly hide from him what he wanted them to hide, and could not deliver him from *It*. And what was worst of all was that *It* drew his attention to itself not in order to make him take some action but only that he should look at *It*, look it straight in the face: look at it and without doing anything, suffer inexpressibly.

And to save himself from this condition Ivan Ilych looked for consolations—new screens—and new screens were found and for a while seemed to save him, but then they immediately fell to pieces or rather became transparent, as if *It* penetrated them and nothing could veil *It*.

In these latter days he would go into the drawing-room he had arranged—that drawing-room where he had fallen and for the sake of which (how bitterly ridiculous it seemed) he had sacrificed his life—for he knew that his illness originated with that knock. He would enter and see that something had scratched the polished table. He would look for the cause of this and find that it was the bronze ornamentation of an album, that had got bent. He would take up the expensive album which he had lovingly arranged, and feel vexed with his daughter and her friends for their untidiness—for the album was torn here and there and some of the photographs turned upside down. He would put it carefully in order and bend the ornamentation back into position. Then it would occur to him to place all those things in another corner of the room, near the plants. He would call the footman, but his daughter or wife would come to help him. They would not agree, and his wife would contradict him, and he would dispute and grow angry. But that was all right, for then he did not think about *It*. *It* was invisible.

But then, when he was moving something himself, his wife would say: "Let the servants do it. You will hurt yourself again." And suddenly *It* would flash through the screen and he would see it. It was just a flash, and he hoped it would disappear, but he would involuntarily pay attention to his side. "It sits there as before, gnawing just the same!" And he could no longer forget *It*, but could distinctly see it looking at him from behind the flowers. "What is it all for?"

"It really is so! I lost my life over that curtain as I might have done when storming a fort. Is that possible? How terrible and how stupid. It can't be true! It can't, but it is!"

He would go to his study, lie down, and again be alone with *It*: face to face with *It*. And nothing could be done with *It* except to look at it and shudder.

CHAPTER VII

How it happened it is impossible to say because it came about step by step, unnoticed, but in the third month of Ivan Ilych's illness, his wife, his daughter, his son, his acquaintances, the doctors, the servants, and above all he himself, were aware that the whole interest he had for other people was whether he would soon vacate his place, and at last release the living from the discomfort caused by his presence and be himself released from his sufferings.

He slept less and less. He was given opium and hypodermic injections of morphine, but this did not relieve him. The dull depression he experienced in a somnolent condition at first gave him a little relief, but only as something new, afterwards it became as distressing as the pain itself or even more so.

Special foods were prepared for him by the doctors' orders, but all those foods became increasingly distasteful and disgusting to him.

For his excretions also special arrangements had to be made, and this was a torment to him every time—a torment from the uncleanliness, the unseemliness, and the smell, and from knowing that another person had to take part in it.

But just through this most unpleasant matter, Ivan Ilych obtained comfort. Gerasim, the butler's young assistant, always came in to carry the things out. Gerasium was a clean, fresh peasant lad, grown stout on town food and always cheerful and bright. At first the sight of him, in his clean Russian peasant costume, engaged in that disgusting task embarrassed Ivan Ilych.

Once when he got up from the commode too weak to draw up his trousers, he dropped into a soft armchair and looked with horror at his bare, enfeebled thighs with the muscles so sharply marked on them.

Gerasim with a firm light tread, his heavy boots emitting a pleasant smell of tar and fresh winter air, came in wearing a clean Hessian apron, the sleeves of his print shirt tucked up over his strong bare young arms;

and refraining from looking at his sick master out of consideration for his feelings, and restraining the joy of life that beamed from his face, he went up to the commode.

"Gerasim!" said Ivan Ilych in a weak voice.

Gerasim started, evidently afraid he might have committed some blunder, and with a rapid movement turned his fresh, kind, simple young face which just showed the first downy signs of a beard.

"Yes, sir?"

"That must be very unpleasant for you. You must forgive me. I am helpless."

"Oh, why, sir," and Gerasim's eyes beamed and he showed his glistening white teeth, "what's a little trouble? It's a case of illness with you, sir."

And his deft strong hands did their accustomed task, and he went out of the room stepping lightly. Five minutes later he as lightly returned.

Ivan Ilych was still sitting in the same position in the armchair.

"Gerasim," he said when the latter had replaced the freshly washed utensil. Please come here and help me." Gerasim went up to him. "Lift me up. It is hard for me to get up, and I have sent Dmitri away."

Gerasim went up to him, grasped his master with his strong arms deftly but gently, in the same way that he stepped—lifted him, supported him with one hand, and with the other drew up his trousers and would have set him down again, but Ivan Ilych asked to be led to the sofa. Gerasim, without an effort and without apparent pressure, led him, almost lifting him, to the sofa and placed him on it.

"Thank you. How easily and well you do it all!"

Gerasim smiled again and turned to leave the room. But Ivan Ilych felt his presence such a comfort that he did not want to let him go.

"One thing more, please move up that chair. No, the other one—under my feet. It is easier for me when my feet are raised."

Gerasim brought the chair, set it down gently in place, and raised Ivan Ilych's legs on to it. It seemed to Ivan Ilych that he felt better while Gerasim was holding up his legs.

"It's better when my legs are higher," he said. "Place that cushion under them."

Gerasim did so. He again lifted the legs and placed them, and again Ivan Ilych felt better while Gerasim held his legs. When he set them down Ivan Ilych fancied he felt worse.

"Gerasim," he said. "Are you busy now?"

"Not at all, sir," said Gerasim, who had learnt from the townsfolk how to speak to gentlefolk.

"What have you still to do?"

"What I to do? I've done everything except chopping the logs for tomorrow."

"Then hold my legs up a bit higher, can you?"

"Of course I can. Why not?" And Gerasim raised his master's legs higher and Ivan Ilych thought that in that position he did not feel any pain at all.

"And how about the logs?"

"Don't trouble about that, sir. There's plenty of time."

Ivan Ilych told Gerasim to sit down and hold his legs, and began to talk to him. And strange to say it seemed to him that he felt better while Gerasim held his legs up.

After that Ivan Ilych would sometimes call Gerasim and get him to hold his legs on his shoulders, and he liked talking to him. Gerasim did it all easily, willingly, simply, and with a good nature that touched Ivan Ilych. Health, strength, and vitality in other people were offensive to him, but Gerasim's strength and vitality did not mortify but soothed him.

What tormented Ivan Ilych most was the deception, the lie, which for some reason they all accepted, that he was not dying but was simply ill, and that he only need keep quiet and undergo a treatment and then something very good would result. He however knew that do what they would nothing would come of it, only still more agonizing suffering and death. This deception tortured him—their not wishing to admit what they all knew and what he knew, but wanting to lie to him concerning his terrible condition, and wishing and forcing him to participate in that lie. Those lies—lies enacted over him on the eve of his death and destined to degrade this awful, solemn act to the level of their visitings, their curtains, their sturgeon for dinner—were a terrible agony for Ivan Ilych. And strangely enough, many times when they were going through their antics over him he had been within a hairbreadth of calling out to them: "Stop lying! You know and I know that I am dying. Then at least stop lying about it!" But he had never had the spirit to do it.

The awful, terrible act of his dying was, he could see, reduced by those about him to the level of a casual, unpleasant, and almost indecorous incident (as if someone entered a drawing-room diffusing an unpleasant odor) and this was done by that very decorum which he had served all his life long. He saw that no one felt for him, because no one even wished to grasp his position. Only Gerasim recognized it and pitied him. And so Ivan Ilych felt at ease only with him. He felt comforted when Gerasim supported his legs (sometimes all night long) and refused to go to bed, saying: "Don't you worry, Ivan Ilych. I'll get sleep enough later on," or when he suddenly became familiar and exclaimed: "If you weren't sick it would be another matter, but as it is, why should I grudge a little trouble?" Gerasim alone did not lie; everything showed that he alone understood the facts of the case and did not consider it necessary to disguise them, but simply felt sorry for his emaciated and enfeebled master. Once when Ivan Ilych was sending him away he even said straight out: "We shall all of us die, so why should I grudge a little trouble?"—expressing the fact that he did not think his work burdensome, because he was doing it for a dying man and hoped someone would do the same for him when his time came.

Apart from this lying, or because of it, what most tormented Ivan Ilych was that no one pitied him as he wished to be pitied. At certain moments after prolonged suffering he wished most of all (though he would have been ashamed to confess it) for someone to pity him as a sick child is pitied. He longed to be petted and comforted. He knew he was an important functionary, that he had a beard turning grey, and that therefore what he longed for was impossible, but still he longed for it. And in Gerasim's attitude towards him there was something akin to what he wished for, and so that attitude comforted him. Ivan Ilych wanted to weep, wanted to be petted and cried over, and then his colleague Shebek would come, and instead of weeping and being petted, Ivan Ilych would assume a serious, severe, and profound air, and by force of habit would express his opinion on a decision of the Court of Cassation and would stubbornly insist on that view. This falsity around him and within him did more than anything else to poison his last days.

CHAPTER VIII

It was morning. He knew it was morning because Gerasim had gone, and Peter the footman had come and put out the candles, drawn back one of the curtains, and begun quietly to tidy up. Whether it was morning or evening, Friday or Sunday, made no difference, it was all just the same: the gnawing, unmitigated, agonizing pain, never ceasing for an instant, the consciousness of life inexorably waning but not yet extinguished, the approach of that ever dreaded and hateful Death which was the only reality, and always the same falsity. What were days, weeks, hours, in such a case?

"Will you have some tea, sir?"

"He wants things to be regular, and wishes the gentlefolk to drink tea in the morning," thought Ivan Ilych, and only said "No."

"Wouldn't you like to move onto the sofa, sir?"

"He wants to tidy up the room, and I'm in the way. I am uncleanliness and disorder," he thought, and said only:

"No, leave me alone."

The man went on bustling about. Ivan Ilych stretched out his hand. Peter came up, ready to help.

"What is it, sir?"

"My watch."

Peter took the watch which was close at hand and gave it to his master.

"Half-past eight. Are they up?"

"No sir, except Vladimir Ivanich" (the son) "who has gone to school. Praskovya Fëdorovna ordered me to wake her if you asked for her. Shall I do so?"

"No, there's no need to." "Perhaps I'd better have some tea," he thought, and added aloud: "Yes, bring me some tea."

Peter went to the door, but Ivan Ilych dreaded being left alone. "How can I keep him here? Oh yes, my medicine." "Peter, give me my medicine." "Why not? Perhaps it may still do me some good." He took a spoonful and swallowed it. "No, it won't help. It's all tomfoolery, all deception," he decided as soon as he became aware of the familiar, sickly, hopeless taste. "No, I can't believe in it any longer. But the pain, why this pain? If it would only cease just for a moment!" And he moaned. Peter turned towards him. "It's all right. Go and fetch me some tea."

Peter went out. Left alone Ivan Ilych groaned not so much with pain, terrible though that was, as from mental anguish. Always and for ever the same, always these endless days and nights. If only it would come quicker! If only *what* would come quicker? Death, darkness? . . . No, no! Anything rather than death!

When Peter returned with the tea on a tray, Ivan Ilych stared at him for a time in perplexity, not realizing who and what he was. Peter was disconcerted by that look and his embarrassment brought Ivan Ilych to himself.

"Oh, tea! All right, put it down. Only help me to wash and put on a clean shirt."

And Ivan Ilych began to wash. With pauses for rest, he washed his hands and then his face, cleaned his teeth, brushed his hair, and looked in the glass. He was terrified by what he saw, especially by the limp way in which his hair clung to his pallid forehead.

While his shirt was being changed he knew that he would be still more frightened at the sight of his body, so he avoided looking at it. Finally he was ready. He drew on a dressing-gown, wrapped himself in a plaid, and sat down in the armchair to take his tea. For a moment he felt refreshed, but as soon as he began to drink the tea he was again aware of the same taste, and the pain also returned. He finished it with an effort, and then lay down stretching out his legs, and dismissed Peter.

Always the same. Now a spark of hope flashes up, then a sea of despair rages, and always pain; always pain, always despair, and always the same. When alone he had a dreadful and distressing desire to call someone, but he knew beforehand that with others present it would be still worse. "Another dose of morphine—to lose consciousness. I will tell him, the doctor, that he must think of something else. It's impossible, impossible, to go on like this."

An hour and another pass like that. But now there is a ring at the door bell. Perhaps it's the doctor? It is. He comes in fresh, hearty, plump, and cheerful, with that look on his face that seems to say: "There now, you're in a panic about something, but we'll arrange it all for you directly!" The doctor knows this expression is out of place here, but he has put it on once for all and can't take it off—like a man who has put on a frock-coat in the morning to pay a round of calls.

The doctor rubs his hands vigorously and reassuringly.

"Brr! How cold it is! There's such a sharp frost; just let me warm myself!" he says, as if it were only a matter of waiting til he was warm, and then he would put everything right.

"Well now, how are you?"

Ivan Ilych feels that the doctor would like to say: "Well, how are our affairs?" but that even he feels that this would not do, and says instead: "What sort of a night have you had?"

Ivan Lych looks at him as much as to say: "Are you really never ashamed of lying?" But the doctor does not wish to understand this question, and Ivan Ilych says: "Just as terrible as ever. The pain never leaves me and never subsides. If only something . . ."

"Yes, you sick people are always like that. . . . There, now I think I am warm enough. Even Praskovya Fëdorovna, who is so particular, could find no fault with my temperature. Well, now I can say good-morning," and the doctor presses his patient's hand.

Then, dropping his former playfulness, he begins with a most serious face to examine the patient, feeling his pulse and taking his temperature, and then begins the sounding and auscultation.

Ivan Ilych knows quite well and definitely that all this is nonsense and pure deception, but when the doctor, getting down on his knee, leans over him, putting his ear first higher then lower, and performs various gymnastic movements over him with a significant expression on his face, Ivan Ilych submits to it all as he used to submit to the speeches of the lawyers, though he knew very well that they were all lying and why they were lying.

The doctor, kneeling on the sofa, is still sounding him when Praskovya Fëdorovna's silk dress rustles at the door and she is heard scolding Peter for not having let her know of the doctor's arrival.

She comes in, kisses her husband, and at once proceeds to prove that she has been up a long time already, and only owing to a misunderstanding failed to be there when the doctor arrived.

Ivan Ilych looks at her, scans her all over, sets against her the whiteness and plumpness and cleanness of her hands and neck, the gloss of her hair, and the sparkle of her vivacious eyes. He hates her with his whole soul. And the thrill of hatred he feels for her makes him suffer from her touch.

Her attitude towards him and his disease is still the same. Just as the doctor had adopted a certain relation to his patient which he could not abandon, so had she formed one towards him—that he was not doing something he ought to do and was himself to blame, and that she reproached him lovingly for this—and she could not now change that attitude.

"You see he doesn't listen to me and doesn't take his medicine at the proper time. And above all he lies in a position that is no doubt bad for him—with his legs up."

She described how he made Gerasim hold his legs up.

The doctor smiled with a contemptuous affability that said: "What's to be done? These sick people do have foolish fancies of that kind, but we must forgive them."

When the examination was over the doctor looked at his watch, and then Praskovya Fëdorovna announced to Ivan Ilych that it was of course as he pleased, but she had sent today for a celebrated specialist who would examine him and have a consultation with Michael Danilovich (their regular doctor.)

"Please don't raise any objections. I am doing this for my own sake," she said ironically, letting it be felt that she was doing it all for his sake and only said this to leave him no right to refuse. He remained silent, knitting his brows. He felt that he was so surrounded and involved in a mess of falsity that it was hard to unravel anything.

Everything she did for him was entirely for her own sake, and she told him she was doing for herself what she actually was doing for herself, as if that was so incredible that he must understand the opposite.

At half-past eleven the celebrated specialist arrived. Again the sounding began and the significant conversations in his presence and in another room, about the kidneys and the appendix, and the questions and answers, with such an air of importance that again, instead of the real question of life and death which now alone confronted him, the question arose of the kidney and appendix which were not behaving as they ought to and would now be attacked by Michael Danilovich and the specialist and forced to amend their ways.

The celebrated specialist took leave of him with a serious though not hopeless look, and in reply to the timid question Ivan Ilych, with eyes glistening with fear and hope, put to him as to whether there was a chance of recovery, said that he could not vouch for it but there was a possibility. The look of hope with which Ivan Ilych watched the doctor out was so pathetic that Praskovya Fëdorovna, seeing it, even wept as she left the room to hand the doctor his fee.

The gleam of hope kindled by the doctor's encouragement did not last long. The same room, the same pictures, curtains, wall-paper, medicine bottles, were all there, and the same aching suffering body, and Ivan Ilych began to moan. They gave him a subcutaneous injection and he sank into oblivion.

It was twilight when he came to. They brought him his dinner and he swallowed some beef tea with difficulty, and then everything was the same again and night was coming on.

After dinner, at seven o'clock, Praskovya Fëdorovna came into the room in evening dress, her full bosom pushed up by her corset, and with traces of powder on her face. She had reminded him in the morning that they were going to the theater. Sarah Bernhardt was visiting the town and they had a box, which he had insisted on their taking. Now he had forgotten about it and her toilet offended him, but he concealed his vexation when he remembered that he had himself insisted on their securing a box and going because it would be an instructive and aesthetic pleasure for the children.

Praskovya Fëdorovna came in, self-satisfied but yet with a rather guilty air. She sat down and asked how he was, but, as he saw, only for the sake of asking and not in order to learn about it, knowing that there was nothing to learn—and then went on to what she really wanted to say: that she would not on any account have gone but that the box had been taken and Helen and their daughter were going, as well as Petrishchev (the examining magistrate, their daughter's fiancé) and that it was out of the question to let them go alone; but that she would have much preferred to sit with him for a while; and he must be sure to follow the doctor's orders while she was away.

"Oh, and Fëdor Petrovich" (the fiancé) "would like to come in. May he? And Lisa?"

"All right."

Their daughter came in in full evening dress, her fresh young flesh exposed (making a show of that very flesh which in his own case caused so much suffering), strong, healthy, evidently in love, and impatient with illness, suffering, and death, because they interfered with her happiness.

Fëdor Petrovich came in too, in evening dress, his hair curled *à la Capoul*, a tight stiff collar round his long sinewy neck, an enormous white shirt-front and narrow black trousers tightly stretched over his strong thighs. He had one white glove tightly drawn on, and was holding his opera hat in his hand.

Following him the schoolboy crept in unnoticed, in a new uniform, poor little fellow, wearing gloves. Terribly dark shadows showed under his eyes, the meaning of which Ivan Ilych knew well.

His son had always seemed pathetic to him, and now it was dreadful to see the boy's frightened look of pity. It seemed to Ivan Ilych that Vasya was the only one besides Gerasim who understood and pitied him.

They all sat down and again asked how he was. A silence followed. Lisa asked her mother about the opera-glasses, and there was an altercation between mother and daughter as to who had taken them and where they had been put. This occasioned some unpleasantness.

Fëdor Petrovich inquired of Ivan Ilych whether he had ever seen Sarah Bernhardt. Ivan Ilych did not at first catch the question, but then replied: "No, have you seen her before?"

"Yes, in *Adrienne Lecouvreur*."

Praskovya Fëdorovna mentioned some roles in which Sarah Bernhardt was particularly good. Her daughter disagreed. Conversation sprang up as to the elegance and realism of her acting—the sort of conversation that is always repeated and is always the same.

In the midst of the conversation Fëdor Petrovich glanced at Ivan Ilych and became silent. The others also looked at him and grew silent. Ivan Ilych was staring with glittering eyes straight before him, evidently indignant with them. This had to be rectified, but it was impossible to do so. The silence had to be broken, but for a time no one dared to break it and they all became afraid that the conventional deception would suddenly become obvious and the truth become plain to all. Lisa was the first to pluck up courage and break that silence, but by trying to hide what everybody was feeling, she betrayed it.

"Well, if we are going it's time to start," she said, looking at her watch, a present from her father, and with a faint and significant smile at Fëdor Petrovich relating to something known only to them. She got up with a rustle of her dress.

They all rose, said good-night, and went away.

When they had gone it seemed to Ivan Ilych that he felt better; the falsity had gone with them. But the pain remained—that same pain and that same fear that made everything monotonously alike, nothing harder and nothing easier. Everything was worse.

Again minute followed minute and hour followed hour. Everything remained the same and there was no cessation. And the inevitable end of it all became more and more terrible.

"Yes, send Gerasim here," he replied to a question Peter asked.

CHAPTER IX

His wife returned late at night. She came in on tiptoe, but he heard her, opened his eyes, and made haste to close them again. She wished to send Gerasim away and to sit with him herself, but he opened his eyes and said: "No, go away."

"Are you in great pain?"

"Always the same."

"Take some opium."

He agreed and took some. She went away.

Till about three in the morning he was in a state of stupefied misery. It seemed to him that he and his pain were being thrust into a narrow, deep black sack, but though they were pushed further and further in they could not be pushed to the bottom. And this, terrible enough in itself, was accompanied by suffering. He was frightened yet wanted to fall through the sack, he struggled but yet cooperated. And suddenly he broke through, fell, and regained consciousness. Gerasim was sitting at the foot of the bed dozing quietly and patiently, while he himself lay with his emaciated stockinged legs resting on Gerasim's shoulders; the same shaded candle was there and the same unceasing pain.

"Go away, Gerasim," he whispered.

"It's all right, sir. I'll stay a while."

"No. Go away."

He removed his legs from Gerasim's shoulders, turned sideways onto his arm, and felt sorry for himself. He only waited till Gerasim had gone into the next room and then restrained himself no longer but wept like a child. He wept on account of his helplessness, his terrible loneliness, the cruelty of man, the cruelty of God, and the absence of God.

"Why hast Thou done all this? Why hast Thou brought me here? Why, why dost Thou torment me so terribly?"

He did not expect a answer and yet wept because there was no answer and could be none. The pain again grew more acute, but he did not stir and did not call. He said to himself: "Go on! Strike me! But what is it for? What have I done to Thee? What is it for?"

Then he grew quiet and not only ceased weeping but even held his breath and became all attention. It was as though he were listening not to an audible voice but to the voice of his soul, to the current of thoughts arising within him.

"What is it you want?" was the first clear conception capable of expression in words, that he heard.

"What do you want? What do you want?" he repeated to himself.

"What do I want? To live and not to suffer," he answered.

And again he listened with such concentrated attention that even his pain did not distract him.

"To live? How?" asked his inner voice.

"Why, to live as I used to—well and pleasantly."

"As you lived before, well and pleasantly?" the voice repeated.

And in imagination he began to recall the best moments of his pleasant life. But strange to say none of those best moments of his pleasant life now seemed at all what they had then seemed—none of them except the first recollections of childhood. There, in childhood, there had been something really pleasant with which it would be possible to live if it could return. But the child who had experienced that happiness existed no longer, it was like a reminiscence of somebody else.

As soon as the period began which had produced the present Ivan Ilych, all that had then seemed joys now melted before his sight and turned into something trivial and often nasty.

And the further he departed from childhood and the nearer he came to the present the more worthless and doubtful were the joys. This began with the School of Law. A little that was really good was still found there—there was light-heartedness, friendship, and hope. But in the upper classes there had already been fewer of such good moments. Then during the first years of his official career, when he was in the service of the governor, some pleasant moments again occurred: they were the memories of love for a woman. Then all became confused and there was still less of what was good; later on again there was still less that was good, and the further he went the less there was. His marriage, a mere accident, then the disenchantment that followed it, his wife's bad breath and the sensuality and hypocrisy: then that deadly official life and those preoccupations about money, a year of it, and two, and ten, and twenty, and always the same thing. And the longer it lasted the more deadly it became. "It is as if I had been going downhill while I imagined I was going up. And that is really what it was. I was going up in public opinion, but to the same extent life was ebbing away from me. And now it is all done and there is only death."

"Then what does it mean? Why? It can't be that life is so senseless and horrible. But if it really has been so horrible and senseless, why must I die and die in agony? There is something wrong!"

"Maybe I did not live as I ought to have done," it suddenly occurred to him. "But how could that be, when I did everything properly?" he replied, and immediately dismissed from his mind this, the sole solution of all the riddles of life and death, as something quite impossible.

"Then what do you want now? To live? Live how? Live as you lived in the law courts when the usher proclaimed 'The judge is coming!' The judge is coming, the judge!" he repeated to himself. "Here he is, the judge. But I am not guilty!" he exclaimed angrily. "What is it for?" And he ceased crying, but turning his face to the wall continued to ponder on the same question: Why, and for what purpose, is there all this horror? But however much he pondered he found no answer. And whenever the thought occurred to him, as it often did, that it all resulted from his not having lived as he ought to have done, he at once recalled the correctness of his whole life and dismissed so strange an idea.

CHAPTER X

Another fortnight passed. Ivan Ilych now no longer left his sofa. He would not lie in bed but lay on the sofa, facing the wall nearly all the time. He suffered ever the same unceasing agonies and in his loneliness pondered always on the same insoluble question: "What is this? Can it be that it is Death?" And the inner voice answered: "Yes, it is Death."

"Why these sufferings?" And the voice answered, "For no reason—they just are so." Beyond and besides this there was nothing.

From the very beginning of his illness, ever since he had first been to see the doctor, Ivan Ilych's life had been divided between two contrary and alternating moods: now it was despair and the expectation of this uncomprehended and terrible death, and now hope and an intently interested observation of the functioning of his organs. Now before his eyes there was only a kidney or an intestine that temporarily evaded its duty, and now only that incomprehensible and dreadful death from which it was impossible to escape.

These two states of mind had alternated from the very beginning of his illness, but the further it progressed the more doubtful and fantastic became the conception of the kidney, and the more real the sense of impending death.

He had but to call to mind what he had been three months before and what he was now, to call to mind with what regularity he had been going downhill, for every possibility of hope to be shattered.

Latterly during that loneliness in which he found himself as he lay facing the back of the sofa, a loneliness in the midst of a populous town and surrounded by numerous acquaintances and relations but that yet could not have been more complete anywhere—either at the bottom of the sea or under the earth—during that terrible loneliness Ivan Ilych had lived only in memories of the past. Pictures of his past rose before him one after another. They always began with what was nearest in time and then went back to what was most remote—to his childhood—and rested there. If he thought of the stewed prunes that had been offered him that day, his mind went back to the raw shriveled French plums of his childhood, their peculiar flavor and the flow of saliva when he sucked their stones, and along with the memory of that taste came a whole series of memories of those days: his nurse, his brother, and their toys. "No, I mustn't think of that. . . . It is too painful," Ivan Ilych said to himself, and brought himself back to the present—to the button on the back of the sofa and the creases in its morocco. "Morocco is expensive, but it does not wear well: there had been a quarrel about it. It was a different kind of quarrel and a different kind of morocco that time when we tore father's portfolio and were punished, and mamma brought us some tarts. . . ." And again his thoughts dwelt on his childhood, and again it was painful and he tried to banish them and fix his mind on something else.

Then again together with that chain of memories another series passed through his mind—of how his illness had progressed and grown worse. There also the further back he looked the more life there had been. There had been more of what was good in life and more of life itself. The two merged together. "Just as the pain went on getting worse and worse, so my life grew worse and worse," he thought. "There is one bright spot there at the back, at the beginning of life, and afterwards all becomes blacker and blacker and proceeds more and more rapidly—in inverse ratio to the square of the distance from death," thought Ivan Ilych. And the example of a stone falling downwards with increasing velocity entered his mind. Life, a series of increasing sufferings, flies further and further towards its end—the most terrible suffering. "I am flying. . . ." He shuddered, shifted himself, and tried to resist, but was already aware that resistance was impossible, and again with eyes weary of gazing but unable to cease seeing what was before them, he stared at the back of the sofa and waited—awaiting that dreadful fall and shock and destruction.

"Resistance is impossible!" he said to himself. "If I could only understand what it is all for! But that too is impossible. An explanation would be possible if it could be said that I have not lived as I ought to. But it is impossible to say that," and he remembered all the legality, correctitude, and propriety of his life. "That at any rate can certainly not be admitted," he thought, and his lips smiled ironically as if someone could see that smile and be taken in by it. "There is no explanation! Agony, death. . . . What for?"

CHAPTER XI

Another two weeks went by in this way and during that fortnight an event occurred that Ivan Ilych and his wife had desired. Petrishchev formally proposed. It happened in the evening. The next day Praskovya Fëdorovna came into her husband's room considering how best to inform him of it, but that very night there had been a fresh change for the worse in his condition. She found him still lying on the sofa but in a different position. He lay on his back, groaning and staring fixedly straight in front of him.

She began to remind him of his medicines, but he turned his eyes towards her with such a look that she did not finish what she was saying; so great an animosity, to her in particular, did that look express.

"For Christ's sake, let me die in peace!" he said.

She would have gone away, but just then their daughter came in and went up to say good morning. He looked at her as he had done at his wife, and in reply to her inquiry about his health said dryly that he would soon free them all of himself. They were both silent and after sitting with him for a while went away.

"Is it our fault?" Lisa said to her mother. "It's as if we were to blame! I am sorry for papa, but why should we be tortured?"

The doctor came at his usual time. Ivan Ilych answered "Yes" and "No," never taking his angry eyes from him, and at last said: "You know you can do nothing for me, so leave me alone."

"We can ease your sufferings."

"You can't even do that. Let me be."

The doctor went into the drawing-room and told Praskovya Fëdorovna that the case was very serious and that the only resource left was opium to allay her husband's sufferings, which must be terrible.

It was true, as the doctor said, that Ivan Ilych's physical sufferings were terrible, but worse than the physical sufferings were his mental sufferings, which were his chief torture.

His mental sufferings were due to the fact that that night, as he looked at Gerasim's sleepy, good-natured face with its prominent cheek-bones, the question suddenly occurred to him: "What if my whole life has really been wrong?"

It occurred to him that what had appeared perfectly impossible before, namely that he had not spent his life as he should have done, might after all be true. It occurred to him that his scarcely perceptible attempts to struggle against what was considered good by the most highly placed people, those scarcely noticeable impulses which he had immediately suppressed, might have been the real thing, and all the rest false. And his professional duties and the whole arrangement of his life and of his family, and all his social and official interests, might all have been false. He tried to defend all those things to himself and suddenly felt the weakness of what he was defending. There was nothing to defend.

"But if that is so," he said to himself, "and I am leaving this life with the consciousness that I have lost all that was given me and it is impossible to rectify it—what then?"

He lay on his back and began to pass his life in review in quite a new way. In the morning when he saw first his footman, then his wife, then his daughter, and then the doctor, their every word and movement confirmed to him the awful truth that had been revealed to him during the night. In them he saw himself—all that for which he had lived—and saw clearly that it was not real at all, but a terrible and huge deception which had hidden both life and death. This consciousness intensified his physical suffering tenfold. He groaned and tossed about, and pulled at his clothing, which choked and stifled him. And he hated them on that account.

He was given a large dose of opium and became unconscious, but at noon his sufferings began again. He drove everybody away and tossed from side to side.

His wife came to him and said:

"Jean, my dear, do this for me. It can't do any harm and often helps. Healthy people often do it."

He opened his eyes wide.

"What? Take communion? Why? It's unnecessary! However . . . ."

She began to cry.

"Yes, do, my dear. I'll send for our priest. He is such a nice man."

"All right. Very well," he muttered.

When the priest came and heard his confession, Ivan Ilych was softened and seemed to feel a relief from his doubts and consequently from his sufferings, and for a moment there came a ray of hope. He again began to think of the vermiform appendix and the possibility of correcting it. He received the sacrament with tears in his eyes.

When they laid him down again afterwards he felt a moment's ease, and the hope that he might live awoke in him again. He began to think of the operation that had been suggested to him. "To live! I want to live!" he said to himself.

His wife came in to congratulate him after his communion, and when uttering the usual conventional words she added:

"You feel better, don't you?"

Without looking at her he said "Yes."

Her dress, her figure, the expression of her face, the tone of her voice, all revealed the same thing. "This is wrong, it is not as it should be. All you have lived for and still live for is falsehood and deception, hiding life and death from you." And as soon as he admitted that thought, his hatred and his agonizing physical suffering again sprang up, and with that suffering a consciousness of the unavoidable, approaching end. And to this was added a new sensation of grinding shooting pain and a feeling of suffocation.

The expression of his face when he uttered that "yes" was dreadful. Having uttered it, he looked her straight in the eyes, turned on his face with a rapidity extraordinary in his weak state and shouted:

"Go away! Go away and leave me alone!"

CHAPTER XII

From that moment the screaming began that continued for three days, and was so terrible that one could not hear it through two closed doors without horror. At the moment he answered his wife he realized that he was lost, that there was no return, that the end had come, the very end, and his doubts were still unsolved and remained doubts.

"Oh! Oh! Oh!" he cried in various intonations. He had begun by screaming "I won't!" and continued screaming on the letter "o."

For three whole days, during which time did not exist for him, he struggled in that black sack into which he was being thrust by an invisible, resistless force. He struggled as a man condemned to death struggles in the hands of the executioner, knowing that he cannot save himself. And every moment he felt that despite all his efforts he was drawing nearer and nearer to what terrified him. He felt that his agony was due to his being thrust into that black hole and still more to his not being able to get right into it. He was hindered from getting into it by his conviction that his life had been a good one. That very justification of his life held him fast and prevented his moving forward, and it caused him most torment of all.

Suddenly some force struck him in the chest and side, making it still harder to breathe, and he fell through the hole and there at the bottom was a light. What had happened to him was like the sensation one sometimes experiences in a railway carriage when one thinks one is going backwards while one is really going forwards and suddenly becomes aware of the real direction.

"Yes, it was all not the right thing," he said to himself, "but that's no matter. It can be done. But what *is* the right thing?" he asked himself, and suddenly grew quiet.

This occurred at the end of the third day, two hours before his death. Just then his schoolboy son had crept softly in and gone up to the bedside. The dying man was still screaming desperately and waving his arms. His hand fell on the boy's head, and the boy caught it, pressed it to his lips, and began to cry.

At that very moment Ivan Ilych fell through and caught sight of the light, and it was revealed to him that though his life had not been what it should have been, this could still be rectified. He asked himself, "What *is* the right thing?" and grew still, listening. Then he felt that someone was kissing his hand. He opened his eyes, looked at his son, and felt sorry for him. His wife came up to him and he glanced at her. She was gazing at him open-mouthed, with undried tears on her nose and cheek and a despairing look on her face. He felt sorry for her too.

"Yes, I am making them wretched," he thought. "They are sorry, but it will be better for them when I die." He wished to say this but had not the strength to utter it. "Besides, why speak? I must act," he thought. With a look at his wife he indicated his son and said: "Take him away . . . sorry for him . . . sorry for you too. . . ." He tried to add, "forgive me," but said "forgo" and waved his hand, knowing that He whose understanding mattered would understand.

And suddenly it grew clear to him that what had been oppressing him and would not leave him was all dropping away at once from two sides, from ten sides, and from all sides. He was sorry for them, he must act so as not to hurt them: release them and free himself from these sufferings. "How good and how simple!" he thought. "And the pain?" he asked himself. "What has become of it? Where are you, pain?"

He turned his attention to it.

"Yes, here it is. Well, what of it? Let the pain be."

"And death . . . where is it?"

He sought his former accustomed fear of death and did not find it. "Where is it? What death?" There was no fear because there was no death.

In place of death there was light.

"So that's what it is!" he suddenly exclaimed aloud. "What joy!"

To him all this happened in a single instant, and the meaning of that instant did not change. For those present his agony continued for another two hours. Something rattled in his throat, his emaciated body twitched, then the gasping and rattle became less and less frequent.

"It is finished!" said someone near him.

He heard these words and repeated them in his soul.

"Death is finished," he said to himself. "It is no more!"

He drew in a breath, stopped in the midst of a sigh, stretched out, and died.

ACKNOWLEDGMENTS

Selected excerpts from Lucretius are reprinted from *The Way Things Are*, trans. by Rolfe Humphries. Copyright © 1968 by the Indiana University Press. Reprinted by permission of Indiana University Press.

"Song of Nezahualcoyotl" and "Song of a Man About to Die in a Strange Land" are reprinted from *Literature of the American Indian*, Abridged Edition, edited by Thomas E. Sanders & Walter W. Peek. Copyright © 1973, 1976 by Benziger Bruce & Glencoe, Inc. Reprinted by permission of Glencoe Publishing Co., Inc.

"This Quiet Dust," "Because I Could Not Stop for Death," "I Heard a Fly Buzz—When I Died," and "How the Waters Closed Above Him" are all reprinted by permission of the publishers and the Trustees of Amherst College from *The Poems of Emily Dickinson*, edited by Thomas H. Johnson, Cambridge, Mass.: The Belknap Press of Harvard University Press. Copyright © 1951, 1955 by the President and Fellows of Harvard College.

"The Journey Nears the Road-End" is reprinted with permission of Macmillan Publishing Co., Inc. from *A Tagore Reader*, edited and translated by Amiya Chakravarty. Copyright © 1961 by Macmillan Publishing Co., Inc.

"For a Dead Lady" is reprinted by permission of Charles Scribner's Sons from *The Town Down the River* by Edwin Arlington Robinson. Copyright 1910 by Charles Scribner's Sons; renewal copyright 1938 by Ruth Nivison.

"There, On the Darkened Deathbed" is reprinted with permission of Macmillan Publishing Co., Inc. from *Poems* by John Masefield. Copyright 1916 by John Masefield; renewed 1944 by John Masefield.

"Blind Date" is reprinted from *Collected Poems* (second edition) by Conrad Aiken. Copyright © 1953, 1970 by Conrad Aiken. Reprinted by permission of Oxford University Press, Inc.

"Story of the Widow's Son" is reprinted by permission of Mary Lavin.

Selected excerpts are reprinted from *The Cancer Ward* by Aleksandr I. Solzhenitsyn and translated by Rebecca Frank. Copyright © 1968 by La Société YMCA-Press and The Dial Press, Inc. Reprinted by permission of The Dial Press.

442 ACKNOWLEDGMENTS

"People" is reprinted from *Selected Poems* by Yevgeny Yevtushenko, translated by Robin Milner-Gulland and Peter Levi. Copyright © by Robin Milner-Gulland and Peter Levi. Reprinted by permission of E. P. Dutton.

"Carol of Death" is reprinted by permission of Doubleday & Co., Inc. from *Leaves of Grass* by Walt Whitman.

"Go Down Death" is reprinted from *God's Trombones* by James Weldon Johnson. Copyright 1927 by The Viking Press, Inc.; © renewed 1955 by Grace Nail Johnson. Reprinted by permission of Viking Penguin Inc.

"Appointment in Samarra" is reprinted by permission of A. P. Watt Ltd.

"I Have a Rendevous with Death" is reprinted by permission of Charles Scribner's Sons from *Poems by Alan Seeger* by Alan Seeger. Copyright 1916 by Charles Scribner's Sons; renewal copyright 1944 by Elsie Adams Seeger.

A selected excerpt from *The Palm-Wine Drinkard* by Amos Tutuola is reprinted by permission of Grove Press, Inc. Copyright © 1953 by George Braziller.

Selected exceprts from *Don Quixote* by Cervantes are reprinted by permission of Macmillan Press Ltd., London and Basingstoke.

"The Jilting of Granny Weatherall" is reprinted from Katherine Anne Porter's *Flowering Judas and Other Stories* by permission of Harcourt Brace Jovanovich, Inc. Copyright 1930, 1958 by Katherine Anne Porter.

"In the Shadow of the Valley of Death" is reprinted from *An Anthology of Modern Arabic Poetry*, edited and trans. by Mounah A. Khouri and Hamid Algar. Copyright © 1974 by The Regents of the University of California. Reprinted by permission.

Selected excerpts from *Death Be Not Proud* by John Gunther are reprinted by permission of Harper & Row, Publishers, Inc. Copyright 1949 by John Gunther.

Selected excerpts are reprinted from *How Could I Not Be Among You?* by Ted Rosenthal by permission of George Braziller, Inc. Copyright © 1973 by Ted Rosenthal.

Selected excerpts from *Stay of Execution* by Stewart Alsop are reprinted by permission of Harper & Row, Publishers, Inc. and by permission of the Estate of the author. Copyright © 1973 by J. B. Lippincott.

Selected excerpts are reprinted from *A Private Battle* by Cornelius Ryan and Kathryn Morgan Ryan. Copyright © 1979 by Kathryn Morgan Ryan. Reprinted by permission of Simon & Schuster, a Division of Gulf & Western Corporation.

Selected excerpts are reprinted from *The Epic of Gilgamesh*, trans. N. K. Sandars (Penguin Classics, Second Revised Edition, 1977), pp. 93–107. Copyright © N. K. Sandars, 1960, 1964, 1972. Reprinted by permission of Penguin Books Ltd.

Selected excerpts from the *Digha-nikaya* are reprinted from *Buddhism in Translations* by Henry Clarke Warren (Cambridge, Mass.: Harvard University Press, 1953). Reprinted by permission of Harvard University Press.

Selected excerpts are reprinted from *Great Dialogues of Plato*, translated by W. H. D. Rouse and edited by Eric H. Warmington and Philip G. Rouse. Copyright © 1956 by John Clive Graves Rouse. Reprinted by arrangement with The New American Library, Inc., New York, N.Y.

Selected excerpts are reprinted from *Eric* by Doris Lund (J. B. Lippincott) by permission of Harper & Row, Publishers, Inc. Copyright © 1974 by Doris Lund.

Selected excerpts from *I Heard the Owl Call My Name* by Margaret Craven are reprinted by permission of Doubleday & Co., Inc.

"The Death of Bed Number 12" is reprinted from *Modern Arabic Short Stories*, selected and translated by Denys Johnson-Davies. Copyright © 1967 by Oxford University Press. Reprinted by permission of Oxford University Press.

"An Elegy on the Death of Furuhi" is reprinted from *Anthology of Japanese Literature*, edited by Donald Keene. Copyright © 1955 by Grove Press, Inc. Reprinted by permission of Grove Press.

"Written on Seeing the Flowers and Remembering My Daughter" is reprinted from *Anthology of Chinese Literature*, edited by Cyril Birch. Copyright © 1972 by Grove Press, Inc. Reprinted by permission of Grove Press.

"To An Athlete Dying Young" is reprinted from "A Shropshire Lad"—Authorized Edition—from *The Collected Poems of A. E. Housman*. Copyright 1939, 1940 © 1965 by Holt, Rinehart and Winston. Copyright © 1967, 1968 by Robert E. Symons. Reprinted by permission of Holt, Rinehart, and Winston, Publishers.

"Out, Out——" is reprinted from *The Poetry of Robert Frost*, edited by Edward Connery Lathem. Copyright 1916, © 1969 by Holt, Rinehart, and Winston. Copyright 1944 by Robert Frost. Reprinted by permission of Holt, Rinehart, and Winston, Publishers.

"Lament" and "Dirge Without Music" are reprinted from *Collected Poems*, published by Harper & Row. Copyright 1921, 1928, 1948, 1955 by Edna St. Vincent Millay and Norma Millay Ellis. Reprinted by permission of Norma Millay Ellis.

Selected excerpts are reprinted from *A Death in the Family* by James Agee. Copyright © 1957 by James Agee Trust. Reprinted by permission of Grosset & Dunlap, Inc.

Selected excerpts are reprinted from *Blood of the Lamb* by Peter De Vries. Copyright © 1961 by Peter De Vries. Reprinted by permission of Little, Brown and Co.

The text of *My Grandpa Die Today* is reprinted by permission of Joan Fassler and the Human Sciences Press.

"To Hell with Dying" is reprinted from Alice Walker's *In Love and Trouble: Stories of Black Women*, published by Harcourt Brace Jovanovich, Inc. Copyright © 1967, 1968 by Alice Walker. Reprinted by permission of Harcourt Brace Jovanovich Inc.

"A Boy Thirteen" is reprinted from *A Boy Thirteen* by Jerry A. Irish. Copyright © 1975 by The Westminster Press. Used by permission.

Selected excerpts are reprinted from *The Iliad*, trans. E. V. Rieu (Penguin Classics, 1950), pp. 400–408, 412–419, 456–458. Copyright © 1950 by the Estate of E. V. Rieu. Reprinted by permission of Penguin Books Ltd.

Selected excerpts are reprinted from *Crime and Punishment* by F. M. Dostoevsky and translated by Jessie Coulson (1953). Reprinted by permission of Oxford University Press.

"The Man He Killed" and "Ah, Are You Digging on My Grave?" are reprinted from Thomas Hardy's *Collected Poems*, published by Macmillan Publishing Co., Inc.

"Dulce et Decorum Est" is reprinted from *The Collected Poems of Wilfred Owen*. Copyright 1946, © 1963 by Chatto & Windus Ltd. Reprinted by permission of New Directions.

Selected excerpts are reprinted by permission of Vallentine, Mitchell & Co., Ltd. from *Journey Through Hell* by Reska Weiss.

Selected excerpts are reprinted from *Hiroshima* by John Hersey. Copyright 1946 and renewed 1974 by John Hersey. Reprinted by permission of Alfred A. Knopf, Inc. Originally appeared in *The New Yorker*.

Selected excerpts are reprinted from *In Cold Blood* by Truman Capote. Copyright © 1965 by Truman Capote. Reprinted by permission of Random House, Inc. Originally appeared in *The New Yorker*.

"Lilith's Child" is reprinted by permission of Edward Francisco. The poem originally appeared in the *Phoenix*, published by the University of Tennessee Press.

Selected excerpts are reprinted from *Epistuale Morales*, vol. II, by Seneca and translated by R. M. Gummere (Cambridge, Mass.: Harvard University Press, 1920). Reprinted by permission of Harvard University Press.

Selected excerpts are reprinted from the *Summa Theologica* by Thomas Aquinas. Reprinted by permission of Benziger Brothers, a division of Glencoe Publishing Co., Inc.

"The Love Suicides at Sonezaki" is reprinted from *Anthology of Japanese Literature*, edited by Donald Keene. Copyright © 1955 by Grove Press, Inc. Reprinted by permission of Grove Press.

Selected excerpts are reprinted from *Madame Bovary* by Gustave Flaubert and translated by Francis Steegmuller. Copyright © 1975 by Francis Steegmuller. Reprinted by permission of Random House, Inc.

"The Mill" is reprinted with permission of Macmillan Publishing Co., Inc. from *Collected Poems* by Edwin Arlington Robinson. Copyright 1920 by Edwin Arlington Robinson; renewed 1948 by Ruth Nivison.

"Richard Cory" is reprinted by permission of Charles Scribner's Sons from *The Children of the Night* by Edwin Arlington Robinson.

"Resume" is reprinted from *The Portable Dorothy Parker*. Copyright 1926 by Dorothy Parker; renewed 1954 by Dorothy Parker. Reprinted by permission of Viking Penguin Inc.

"A Summer Tragedy" is reprinted by permission of Dodd, Mead & Company, Inc. from *The Old South* by Arna Bontemps. Copyright 1933, 1961 by Arna Bontemps. Copyright © 1944 by Random House, Inc. Copyright © 1973 by Alberta Bontemps, Executrix.

"The Last Letter" by Isao Matsuo is reprinted from *The Divine Wind* by Rikihei Inoguchi, Tadashi Nakajima, and Roger Pineau. Copyright © 1958 by the United States Naval Institute. Reprinted by permission from Roger Pineau.

Selected excerpts are reprinted from pp. 127–131, 137–138 in *The Bell Jar* by Sylvia Plath. Copyright © 1971 by Harper & Row, Publishers, Inc. Reprinted by permission of Harper & Row, Publishers, Inc.

"Tract" is reprinted from *Collected Earlier Poems* of William Carlos Williams. Copyright 1938 by New Directions Publishing Corporation. Reprinted by permission of New Directions.

A selected excerpt is reprinted by permission of Charles Scribner's Sons from *Look Homeward, Angel* by Thomas Wolfe. Copyright 1929 by Charles Scribner's Sons; renewal copyright © 1957 by Edward C. Aswell, Administrator, C.T.A. and/or Fred Wolfe.

Selected excerpts are reprinted from *The Grapes of Wrath* by John Steinbeck. Copyright 1939 by John Steinbeck. Reprinted by permission of Viking Penguin Inc.

Selected excerpts are reprinted from *Grateful to Life and Death* by R. K. Narayan. Reprinted by permission of Michigan State University Press.

Selected excerpts are reprinted from *The Stranger* by Albert Camus and translated by Stuart Gilbert. Copyright 1946 and renewed 1974 by Alfred A. Knopf, Inc. Reprinted by permission of Alfred A. Knopf, Inc.

Selected excerpts are reprinted from *Trying Hard to Hear You* by Sandra Scoppettone. Copyright © 1974 by Sandra Scoppettone. Reprinted by permission of Harper & Row, Publishers, Inc.

A selected excerpt of the *Chuang Tzu* is reprinted from *A Source Book in Chinese Philosophy*, trans. and compiled by Wing-tsit Chan. Copyright © 1963 by Princeton University Press. Reprinted by permission of Princeton University Press.

"Lament of a Young Man for His Son" is reprinted from *The American Rhythm* by Mary Austin. Copyright renewed 1958 by Kenneth M. Chapman and Mary C. Wheelwright. Reprinted by permission of Houghton Mifflin Co.

"Heartache" is reprinted from *The Image of Chekhov* by Anton Chekhov and translated by Robert Payne. Copyright © 1963 by Alfred A. Knopf, Inc. Reprinted by permission of Alfred A. Knopf, Inc.

"Patterns" is reprinted from *The Complete Poetical Works* of Amy Lowell. Copyright 1955 by Houghton Mifflin Company. Reprinted by permission of the publisher.

"nobody loses all the time" is reprinted from *IS 5*, poems by E. E. Cummings, with the permission of Liveright Publishing Corporation. Copyright 1926 by Horace Liveright. Copyright renewed 1953 by E. E. Cummings.

Selected excerpts are reprinted from *A Grief Observed* by C. S. Lewis. Copyright © 1961 by N. W. Clerk. Reprinted by permission of The Seabury Press, Inc.

A selected excerpt from "Letter to Menoeceus" is reprinted from *The Stoic and Epicurean Philosophers*, edited by Whitney Oates. Reprinted by permission of Random House, Inc.

Selected excerpts are reprinted from *The Bhagavad Gita*, trans. by Franklin Edgerton (Cambridge, Mass.: Harvard University Press, 1944). Copyright 1944 by the President and Fellows of Harvard College; © 1972 by Eleanor H. Edgerton. Reprinted by permission of Harvard University Press.

A selected excerpt is reprinted from Goethe's *Faust*, trans. by Walter Kaufmann. Reprinted by permission of Doubleday & Company Inc.

"Laura" is reprinted from *The Complete Short Stories of Saki*. Copyright 1930 by The Viking Press, Inc.; © renewed 1958 by The Viking Press, Inc. Reprinted by permission of Viking Penguin Inc.

A selected excerpt is reprinted from *The Prophet* by Kahlil Gibran. Copyright 1923 by Kahlil Gibran and renewed 1951 by Administrators C.T.A. of Kahlil Gibran Estate and Mary G. Gibran.

"The Kidd Will" is reprinted from an official copy of the document provided by the Superior Court Clerk, Phoenix, Arizona.

"Do Not Go Gentle into That Good Night" is reprinted from *The Poems of Dylan Thomas*. Copyright 1952 by Dylan Thomas. Reprinted by permission of New Directions.

The Death of Ivan Ilych is reprinted from *The Death of Ivan Ilych and Other Stories* by Leo Tolstoy and translated by Louise and Aylmer Maude (1935). Reprinted by permission of Oxford University Press.

INDEX